RECLAIMING
THE
INNER
CHILD

. . . .

RECLAIMING
THE
INNER
CHILD

. . . .

EDITED BY

JEREMIAH ABRAMS

Mandala

An Imprint of HarperCollins*Publishers*

For Phillip, Rachael, and Barbara
my best boy, my best girl, their best mom:

"Anyway it wouldn't ring true,

If not for you."

Mandala
An Imprint of HarperCollins*Publishers*
77-85 Fulham Palace Road,
Hammersmith, London W6 8JB

Published by Mandala 1991
First published by Jeremy P. Tarcher, Inc.,
5858 Wilshire Blvd, Los Angeles, CA 90036, 1990

1   3   5   7   9   10   8   6   4   2

Jeremiah Abrams and the contributors assert
the moral right to be identified as the authors
of this work

A catalogue record for this book
is available from the British Library

ISBN 1 85274 118 X

Printed in Great Britain by
Mackays of Chatham, Kent

I thought finally that of all the nostalgias that haunt the human heart the greatest of them all, for me, is an everlasting longing to bring what is youngest home to what is oldest, in us all.

—LAURENS VAN DER POST

CONTENTS

. . . .

Jeremiah Abrams
Introduction: The Inner Child   1

PART I
The Promise of the Inner Child

Introduction   15

1. Edith Sullwold
   A Fresh Experiment:
   The Archetype of the Inner Child   17

2. C. G. Jung
   The Psychology of the Child Archetype   24

3. James H. Young
   The Child Archetype in the Poetry of Wordsworth   31

4. Gaston Bachelard
   Reveries Toward Childhood   40

5. June Singer
   The Motif of the Divine Child   49

6. Ralph Metzner
   Rebirth and the Eternal Child   54

PART 2
The Abandoned Child

Introduction   61

7. Gilda Frantz
   Birth's Cruel Secret: O I Am My Own Lost Mother
   to My Own Sad Child   64

8. James Hillman
   Abandoning the Child   77

9. Rose-Emily Rothenberg
   The Orphan Archetype   87

10. Marion Woodman
    The Soul Child   98

11. M. Scott Peck
    Love and the Fear of Abandonment   103

12. Ursula K. LeGuin
    The Ones Who Walk Away from Omelas   108

PART 3
Eternal Youth and Narcissism:
The Child's Dilemma

Introduction   117

13. Joel Covitz
    Narcissism: The Disturbance of Our Time   120

14. Alice Miller
    The Search for the True Self   126

15. Marie-Louise von Franz
    Puer Aeternus   138

16. Jeffrey Satinover
    The Childhood Self and the Origins of Puer Psychology   144

17. Helen M. Luke
    The Little Prince   156

PART 4
The Wounded Child Within

Introduction   167

18. Charles L. Whitfield
    How Can We Heal Our Child Within?   170

19. Hal Stone and Sidra Winkelman
    The Vulnerable Inner Child   176

20. Alexander Lowen
    Why Are You So Angry with Me?   185

21. Alice Miller
    Advocating for the Child   189

22. Robert M. Stein
    On Incest and Child Abuse   193

23. Susanne Short
    The Whispering of the Walls   198

PART 5
Recovering the Child

Introduction   207

24. Lucia Capacchione
    The Power of Your Other Hand   209

25. Joyce C. Mills and Richard J. Crowley
    Contacting the Child Within   217

26. John Bradshaw
    Liberating Your Lost Inner Child   224

27. John Loudon
    Becoming a Child   234

28. Nathaniel Branden
    Integrating the Younger Self   242

29. Jean Houston
    Recalling the Child   248

30. Adelaide Bry
    Replaying the Movies of Your Childhood   252

31. Joseph Campbell
    Killing the Dragon   259

32. Robert M. Stein
    Redeeming the Inner Child in Marriage and in Therapy   261

PART 6
Inner Child/Outer Child:
The Future of Parenting

Introduction   275

33. James Hillman
    A Note on Story   277

34. Bruno Bettelheim
    Exploring Childhood as an Adult   280

35. Erik H. Erikson
    The Historical Relevance of Human Childhood   287

36. Theodore Reik
    Out of the Mouths of Babes   289

37. Samuel Osherson
    The Wounded Father Within   295

Epilogue
"May You Stay Forever Young"   301

Notes   303

Notes on Contributors   313

Bibliography   317

Permissions and Copyrights   321

ACKNOWLEDGMENTS

· · · · · · ·

A project such as this is the work of many hands. Without the generous, creative, and cooperative energies of the many, the one work would not exist.

I am especially indebted to my loving wife, Barbara Shindell, who has sacrificed to keep things going during my distraction, and who has been my mainstay, chief reader, and enthusiastic supporter.

I am most grateful to my editor, Connie Zweig, that rare and gifted kind of person who has been able to be a dear friend as well as book-mother and book-midwife to this endeavor.

Many other individuals also deserve special thanks for their specific aid to this book: Bob Stein and Joel Covitz gave unflinching intellectual and emotional support to this endeavor throughout, as readers, believers, critics, and contributors. Mark Dowie and Mark Libarle helped me to get the book off to a great start. Bill and Vivienne Howe generously allowed me to turn their library into a research facility. Sharon Heath gave infusions of support from her parallel project. Lotte Stein, Joanna Karp, Bruce and Carla Burman, and Alys Graveson provided invaluable critical support as readers. Kathleen Dickey rescued and commandeered the manuscript preparation with grace. The support from Jeremy Tarcher and his staff has been attentive and professional throughout. And, obviously, I am indebted to the individual authors and publishers who have generously allowed their written work to be woven into this tapestry.

I especially want to acknowledge those clients and personal friends who have shared their innermost beings with me over the years, who have given reality to my own experience of the inner child and to the healing possibilities within us all.

INTRODUCTION: THE INNER CHILD

. . . .

JEREMIAH ABRAMS

> It is the Child that sees the primordial se-
> cret in Nature and it is the child of our-
> selves we return to. The child within us
> is simple and daring enough to live the
> Secret.
>
> —CHUANG TSU

Most of us feel a strong resonance with the inner child. We know intuitively what it is, what its meaning is for us. We sense, perhaps secretly, that a part of us remains whole, untouched by life's sorrows, capable of great joy and wonder at small things.

This child image is one of subtle complexity and truth. Its message is that *we all carry within us an eternal child*, a young being of innocence and wonder. *And that symbolic child also carries us*, who we have been, the record of our formative experiences, our pleasures and pains.

As a symbolic and poetic reality, the inner child appears in our imaginations, our dreams, our art, and in mythologies throughout the world representing renewal, divinity, a zest for life, a sense of wonder, hope, the future, discovery, courage, spontaneity, and immortality. As such, the inner child is a uniting symbol and brings together the separated or dissociated parts of the individual personality. Marie-Louise von Franz, eminent Jungian analyst and scholar, says: "If I trust my naive reaction, then I am whole; I am wholly in the situation and wholly in life. . . . That is why child therapists let children play, and in two minutes they reveal their whole problem, for in that way they are themselves."

The inner child is both a developmental actuality and a symbolic possibility. It is the soul of the person, created inside of us through the experiment of life, and it is the primordial image of the Self, the very center

I

of our individual being. As Carl Gustav Jung suggested, the child represents a "wholeness which embraces the very depths of Nature."

"The Child is the father of the Man," said Wordsworth. The child is father to the whole person.

Most of us continue to have contact with the child in adulthood through childish habits and desires and childlike behavior, and through contact with real children. Jung said that the tendency to engage in regressive activity has the positive function of keeping us connected to the child, of activating the inner child. He said regression is a "genuine attempt to get at something necessary: the universal feeling of childhood innocence, the sense of security, of protection, of reciprocal love, of trust, of faith—a thing that has many names."[1]

WE HAVE ALL BEEN CHILDREN

Our inner child possesses the spirit of truthfulness, absolute spontaneity, and genuineness. Its actions bespeak a naturalness in us, the ability to do the right thing, the capacity to save a situation. Culver Barker, a British psychologist, observed how important it is to become aware of the child within, to relate to it consciously and be reinforced by it. He wrote:

> When I talk about the child within, I mean that aspect within us adults which still reflects some of the qualities of the divine child. . . . When we are too unconscious of it, for whatever reason, and so do not mediate it, this force contains all the potentialities for constructive and destructive activities. So it can hold the creative dynamics of the human personality, its motive power.[2]

"Only when I make room for the voice of the child within me," says renowned Swiss psychoanalyst Alice Miller, "do I feel myself to be genuine and creative."

The child's voice is essential to the process of becoming oneself. Individuation, the lifelong process of personality development, is tied to and circles around the unique identity of the childhood self. Von Franz concurs with Miller on this point when she says, "The child within is the genuine part, and the genuine part within one is that which suffers. . . . Many grown-ups split off this part and thereby miss individuation, for only if one accepts it and the suffering it imposes on one, can the process of individuation go on."

The inner child's voice is one that each and every one of us will recognize, for we know it well. We have all been children. And the child we have been remains within us—for better or worse—a container of our personal history and an ever-present symbol of our hopes and creative possibilities.

The child, by whatever means we achieve contact with it, is the key to our achieving fullest expression as individuals. This child entity, the self we truly are and have always been, lives within us in the here and now. If, for instance, we observe the self-image of exceptionally gifted individuals—people who have fully realized their talents in life—it is striking how much their self-concept is tied to the unique and personal experience of the childhood self.

Albert Einstein is a well-known example of the genius forever wedded to the inner child's naturalness. It is said that Einstein didn't even speak until he was nearly five years old! "Even at the age of nine he was not fluent," says biographer Ronald W. Clark.[3] The authenticity of his child self was not contaminated by words, but rather contained in a nonverbal sense of wonder. Einstein recognized this quality of the child in himself. He honored it faithfully in the face of adversity. In his autobiographical notes, written at the age of sixty-seven, he mused:

> It is, in fact, nothing short of a miracle that the modern methods of instruction have not yet entirely strangled the holy curiosity of inquiry; for this delicate little plant, aside from stimulation, stands mostly in need of freedom; without this it goes to wreck and ruin without fail. It is a very grave mistake to think that the enjoyment of seeing and searching can be promoted by means of coercion and a sense of duty.[4]

This naturalness, freedom, and perpetual sense of wonder, assiduously preserved into adult life, remained the mark of Einstein's character even in old age.

In contrast, the life of Wolfgang Amadeus Mozart provides an example of a one-sided inversion of the positive tendencies in the inner child. Here we have a childhood genius who, according to his biographers, was unable to achieve balance by developing the socialized adult self in his personality. His child self was a prisoner of conditional love, inflated with grandiosity and compelled to seek the approval of his father, his monarch, and his world. His musical gift burned pure, but his puerile behavior led to a premature demise.

For other gifted individuals, maturity and adulthood result in a diminution of the vibrant power of the child. Consider, for example, the flattening effects of maturation on the gifts of many child prodigies. The process of socialization somehow has a stifling effect on the natural gifts of most children. This is the narcissistic dilemma.

Perhaps the scenario goes like this: The real child, being forced to adapt, becomes a little adult and identifies with a false self. The treasures of the true child self are then hidden protectively in such a well-concealed sanctum that when the adult self matures, it fails to recall and to reclaim the inner child. The child within is abandoned, lost. Eventually, rationalization or bitterness replaces the natural spontaneity and clarity of that radiant self. As J. Robert Oppenheimer, the dark genius who fathered the atomic age, lamented, "There are children playing in the street who could solve some of my top problems in physics, because they have modes of sensory perception that I lost long ago."[5]

"WHERE IS THE LIFE WE
HAVE LOST IN LIVING?"

For others, the child within has been far from inspiring, for it is hardly a reality. The experience of their childhood stories has been obliterated by pain and time, obscured by rationality, driven out by ambition, or distorted by the pressure to grow up and conform.

Few of us had a childhood free of anxiety, filled with contact and understanding involvement with adults, a childhood of freedom to engage in imaginative play and to follow distraction to delight, an emotional environment where it was safe to feel vulnerable. For many, the inner child is a traumatized and wounded being, a sufferer we would rather not acknowledge, stunted by experiences we would rather not remember as adults.

The child of our experience, says child therapist Edith Sullwold, "is the child which we all desire to heal, so that we can reclaim the energy for adult action that still resides in the reactive patterns of defense and protection, which developed in response to early painful experiences."

We have played and suffered, grown and learned. The youthful, soulful part persists, though for some only as an occasional twinkle in the eyes or an intonation of voice. Many people experience the inner child unconsciously as one who has not had its needs recognized or met. This experience and the longing that accompanies it are a great source of humiliation and shame, very difficult to identify or share with others. Thus the child can be a tremendous inhibition in adult human relatedness.

We always encounter the inner child in marriage and other close associations with others, where the wounding love relationships of our past are most deeply felt. "Those childhood wounds to the soul," says author and Jungian analyst Robert M. Stein, "make it extremely difficult, if not impossible, for one to experience an intimate and creatively evolving human connection. In this sense the wounded child also represents that aspect of the soul which needs and demands union with another."

Healing this wounded problem child is possible, and necessary if we are to achieve inner wholeness. Healing requires an internal transformation, the creation of a positive inner attitude that supports and nourishes the child within compassionately. In her book *The Drama of the Gifted Child*, Alice Miller describes the shift that takes place during the healing process:

> If a person is able . . . to experience that he was never "loved" as a child for what he was, but for his achievements, success, and good qualities, and that he sacrificed his childhood for this "love," this will shake him very deeply but one day he will feel the desire to end this courtship. He will discover in himself a need to live according to his "true self" and no longer be forced to earn love, a love that at root, still leaves him empty-handed since it is given to the "false self," which he has begun to relinquish.

THE LIGHT OF THE WORLD
CAN SHINE THROUGH

The inner child is the carrier of our personal stories, the vehicle for our memories of both the actual child and an idealized child from the past. It is the *truly alive* quality of being within us. It is the soul, our experiencer throughout the cycles of life. It is the sufferer. And it is the bearer of renewal through rebirth, appearing in our lives whenever we detach and open to change.

In the poem "The Holy Longing," Goethe, the great European renaissance man of the eighteenth and nineteenth centuries, sang his praise to this remarkable quality in the human being:

> *Tell a wise person, or else keep silent,*
> *because the massman will mock it right away.*
> *I praise what is truly alive,*
> *what longs to be burned to death . . .*
>
> *And so long as you haven't experienced*
> *this: to die and so to grow,*
> *you are only a troubled guest*
> *on the dark earth.*[6]

To experience this process of renewal is to experience the creative possibilities of the symbolic inner child. To "die"—that is, to let go at a time of transition—allows some new possibility to be born. "Give up what thou hast and thou shalt receive," goes the Latin proverb. When something passes out of being, the child is constellated as an inner possibility. It enters our sphere filled with a naive vitality.

"The process of psychologically dying while one is still alive is followed by a psychological rebirth, or renewal," says Ralph Metzner in his book *Opening to the Light*. A new being is born—a new way of being—imagined as the symbolic radiant child. "The newborn child is still connected to the Tao, to the source of its life and its arising, and this is why we should emulate it," adds Metzner. "As Chuang Tsu says, 'Can you be like a newborn child? The baby cries all day and yet his voice never becomes hoarse. That is because he has not lost nature's harmony.' "

At the core of our being this eternal child exists, truly alive, awaiting embodiment in our actions and our attitudes. And the light of the world can shine through it.

"IT TAKES A LONG TIME
TO BECOME YOUNG"

The inner child motif, though it has emerged as a concept in the popular culture only in the past thirty years, is both timeless and contemporary. It is as ancient as religion, and as current as a Hollywood comedy. In the film *Big*, for instance, a boy gets his wish to be grown-up instantaneously, and we see him succeed in the adult world in his new adult's body by simply remaining his natural child self, innocent and ebullient. This is not substantially different from the child-god Hermes we meet in the Homeric Hymns, who, through his cleverness (and all on the very day he is born!) invents music and song by creating a lyre as a toy from a tortoise's shell, steals from and appeases his older brother, the archer Apollo, and wins the approval of his most famous father, Zeus.

The child within is an evolving concept, originating in primordial times with the very earliest forms of nature worship and solar religions. Those child-gods gave way before the beginning of our eon to the emergence of divine mythological children thoughout the world. The Romulus and Remus fable gave us the glory that was Roman civilization. The messiah concept of the Hebrews eventually produced what has become the primary inner symbol of the self in our times, the Christ child. During the Middle Ages, when unsanctioned religious practices were forced underground, the alchemists imagined their great work accomplished in a synthesis of the opposites, the creation of an inner soul child, the Philosopher's Child. In the East, to this day, devotion to the child Krishna suffuses family life with an awareness of divine presence in everyday living.

In the West, religious thought has given rise to secular thought on the subject of the child. Tremendous growth has taken place in the social sciences in our era—a period of time once imagined by Victorian scientistic sensibilities to be the coming "century of the Child." Most especially expanded in our immediate times is the realm of psychological ideas. By the 1960s, revisionist work in educational theory and practice had fully taken hold of modern ideas of child psychology and developmental theory. The analytic insights of the depth psychologies of Freud, Adler, Jung, Reich, Reik, and others had grown in influence and were making perfectly clear what the more mystical traditions had valued through the ages—namely, that we are not all of a piece, that each of us contains a multitude of internal influences, the child and childhood being the most immediate and important.

This ripe intellectual context gave ferment to the rising idea of the inner child. The concept emerges in the serious and the popular psychological literature of the 1960s, most notably in the works of the preeminent Swiss psychologist C. G. Jung ("The Psychology of the Child Archetype," 1959 American edition), who wrote about the inner child as a symbol of wholeness in the psyche, as a bridge between the personal and collective realms. American psychiatrist W. Hugh Missildine (*Your Inner Child of the Past*, 1963) wrote one of the original books in the self-help genre, giving encouraging advice on how to bring the inner child of experience into harmony with the outer adult's personality. The extremely popular work of California psychiatrist Eric Berne (*Transactional Analysis*, 1961) placed the inner child in an interactive role with an inner parent and inner adult, a versatile model that worked well in psychotherapeutic settings, enabling the inner child to take a constructive role in healing the whole person.

There are important reasons why the image of the inner child has such a compelling message for us today. The following six catalyzing factors, though not a complete explanation in themselves, are what make the inner child a theme of pressing interest.

The Expansion of Interest in Psychology

Psychology—itself a child of this century—has brought us to an appreciation of the relevance of human childhood, stressing its developmental importance and emphasizing the reality of childhood experience. Sigmund Freud, whose brilliance was midwife to modern psychological inquiry, is reported to have said at the end of his pioneering career that "the real value of psychoanalysis is to improve parenting." Almost all subsequent thought in the field of psychology has given a prominent place to the child and child studies.

Jung, whose discoveries have advanced psychological thinking well into the next century, did not underestimate the promise of psychology for the modern temperament when he asked waggishly:

> Why is it that just now especially we interest ourselves in psychology? The answer is, everyone is in dire need of it. Humanity seems to have reached today a point where previous concepts are no longer adequate and where we begin to realize that we are confronted with something strange, the language of which we no longer understand. We live in a time when there dawns upon us a realization that the people living on the other side of the mountain are not made up exclusively of red-headed devils responsible for all the evil on this side of the mountain.[7]

A Parallel Growth in Psychotherapy

The "talking cure," which originated with Freud and his followers, has evolved and become differentiated in its focus, but nevertheless continues to honor the soul, to validate the inner life of the adult, and to acknowledge the existence of the inner child in need of healing.

In the past three decades the phenomenon of the inner child has risen in prominence largely because of a growing interest in Jungian depth psychology in general and in the treatment of narcissistic personality disorders in particular. Both of these disciplines identify the image of the inner child as the vulnerable soul, the wounded child in need of integration, and the injured Self. Archetypal psychologist James Hillman echoes Jung when he says, "What depth psychology has come to call regression is nothing other than a return to the child."

With the rise and popularization of psychotherapy, therapists have come into contact with the neglected child within themselves and have found it necessary to heal their own inner children in order to effectively help others. According to author Charles L. Whitfield, many therapists have in turn extended this work to their clientele and have made recovery of the inner child a key feature of the therapeutic relationship, expanding the currency of the inner child in many circles.

The Adult Children of Alcoholics (ACA) Program

This rapidly growing phenomenon, a spin-off of the enormously popular twelve-step self-help recovery movement of the Alcoholics Anonymous fellowship, makes broad use of the child-within concept. It has been estimated that the *ACA* program is growing at a rate of one new group nationwide every day. The success of the concept seems to lie in the identification of the previously unacknowledged suffering of those who were raised in alcoholic households; specifically, the recognition of the disastrously damaging effects on the child self of such persons. Utilizing a family and systems approach to alcoholism recovery, the *ACA* model makes it plain that families that are dysfunctional for any reason, not just alcoholic or chemically dependent ones, do incalculable damage to the children and to the inner childhood of their members. This is a very influential phenomenon, with a burgeoning membership and literature, helping to break the denial of the genuine, suffering part of us that is the inner child.

The Ever-Widening Acknowledgment of Child Abuse

The rise in incidence, reporting, prosecution, and publicity of child abuse forces us to consider the perpetuation of such behavior by the abused inner children of adult offenders. Jungian analyst and author Joel Covitz, in his book *Emotional Child Abuse*, calls this cross-generational phenomenon "the family curse." He says that when we look at the adult perpetrator of abuse,

> we almost always find this root: as a child, this person's healthy narcissistic needs were not met . . . and when the child grows up, the devastating effects of these disturbances are passed on to his own children. Patterns of abuse will not be altered until parents realize more fully the effect their actions have on their children.

What is it in our culture that is manifesting in this epidemic of child abuse? This is a complicated problem, requiring a deeper consideration of collective attitudes toward the inner child. "Actual child abuse always reflects a lack of connection to and respect for the internal or psychic child," according to Robert M. Stein, a leading thinker in the field, whose writing challenges us to look at this problem with greater sensitivity and awareness. The growing attention and awareness of child abuse in our culture, and the insight that most perpetrators have been abused themselves, give work on the inner child an important mandate.

Today's Increased Parental Burden

The child-rearing task, under siege now as never before, cries out for support and attention. Attitudes toward children and their development are changing rapidly. What would have been thought of as inappropriate thirty years ago, such as widespread child care outside the home for six-month-old babies, is now widely accepted practice. Rapidly changing values in postindustrial culture have irrevocably altered the family structure and are radically affecting child-rearing practices. Women have entered the workforce in large numbers in response to economic pressures and in an effort to expand their sense of identity and purpose. This trend, along with the increased incidence of single-parent households, has necessitated wholesale rethinking of the parental task as we approach the end of the century. The cohort, tidal-wave generation of new parents, the postwar baby boom, is now proliferating in considerable numbers. These people need and want to expand the collective awareness of good parenting. Parents more than ever *want* all the help they can get. Yet parenting and the art of child-rearing seem to be subject to greater isolation and social abandonment, as are our children.

These circumstances bring special attention to the child within the parent, as well as to the inner life of the child: The quality and success of parenting is deeply enhanced when parents can realize their own neglected child selves and transform them into compassionate resources for the care of their own children. The way one treats the inner child strongly determines the way one treats the outer child.

Hunger for Spirituality and Meaning

The spiritual uncertainty of the times calls for a birth of new meaning and hope in each of us.

> *Things fall apart; the centre cannot hold;*
> *Mere anarchy is loosed upon the world,*
> *The blood-dimmed tide is loosed, and everywhere*
> *The ceremony of innocence is drowned . . .*[8]
>
> —W. B. YEATS, "The Second Coming"

We suffer from what Jung has called "an unprecedented impoverishment of symbols." There is a great hunger for spirituality and meaning in our era, a longing for a second coming of a divine inner child whose appearance would announce the beginning of a new millennium of hope. On the personal level, we feel a compelling necessity to contact and to live the inner child's destiny in order to find spiritual salvation. "Our childhood bears witness to the childhood of man, of the being touched by the glory of living," said Gaston Bachelard.

Or as Jungian psychologist June Singer puts it, "The divine child within us gives meaning to our immature strivings; he shows us the unconscious side of the limitations which we experience, and that is a vision of potentiality coming into flower."

In psychological terms, we might say the appearance of the divine child is a manifestation of the Self, causing a restructuring of the personality to accommodate an expanded comprehension of meaning and a fuller expression of vitality.

"As one searches the literature of mysticism and spiritual guidance and the life stories of those who seem to have become mature selves," writes John Loudon in his essay "Becoming a Child," "the goal seems common: an integration that embraces the fullness of human potentiality that is at the same time uncomplicated, wise, joyful, and even playful." In short, a return to the child. This motif is reflected in the great mythologies of the world's religions, where the birth of a special child means that the old gods have to go, and a new beginning emerges.

The appearance of the archetype of the divine child—the collective inner child—presages a transformation in the individual or the collective psyche, the possibility of renewal and expansion. "There is within us," writes Edith Sullwold in the opening essay of this book, "a creative force which is beckoning, forcing us out of its own essential nature, to leave the old and familiar world view and step forward into the new."

"SING, MUSE, THE CHILD!"

This child awareness in our midst is a healthy sign for our culture, portending good things for our children. As Homer made his ancient invocation, "Sing, Muse, the Child!," so we might now look to the child within for inspiration.

This book has come into being to satisfy that objective. It brings together, for the first time, major writings on the subject of the inner child. The intentions of the book are simple and direct: to give structure to a field of inquiry that is both compelling and timely; and to supply the reader with the best, most readable, inspiring material available. The project has been guided by synchronicity, persistence, and the good faith of many people. Chance encounters and suggestions from many unnamed helpmeets have played no small part. Such an endeavor becomes itself a practice in discovery, in developing that sense of choosing the right thing to do, and in trusting one's naive reaction as it occurs. This has been an unexpected blessing, a beneficial gift which the child has brought along.

The selection of material for this collection has been made after an extensive literature search, each contribution chosen for its particular quality of thought, point of view, and passion for the subject. The selections are clustered around six major themes, focused topics that emerged once the breadth of the subject was fully surveyed. The section introductions provide a skeletal structure for the book, describing each main theme and giving a general context for the essays in each section. Shorter, lead-in descriptions preceding each essay provide more specific contextual information.

Part 1 examines the mythic dimensions of the inner child theme, the innate images of childhood and childlikeness that we all carry. Here we meet the archetype of the child and the divine child, the poetic and mysterious child-god filled with promise and possibility, reverie and wonder, rebirth and renewal, the very highest and best in all of us.

Part 2 carries the theme of abandonment—figurative, literal, intentional, unintentional; the abandoned, repressed, unloved, or lost child, the victim of fate, circumstance, and neglect.

Part 3 focuses on the paradigmatic problem of narcissistic disturbances, the minefield most children have to cross, the inner dilemma of our time. Here we learn about the effects of inner conflicts on the formation of self, self-concept, and character. We meet the *puer aeternus*, the eternal youth who, in order to avoid further loss, hovers above life, living only provisionally. Though exuberant and charming, this disturbed inner child is not yet willing to take life for real.

Part 4 is about the wounded child, the child as victim, abused, abandoned, neglected, a product of dysfunctional family life or societal indifference. Where there is wounding there is also healing, and all the pieces in this section also address the healing of that wounded inner child.

Part 5 moves up and out, beyond the vale of tears and injury, to the practical tasks of recovering the younger self, of realizing the child's gifts and embracing its vitality.

Finally, Part 6 examines the revitalization of child-rearing practices through knowledge and awareness of the child within.

• • • • • • •

We came on this trek
To find our life.
For we are all,
We are all,
We are all the children of . . .
A brilliantly colored flower,
A flaming flower.
And there is no one,
There is no one,
Who regrets what we are.

—HUICHOL INDIAN CHANT[9]

PART 1

· · · · · · ·

THE PROMISE OF THE INNER CHILD

INTRODUCTION

. . . .

> In every adult there lurks a child—an eternal child, something that is always becoming, is never completed, and calls for unceasing care, attention, and education. That is the part of the human personality which wants to develop and become whole.
>
> —C. G. JUNG

We begin, first of all, with the archetype of the child, what we might call the "big" image of the child within, since it is the child each of us carries, both as a part of ourselves and as an encoded form of the collective human experience of the child. In the beginning was the newly created being, the child, as in the garden of Eden, filled with innocence, wonder, happiness, all the possibilities of human life and the future. The promise that child holds is within us. It is in our origins and in our hopes.

This promise begins with a birth. When a child is born a star lights up, a world of possibilities opens. Each writer in this section discusses the inner possibilities that the child carries for both the individual life and for the collective life of man.

Edith Sullwold introduces us to the archetypal world of the child, suggesting that each birth, each child's life, is a fresh experiment in humankind's spiritual evolution. She differentiates for us the personal world of the inner child from the larger realm of the mythic child.

Carl Jung's essay, laden with the freight of complex ideas, is the definitive work on the mythic dimensions of the inner child. The child is a symbol, says Jung, that expresses "the all-embracing nature of psychic wholeness." In describing the child archetype, he says that "it is a well-nigh hopeless undertaking to tear a single archetype out of the living tissue of the psyche; but despite their interwovenness they do form units of meaning that can be apprehended intuitively." (Therefore, we recommend using your intuitive faculties, rather than your analytic ones, in tackling Jung's article.)

In James H. Young's study of the child archetype, we find an amplification of these psychological ideas through the inspired poetic vision of Wordsworth. The English Romantic's poems emphasize the duality of the child's spiritual awareness and the adult's prosaic vision, the living conflict we all embody and experience internally as a discrepancy between the child's genius and the adult's pragmatics. Usually the adult wins in this battle and the child's view is neglected. Young treats this dualism in both Jung and Wordsworth, suggesting the ways in which both men envisioned transcending this problem. The theme of abandonment, which Jung regarded as a special phenomenon of the child archetype, is a related aspect of this dualism. We take up the abandoned inner child as the focus of Part 2.

Gaston Bachelard's selection, the fourth chapter in this section, is a song to the inner child, to memory, to all the childhoods in us that still remain potentials in the form of our child within. It is really a joyous prose poem incantation, reminding us that, as contemporary novelist Tom Robbins says, "it's never too late to have a happy childhood."

June K. Singer, whose essay forms Chapter 5, treats the divine child as an extension of our collective awareness, saying it symbolically represents "the ideals of a culture which it is not able, in reality, to fulfill." Her provocative ideas on the child motif expand on the Jungian archetypal perspective. She also introduces us to the *puer aeternus* archetype, the eternal child who is the subject of Part 3 of this book.

This section ends with the great mystery of rebirth and the idea of becoming a child again through a metaphoric process of death-rebirth. Ralph Metzner's succinct essay makes it clear that renewal is the birth of a spiritual attitude, often taking the form of a realization of the inner child. "Out of the turmoil and darkness of dying," he says, "comes the sparkling vitality of the newborn self. This new self is connected to the eternal source of all life, that source from which we all derive, the divine essence within. It is therefore aptly named 'the eternal child.' "

1 · A FRESH EXPERIMENT: THE ARCHETYPE OF THE INNER CHILD

· · · · · · ·

EDITH SULLWOLD

Edith Sullwold brings considerable energy, understanding, and sensitivity to the difficult task of distinguishing the personal from the archetypal qualities of the inner child. Her warm and particular feelings for the child's inner life are blended here with scholarship, interpretive skill, and a storyteller's knowledge of her material. This essay was originally delivered by the author on November 20, 1987, as the keynote address at the conference Reawakening the Inner Child, in Washington, D.C. Dr. Sullwold, who is a child therapist and therapist supervisor, generously agreed to expand and adapt her talk expressly for this collection, to once again sound the keynote on the inner child.

One of my favorite quotations regarding the child comes from a rather unlikely source, the pen of George Bernard Shaw. In an essay that asks, what is a child?, he answers:

> An experiment. A fresh attempt to produce the just man made perfect, that is, to make humanity divine. And you will vitiate the experiment if you make the slightest attempt to abort it into some fancy figure of your own, for example, your notion of a good man or a womanly woman. . . . If you begin with its holiest aspirations, and suborn them for your own purposes, there is hardly any limit to the mischief you may do.[1]

This statement seems to speak with a profound understanding of the nature of both the outer and inner child. The idea that a child is a "fresh experiment" implies that the child is viewed as an individual with gifts and limitations particular to his or her own unique nature—a being who can contribute to the exploration of life's meaning, who can contribute to the richness of life's possibilities.

This new being, out of necessity for nurturance and guidance, finds himself in a particular family, a particular culture, a particular education. Within these particulars are rules, values, and systems to which the child begins to adapt, becoming shaped by them. This shaping often happens to such an extent that the child is no longer connected to those aspects of his being which do not fit within the structure of these outer forms and expectations. For some, adaptation means that those gifts which do not fit within the structure or are not valued are submerged and consequently lost, not only to the individual but to the culture as well.

In others, the vitality of these gifts cannot be so easily submerged. Lacking appropriate channels for expression, the energy behind these gifts will cause pain, as can any energy when it is blocked and pushes for a chance to live.

This experience can be like that which Wordsworth so well describes, "Shades of the prison-house begin to close / Upon the growing Boy"[2] ("The Boy" refers to the Divine or Self aspect). Every time I read this line I feel within my own body the double strain of restriction from the outside and the organic pressure of growth from the inside.

While writing this, on the first glorious day of spring, I went outside to watch our tulips open in the sun. I noticed some day lilies that had struggled to come up through a few boards left over from our winter building project. The force of these fragile shoots in a vital push for growth was amazing, but because of the restriction of the boards they were bent, distorted, and somewhat yellow. Once out into the light and free of the boards, perhaps they would be able to straighten up, continue to grow, and eventually to blossom. But they might never gain the fullness of other flowers nearby that had only the open space of sun, air, and rain to meet as they emerged.

So it is often with the child. The board once used to provide structure may crush or distort the natural organic life of our children. We need to be continually vigilant in looking under those boards—examining our value systems and our assumptions about reality.

Where shall we turn for the inspiration and encouragement to lift up the debris of the old and restricting structure—our notions of the "good man" or "womanly woman" of which Shaw speaks? Unfortunately, these images are often formed out of an unconscious acceptance of the collective definitions of success, health, and normality.

Here Shaw's last phrase is important—the idea that the child has his or her own "holiest aspirations," own unique path. In this context, the word "holiest" may have two meanings. The aspirations or intentions are seen to have a holy or spiritual source. And we know the word "holy" is related to "whole." To take this gift of life we are given and carefully, respectfully help it to grow to its fullest can be the "holiest" task. This growth must include all aspects of our being as individuals, not only those that are sanctioned by collective values. This urge to grow is as natural in each of us as the urge to push up past the boards was in the day lily. C. G. Jung says in his essay on "The Psychology of the Child Archetype" that the image of the child "represents the strongest, the most ineluctable urge in every being, namely the urge to realize itself."[3]

The divine aspect of the inner child that resides in us all is a source that when consciously realized can give us the courage and enthusiasm of exploration to break out of our "prison doors." I use the word "divine" to distinguish this aspect from the inner child which has been formed by memory of personal experience—that is, the neglected, abused, unfed, unloved, overdisciplined, overjudged child, as well as the vulnerable and needful aspects of the child we once were. This is the child—our child of experience—which we all desire to heal, so that we can reclaim the energy for adult action that still resides in the reactive patterns of defense and protection that we developed in response to early painful experiences. To heal this child also means that we will not unconsciously continue these patterns with the "fresh experiments" that are our own children.

The actual child of our memory is no longer who we are. Though we have survived beyond it, we frequently continue to live our lives unaware of patterns we adopted when we were young, and thus we limit the scope of our living in the present. The consequences of the hurt, fear, anger, and loneliness of early years have been given much recognition in recent years in psychological theory and therapeutic practice. However, when the spotlight is thrown on early experiences, other memories also can return—positive images of events that supported the child's natural exuberance, curiosity and adventurous exploration, the deliciousness of the senses and the richness of the imagination. These memories, allowed to emerge, give us a sense of the history of our pleasure and pains, reconnecting us to the being we are now as adults. How we live in the present is a consequence of all the events which have come to us in our experiment with living.

In addition to memories of actual events, we often carry within us an image of the ideal childhood, one with perfect nurturance and guidance. It is the childhood we would have liked, constructed out of the limitations of our own experience. By comparison, we find our own childhood wanting. This image is sometimes projected on others whom we perceive as having had a perfect childhood, and we increase our loneliness and pain as we mourn for the ideal. Frequently this image is also projected on our children as we try to provide a perfect childhood for them, at the same time creating an image of ourselves as the perfect parents.

One antidote for this paradisical idealization of childhood is to share our stories and history with others, discovering thereby that the common human condition of children and parents is a complex blend of successes and failures, gifts and limitations.

Behind these images of the actual and the ideal childhood is the image of the divine inner child mentioned earlier, which comes from the deepest archetypal level of our being. This archetypal image has as its universal function the task of seeing that our experiment with living remains fresh. The divine inner child has innocence, which the Zen master Suzuki Roshi called "beginner's mind." It represents spontaneity and the deep urge of the human soul to expand, to grow, and to explore vast and unlimited territories.

Sometimes this inner child makes very strong demands, presenting itself in emotions of anxiety, depression, anger, hopelessness, or in physical symptoms. Sometimes it brings us subtle and fragile new shoots of inspiration—a sudden idea, a dream, a fantasy, or a feeling of longing for something renewing. The natural, vital force of this archetype wants recognition by us and cannot be ignored without consequences. If we do not claim its enlivening energy for ourselves, we often project it outwardly. If we place the archetypal child onto our outer, physical children, then they will carry the burden of our own creative development.

This inspiring image of the inner child represents the creative aspects of life, both within the individual human being and in the collective. It is expressed in myth, the metaphorical realm of history. In every culture there are stories of the birth of the special child—child of the gods, goddesses, and heroes—timeless stories that belong to the species. As we hear these ancient stories we can perhaps resonate with them as songs of our primal origins. Here we can rediscover and remember the roots of our own nature, our instincts, and creativity, and recognize elements of our being we once knew instinctively. They can remind us of our incipient wholeness, which was in our origins.

Perhaps it is best to give an example of such a story. My favorite one among the Greek epiphanies is the story of Hermes as a child. Hermes is born of a union of Zeus and the wood nymph Maia. Maia's name reminds us of the month of May; of Mary the mother of another Divine Child, Jesus; and of Maya, the mother of Buddha. To protect Hermes from Zeus's jealous wife Hera, Maia keeps the infant in a cave, as if in a second womb. Zeus has abandoned his new son and has returned to Olympus and his old family.

Maia, a spirit of nature, cares for Hermes. A trickster in character, the child escapes the cave in the early morning of the first day of his life, creates a lyre from a tortoise shell, and steals his brother Apollo's cattle. Apollo apprehends his young brother and takes him to trial at the court of Zeus. Hermes, according to Homer, replies to all-knowing Zeus's accusations, "How could I have done such a thing? I was only born yesterday," and winks at Zeus. At that, Zeus laughs, and all those on Olympus laugh with him. Zeus's only dictum is that harmony be established between the two brothers, a feat that is ultimately achieved when Hermes plays the new instrument of harmony he has created, the lyre.

In this story we find the universally common elements of mythic tales recounting the birth of the divine child. Although there are variations of plot, circumstance, and costume, these mythic dramas seem to share a skeletal structure that defines the general qualities and characteristics of the inner child, attributes that have much meaning to us psychologically.

In the first place, these children are born under circumstances of unusual conception and delivery—unusual from the point of view of ordinary human birth. These conceptions are sometimes the result of the union of spirit and human, as in the immaculate conception of Mary or in the case of Buddha's mother, who is impregnated by an elephant. Sometimes the union is that of a god with some aspect of nature, as Hermes born from Zeus and the wood nymph. The birth itself can be unusual, directly out of primal elements of water or fire (Venus), or out of the head of Zeus (Athena), or from his thigh (Dionysus).

These unusual births speak metaphorically of the emergence in us of a new beginning that comes from unknowable, unexpected, out-of-the-ordinary sources and creates spontaneous birthings within our own psyches. These may come as hunches, dreams, visions, or emotions. If the outer personality or the culture has developed in a one-sided, restricted manner, the appearance of the divine inner child will presage the possibility of renewal and expansion. The inner birth may be conceived through an outer event that startles or surprises us. Perhaps seen as an accident of fate, it awakens us to a new insight of life possibility.

The child, so unusually conceived and delivered, comes into a particular situation, culture, or order that is already formed, whether in the realm of the gods, the underworld, or the human sphere. This world has its own established patterns and principles represented by those in power, and this unusually created and creative child is in most cases in great danger from the old order. Even Apollo attempts to destroy his precocious baby brother, Hermes. Herod kills the young in order to be sure of destroying the Christ child. Hera, always jealous of Zeus's mating with the new and virginal elements, seeks to destroy the progeny of such unions. These rulers represent in us the old structure that does not want to lose its power to the new and divinely conceived being. To incorporate the new, the old must give way to change.

To be sensitive and responsive to the promptings and demands of this inner child, who is constantly urging us to be more, opens us for change. On the other hand, the discomfort of this experience will often result in attempts to placate, distract, or tranquilize this inner child, or to ignore it and deny it time and attention. Thus we jeopardize our own "holiest aspirations."

In addition to danger from the existing order that wants to maintain its established power, these divine children of myth and psyche are exposed and vulnerable because they are often abandoned by one or both parents, as Zeus abandons Hermes. Within our own psyches this may indicate that the ordinary familiar parents, patterns of what we already know, abandon this child to his own devices to find his own singular, nonconventional place in the order of things.

Although abandoned by his divine parents, the child is often protected by guardians from the earth realm, representations of the natural forces in our own simple, primitive nature that can nurture this special child quietly, with a kind of earth-peasant knowledge. This natural force can allow the child to become earthed, to become incarnated in us in its own natural organic timing.

The child's place of birth often offers some protection. Hermes is born in a cave, a kind of second womb. So was his father, Zeus, protecting him from being devoured by *his* father, Chronos. Christ is born in a stable, since there is no room at the collective inn. And here again it is the animals and shepherds who first surround him. In this protected place, the child can gain strength until ready to enter the threatening world. Psychologically, this protection may represent some development in us—a creative idea, a dream, or a new attitude or relation to life—that should not be manifested or brought out into the light before it has a certain maturity and can survive on its own and, consequently, can bring effective and integrated change to the old order. Christ is twelve when he returns and speaks to the elders in the temple.

Paradoxically, this abandoned and threatened child that needs protection is already full of creative individuality and indestructible power. It is the extraordinary gift of Hermes that creates the lyre and threatens Apollo with the magical power of trickery. Buddha, just born, walks seven steps from his mother and, pointing both upward and downward, declares himself Prince of all that is above and below. It is this power that draws the three Kings of the Orient to come and worship the Christ child.

In fact, it is precisely this recognized, prophesized, intuited power that is such a threat to the old order. It is not just an ordinary event, this birth. In psychological terms it can be seen as a manifestation of the Self, which demands a restructuring of the personality. This can lead to a painful disintegration of the old form and often a time of confusion, loneliness, and disorientation before the new order is established.

These potentially painful trials are sensed by the currently ruling principle in the personality, the ego. The ego may set up resistances in an attempt to silence the new voice. But being divine, it will not be silenced. We always have before us the choice of listening to it cry to us out of its prison, or to join its exuberant, joyful movement toward an expanded, more humane life. Then we can enter with it into the world of divine play.

Hermes brought laughter and the sound of soothing, harmonious music into the world of Olympus—a new ingredient in the kingdom to be acknowledged and appreciated, changing the quality of the realm forever.

In the modern adult, the energy of the inner child may result in dramatic changes in lifestyle and image. It may lead only to the pursuit of new interests or habits. But once born in us, this child will demand that we expand our world to include it, to suffer the abandonment of our own inner familiarities that sustained us, and to tolerate the loneliness arising from creative action conceived out of an inspired connection to the new. The prize to be won is our totality, a totality hinted at in our beginnings and to which we are inexorably drawn. It is possible that cultures can also be so renewed, old orders reexamined and reconstructed, leading toward a more harmonious world for the human race.

The archetype of the inner child, then, can bring a sense of hope to the hopelessness of our personal history and world history. It reminds us of a time as it was in the beginning, the moment of creation, the new, the unexpected, the individual difference that changes the whole. This is the promise of the "fresh experiment," the promise of the inner child.

2 · THE PSYCHOLOGY OF THE CHILD ARCHETYPE

. . . .

C. G. JUNG

This is an excerpt from the pioneering study of the inner child. To understand the child archetype requires some grounding in Jung's background notion of the collective unconscious, which he conceived of as the repository of humanity's psychic heritage and possibilities. It also requires some understanding of the nature of the archetype, one of Jung's major discoveries, perhaps the fundamental concept in his work. He developed his theory of the archetypes in stages, beginning around 1912. The realization of his own inner child came from personal encounters around the same time (see Chapters 7 and 26 for details of these experiences). This essay contains the quintessential musings on the inner child. It is pregnant with the very thoughts that have spawned and given reality to our subject; it is referenced by several contributors in this volume.

The archetype, according to Jung, "is an irrepresentable unconscious, pre-existent form that seems to be part of the inherited structure of the psyche. Its form might perhaps be compared to the axial system of a crystal, which, as it were, preforms the crystalline structure in the mother liquid, although it has no material existence of its own. . . . The archetype in itself is empty and purely formal, nothing but a preformed faculty, a possibility of representation which is given a priori. The representations themselves are not inherited, only the forms, and in that respect they correspond in every way to the instincts, which are also determined in form only. The existence of the instincts can no more be proved than the existence of the archetypes, so long as they do not manifest themselves concretely" (CW, vol. 9, i, para. 155).

Jung also said: "Archetypes were, and still are, living psychic forces. . . . Always they were the bringers of protection and salvation, and their violation has as its consequence the 'perils of the soul' known to us from the psychology of primitives. Moreover, they are the unfailing causes of neurotic and even psychotic disorders, behaving exactly like neglected or maltreated physical organs or organic functional systems" (CW, vol. 9, i, para. 266).

The Critical Dictionary of Jungian Analysis *(Samuels, et al., 1986) says the following:*

> *All psychic imagery partakes of the archetypal to some extent. That is why dreams and many other psychic phenomena have numinosity. Archetypal behaviors are most evident at times of crisis, when the ego is most vulnerable. Archetypal qualities are found in symbols and this accounts in part for their fascination, utility and recurrence. Gods are metaphors of archetypal behaviors and myths are archetypal enactments. The archetypes can neither be fully integrated nor lived out in human form. Analysis involves a growing awareness of the archetypal dimensions of a person's life. . . . Jung's concept of the archetype is in the tradition of Platonic Ideas, which are present in the minds of the gods and serve as the models of all entities in the human realm.*

This essay in its complete form was published originally in 1940; an English translation was made in 1949, the current translation in 1963.

THE ARCHETYPE AS A LINK WITH THE PAST

As to the *psychology* of our theme I must point out that every statement going beyond the purely phenomenal aspects of an archetype lays itself open to criticism. Not for a moment dare we succumb to the illusion that an archetype can be finally explained and disposed of. Even the best attempts at explanation are only more or less successful translations into another metaphorical language. (Indeed, language itself is only an image.) The most we can do is to *dream the myth onwards* and give it a modern dress. And whatever explanation or interpretation does to it, we do to our own souls as well, with corresponding results for our own well-being.

The archetype—let us never forget this—is a psychic organ present in all of us. A bad explanation means a correspondingly bad attitude to this organ, which may thus be injured. But the ultimate sufferer is the bad interpreter himself. Hence the "explanation" should always be such that the functional significance of the archetype remains unimpaired, so that an adequate and meaningful connection between the conscious mind and the archetype is assured. For the archetype is an element of our psychic structure and thus a vital and necessary component in our psychic economy. It represents or personifies certain instinctive data of the dark, primitive psyche, the real but invisible roots of consciousness. Of what elementary importance the connection with these roots is, we see from the preoccupation of the primitive mentality with certain "magic" factors, which are nothing less than what we would call archetypes. This original form of *religio* ("linking back") is the essence, the working basis of all religious life even today, and always will be, whatever future form this life may take.

There is no "rational" substitute for the archetype any more than there is for the cerebellum or the kidneys. We can examine the physical organs anatomically, histologically, and embryologically. This would correspond to an outline of archetypal phenomenology and its presentation in terms of comparative history. But we only arrive at the *meaning* of a physical organ when we begin to ask teleological questions. Hence the query arises: What is the biological purpose of the archetype? Just as physiology answers such a question for the body, so it is the business of psychology to answer it for the archetype.

Statements like "The child motif is a vestigial memory of one's own childhood" and similar explanations merely beg the question. But if, giving this proposition a slight twist, we were to say, "The child motif is a picture of certain *forgotten* things in our childhood," we are getting closer to the truth. Since, however, the archetype is always an image belonging to the whole human race and not merely to the individual, we might put it better this way: "The child motif represents the pre-conscious childhood aspect of the collective psyche."[1]

(It may not be superfluous to point out that lay prejudice is always inclined to identify the child motif with the concrete experience "child," as though the real child were the cause and precondition of the existence of the child motif. In psychological reality, however, the empirical idea "child" is only the means [and not the only one] by which to express a psychic fact that cannot be formulated more exactly. Hence by the same token the mythological idea of the child is emphatically not a copy of the empirical child but a *symbol* clearly recognizable as such: it is a wonder-child, a divine child, begotten, born, and brought up in quite extraordinary circumstances, and not—this is the point—a human child. Its deeds are as miraculous or monstrous as its nature and physical constitution. Only on account of these highly unempirical properties is it necessary to speak of a "child motif" at all. Moreover, the mythological "child" has various forms: now a god, giant, Tom Thumb, animal, etc., and this points to a causality that is anything but rational or concretely human. The same is true of the "father" and "mother" archetypes which, mythologically speaking, are equally irrational symbols.)

We shall not go wrong if we take this statement for the time being *historically*, on the analogy of certain psychological experiences which show that certain phases in an individual's life can become autonomous, can personify themselves to the extent that they result in a *vision of oneself*—for instance, one sees oneself as a child. Visionary experiences of this kind, whether they occur in dreams or in the waking state, are, as we know, conditional on a dissociation having previously taken place between past and present. Such dissociations come about because of various incompatibilities; for instance, a man's present state may have come into conflict with his childhood state, or he may have violently sundered himself from his original character in the interests of some arbitrary persona[2] more in keeping with his ambitions. He has thus become unchildlike and artificial, and has lost his roots. All this presents a favorable opportunity for an equally vehement confrontation with the primary truth.

In view of the fact that men have not yet ceased to make statements about the child god, we may perhaps extend the individual analogy to the life of mankind and say in conclusion that humanity, too, probably always comes into conflict with its childhood conditions, that is, with its original, unconscious, and instinctive state, and that the danger of the kind of conflict which induces the vision of the "child" actually exists. Religious observances, i.e., the retelling and ritual repetition of the mythical event, consequently serve the purpose of bringing the image of childhood, and everything connected with it, again and again before the eyes of the conscious mind so that the link with the original condition may not be broken.

THE FUNCTION OF THE ARCHETYPE

The child motif represents not only something that existed in the distant past but also something that exists *now*; that is to say, it is not just a vestige but a system functioning in the present whose purpose is to compensate or correct, in a meaningful manner, the inevitable one-sidedness and extravagances of the conscious mind. It is in the nature of the conscious mind to concentrate on relatively few contents and to raise them to the highest pitch of clarity. A necessary result and precondition is the exclusion of other potential contents of consciousness. The exclusion is bound to bring about a certain one-sidedness of the conscious contents. Since the differentiated consciousness of civilized man has been granted an effective instrument for the practical realization of its contents through the dynamics of his will, there is all the more danger, the more he trains his will, of his getting lost in one-sidedness and deviating further and further from the laws and roots of his being. This means, on the one hand, the possibility of human freedom, but on the other it is a source of endless transgressions against one's instincts. Accordingly, primitive man, being closer to his instincts, like the animal, is characterized by fear of novelty and adherence to tradition. To our way of thinking he is painfully backward, whereas we exalt progress. But our progressiveness, though it may result in a great many delightful wish-fulfillments, piles up an equally gigantic Promethean debt which has to be paid off from time to time in the form of hideous catastrophes. For ages man has dreamed of flying, and all we have got for it is saturation bombing! We smile today at the Christian hope of a life beyond the grave, and yet we often fall into chiliasms a hundred times more ridiculous than the notion of a happy Hereafter. Our differentiated consciousness is in continual danger of being uprooted; hence it needs compensation through the still existing state of childhood.

The symptoms of compensation are described, from the progressive point of view, in scarcely flattering terms. Since, to the superficial eye, it looks like a retarding operation, people speak of inertia, backwardness, scepticism, fault-finding, conservatism, timidity, pettiness, and so on. But inasmuch as man has, in high degree, the capacity for cutting himself off from his own roots, he also may be swept uncritically to catastrophe by his dangerous one-sidedness. The retarding ideal is always more primitive, more natural (in the good sense as in the bad), and more "moral" in that it keeps faith with law and tradition. The progressive ideal is always more abstract, more unnatural, and less "moral" in that it demands disloyalty to tradition. Progress enforced by will is always *convulsive*. Backwardness may be closer to naturalness, but in its turn it is always menaced by painful awakenings. The older view of things realized that progress is only possible *Deo concedente* ("God willing"), thus proving itself conscious of the opposites and repeating the age-old *rites d'entree et de sortie* ("rites of passage") on a higher plane. The more differentiated consciousness becomes, the greater the danger of severance from the root-condition. Complete severance comes when the *Deo concedente* is forgotten. Now it is an axiom of psychology that when a part of the psyche is split off from consciousness it is only *apparently* inactivated; in actual fact it brings about a possession of the personality, with the result that the individual's aims are falsified in the interests of the split-off part. If, then, the childhood state of the collective psyche is repressed to the point of total exclusion, the unconscious content overwhelms the conscious aim and inhibits, falsifies, even destroys its realization. Viable progress only comes from the cooperation of both.

THE FUTURITY OF THE ARCHETYPE

One of the essential features of the child motif is its futurity. The child is potential future. Hence the occurrence of the child motif in the psychology of the individual signifies as a rule an anticipation of future developments, even though at first sight it may seem like a retrospective configuration. Life is a flux, a flowing into the future, and not a stoppage or a backwash. It is therefore not surprising that so many of the mythological saviors are child gods. This agrees exactly with our experience of the psychology of the individual, which shows that the "child" paves the way for a future change of personality. In the individuation process, it anticipates the figure that comes from the synthesis of conscious and unconscious elements in the personality. It is therefore a symbol which unites the opposites;[3] a mediator, bringer of healing, that is, one who makes whole. Because it has this meaning, the child motif is capable of the numerous transformations mentioned above: it can be expressed by roundness, the circle or sphere, or else by the quaternity as another form of wholeness.[4] I have called this wholeness that transcends consciousness the "self.[5] The goal of the individuation process is the synthesis of the self. From another point of view the term "entelechy" might be preferable to "synthesis" [entelechy = a vital force urging an organism toward self-fulfillment]. There is an empirical reason why "entelechy" is, in certain conditions, more fitting: the symbols of wholeness frequently occur at the beginning of the individuation process, indeed they can often be observed in the first dreams of early infancy. This observation says much for the *a priori* existence of potential wholeness,[6] and on this account the idea of entelechy instantly recommends itself. But insofar as the individuation process occurs, empirically speaking, as a synthesis, it looks paradoxically enough, as if something already existent were being put together. From this point of view, the term "synthesis" is also applicable.

THE CHILD AS BEGINNING AND END

Faust, after his death, is received as a boy into the "choir of blessed youths." I do not know whether Goethe was referring, with this peculiar idea, to the *cupids* on antique grave-stones. It is not unthinkable. The figure of the *cucullatus* points to the hooded, that is, the *invisible* one, the genius of the departed, who reappears in the childlike frolics of a new life, surrounded by the sea-forms of dolphins and tritons. The sea is the favorite symbol for the unconscious, the mother of all that lives. Just as the "child" is, in certain circumstances (e.g., in the case of Hermes and the Dactyls), closely related to the phallus, symbol of the begetter, so it comes up again in the sepulchral phallus, symbol of a renewed begetting.

The "child" is therefore *renatus in novam infantiam* ("reborn into a new childhood"). It is thus both beginning and end, an initial and a terminal creature. The initial creature existed before man was, and the terminal creature will be when man is not. Psychologically speaking, this means that the "child" symbolizes the pre-conscious and the post-conscious essence of man. His pre-conscious essence is the unconscious state of earliest childhood; his post-conscious essence is an anticipation by analogy of life after death. In this idea the all-embracing nature of psychic wholeness is expressed. Wholeness is never comprised within the compass of the conscious mind —it includes the indefinite and indefinable extent of the unconscious as well. Wholeness, empirically speaking, is therefore of immeasurable extent, older and younger than consciousness and enfolding it in time and space. This is no speculation, but an immediate psychic experience. Not only is the conscious process continually accompanied, it is often guided, helped, or interrupted, by unconscious happenings. The child had a psychic life before it had consciousness. Even the adult still says and does things whose significance he realizes only later, if ever. And yet he said them and did them as if he knew what they meant. Our dreams are continually sayings things beyond our conscious comprehension (which is why they are so useful in the therapy of neuroses). We have intimations and intuitions from unknown sources. Fears, mood, plans, and hopes come to us with no visible causation. These concrete experiences are at the bottom of our feeling that we know ourselves very little; at the bottom, too, of the painful conjecture that we might have surprises in store for ourselves.

Primitive man is no puzzle to himself. The question "What is man?" is the question that man has always kept until last. Primitive man has so much psyche outside his conscious mind that the experience of something psychic outside him is far more familiar to him than to us. Consciousness hedged about by psychic powers, sustained or threatened or deluded by them, is the age-old experience of mankind. This experience has projected itself into the archetype of the child, which expresses man's wholeness. The "child" is all that is abandoned and exposed and at the same time divinely powerful; the insignificant, dubious beginning, and the triumphal end. The "eternal child" in man is an indescribable experience, an incongruity, a handicap, and a divine prerogative; an imponderable that determines the ultimate worth or worthlessness of a personality.

3 · THE CHILD ARCHETYPE IN THE POETRY OF WORDSWORTH

· · · · · · ·

JAMES H. YOUNG

James H. Young amplifies Jung's child archetype through the many children in Wordsworth's poetry. He also demonstrates how the ideas of childhood illuminate the mysterious quality in the work of this most accomplished English Romantic poet. Wordsworth's poetry beautifully illustrates Jung's conception of the inner child, showing us the child's access to what the poet called "unknown modes of being." Young's analysis and comparison expands on the inner child theme in both of these writers: Jung's symbolic understanding of the inner child is an excellent balance to Wordsworth's struggle with the literalism of recovering the child in adulthood. This essay originally appeared in the Winter, 1977, volume of the journal Quadrant.

The child, prattling, bashful, or curious, is a recurrent image in the poetry of William Wordsworth. Some of Wordsworth's poems are addressed to particular children, such as Coleridge's son Hartley or Wordsworth's own sons and daughters. Children usually appear in Wordsworth's poems simply as an essential element in the panorama of life. Sometimes, however, children take on the special aura of the divinity; they are invested with holy light or they function as inspirations to others. These special, rather superhuman children in Wordsworth's poems show many of the features of what C. G. Jung has called the "child archetype," and consequently these special children are of particular interest.

    Because of the similarities between certain of the children in Wordsworth's poetry and the child archetype, it is reasonable to consider to what degree Jung's concept of the child archetype sheds light on Wordsworth's poems. It is the purpose of this study to demonstrate that Jung's comments on the child archetype are indeed very useful in the interpretation of Wordsworth's poetry. Particularly, Jung's ideas illuminate Wordsworth's *Ode: Intimations of Immortality from Recollections of Early Childhood*—a poem that affirms the possibility that the adult may regain something like the lost "vision splendid" of childhood.

The child archetype is the image of a child that appears in myths and legends from all over the world; it appears in dreams, and sometimes in works of the imagination such as poems. Jung notes the importance of the unusual features of the child archetype. He says, "The mythological idea of the child is emphatically not a copy of the empirical child, but a symbol clearly recognizable as such; it is a wonder-child, a divine child, begotten, born, and brought up in quite extraordinary circumstances, and not—this is the point—a human child."[1]

Examples of the child archetype in myths and legends are numerous. A few instances will suffice here to suggest the exotic quality of the archetypal child. In Indian legend, one such child appears to Indra, who has slain "the dragon" and released the "flood of life."[2] Indra commands the "miraculous genius" Vishvarkarman to erect a magnificent palace to commemorate this triumph. Vishvarkarman, however, cannot keep up with Indra's architectural demands and complains to the demiurgic creator, Brahma, who promises to help. The next morning a boy with "luminous features" and "radiant with the luster of wisdom" appears and describes to Indra how he has seen eons come and go. Indra addresses him as "Ocean of Virtues" and "Wisdom Incarnate" and asks to be taught the "secrets of the ages." The boy's words lead Indra to "wisdom"; he no longer wishes to build a palace.

Another example is seen in Merlin of the Arthurian legends, who "can also appear as a child . . . pouring forth wisdom all age and time."[3] For example, in one tale a white stag raced into Arthur's hall and around the round table, pursued by a pack of dogs, one of which, still pursuing the stag, dragged Gawain out of the hall. The dogs were followed by a black huntsman, and finally came a fair damsel who paused long enough to request aid from the bewildered knights. Arthur looked to Merlin for an explanation. "Merlin threw back the hood that concealed his lined face, and the moment his features became visible they were transformed. The familiar countenance with its long white beard and crowned with druidic mistletoe had become the radiant visage of an ageless boy, with leaves of laurel in his golden hair." The transformed Merlin makes an oracular statement and disappears.[4]

These illustrations demonstrate some of the particular qualities and functions Jung saw as characteristic of the archetypal child. The child is often divinely inspired and in some cases literally radiates light or is shrouded in an aura of divinity. The child is sometimes seen as hopelessly fragile, surrounded by forces that threaten to consume or destroy it, yet the child in such a setting may miraculously surmount all the dark forces that oppose it, in some cases emerging as a hero figure. The child is sometimes portrayed as having a special affinity with nature, or of being attuned to a divine presence permeating nature. Finally, the child often functions as a herald bringing spiritual revelation, or as a healer capable of miraculously curing or saving the sick and the lost.[5]

These qualities and functions of the archetypal child may all be found in child-images of Wordsworth's poetry. Wordsworth often portrays children, for example, as illuminated or enlightened by their special sensibilities. In the sonnet "Oh What a Wreck" Wordsworth suggests that children are "privileged to hold / Divine communion," and in the sonnet "Young England" he advised England to "Let Babes and Sucklings be their oracles."[6] Similarly a comparably wise child figure, according to Erich Neumann, appears in the Jewish Midrash, an ancient exposition of biblical texts. In describing the child archetype, Neumann notes that the Midrash "ascribes knowledge to the unborn babe in the womb, saying that over its head there burns a light in which it sees all the ends of the world."[7]

Wordsworth's archetypal children are sometimes not only inspired by the light of higher knowledge but literally radiant. In "The Widow on Windermere Side" the widow, burdened by "blameless debt" and deeply grieved by the deaths of all her children, is transported into "earthly ecstacies" by visions of her dead son:

> His raiment of angelic white, and lo!
> His very feet bright as the dazzling snow
> Which they are touching; yea far brighter, even
> As that which comes, or seems to come, from heaven,
> Surpasses aught these elements can show.

The child here is clearly unearthly; his radiance surpasses any brightness of earthly things. The widow accepts him as an "Angel." Other children in Wordsworth's poems are similarly illuminated by divine light. In *The Borderers* the blind Herbert says after a flash of lightning that he has seen "his Child / A face no cherub's face more beautiful / Revealed by lustre brought with it from Heaven" (11. 716–718). Again, in "Maternal Grief" a child "partook / Reflected beams of that celestial light."

The fragile, vulnerable quality of the child archetype is apparent in *The Prelude, VII*, where Wordsworth portrays a child threatened by the hostile environment of London:

> . . . I see
> The lovely Boy as I beheld him then
> Among the wretched and the falsely gay,
> Like one of those who walked with hair unsinged
> Amid the Fiery furnace.

—(11. 366–369)

Another example may be found in "Lucy Gray," in which little Lucy disappears in a blizzard, leaving her parents "wretched." In an odd twist, the ending of the poem suggests that she has somehow surmounted the forces of nature, and that "to this day / She is a living child; / That you may see sweet Lucy Gray / Upon the lonesome wild."

Many of the children in Wordsworth's poetry share with the child archetype the quality of being especially attuned with nature. Jung at one point describes the archetypal child as a "personification of vital forces quite outside the limited range of our one-sided conscious mind; of ways and possibilities of which our conscious mind knows nothing; a wholeness which embraces the very depths of Nature."[8] In Wordsworth's poems children are often regarded as having a special wholeness because of their affinity with nature. In the *Ode*, to cite one example, Wordsworth describes the "Youth" as "Nature's Priest."

One of the most significant features of Jung's child archetype is its frequent function as a herald, a bringer of redemptive grace, or its ability to heal the sick and guide the lost. As Jung puts it, "The 'child' distinguishes itself by deeds which point to the conquest of the dark."[9] Among Wordsworth's poems an early example of such a child appears to Herbert in *The Borderers*. Herbert has returned from the Holy Land blinded, and has been denied his barony. Cast out, resting under a tree with his infant daughter in his arms, Herbert miraculously receives a child guide:

> . . . I heard a voice
> Such as by Cherith on Elija called;
> It said, "I will be with thee!" A little boy,
> Hailed us as if he had been sent from heaven,
> And said, with tears, that he would be our guide.

—(ll. 1362–1367)

Of interest here are the association of the child with the patriarchal voice of the Old Testament, and the auspicious appearance of the child to guide the sightless man across the desolate wastes of the Scottish moors.

Wordsworth again suggests the redemptive power of the child in a description of Lear from "Artegal and Elidure."

> . . . Lear
> By his ungrateful daughters turned adrift.
> Ye lightnings hear his voice!—they cannot hear,
> Nor can the winds restore his simple gift.
> But One there is, a Child of nature meek,
>   Who comes her Sire to seek;
> And he, recovering sense, upon her breast
> Leans smilingly, and sinks into a perfect rest.

—(ll. 41–48)

Even the winds, often symbolic of inspiration in Wordsworth's poetry, cannot "restore" Lear. It is the "Child" who restores "sense" and brings "perfect rest." The healing power of the Angel child in "The Widow on Windermere Side" also may be recalled as an example of an unearthly child with miraculous healing power.

Two child images that seem particularly archetypal appear in Wordsworth's poems "To H. C." and his *Ode: Intimations of Immortality from
Recollections of Early Childhood.* The ethereal quality and fragility of a child
archetype are apparent in a passage of "To H. C.," ostensibly addressed to
Hartley Coleridge:

> *Thou faery voyager! that dost float*
> *In such clear water that thy boat*
> *May rather seem*
> *To brood on air than on an earthly stream;*
> *Suspended on a stream as clear as sky,*
> *Where earth and heaven do make one imagery;*
>
> . . . .
> *Thou art a dew-drop which the morn brings forth,*
> *Ill fitted to sustain unkindly shocks,*
> *Or to be trailed along the soiling earth;*
> *A gem that glitters while it lives,*
> *And no forewarning gives;*
> *But at the touch of wrong, without a strife,*
> *Sips in a moment out of life.*

It might be objected that this passage from "To H. C." has nothing to do
with the child archetype, that it was addressed to Hartley Coleridge, who
was, after all, only Hartley Coleridge, not a mythical child-god. It must
be admitted, however, that there are aspects of the description of Hartley
Coleridge that make him seem larger than life. He is a "faery voyager," a
"gem that glitters," and most significant, he is able to conjoin "earth and
heaven" into "one imagery." The "H. C." of the poem is far more than
Hartley Coleridge, and he is more than a simple image of childlike freshness
and innocence. He is possessed of that "blessed vision" which enables him
to transcend the dichotomy between heaven and earth so that he seems
"suspended in a stream as clear as a sky." The H. C. of the poem is a fragile
but definitely transcendent being, for which the real Hartley Coleridge could
have been little more than the initial inspiration.

The image of the divine child is equally important in Wordsworth's
Ode. There, the child's special purity and higher wisdom are clear in stanza
eight:

> *Thou, whose exterior semblance doth belie*
> *Thy soul's immensity;*
> *Thou best Philosopher, who yet dost keep*
> *Thy heritage, thou Eye among the blind,*
> *That, deaf and silent, read'st the eternal deep,*
> *Haunted forever by the eternal mind,*
> *Mighty Prophet! Seer blest!*
> *On whom those truths do rest,*
> *Which we are toiling all our lives to find,*

In darkness lost, the darkness of the grave;
Thou, over whom thy Immortality
Broods like the Day, a Master o'er a Slave,
A presence which is not to be put by;

. . . .

Thou little Child, yet glorious in the might
of heaven-born freedom . . .

Some images of children in Wordsworth's poems, then, show the attributes Jung held to be typical of the child archetype. They often have special spiritual awareness, they may function as heralds or healers, they may show a special affinity to nature, they may seem fragile or threatened. The child archetype in various guises recurs often enough in Wordsworth's poems so that Jung's discussion of the significance of the child archetype may add to our understanding of Wordsworth's poetry. In particular, Jung's interpretation of the child archetype may contribute to an understanding of Wordsworth's *Ode: Intimations of Immortality from Recollections of Early Childhood.*

The *Ode* is, of course, a much-discussed poem. The prevailing critical view for a time was that the *Ode* was Wordsworth's lament for the lost spiritual awareness of his childhood. According to this view the closing stanzas of the poem conveyed a sense of resignation, as in the lines, "What though the radiance that was once so bright / Be now forever taken from my sight." More recently, the view that the close of the poem is some kind of affirmation has gained gradual acceptance. Certainly the lines in stanza ten of the *Ode*, "Then sing, ye birds, sing, sing a joyous song / And let the young lambs bound," seems to be at least affirmative, if not euphoric. Jung's interpretation of the child archetype lends support to the view of the close of the *Ode* as an affirmation. Furthermore, Jung's ideas may help to establish a clearer understanding of what the poem affirms.

Jung says that the appearance of the child archetype is "conditional to a dissociation having previously taken place between past and present." Such dissociations, Jung adds, "come about because of various incompatibilities." An example of a victim of such an incompatibility, notes Jung, would be a man who has "come into conflict with his childhood state." Such a man would feel "unchildlike and artificial," as if he had "lost his roots." Such a man's mind would be confronted by a "collision of opposites" between his present state and the childhood state, and the archetypal child would symbolize a "nascent state of consciousness," a developing state of mind of which the man is not yet aware. When fully developed and thus conscious, this new state of mind would transcend the apparent "collision of opposites," incorporating elements of both poles of the opposition between child and man.[10]

Jung's interpretation accounts for the phenomonology of the child archetype. The child may seem ethereal, radiant, or especially wise because it represents a higher level of awareness. It is one with natural forces because it represents a higher level of awareness. It is one with natural forces because, as Jung says, it represents a "wholeness which embraces the very depths of Nature."[11] The child functions as a herald or healer because it symbolizes the state of awareness which will transcend the painful "collision of opposites." And the fragile quality sometimes apparent in the child archetype derives from the tentative nature of the developing state of mind. As Jung remarks, "the motifs of insignificance, exposure, abandonment, danger, etc., try to show how precarious is the psychic possibility of wholeness."[12]

Wordsworth's poems often reflect such a Jungian "collision of opposites." In the *Ode* and elsewhere Wordsworth portrays two apparently incompatible modes of awareness: the "vision splendid" of the simple child and the prosaic sight of adulthood. In the *Ode* Wordsworth describes the gradual drawing away from the spiritual awareness of childhood that accompanies growing up. "Heaven lies about us in our infancy," he says, but "shades of the prison house begin to close / Upon the growing boy," though he still "beholds the light." "The Youth," Wordsworth says, "still is Nature's Priest" although he "daily farther from the east / Must travel." Finally, "Man" loses this special vision of childhood. He "perceives it die away / And fade into the light of common day." Thus, Wordsworth describes two modes of awareness which appear irreconcilably incompatible; he is caught in a Jungian collision of opposites.

Wordsworth's perception of these two modes of seeing (in fact, of two modes of being) and his preference for the naturalness and simplicity of the childlike mode, as opposed to the artificiality and narrowness of the adult mode, produced some unusual developments in his poetry. For example, in "The Widow on Windermere Side," in order for the widow to regain childlike spirituality she must give up her reason, her adult way of thinking, and exist in a state of sublime insanity. Even more drastic than this, in some poems natural children are seen as escaping the death in life of adulthood by dying; death, in other words, seems preferable to growing up. One might call it the "Peter Pan syndrome." Lucy Gray, it may be recalled, disappears in a blizzard, but instead of dying she is suspended in a blissful childlike state. "Three Years She Grew" suggests that Lucy, who is claimed by "Nature," may be fortunate in dying. In *The Prelude, VII*, Wordsworth recalls a "lovely boy" he had seen in London, and remarks that it might have been best "that this fair creature, checked / By special privilege of Nature's love / Should in his childhood be detained forever!" (11. 374–376). Richard J. Onorato, in discussing this passage, affirms that "Wordsworth can imagine death . . . as a suitable withdrawal from the life of the historical present which often kills the spirit before the man."[13]

Death, however, is a rather drastic alternative to growing up, and becomes scarcely more appealing even if growing up does mean the loss of one's awareness of the spiritual essences of things. What would be preferable, clearly, would be the achievement of a mode of seeing, or of being, that transcended the dichotomy, that enabled one to see either as a child or as a man, or perhaps as both at once.

In the *Ode* Wordsworth initially presents the duality of the child's and the man's ways of seeing, expressing regret that "The things which I have seen I now can see no more." Some critics have felt that the poem does not move beyond this duality, that if there is anything positive about the end of the poem, it is only that Wordsworth has achieved some sort of resignation. Babenroth, for example, concludes that in the *Ode* Wordsworth is "satisfied to rest in childhood, because there the sense of unity has not been disturbed by the interposition of reason."[14] This view fails to account fully for the conclusion of the poem, however, which clearly suggests the attainment of a level of awareness that combines the child's rapture and man's reason, and thus transcends dualism.

In stanza nine of the *Ode* Wordsworth asserts that "Nor Man nor Boy" can "utterly abolish or destroy" the "Truths that wake to perish never." By saying so, Wordsworth implies that both Man and Boy are in some way threats to truth, and we may infer that they are threats because neither Man nor Boy has broad enough vision to fully apprehend reality. Wordsworth, consequently, would not choose to be either, but to be a mixture of the best qualities of both. The same stanza reveals that he must use man's reason to regain the child's faith in the "glory and the dream." By contemplating those moments when he has glimpsed "the fountain light of all our day," and by "obstinate questioning / Of sense and outward things," he is able to see again "that immortal sea" and to "hear the mighty waters rolling evermore." In the conclusion of the *Ode* Wordsworth affirms that the pure intuitive simplicity of the child may be restored by means of the synthetic reasoning of the man. He achieves a mode of seeing that transcends the duality of child and man. The contemplation in tranquility of those times in one's past when the "glory and the dream" were perceptible enables one to travel "in a moment" back to the "immortal sea." The speaker of the poem thus achieves a third level of vision, much like that achieved by Owain, a mythical predecessor of Gawain, as described by Zimmer:

> He achieves a harmonious fusion of the conscious and the unconscious personalities, the former aware of the problems and controls of the visible, phenomenal world, the latter intuitive of those deeper springs of being from which both the phenomonal and its conscious witness perennially proceed. Such a harmoniously integrated style of life is the boon which nature bestows upon every infant, in a preliminary, indecisive way, and which the growing child then loses with the development of its self-conscious individuality.[15]

Thus the *Ode* affirms the possibility of a synthesis of child and man.

The significance of archetypal children in Wordsworth's poetry then is twofold. First, they often embody the ability to directly apprehend reality, to achieve a mystical awareness of essential truths without the mediation of reason. Second, as Jung suggests, the child-symbol affirms the fragile potential for wholeness. In Wordsworth's *Ode* the appearance of children shrouded in divinity early in the poem is emblematic of the potential to transcend the duality of child and man. The speaker by the end of the poem has transcended this duality: he is both contemplative since he has attained the "philosophic mind," as well as childlike in that he can again see and hear "the immortal sea." Hence the euphoric tone of the lines that begin stanza ten: "Then, sing, ye birds, sing, sing a joyous song / And let the young lambs bound." Admittedly, the man's perceptions are not identical to the child's, for the "radiance which was once so bright" has not returned. Unlike the child, however, who is "deaf and silent," the speaker can see, hear, and speak. Thus, through the poem, the speaker can share his transcendent perceptions with us.

4 · REVERIES
TOWARD
CHILDHOOD

. . . .

GASTON BACHELARD

The highest, the purest, and the best of the child are praised repeatedly by Gaston Bachelard in this excerpt from his 1971 book The Poetics of Reverie. *The author, a significant thinker of modern-day France, explores not only the experience of childhood, the child in the adult, and the archetype of the child, but also the unexperienced childhood, the promise of the inner child, the potential, unlived child: "A potential child is within us. When we go looking for it in our reveries, we relive it even more in its possibilities than in its reality."*

Bachelard doesn't write; he soars. He doesn't understand; he sees. Read his essay and discover the poetic basis for the reality of the child: "Within us, still within us, always within us, childhood is a state of mind."

I

When, all alone and dreaming on rather at length, we go far from the present to relive the times of the first life, several child faces come to meet us. We were several in the trial life, in our primitive life. Only through the accounts of others have we come to know of our unity. On the thread of our history as told by others, year by year, we end up resembling ourselves. We gather all our beings around the unity of our name.

But reverie does not recount. Or, at least there are reveries so deep, reveries which help us descend so deeply within ourselves that they rid us of our history. They liberate us from our name. These solitudes of today return us to the original solitudes. Those original solitudes, the childhood solitudes, leave indelible marks on certain souls. Their entire life is sensitized for poetic reverie which knows the price of solitude. Childhood knows unhappiness through men. In solitude, it can relax its aches. When the human world leaves him in peace, the child feels like a son of the cosmos. And thus, in his solitudes, from the moment he is master of his reveries, the child knows the happiness of dreaming which will later be the happiness of poets. How is it possible not to feel that there is communication between our solitude as a dreamer and the solitudes of childhood? And it is no accident that, in a tranquil reverie, we often follow the slope which returns us to our childhood solitudes.

Let us leave to psychoanalysis then the task of curing badly spent childhoods, of curing the puerile sufferings of an *indurate childhood* which oppresses the psyche of so many adults. There is a task open to a poetico-analysis which would help us reconstitute within ourselves the being of liberating solitudes. Poetico-analysis ought to return all the privileges of the imagination to us. Memory is a field full of psychological ruins, a whatnot full of memories. Our whole childhood remains to be reimagined. In reimagining it, we have the possibility of recovering it in the very life of our reveries as a solitary child.

From then on, the theses which we wish to defend in this chapter all return to make us recognize within the human soul the permanence of a nucleus of childhood, an immobile but ever-living childhood, outside history, hidden from the others, disguised in history when it is recounted, but which has real being only in its instants of illumination, which is the same as saying in the moments of its poetic existence.

When he would dream in his solitude, the child knew an existence without bounds. His reverie was not simply a reverie of escape. It was a reverie of flight.

There are childhood reveries which surge back with the brilliance of a fire. The poet finds his childhood again by telling it with a tone of fire.

Tone of fire. I shall tell what my childhood was.
We unearthed the red moon in the thick of the woods.[1]

An excess of childhood is the germ of a poem. One would laugh at a father who, for love of his child, would go "unhook the moon." But the poet does not shy away from this cosmic gesture. In his ardent memory, he knows that that is a childhood gesture. The child knows very well that the moon, that great blond bird, has its nest somewhere in the forest.

Thus, childhood images, images which a child could make, images which a poet tells that a child has made are, for us, manifestations of the permanent childhood. Those are the images of solitude. They tell of the continuity of the great childhood reveries with the reveries of the poet.

II

So it seems that, with the aid of the poet's images, childhood will be revealed as psychologically beautiful. How can we avoid speaking of psychological beauty when confronted with an attractive event from our inner life? This beauty is within us, at the bottom of memory. It is the beauty of a flight which revives us, which puts the dynamism of one of life's beauties within us. In our childhood, reverie gave us freedom. It is striking that the most favorable field for receiving the consciousness of freedom is none other than reverie. To grasp this liberty when it intervenes in a child's reverie is paradoxical only if one forgets that we still dream of liberty as we dreamed of it when we were children. What other psychological freedom do we have than the freedom to dream? Psychologically speaking, it is in reverie that we are free beings.

A potential childhood is within us. When we go looking for it in our reveries, we relive it even more in its possibilities than in its reality.

We dream of everything that it could have been; we dream at the frontier between history and legend. To reach the memories of our solitudes, we idealize the worlds in which we were solitary children. So it is a problem in practical psychology to take into account the very real idealization of childhood memories and the personal interest we take in all childhood memories. And for that reason there is communication between a poet of childhood and his reader through the intermediary of the childhood which endures within us. Furthermore, this childhood continues to be receptive to any opening upon life and makes it possible for us to understand and love children as if we were their equals in original life.

A poet speaks to us and we are a living water, a new wellspring. Let us listen to Charles Plisnier:

> Ah, provided I consent to it
> my childhood there you are
> as alive, as present
> Firmament of blue glass
> tree of leaf and snow
> river that runs, where am I going?[2]

Reading these lines I see the blue sky above my river in the summers of the other century.

The being of reverie crosses all the ages of man from childhood to old age without growing old. And that is why one feels a sort of redoubling of reverie late in life when he tries to bring the reveries of childhood back to life.

This reinforcement of reverie, this deepening of reverie which we feel when we dream of our childhood explains that, in all reverie, even that which takes us into the contemplation of a great beauty of the world, we soon find ourselves back to old reveries, suddenly so old that we no longer think of dating them. A glimmer of eternity descends upon the world. We are standing before a great lake whose name is familiar to geographers, high in the mountains, and suddenly we are returning to a distant past. We dream while remembering. We remember while dreaming. Our memories bring us back to a simple river which reflects a sky leaning upon hills. But the hill gets bigger and the loop of the river broadens. The little becomes big. The world of childhood reverie is as big, bigger than the world offered to today's reverie. From poetic reverie, inspired by some great spectacle of the world, to childhood reverie, there is a commerce of grandeur. And that is why childhood is at the origin of the greatest landscapes. Our childhood solitudes have given us the primitive immensities.

By dreaming on childhood, we return to the lair of reveries, to the reveries which have opened up the world to us. It is reverie which makes us the first inhabitant of the world of solitude. And we inhabit the world better because we inhabit it as the solitary child inhabits images. In the child's reverie, the image takes precedent over everything else. Experiences come only later. They go against the wind of every reverie of flight. The child sees everything big and beautiful. The reverie toward childhood returns us to the beauty of the first images.

Can the world be as beautiful now? Our adherence to the original beauty was so strong that if our reverie carries us back to our dearest memories, the present world is colorless. A poet who writes a book of poems entitled *Concrete Days* can say:

> . . . *The world totters*
> *when from my past I get*
> *what I need to live in the depths of myself.*[3]

Ah! how solid we would be within ourselves if we could live, live again without nostalgia and in complete ardor, in our primitive world.

In short, isn't that opening on the world of which philosophers avail themselves, a reopening upon the prestigious world of original contemplations? But put another way, is this intuition of the world, this *Weltanschauung* anything other than a childhood which dares not speak its name? The roots of grandeur of the world plunge into a childhood. For man, the world begins with a revolution of the soul which very often goes back to a childhood. A passage by Villiers de L'Isle-Adam will give us an example of this. In 1862 in his book *Isis*, he wrote of his heroine, the dominating woman: "The character of her mind was self-determining, and by obscure transitions it attained the immanent proportions where the self is affirmed for what it is. The nameless hour, the eternal hour when children cease to look vaguely at the sky and the earth rang for her in her ninth year. From this moment on, what was dreamed confusedly in the eyes of this little girl took on a more fixed glint: one would have said she was feeling the meaning of herself while awakening in our shadows."[4]

Thus, in "a nameless hour," the world is affirmed for what it is, and the soul which dreams is a consciousness of solitude. At the end of Villiers de L'Isle-Adam's account, the heroine will be able to say: "My memory, suddenly damaged in the deep domains of the dream, felt inconceivable memories." Thus, the soul and the world are both open to the immemorial.

So, like a forgotten fire, a childhood can always flare up again within us. The fire of yesteryear and the cold of today meet in a great poem by Vincent Huidobro:

In my childhood is born a childhood burning like alcohol
I would sit down in the paths of the night
I would listen to the discourse of the stars
And that of the tree.
Now indifference snows in the evening of my soul.[5]

These images which arise from the depths of childhood are not really memories. In order to evaluate all their vitality, a philosopher would have to be able to develop all the dialectics that are summed up too quickly in the two words "imagination" and "memory." We are going to devote a short paragraph to pointing up the boundaries between memories and images.

III

. . .The past is not stable; it does not return to the memory either with the same traits or in the same light. As soon as the past is situated within a network of human values, within the inner values of a person who does not forget, it appears with the double force of the mind which remembers and the soul which feasts upon its faithfulness. The soul and the mind do not have the same memory. Sully Prudhomme, who experienced this division, wrote:

Oh, memory, the soul renounces,
Frightened, to conceive you.

It is only when the soul and mind are united in a reverie by the reverie that we benefit from the union of imagination and memory. In such a union we can say that we are reliving our past. Our past being imagines itself living again.

From then on, in order to constitute the poetics of a childhood set forth in a reverie, it is necessary to give memories their atmosphere of images. In order to make our philosopher's reflections on remembering the reverie clearer, let us distinguish a few polemical points between psychological facts and values.

In their psychic primitiveness, imagination and memory appear in an indissoluble complex. If they are attached to perception, they are being badly analyzed. The remembered past is not simply a past of perception. Since one is remembering, the past is already being designated in a reverie as an image value. From their very origin, the imagination colors the paintings it will want to see again. For facts to go as far as the archives of the memory, values must be rediscovered beyond the facts. Familiarity is not analyzed by counting repetitions. The techniques of experimental psychology can scarcely hope to undertake a study of the imagination from the point of view of its creative values. In order to relive the *values of the past*, one must dream, must accept the great dilation of the psyche known as reverie, in the peace of a great repose. Then memory and imagination rival each other in giving us back the images which pertain to our lives. . . .

Such a phenomenological project of gathering the poetry of childhood reveries in its personal actuality is naturally much different from the very useful objective examinations of the child by psychologists. Even by letting children speak freely, by observing them uncensored while they are enjoying the total liberty of their play, by listening to them with the gentle patience of a child psychoanalyst, one does not necessarily attain the simple purity of phenomenological examination. People are much too well educated for that and consequently too disposed to apply the comparative method. A mother who sees her child as someone *incomparable* would know better. But alas! a mother does not know for very long. . . . From the time a child reaches the "age of reason," from the time he loses his absolute right to imagine the world, his mother, like all educators, makes it her duty to teach him to be *objective*—objective in the simple way adults believe themselves to be "objective." He is stuffed with sociability. He is prepared for his life as a man along the lines of the ideal of stabilized men. He is also instructed in the history of his family. He is taught most of the memories of early childhood, a whole history which the child will always be able to recount. Childhood—that dough!—is pushed into the die so that the child will follow closely in the path of the lives of others.

The child thus enters into the zone of family, social and psychological conflicts. He becomes a premature man. This is the same as saying that this premature man is in a state of repressed childhood.

The questioned child, the child examined by the adult psychologist, . . . does not surrender his solitude. The solitude of the child is more secret than the solitude of a man. It is often late in life that we discover our childhood and adolescent solitudes in their depths. In the last quarter of life one understands the solitudes of the first quarter by reflecting the solitude of old age off the forgotten solitudes of childhood.[6] The child dreamer is alone, very much alone. He lives in the world of his reverie. His solitude is less social, less pitted against society, than the solitude of men. The child knows a natural reverie of solitude, a reverie which must not be confused with that of the sulking child. In his happy solitudes, the dreaming child knows the cosmic reverie which unites us to the world.

In our opinion, it is in the memories of this cosmic solitude that we ought to find the nucleus of childhood which remains at the center of the human psyche. It is there that imagination and memory are most closely bound together. It is there that the being of childhood binds the real with the imaginary, that it lives the images of reality in total imagination. And all these images of its cosmic solitude react in depth in the being of the child; aside from his being for men, a being for the world is created under the inspiration of the world. That is the being of cosmic childhood. Men pass; the cosmos remains, an ever primitive cosmos, a cosmos that the world's greatest spectacles will not erase in the entire course of life. The cosmicity of our childhood remains within us. In solitude, it reappears in our reveries. This nucleus of cosmic childhood is then like a false memory within us. Our solitary reveries are the activities of a meta-amnesia. It seems that our reveries toward the reveries of our childhood introduce us to a being preconditional to our being, a whole perspective on the *antecedence of being*.

Were we or were we dreaming of being, and now in dreaming on our childhood, are we ourselves? . . .

If the senses remember, aren't they going to find, within some archaeology of the perceptible, these "mineral dreams," these dreams of the "elements," which attach us to the world in an "eternal childhood"?

"Upstream from myself," says the poet; "Upstream from upstream," says the reverie which looks to go back up to the springs (*sources*) of the being; those are the proofs of the antecedence of being. Poets look for this antecedence of being; therefore it exists. Such a certainty is one of the axioms of a philosophy of the oneirism.

In what beyond are poets not capable of remembering? Isn't early life a trial for eternity? Jean Follain can write:

> *While in the fields*
> *of his eternal childhood*
> *the poet wakes*
> *and doesn't want to forget anything.*[7]

How vast life is when one meditates upon its beginnings! Isn't meditating upon an origin dreaming? And isn't dreaming upon an origin going beyond it? Beyond our history extends "our incommensurable memory" to take an expression which Baudelaire borrowed from de Quincey.[8]

In order to force the past, when forgetfulness is hemming us in, poets engage us in reimagining the lost childhood. They teach us "the audacities of the memory."[9] One poet tells us the past must be invented:

> *Invent. There is no lost feast*
> *At the bottom of memory.*[10]

And when the poet invents those great images which reveal the intimacy of the world, isn't he remembering? . . .

Thus the poet says:

> *Of childhoods I have so many*
> *That I would get lost counting them.*[11]

. . . And we shall always return to the same oneiric certainty: Childhood is a human water, a water which comes out of the shadows. This childhood in the mists and glimmers, this life in the slowness of limbo gives us certain layer of births. What a lot of lost springs which have, nevertheless, flowed! Reverie toward our past, then, reverie looking for childhood, seems to bring back to life lives which have never taken place, lives which have been imagined. Reverie is a mnemonics of the imagination. In reverie we re-enter into contact with possibilities which destiny has not been able to make use of. A great paradox is connected with our reveries toward childhood: in us, this dead past has a future, the future of its living images, the *reverie future* which opens before any rediscovered image.

IV

Every childhood is prodigious, naturally prodigious. It is not that it lets itself be impregnated, as we are tempted to believe, by the ever so artificial fables which are told to it and which serve only to amuse the ancestor doing the telling. What a lot of grandmothers take their grandson for a little fool! But the child being born malicious stirs up the mania for storytelling, the eternal repetitions of romancing old age. The child's imagination does not live from these fossile fables, these fossiles of fables. It is in his own fables. The child finds his fables in his reverie, fables which he tells no one. Then the fable is life itself: "I have lived without knowing I was living my fable." This great line is found in a poem entitled "I am sure of nothing."[12] The *permanent child* alone can return the fabulous world to us. Edmond Vandercammen appeals to childhood to "sweep closer to the sky."[13]

> The sky is waiting to be touched by a hand
>   Of fabulous childhood
> —Childhood, my desire, my queen, my cradlesong—
>   By a breath of the morning.

Besides, how could we tell our *fables* when, precisely, we speak of them as "fables"? We hardly know what a *sincere fable* is any more. Grown-ups write children's stories too easily. Thus they make childish fables. To enter into the fabulous times, it is necessary to be serious like a dreaming child. The fable does not amuse, it enchants. We have lost the language of enchantment. Thoreau wrote: "It seems that we only languish during maturity in order to tell the dreams of our childhood, and they vanish from our memory before we were able to learn their language."[14]

In order to rediscover the language of fables, it is necessary to participate in the existentialism of the fabulous, to become body and soul an admiring being and replace perception of the world with admiration. Admiration in order to receive the qualities of what is perceived. And even in the past, to admire the memory. When Lamartine returned to Sant-Point in 1849, at a site where he was about to relive the past, he wrote: "My soul was nothing but a canticle of illusions."[15] Confronted with witnesses to the past, with objects and site which recall memories and make them precise, the poet discovers the union of the poetry of memory and the truth of illusions. Childhood memories relived in reverie are really "canticles of illusions" at the bottom of the soul.

Ah! does the child who exists within us remain under the sign of the forbidden childhood? We are now in the realm of images, of images which are freer than memories. The prohibition to be lifted in order to dream freely does not depend upon psychoanalysis. Beyond parental complexes, there are anthropocosmic complexes against which reverie helps us to react. These complexes block the child in what we shall call, as Bosco does, the forbidden childhood. All our child dreams have to be taken up again so that they will take on their full poetic flight. This task should be accomplished by poetico-analysis. But in order to try it out, it would be necessary to be both poet and psychologist. That is a great deal to ask of one man.

In our dreams toward childhood, in the poems we would all want to write in order to make our original reveries live again, to give us back the universe of happiness, childhood appears, in the very style of the psychology of the depths, like a real *archetype*, the archetype of simple happiness. It is surely an image within us, a center for images which attract happy images and repulse the experiences of unhappiness. But this image, in its principle, is not completely ours; it has deeper roots than our simple memories. Our childhood bears witness to the childhood of man, of the being touched by the glory of living.

From then on, personal memories, clear and often retold, will never completely explain why reveries which carry us back toward our childhood have such an attraction, such a soul quality. The reason for this quality which resists the experiences of life is that childhood remains within us a principle of deep life, of life always in harmony with the possibilities of new beginnings. Everything that begins in us with the distinctness of a beginning is a madness of life. The great archetype of life beginning brings to every beginning the psychic energy which Jung has recognized in every archetype.

Like the archetypes of fire, water and light, childhood, which is a water, a fire which becomes a light, causes a great abundance of fundamental archetypes. In our reveries toward childhood, all the archetypes which link man to the world, which provide a poetic harmony between man and the universe, are, in some sort, revitalized.

Within us, still within us, always within us, childhood is a state of mind.

5 · THE MOTIF OF THE DIVINE CHILD

· · · · · · ·

JUNE SINGER

The divine child is a universal manifestation of the child archetype. We see it in examples such as the madonna and child and the child-hero gods of myth. June Singer, practicing Jungian analyst and author, utilizes both her consulting room experience and her authoritative grasp of mythology to draw a portrait of the divine quality of the inner child. This piece is excerpted from her book Boundaries of the Soul, *a rich study of psychotherapy from a Jungian perspective.*

The archetype of the divine child tends to appear in advance of a transformation in the psyche. His appearance recalls the marking of aeons in the history of the world which were heralded by the appearance of an infant who overthrows an old order and, with passion and inspiration, begins a new one. I know of no place where the power of this archetype is better expressed than in William Blake's poem, *A Song of Liberty*. The Eternal Female, the anima, gives birth to the divine child, a sun god with flaming hair. This evokes the jealous rage of the old king, the "starry king" of night and darkness and all the decadence that has come upon the world. Though the king flings the divine child into the western sea, the child will not be drowned. A night sea journey will take place and when it is finished the son of morning will rise in the east to bring his light to the world:

> The Eternal Female groan'd! it was heard all over the Earth!
> . . . In her trembling hands she took the new born terror,
>   howling:
> On those infinite mountains of light, now barr'd out by the
>   atlantic sea, the new born fire stood before the starry
>   king!
> Flag'd with grey brow'd snows and thunderous visages, the
>   jealous wings wav'd over the deep.
> The speary hand burned aloft, unbuckled was the shield;
>   forth went the hand of jealousy among the flaming hair,

49

and hurl'd the new born wonder thro' the starry night.
The fire, the fire is falling! . . .

The fiery limbs, the flaming hair, shot like the sinking sun
* into the western sea . . .*
With thunder and fire, leading his starry hosts thro' the
* waste wilderness, [the gloomy king] promulgates his ten*
* commands, glancing his beamy eyelids over the deep in dark*
* dismay,*
Where the son of fire in his eastern cloud, while the
* morning plumes her golden breast.*
Spurning the clouds written with curses, stamps the stony
* law to dust, loosing the eternal horses from the dens of*
* night, crying:*
Empire is no more! And now the Lion & Wolf shall cease.[1]

In [Jungian] analysis, the motif of the child frequently appears in the course of the individuation process. At first the analysand tends to identify this with his own infantilism, and this may be appropriate to a degree. Wherever the appearance of the child in dreams or other kinds of imagery bears a resemblance to the dreamer himself, or to a form of the dreamer's behavior, the image may be helpful in understanding the personal aspects of the material itself. It may be helpful in tracing back neurotic elements to an earlier stage of development in the individual.

However, just as fantasy material may, in part, be identifiable with the history of the one who produces it, in part, the image of the divine child may also be new, bearing no resemblance whatever to the previous experience of the individual. It is this latter element that encourages the imagination to dwell on the futurity of the archetype—that is, to ask what this image may suggest about developments which are still embryonic in the psyche but which have the potentiality for growth and change.

As our own children are, to a certain extent, extensions of our own egos, so the "divine child" may be thought of as an extension of the collective consciousness. As we pin our hopes and dreams on our children, wishing for them the fulfillment of our unfinished tasks, the realization of what we were never able to realize, so the "divine child" represents the ideals of a culture which it is not able, in reality, to fulfill. Often the "savior" becomes the scapegoat for the sins of his society, and by reason of his suffering and his sacrifice the society is enabled to continue, to have another chance.

The divine child is unusual from the very circumstances of his birth, or even of his conception. Perhaps he is taken from his mother in order to prevent some dire fate to the family or the community. Moses, Oedipus and Krishna were taken from their mothers and reared by strangers; Romulus and Remus were abandoned to the wilderness; all of these children were saved for a special mission. Some miraculous design kept them safe until the time was ripe for their task to be fulfilled. In the intervening years the child would overcome many difficulties and develop his own sense of meaning and a style of living which expresses that meaning. At the appropriate time he manifests himself and brings into reality that dynamic change for which he was appointed. Shortly thereafter he dies, having accomplished that for which he came.[2]

In our own dreams the appearance of the special child often carries with it a profound meaning. In my practice I have found that it is common for a child who is maimed or ill or dying to appear in a dream. This may have no correspondence to the life of the individual, and so I find myself wondering—in what way is the dreamer's innate potential being distorted or cut off? The analysis of the specific details in the unconscious material and some comparison with similar details as they appear in the archetypal situations in the literature of myth and comparative religion may enable the individual to get beyond his immediate concern and to see where he is going in terms of his life task. As Viktor Frankl pointed out in *Man's Search for Meaning*, his report on his concentration camp experiences, those who regarded their lives in the camp as "provisional" and lived only from day to day quickly lost their strength. The few who were able to find, through their suffering in a place where their physical bodies were imprisoned, the challenge to free their spirits, these few tended to survive against nearly impossible odds. The divine child within us gives meaning to our immature strivings; he shows us the unconscious side of the limitations which we experience, and that is a vision of potentiality coming into flower.

Another archetype which we are likely to meet along the way of individuation has been called by Jung the *puer aeternus*, after the child god Iachhus in the Eleusinian mysteries.[3] He is described by Ovid in *Metamorphoses* as a divine youth, born into the mother-cult mysteries. A god of vegetation and resurrection, he has some of the qualities of the redeemer. The man who is identified with the archetype of the *puer aeternus*, with eternal youth, is one who has remained too long in adolescent psychology. In him, characteristics which are normal in a youth in his teens are continued into later life.[4] Perhaps the expression "high living" best describes what this archetype is about: the young man indulges his high-flying fantasies, living out experiences for their sheer excitement, picking up friends when he wants amusement and dropping them when they become in any sense a responsibility. Some of the heroes of the youth culture fall into this category, and again, for some "getting high" is the objective in and of itself. The aimless traveling, moving in and out of various groups, is characteristic of the *puer*. Homosexuality is an expression of this archetype, especially when homosexuality takes the form of casual and promiscuous relationships, compulsively arrived at. If he is heterosexually inclined, he forms one liaison after another, only to drop each one at the first suggestion that some commitment may be required of him.

Von Franz, in her study of the *puer aeternus* archetype,[5] suggests that the man who is identified with this archetype often seeks a career in flying, but that he is usually rejected on application for the reason that psychological tests how up his instability and the neurotic reasons for his interest in this profession.

The dreams of an individual who is established in his life in a secure position, who may be already middle-aged, may disclose the operation of the *puer aeternus* archetype. The motifs of flying (sometimes without any plane, just by flapping the arms), high-speed driving, deep-sea diving, climbing precarious mountain cliffs, are all typical of one whose unconscious is dominated by this archetype. They may be taken as a warning signal to be aware of the ways in which the unconscious may be preparing to intrude its autonomous will in the way of consciously determined functioning.

There is, of course, a feminine counterpart to the *puer* and that is the *puella aeterna*, the woman who is afraid to grow old, although she will never admit it. Still, the fear dominates much of her existence. She is the one who never tells her age, who falls for every diet fad and for every new make-up with the fantastic promise of rejuvenation written into the advertisements. She is a "pal" to her children, and an everlasting coquette where men are concerned. In her dreams she is often on a pedestal, inspiring the adoration of men, or she is a siren or a whore or a nymphet. In life she generally is reckless and impulsive. When it comes to making an important decision, however, she vacillates a good deal and asks many people for advice. She then acts with surprising suddenness, and she regrets her actions almost before they are completed.

Living the archetype of "eternal youth" is not altogether negative, as may be inferred from some of the ways we see it manifest itself. Some aspects of the *puer aeternus* or the *puella aeterna* which are most helpful are youthful enthusiasm and the boundless energy to carry it along, spontaneity of thinking, production of new ideas and new ways to solve problems, willingness to strike out in a different direction without being held in by a desire to conserve the past and its values.

The *puer* and *puella* as unconscious factors provide the needed impetus to start out on new paths. They do not necessarily offer the wisdom to discern whether the endeavor is worth the struggle, and they often do not provide the steadying and staying power to carry it through if, indeed, it is worth while. When this archetype is active great dreams and schemes will be hatched. If they are to succeed, even in the smallest part, a compensatory archetype must come into play. This is the "senex" archetype.[6]

Senex means old or aged and, as archetype, it stands behind the forces that would preserve the traditional values, that hold out for keeping things the way they are, for applying sober judgment and consideration in the schemes of the eternal youth. At best this factor in the unconscious is expressed in mature wisdom born of experience and, at worst, it represents a hidebound orthodoxy that tolerates no interference from those who would break with established patterns.

A variant of the figure of the *puer aeternus*, sometimes even incorporating aspects of the senex, is the enchanting archetypal figure who is known as the *trickster*.

In dreams the trickster is the one who sets obstacles in our path for his own reasons; he is the one who keeps changing shape and appearing and disappearing at the oddest moments. He symbolizes that aspect of our own nature which is always nearby, ready to bring us down when we get inflated, or to humanize us when we become pompous. He is the satirist par excellence, whose trenchant wit points out the flaws in our haughty ambitions, and makes us laugh though we feel like crying. In society we find him as critic or gadfly, and he even pops up in the highest offices of our land.

6 · REBIRTH AND THE ETERNAL CHILD

· · · · · · ·

RALPH METZNER

Rebirth and renewal are often experiences of renewed hope and possibilities. The child is the promise of the future, the symbol for these transformative processes. In this short excerpt from his book Opening to Inner Light, *Ralph Metzner describes the rebirth experience and its path of intersection with the eternal inner child.*

The process of psychologically dying while one is still alive is followed by a psychological rebirth, or renewal. In the words of Ramana Maharshi, "He who finds his way to the core of the Self, whence arise all levels of the I, all spheres of the world, he who finds his way home to his first source with the question 'whence am I' is born and reborn. Know that whoever is so born is the wisest of the wise—each moment of his life he is born anew."[1]

This rebirth phase of transformation may be experienced in several different ways. (a) First, there is the idea of a resurrection, a restoring to life of a personality that has died. (b) Alternatively, rebirth is seen as the replacement of the small self by another, greater Self or Spirit. (c) Third, it is said that one who has died, whether actually or metaphorically, lives afterward in a different world, a different state. (d) In the fourth variant, the new being is actually imagined as a child: this is the archetype of the radiant, divine, or eternal child, which, as Jung points out, symbolized "the potential future."[2]

(a) The idea of resurrection, the restoration to life of an adult body that has died, is described in many mythic and shamanic tales: Osiris is put together again by Isis; the twins Hunter and Jaguar of the Popul Vuh reassemble themselves after being dismembered; shamans who have "died" may be reconstituted by their power animal or ally. Many modern practitioners of shamanic work recount how they were "cut up," "pulverized," "burned," "eviscerated," or otherwise "killed," then reconstructed by their animal helper.[3] For example, one man reported how his animal, a "horse," stood over his lifeless "corpse" and passed its huge nostrils gently all over his body, "breathing" life back into him. While, from a skeptical point of view, we could dismiss all this as the deluded fantasy of an overactive imagination, we would still have to account for the fact that this man, like others, felt better and healthier after this experience.

In the New Testament, the story of Lazarus, as well as that of Jesus himself, exemplifies this kind of physical resurrection. To a lesser degree, the modern accounts of near-death experience (NDE) coincide with this kind of pattern. In the case of Jesus, the resurrection was into a nonphysical, "spiritual" body that yet resembled the physical in all significant respects, even to having the wounds that the physical body had suffered. The closest most of us come to this kind of experience is in suffering a near-fatal illness and then recovering—the body appears to be fully restored to health. A common feature in all these accounts, when the individual is intentionally pursuing a death-rebirth transformation, is that the new body is better than the old; it is stronger, healthier, and lighter.

(b) Another aspect of this rebirth and renewal experience is that the little self is overshadowed or replaced by the Great Self, the personal-physical ego replaced by the transpersonal Spirit, the mortal by the Immortal. Meister Eckhart says, in this experience "the soul . . . is dead to self and alive to God."[4] A Sufi saint wrote, "thy being dies away, and His person covers thy person."[5] Or, in the words of the Gospel of John, "No one can enter the Kingdom of God without being born from water and Spirit. That which is born of the flesh is flesh, that which is born of the Spirit is spirit."[6] People in such states feel their own ego concern and interests fade into insignificance or nothingness in the face of the awesome power and light of the Great Self, the god within, the "diamond essence," the Atman.

The enounter with the Self can be an overwhelming and annihilating self-confrontation, as was pointed out by C. G. Jung In his essay "Concerning Rebirth," Jung wrote that

> He who is truly and hopelessly little will always drag the revelation of the greater down to the level of his littleness, and will never understand that the day of judgment for his littleness has dawned. But the man who is inwardly great will know that the long-expected friend of his soul, the immortal one, has now really come, "to lead captivity captive"; that is, to seize hold of him by whom this immortal had always been confined and held prisoner, and to make his life flow into that greater life—a moment of deadliest peril.[7]

As this quotation makes clear, the deadly danger exists for those identified with the small self, the personal ego. Not all encounters with Self, however, need be traumatic or even painful. There is, after all, the vast literature of mysticism that sings in rapturous tones of ecstatic union with the divine, of dyings that are peaceful and blissful, of unitive experiences that have the character of a nuptial or are likened to dissolving in an oceanic feeling of oneness.

(c) Some accounts of death-rebirth experiences emphasize the new quality of awareness and perception that comes into existence afterward. It is as if we had entered a new world in which everything looks and feels different, and a kind of pristine, shining radiance suffuses everything we perceive. Mental and emotional responses to what is perceived are also new; there is a quality of joy and spontaneity and an outpouring of affection and enthusiasm. In an anonymous medieval Hermetic treatise we read, "The resurrection is the revelation of what is, and the transformation of things, the transition [*metabole*] into newness. For imperishability descends upon the perishable; the light flows down upon the darkness, swallowing it up."[8] Here we find the metaphor of the newly born paralleling the metaphor of vision with the veils removed, the doors of perception having been cleansed. The mystics say that after the death-rebirth revelation, everything is seen with love and wisdom, from the perspective of the infinite and eternal (*sub specie aeternitatis*).

(d) The biblical admonition that "except ye become as children, ye cannot enter the Kingdom of Heaven" follows naturally from the teaching that one needs to die before entering the blessed, enlightened state of this Kingdom. Here the death-rebirth metaphor leads us to the archetype of the divine child, the *puer aeternus*. While most discussions by Jungians of the *puer* or *puella* focus on the shadow side of this archetype and on its clinical manifestations in flighty, immature "playboys" or "babies," these represent only a limited interpretation of this powerful image. Chinese and Western alchemists spoke of the fetus of immortality, the philosophers' child that is born as a consequence of the inner conjunction of male and female. The idea of the eternal child, who comes into manifestation after a conscious "death" experience is connected to the numerous myths, which play a central role in most religions, of the birth of a god in human form. The Indian legends of the boy Krishna and the Christian legends of the infant Jesus are only the best-known examples.

Jung, in his essay on "The Psychology of the Child Archetype," pointed out several of the significant features or meanings of this profound symbol. He described it as an anticipation of the synthesis of conscious and unconscious, as a symbol of wholeness, or the Self. The child-god or child-hero always has an unusual, miraculous birth or a virgin conception—which corresponds to the "psychic genesis" of the new being. The child image represents a link to the past, to our childhood, as well as a link to the future, as it anticipates a "nascent state of consciousness." The "golden child" or "eternal youth" is androgynous, because he/she represents the perfect union of opposites. Only the old self, the ordinary ego, identifies itself as male or female—and this self has now died. The "child" is both beginning and end, "an initial and a terminal creature," because the wholeness that it symbolizes is "older and younger than consciousness, enfolding it in time and space."[9]

The divine child is invincible. He/she overcomes dangerous enemies in infancy: one of the images of the boy Krishna shows him trampling a giant serpent underfoot in a dance—a metaphor for the overcoming of reptilian instinctual aggressiveness. An example from Greek mythology is the story of the baby Herakles, who strangled a serpent that attacked him in his crib. The Child has all the power of a god, since it is a god: it is the Immortal One that replaces the mortal personality that has "died." Here, too, we find the notion of the divine child as representing the triumph over death. Christ demonstrated the power to resurrect—himself as well as another (Lazarus)—and many other divine heroes and yogic adepts of high degree have demonstrated similar powers, as documented particularly in Eastern mystical literature. While such powers might seem remote to the average person, the myths and images that convey them show potentials; they reveal what humans *can* attain.

In the Russian Orthodox liturgy, the triumph over death is expressed in the following words: "Christ is risen from the dead, trampling down death by death, and upon those in the tomb bestowing life." I suggest that this imagery refers to the change that occurs in the psyche as the healing, transformative power of the intentional dying is experienced. The unconscious death tendencies (*thanatos*), which function to oppose the body's life-preserving tendencies (*eros*) through disease and other destructive operations are gradually reduced; or rather, brought into balance. One of my teachers referred to "pockets of death" within our nature that are opened up and dissolved by enlightened awareness, thus bringing about the death of death. As we consciously accept dying and "dying," the process provides spiritual nourishment. Shakespeare expresses this idea in one of the sonnets:

> So shalt thou feed on death,
>   That feeds on men,
> And death once dead, there's
>   No more dying then.

In the nontheistic Chinese Taoist tradition, the archetype of the eternal child also is known and treasured. The newborn child is still connected to the Tao, to the source of its life and its arising, and this is why we should emulate it. As Chuang Tsu says: "Can you be like a newborn child? The baby cries all day and yet his voice never becomes hoarse. That is because he has not lost nature's harmony."[10] Characteristically, the Taoists emphasize the practical value, in terms of health and well-being, of attunement to the awareness of the infant.

For the individual in a process of transformation, the imagery and mythology of the eternal child fosters a positive and life-affirming attitude: we are encouraged to confront and transform our fear of death, to embrace the process of "dying" as liberating and as bringing wisdom. We thus come to know that out of the turmoil and darkness of dying comes the sparkling vitality of the newborn self. This new self is connected to the eternal source of all life, that source from which we all derive, the divine essence within. It is hence aptly named "the eternal child."

PART 2

. . . .

THE
ABANDONED
CHILD

INTRODUCTION

• • • • • • •

> Mankind is an orphan were it not for God,
> according to St. Augustine. Psychologi-
> cally translated this would imply that for
> the abandoned child there are no "good
> enough" parents. . . . We are indeed all,
> in part, orphans, and it is through the suf-
> fering of this archetypal fact of abandon-
> ment (and abandoning) that we can join
> together in community. This communal
> feeling, based on a recognition of our mu-
> tual aloneness and suffering, is a religious
> emotion, an existential reality, and a re-
> turn to the world with a recognition that
> the world is all we have, and that maybe
> it is "good enough."
>
> —PATRICIA BERRY, *Chiron*, 1985

The child begins life in a state akin to paradise. Pure and abounding with possibilities—its needs fulfilled in a maternally enfolding, watery world that is timeless, seamless, and without end—the innocent child enters, carrying the great promise of humanity.

But, alas, innocence cannot endure. What begins with infinite potential must eventually move out into the finite, unpredictable world in order to be fulfilled. Hence, an abrupt separation or abandonment is one of the early transitional experiences for each human being, a passage in which the child becomes internalized as the individual personality adapts to the demands of his or her outer circumstance. According to C. G. Jung, abandonment is, in fact, what initially defines the inner child. " 'Child,' " he said, "means something evolving toward independence. This it cannot do without detaching itself from its origins: abandonment is therefore a necessary condition, not just a concomitant symptom."

The experience of abandonment—actual, emotional, psychological—is therefore an initiation into life. It is a reenactment of the fall from Eden, a loss of innocence, both a disappointment and a betrayal. Yet, it is a positive event because it sets us in motion on our journey, circling on our way in search of experience and identity. The poet Rainer Maria Rilke gave voice to the positive side of the solitary quest:

> *I live my life in growing orbits,*
> *which move out over the things of the world.*
> *Perhaps I can never achieve the last,*
> *but that will be my attempt.*
> *I am circling around God, around the ancient tower,*
> *and I have been circling for a thousand years.*
> *And I still don't know if I am a falcon,*
> *Or a storm, or a great song.*

—(*Book for the Hours of Prayer*, 1899 TRANSLATED BY ROBERT BLY)

Abandonment requires us to adjust, to accept our predicament. "It is only when one is truly alone," says analyst Rose-Emily Rothenberg, "that the creative potential [the 'child'] that is carried deep inside has the space and room to emerge into the light of day." We must take up the challenge of our separateness. The pain of our aloneness forces us to become aware, to open to the experience of our Self as apart from others. Perhaps we will eventually come around and, as T. S. Eliot said, " . . . arrive where we started / And know the place for the first time" (*The Four Quartets*).

For some, abandonment is a wound to the childhood Self that results in a narrowing adaptation in which the child is buried deep inside under layers of resentment, entitlement, and cynicism. In the heart of every cynic, however, is a bleeding romantic, an innocent inner child who has been wounded early in life by disillusionment with parents or by a discovery that the world is not all it had been cracked up to be.

For all of us, the challenge of abandonment is to accept our orphanhood, to acknowledge that we are ultimately on our own, which means a lifelong responsibility for the care and nurturance of our inner child. The person who tries to avoid the experience of abandonment and to preserve idealistic innocence into adulthood does so at great peril. Such denial requires a great deal of energy and can only result in the futility of the narcissistic dilemma (a theme we will take up in Part III).

As long as the inner child is not actually brought into being, if it is not a reality for the individual, it is abandoned. Jung went so far as to suggest that inner-child awareness requires periodic renewal through ritual if it is to be realized as something real and internal. "The Christ Child," he wrote in his essay on the child archetype, "is a religious necessity only so long as the majority of men [and women] are incapable of giving psychological reality to the saying: 'Except ye become as little children. . . . ' "

Gilda Frantz, who opens this section, suggests that some people have the experience of abandonment before they can understand or integrate it: They are either an unwanted child, are abandoned at birth, or are born to deficient mothers who fail to bond. "This is akin to being born into the archetype of the abandoned one," she says, "and this child has the fate of having to integrate the inner nurturing mother as well as the inner abandoned child at some point in his or her life." Frantz's piece is confessional and informational, and her concluding remarks about Jung should not be overlooked.

James Hillman's contribution, on the other hand, challenges us to move beyond the literalism of actual abandonment and to consider a variety of inner-child scenarios: abandonment of the child in our collective thinking about childhood and in our psychologizing; abandonment of the child in our dreams, in our relationships, and in our models of imagination and maturity.

Rose-Emily Rothenberg's article is a definitive piece on the orphan archetype, that part of the child that is "hidden in the innermost soul of man." From her own experience of abandonment, she reminds us that we are all orphans, and that through the suffering of our abandonment we can realize our own inner resources.

Marion Woodman's concise words bring us to consider the issues of identity that are constellated by our forsaken inner child: "If we have lived behind a mask all our lives, sooner or later—if we are lucky—that mask will be smashed. . . . Perhaps we will look into the terrified eyes of our own tiny child, that child who has never known love and who now beseeches us to respond."

M. Scott Peck isolates the abandonment theme in parenting and identifies the destructive consequences of using the threat of abandonment—consciously or unconsciously—as a child-rearing tool. "Children, abandoned either psychologically or in actuality, enter adulthood lacking any deep sense that the world is a safe and protective place," he writes.

And finally, in a literary *tour de force*, science fiction writer Ursula K. LeGuin asks us to consider the moral dilemma of abandoning our inner child.

7 · BIRTH'S CRUEL SECRET: O I AM MY OWN LOST MOTHER TO MY OWN SAD CHILD

. . . .

GILDA FRANTZ

Gilda Frantz's personal warmth comes through strongly in this consideration of fate and abandonment, their effects on the inner child and on the life of the adult. Frantz, a Jungian analyst, has had a lifelong involvement in the work of Carl Jung. Her revelations about Jung's recovery of his own lost inner child and its relationship to his creative life are enlightening. This piece appeared originally in the journal Chiron, 1985.

INTRODUCTION

The most difficult aspect in writing this paper had to do with the recollection of my own abandonment as an infant. I was abandoned by my father. In the loss of that relationship, the maternal archetype also was damaged and not able to be carried by my mother. This early abandonment has shaped my life and has colored almost everything I have done in terms of creativity, ambition, and a desire to find ways to nurture myself. Children like me possess an early awareness, a knowing that they are born into a more difficult situation, and this may make them more cautious and watchful. These qualities can be an enormous help in later life if they do not cause isolation.

The Great Goddess came into my life through active imagination and dreams in analysis. She watched over me and helped nourish me. My relationship with the positive mother archetype clearly came about through my contact with a woman analyst. But the relationship to the "good father" came with my marriage, and the nurturing masculine was as much the "lost mother" as was the feminine. I hope it is understood that in speaking of this "lost mother" I am speaking of that which nurtures us spiritually. I submit the following material with deep gratitude for all that the gods have given to me, both good and bad.

I chose the title from a scrap of paper I found in my late husband's desk. Its cryptic meaning was numinous and touched me in the place of my own experience of abandonment: it seemed a poetic image of the suffering child.

" 'Child' means something evolving toward independence. This it cannot do without detaching itself from its origins: abandonment is therefore a necessary condition, not just a concomitant symptom."[1] There are some for whom the necessary condition of abandonment comes before they can integrate its purpose or meaning. There are those whose experience begins *in utero*, children whose mothers are ill or depressed or die in childbirth or have been abandoned or whose birth is unwanted. There are those mothers who are unwed and offer the child for adoption with great suffering and reluctance. The result of these fateful births is that the lives of child and parents are deeply affected.[2] This is akin to being born into the archetype of the abandoned one, and this child has the fate of having to integrate the inner nurturing mother, as well as the inner abandoned child at some point in his or her life. Orphans are particularly prone to this path as are children of narcissistically wounded mothers.[3]

What about the child who did not suffer any of the above circumstances? This child's abandonment comes through the lack of special nurturing by a mother who is not capable of such. The child can feel abandoned even though the outer circumstances of his or her life imply the opposite. Fate intensifies the already intense relationship between parent and child. While the fate of a child is restricted to the parents, the fate of an adult is not limited to the parents.[4] In the case material about Anne, which follows, I will say more about this.

FATE AND ABANDONMENT

We make certain decisions in life and can avoid this or that, or decide when to marry and whom, but even those decisions send us in a direction that can seal our fate. "Humanity may possibly draw the conclusion that only one side of fate can be mastered with rational intentions."[5] But again, the use of the rational will is only one-half of the picture. The other half is a hurtling toward a destination which we did not choose and which we cannot change. The Stoics called that "the compulsion of the stars," or Heimarmene.

A common thread I can observe in the people I see analytically is fate. Some have difficult lives, and not all the difficulty is earned. It is not always something they have or have not done that causes them to be abandoned. Often it is the so-called accident of birth that determines their fate. The challenge is to see what each one of us can do with the raw material of life. Life itself is an experiment and, as Emerson puts it, the more experiments we make, the better.

Abandonment is a fateful experience in which we feel we have no choice. We feel alone, as if the gods are not present. If we feel the gods are present and supportive, then we are not abandoned. The word abandonment means literally "not to be called." It is etymologically connected with the word "fate." Fate means "the divine word" and is from *fari* and *fatum*, meaning "to speak."

Who is it that either summons us or does not? Let us discuss the Fates. They were divine beings who determined the course of human lives and were called Moerae (Moira) by the Greeks and Fata by the Romans, as well as Parcae. The Fates were the daughters of Nyx and their names were Klotho, Lachesis, and Atropos. Klotho means the one who weaves the thread; Lachesis, the one who spins the thread; and Atropos, the one who is unyielding and cuts the thread. Homer repeatedly referred to these three in writing about the destinies allotted to man by the gods. The sisters were always represented as spinning, measuring, and cutting the thread of life. The word shroud is from the root "to cut." Though there are many contradictions as to whether the Fates did the gods' will, it is evident that even Zeus was bound by their decisions.

The Fates and the Erinyes have a connection. The Erinyes were called the Furies by the Romans and were born from earth fertilized by drops of blood from the castrated Uranus. Aeschylus described them as hideous and frightening, but in sculpture and paintings they are not thus depicted. In their deeds the Erinyes were not regarded as unjust or even malign, even though they were said to inflict punishment. The retribution they meted out was considered a protection of those that human law had failed to protect, such as those who were injured by members of their own families.[6]

The three Graces are associated with the Erinyes and the Fates as well. They were the Eumenides, the kindly ones. The combination of terrible and benign is frequently found in chthonic deities. Spirits, demons, deities, as well as heroes, were thought to live in or beneath the earth, and their concern was with the dead or with the fertility of the earth. Many of the chthonic divinities combined these two functions of punishing and kindness, fertilization and death. Those spirits who lived in the earth where the dead were buried and crops arose inevitably came to be associated with both events.

During the process of thinking about abandonment, I had a dream. The word used for fate in my dream was *bashart*, a Yiddish word meaning "that which is meant is meant." As Dr. Clara Zilberstein interprets it, *bashart* means it *has* to happen at a certain moment in time. It is a semi-mystical concept that has to do with who has been promised to a person, one's intended. There is a genuine affection for the word among Jewish people, and it implies a true acceptance of what God gives us, good or bad. For me it implied that the unconscious accepted the presentation of this material—that it was "meant"—and that it focused me upon my fate as a Jewish woman, wife, and widow as well as on my having to deal with "what was intended by the fates."

"Without necessity nothing budges, the human personality least of all. It is tremendously conservative, not to say torpid. Only acute necessity is able to rouse it."[7] Suffering and abandonment awaken us. Through the awesome pain of not being called, we may find a way to change what needs changing in our lives. Alchemy says it this way:

> [*Liquefactio*] is one of the ways of first dissolving consciousness and getting closer to the unconscious which plays a great role in alchemy as well. One of the beginning stages of the alchemical is very often the *liquefactio*, the turning into liquid in order to undo the *prima materia* which is often hardened or solidified in a wrong way and therefore cannot be used to make the philosopher's stone. The materials must first be liquefied. Naturally, the underlying chemical image is the extraction of a metal from its ore through melting, but *liquefactio* often has the alchemical connotation of a dissolution of the personality in tears and despair.[8]

A flame applied externally to melt the metals is alternately raised and lowered in intensity. The raising and lowering of the flame is the agony of abandonment. The flame is Fate.

TEARS AND ABANDONMENT

In the practice of analytical psychology, it is a common experience to have a patient enter analysis in the stage where there is death and mourning. The condensation of these vapors comes in the form of tears.

In an unpublished paper on depression, Kieffer Frantz (1966) did a survey of the literature, which included the then-current psychoanalytic position. He wrote the following:

> These characteristics would seem to be the most consistent observable evidence of the presence of depression. Yet, if we are not to accept a pathological evaluation as being the only point of view, how are we to appraise the observable phenomenon of depression?
>
> Let us begin with the dream of a woman who began therapy in a depression. The dream was that the dreamer was crying and tears were rolling down her cheeks. As the tears were rolling, they gradually turned into diamonds. The tears would certainly seem to substantiate the characteristics of hopelessness, helplessness, sadness and internal suffering described above. But what of the diamonds? A definite change has occurred. In *Two Essays on Analytical Psychology*, Jung states, "This transformation is the aim of the analysis of the unconscious. If there is no transformation it means that the determining influence of the unconscious is unabated and that it will, in some cases, persist in maintaining neurotic symptoms in spite of all our analysis and all our under-

standing. Alternatively, a compulsive transference will take hold, which is just as bad as a neurosis."[9]

The dream points to a process that begins with tears and changes or is transformed to diamonds, the "pure water." The depression from this point of view may be conceived as the descent into the unconscious for the purpose of beginning the journey. Between the beginning and the ending there are many different stages and perhaps many depressions.

My interest in tears as a *creative* expression of abandonment began with my reading of the paper, when an acquaintance asked me to find the afore-mentioned reference to tears and diamonds. The tears are the expression par excellence of abandonment. But what about the diamonds?

Diamond means "invincible." It is also called "adamantine," and from this we get our word "adamant." While adamant means "a very hard substance," it also means "to tame," "to conquer." Metaphorically, nature has to suffer in order to produce a diamond because of the enormous pressure and heat the earth has to sustain to turn carbon into diamonds. In the dream, diamonds evolve from tears. Through the operation of *liquefactio*, the wash-ing away of an encrusted and improperly hardened *prima materia*, jewels are revealed. Thus, the dreamer is given some hope that something valuable may result from her intense suffering.

The diamond body is the Self that is within each of us.[10] Consciousness of the Self shapes and polishes this diamond, and upon our physical death the body drops away and this diamond is revealed in all its dazzling beauty.[11] In the example used, the diamond is revealed through the process of depres-sion, or *nigredo*, and "conscious suffering."

In writing about her long relationship with Jung, Hilde Kirsch says: "The most important gift Jung has given me, and hopefully to mankind, is the acceptance of suffering as a necessity." In her paper, she quoted a letter he wrote to a friend about suffering: "Try to apply seriously what I have told you, not that you might escape suffering—nobody can escape it—but that you may avoid the worst—blind suffering." Jung also wrote about himself,

> I think that God in turn has bestowed life on me and has saved me from petrification. Thus I suffered and was miserable, but it seems that life was never wanting and even in the blackest night . . . by the grace of God I could see a great light. Somewhere there seems to be a great kindness in the abysmal darkness of the Deity.[12]

The dreamer above had the experience of conscious suffering, not of blind suffering. She was aware of her suffering and possibly knew the cause. I was once told by a victim of a disaster that "without this I would have been an ordinary housewife, but this loss forced me to change and now I have developed into a deeper person."

The symbolism of tears and abandonment is found in myths where creation is formed out of tears or by crying. Creation is also brought about by the loneliness of the gods. There is a Baluba myth in which the tears of the animals soften the earth and provide a place for the seeds to grow and become shelter for the animals. [13] In the Grimm's fairy tale "The Handless Maiden," the daughter is sold to the devil and is saved by her tears. When the devil asks to buy everything behind the mill, the father, unaware that his only daughter is there, sells the property to him. This abandonment of the daughter and subsequent betrayal is what provoked the tears that ultimately save her.

Cinderella is also abandoned by her father. After the death of her mother, the father remarries and she becomes part of what today would be known as a "blended family." Her stepsisters are treated as more important than Cinderella. When the father asks the sisters what they want from town, they ask for precious and costly gifts. As an afterthought, he asks Cinderella, and she only desires a branch from a tree that brushes his hat as he rides home. He forgets all about her after buying the stepdaughters their gifts, but his hat does brush the branch, causing him to remember. Cinderella plants the branch and a tree grows up. A bird comes to the tree and grants Cinderella three wishes. This bird is the spirit of her dead (lost) mother. The story of Cinderella is a beautiful example of the sad child redeeming the lost mother and the abandoning father through her relationship to the Prince.

What has been spoiled by the mother can only be healed by the mother, and what has been spoiled by the father can only be healed by the father. [14] Relationship itself can often be the healing "father" and can heal a wounded child and be a nurturing parent. We think we find a father in a man, but he may also be a good mother. In the Boddisattva of Compassion, [15] Kuan Yin was masculine and remained so until the twelfth century, when He became a Goddess and feminine. The masculine offers its own kind of nurturing. [16]

"The one who hears the cries" is how Kuan Yin is known. This myth is an ancient affirmation of the existence of abandonment and suffering and healing. In Tibetan Buddhism there is the concept of Dukkha, which loosely translated means "suffering," but which can also mean "unsatisfactoriness." [17] Suffering, in the Buddhist tradition, is understood to be "within one's 'own' mind and body and when it is understood one will know true happiness." Dukkha may be physical pain or mental anguish and it refers to the facts of "birth, old age, disease and death" and to human conditions common to all, like "grief, lamentation (crying out), pain, anguish and despair." [18]

Weeping often accompanies the sowing of corn. It is the weeping and bewailing the death of the fertility god that ensures his return in the spring. [19] When we cry out in despair, we cry tears and hope that someone hears our cries. Water is the living power of the psyche. When weeping and water symbolism occur during analysis, it calls for a sense of containment and at the same time is a purifying experience.

Lily was in her 50s when she came to see me. Her adult life had been spent in having babies, and she had a family of 12 sons and daughters. She found time only for her husband's and children's needs. She felt she had betrayed something within herself in sacrificing her inner child by mothering all those children. Everything made her cry—happiness, sadness, anger, frustration. There were times when it seemed she used an entire box of tissues within an hour. The tears robbed her of a chance to express her feelings; instead of talking, she wept. Her sad child had emerged.

Lily was an abandoned child in that her mother was so self-involved that she was unaware of her daughter's true nature. I sat with Lily through many, many hours of crying, as container for her tears. One day I asked her a question: "Where do all these tears go?" She looked up in amazement and began to descibe a deep and vast natural pool or lake that had become filled by her tears. She began a dialogue with her tears, and these dialogues brought old and buried memories up from the depths. Often she recalled wrongs done to her (usually of omission) by parental figures or siblings. She wrote: "I hear the water running down the stream. I locate its site and watch the flow of water. Its movement is suddenly obstructed by an unforeseen obstacle . . . of several rocks falling, disturbing its current and redirecting it toward a new challenge."

These dialogues between Lily's ego and the unconscious, depicted as her tears, were truly healing. I am not reproducing the entire dialogue out of respect for the organic and ongoing quality of the relationship, but it was active imagination, as opposed to unconscious fantasy. Contact with the unconscious through written dialogue, to use one example of the ways to make the connection, occurs when the ego makes way for the unconscious by lowering its hold (voluntarily), thus allowing archetypal energies a voice.[20] This is how Lily was able to come to a deeper relationship to her tears, by encountering them within herself.

Lily's sad child was a child of the "earth and of starry heaven,"[21] and was parched and dry and needed the water of memory. She needed to remember, to take what had been dismembered and lost. By drinking her fill of the cold water of Osiris,[22] she could speak to the inner lost mother of her sadness and mourning.

ABANDONMENT AND THE CREATIVE CHILD

Etymologically, the word *mourning* means "to remember" and stems from the same root as *memory*. In mourning we are held in the memory of what has been lost or abandoned until we have found a replacement for it. Mourning occurs whether we have ever experienced actual death or not. Most of us enter analysis in a state of keep grief and mourning. Mourning and depression are the other names of abandonment.

Anne came into analysis when *I* was still feeling abandoned and in mourning over the loss of my husband. It was a synchronistic moment.

Being in that state myself I could see that she, too, was mourning a loss. Her presenting complaint had to do with many fears about so-called little things. She was reclusive and inclined not to answer her phone. As her story came out, it became apparent that some years before she had suffered the loss of a cherished goal. Perhaps what was lost was the illusion of this possibility in her life.

She had studied to be an actress from the age of seven or eight. At a crucial point in her studies, when she was around twenty, she felt she just didn't have what it took to be an actress, and she didn't feel tough enough. She had planned to study in New York with a famous acting coach, and with almost no reflection she swiftly gave up her dream. This termination of her career deeply wounded the inner child.

Anne's mother was a strong, opinionated woman, and Anne was under the influence of a powerful negative mother archetype. She was used to having others determine her destiny, but she didn't count on what the loss of her dream would mean to her. In the 1970s she became interested in drugs and found some comfort in them, but this was no solution. Although she was now out of college and had another career in teaching, she often contemplated suicide because of the lack of meaning in her life. She was, in a spiritual sense, half alive. She didn't know she was grieving for her lost ambition, her abandoned career; she only knew she thought about death a great deal. The neurotic perpetually hesitates entering into life and is inclined to avoid the "dangerous struggle for existence." Refusing to really experience life forces him/her to deny life and thus they "commit partial suicide."[23]

My own loss experience had changed me. When I went back to work after my husband's death, I found that a gauzy veil that had formerly existed had disappeared. The veil could be called a "professional attitude." Through my bereavement, an almost egoless state, my psyche was more permeable, more open to the unconscious. I was less defended and more "there." It was almost as though there were trails of smoke, like those from a Bushman's fire, that circled between Anne and me. I became conscious of the presence of the healing power of the mother for the inner child.

Anne's dreams were frightening to her, yet they showed me that she had the ego strength for the journey and that the journey would take time. Gradually she began to consider the idea that the acting she loved and had given up so many years ago might be in her life in another form. The idea to work in amateur theater was repugnant, but she did like studying, so she enrolled in some classes with local teachers and began to enjoy the contact with the world of acting. Instead of feeling helpless and identified with the sad child, she was beginning to find the lost mother. She was beginning to nurture herself.

Rather than being related to her inner sad child's needs, Anne had been *identified* with the child. Her destiny was tied to her parents. She feared what would happen to her if they died. She feared abandonment. If she could accept her abandoned goal, she might begin a new relationship to the

Self. Recently, she has begun to grow up and enter the adult world, a world she had always identified with death and dying and abandonment. It is not to say that now she is without fears, or that her life is "perfect," but she is more in it and more alive to possibilities yet unknown to her.

ABANDONMENT AND LOSS

One instance of the "sad child/lost mother" abandonment is widowhood. Occasionally, we wounded children find in a mate the mother and/or father we have been deprived of in our early years. With the death of the spouse, we are plunged once again into the deepest mourning. Then the "child" is out, bewildered and in great pain. It is as though one connects with the mourning of Demeter and Persephone, or of Christ on the cross, asking why God has forsaken him.

Let me encapsulate widowhood so that something about the problem the widow faces in relation to the sad child can be understood.

> The position of widows in many cultures is one of the saddest in society. The simple fact that they were born women ensured their fate. The moment their husbands died, their own function in life was regarded as ended. Often they were destroyed to accompany and serve their dead spouses in the new life beyond death, as they had in his earthly life.[24]

While we are too civilized today to allow widows to be put into the grave, the fact remains that many women live their lives through their husbands. Sylvia was a newly widowed woman. Her husband died quite unexpectedly and suddenly. She was a well paid journalist, in a profession she enjoyed. She was left with two children, her grief, and her anger. "How dare he do this to me?" she raged. What he "did" soon became clear. Her wounded, shy inner child had found a home within the breast of her husband. He was outgoing and aggressive. She was able to meet the outer world through his protection, and now she was abandoned.

When he died, she no longer felt able to meet the world and that part of her went into the grave. Her task, like Persephone's, would be to bring it back into consciousness or find another outgoing and aggressive partner. If she did not find such a replacement, then what was being lived unconsciously through him would have to be made conscious. This step requires an enormous change in attitude and consciousness and a new vessel for the sad child. The change is difficult: it is not desired; and it is not what one seeks willingly.

The experience of widowhood reconstitutes the abandoned child archetype. The feelings around the death of a significant other, especially a spouse, often are guilt, shame, anger, abandonment, depression, lack of libido, and hope. I think the *shame* and *guilt* directly connect to the tradition of widow murder, wherein the one closest to the deceased went with him or her into the land of the dead. By being alive, we feel guilty and ashamed that for us life goes on. This wilderness experience is one we all have, but the widowed need all the encouragement possible to leave the land of the dead and return to life. The pull away from life is very strong at such times.

In modern life one has the automobile, where one who feels abandoned may contemplate death or find a place to cry alone. The car is now the place of sanctuary, and as such it is the place that can allow for thoughts of death and dying. Not that this implies that the car is used to bring about death, but it is there that death is contemplated. Ask any newly widowed person if they use the car as a place to rage and cry and think of death, and the answer will be affirmative.

Another thing to observe about widows has to do with money. Many newly widowed men and women obsess about money. Anxiety about money becomes a substitute for the fear of being on one's own. I have known wealthy individuals who become terrified that they are being cheated or robbed by the lawyers and accountants around them. This also applies to individuals without a great deal of money. They, too, find themselves obsessing about money when, in fact, they are grieving about their loss. While there *are* concerns, there is a special kind of concern the newly widowed express, and I think it is due to the feelings of abandonment and the "child." The newly bereaved feel so helpless and naked, so overwhelmed with the feelings of love, hate, loss, etc., that money anxiety becomes the container for all of the above.

> Widow murder was a natural consequence of the belief that the wife's life ended with the death of the spouse. And they were often killed with prescribed ritual. . . . As late as 1857 there was a law in Oyo, in Western Nigeria, ensuring that certain individuals in the king's retinue, including his official mother, various priestesses, as well as the king's favorite wife, all died when he died and by their own hand.[25]

Today, widow murder is practiced in a much subtler form. We don't kill the widow: She is abandoned and becomes invisible. The more a woman is identified with her husband, the more prone she is to feelings of abandonment and desertion. In my own experience, I had a "life of my own," but the body blow of grief that I was experiencing was that my marriage had been a safe container for my inner sad child. Alone I avoided this child, but with my husband it was safe to bring her out from time to time. I hated the idea that I would have to face her alone. But it was either that, or like one of the widows in the Melanesian New Hebrides, where a conical cap made of spider's web was used for smothering them, I would be smothered by being stuck in isolation and abandonment.

> When widows were permitted to stay alive, the problem of what to do with them had to be resolved by her own or her husband's relatives. Often she was regarded with suspicion and suspected of witchcraft, because of her contact with death, and the . . . fear that she might have caused her husband's death.

In societies where a widow was allowed to remain alive she had to be ritually freed from contact with her dead partner before anyone could touch her or go near her, as death was believed to be very contagious. After a period of isolation she was permitted to re-enter her family in the unenviable new widow's role. The isolation of the widow continues to this day even in the Western world.[26]

In Victorian times the term "widows' weeds" were used to describe the clothing the widows wore. This expression can be traced etymologically to the word *wadmal*, which is a strong, woven cloth. The word encompasses two meanings: *wad*, meaning "a tied bundle," and *mal*, meaning "time." Widows' weeds can imply a limit of time for the mourning period or the isolation, but to me the connotation of strong cloth indicates that the garment is made to last a lifetime.

It is not widely known outside of religious life that Catholic nuns took their habit from the garb widows wore. Sister Mary Patricia Sexton told me that, in and around the seventeenth century in France nuns could go to rough waterfront dives to do the work of the Church knowing that no one would look at them or bother them if they dressed like widows. The symbolism of marriage to Christ in mourning clothes has other meanings but from the standpoint of this paper, it is interesting to muse about what it was the widows and nuns had in common. Many early convents were started by widows. The clothes they wore were designed to be unchanging and to disguise their sexuality. This outfit, this attitude, was meant to last forever.[27]

In certain tribes a ban was imposed on remarriage until the body of the dead husband had decomposed. The New Zealand Maori widow wore two special feather cloaks called "cloak of tears." The bones were eventually exhumed, wrapped in the feather cloaks, and reburied. Then the widow was free to remarry.[28]

In contemporary times words about death may be included in marriage vows. Yet, of all the widows and widowers I have asked, only one recalls actually hearing the words, " 'til death do us part" at the wedding. "Attempts to expel death or not to take death into account are a deception committed by man upon himself. No matter how hard man tries to shelve and hush up knowledge of the inevitable end of his earthly life, he never quite succeeds."[29]

CONCLUSION

Analytical psychology encourages individuals to give up attitudes that are too conventional or too collective and stifling. From the history of widow murder, it can be seen that within each of us there is a powerful, archaic pull to abandonment. I encourage analysands who are grieving to be "different," that is, to be true to what the soul wants. A relationship to the fantasies and inner world is an appropriate counterbalance to the forces of

the collective consciousness that are inclined to isolate the abandoned one
and are often destructive to his or her development. There is a journey to
the underworld which the sad child makes. He or she becomes intimate
with the dark, with fear, and with what can be the most decisive experience,
that of being alone with our own self. Before we experience this, something
we treasure is sacrificed and/or lost, abandoned. We have to become dis-
identified from the oneness of subject and object, from unconsciousness
participation mystique.[30]

Abandonment is to be in a state of constant connectedness to the lost
object. There is a time in the mourning process when there is a serenity in
the bereaved, a time of grace. The journey to the underworld is a rite of
passage and must be seen as such. One must cross the river and return
again, alone. The danger is getting stuck halfway between one shore and
the other. How many of us still mourn a childhood which was not what
we wished for?

Next to the well of Mnemosyne stands the forbidden well of Lethe,
forgetfulness. The notion of forgetfulness is that in death we can forget the
sorrows of this world and forget the difficult journey to the next. This
theme is elemental and human, and it belongs not just to the Greek and
Orphic myths but occurs everywhere.[31]

Forgetfulness can be an obstacle on this journey. When childhood dreams
or fantasies are recalled in the process of analysis, healing can occur. These
memories have been hidden away to protect them. But if they are hidden
forever, one can remain stuck in the sadness and mourning. A woman
recalls a secret game played in childhood. She was an alchemist and invented
the perfect food that would stamp out hunger in the world. This game was
an attempt on the part of her unconsciousness to compensate for not getting
the right food from her parents. I think that secret games from childhood
are an attempt on the part of the psyche to protect what is healing and
precious from the too close scrutiny of the negative parental image. This
is also why children often stop drawing or coloring at an early age if the
work is criticized by an authority figure. This protects further damage to
the expression of the imaginatal child's psyche until adulthood when, it is
hoped, he or she can begin to allow it out once more.[32]

The archetypes of the sad child and the lost mother emerge during
times of intense loss and suffering and abandonment. Jung himself had such
an experience after his break with Freud. A memory came to him with
intense affect about himself as a young boy of 10 or 11. He remembered
that as a child he liked to play with sand and stones and make castles and
such. He realized that he had forgotten this young lad, but it was obvious
to Jung that the child was still alive and wanted something from him. Jung
proceeded to do whatever the inner child wished, carefully noting the images
and fantasies that were activated by the contact. He called this activity
"serious play."[33] This occurred during the time that Jung was in despair
over the loss of his relationship to Freud, as well as over his professional
direction and life course.

Through this "serious play," Jung made contact with his forgotten and abandoned child and brought the child into his life. You might say that he became the lost mother to his own sad child. Through contact with this inner child came a burst of creativity. In the film, "Matter of Heart," von Franz said that whenever Jung was about to begin writing a book, he would go to the shore of the lake and dig in the sand and make passages for the water to flow. He did not allow that inner child to be forgotten again.

What happens to many of us is that we allow the child to emerge within the vessel of relationship and often seek a relationship in which the child can come out into the open and play. When this container is broken by death or divorce or some separation of an abandoning nature, the child goes into hiding and suffers. Many have had this experience of bringing an abandoned, sad child into a relationship so that the other could nurture the child. When this occurs, the union can become a sacred vessel for the inner creative child or a substitute for a relationship to this child.

8 · ABANDONING
THE CHILD

· · · · · · ·

JAMES HILLMAN

James Hillman writes passionately, no matter what his subject. Here, writing on the child nature in all of us, he is perhaps at his most eloquent. Hillman's sense of abandonment is not that of a literal plight, not the orphan-without-parentage scenario. He sees an unhealthy sentimentalization of childhood that relegates the inner child to some romantic (though immature) state, a cultural attitude that divides the individual into adult vs. child, where the child and its imaginal power have to be regained from a lost, forgotten, and childish status. Hillman is not afraid to tackle the ambiguities of language and concept in order to provoke an awareness of the reader's own psychology and, especially, of that aspect that is "perennially child."

This essay is excerpted from a lecture delivered by Dr. Hillman in the summer of 1971 at the Eranos Conference, Ascona, Switzerland. Hillman is one of the most exciting voices in psychology today. He was formerly director of studies at the C. G. Jung Institute, Zurich, and is today the foremost proponent of archetypal psychology. He is a prolific writer and lecturer, a Jungian analyst, and editor of the respected journal Spring.

WHAT IS THE CHILD?

What is this "child"—that is surely the first question. Whatever we say about children and childhood is not altogether really about children and childhood. We need but consult the history of painting to see how peculiar are the images of children, particularly when comparing them in their distortions with contemporary exactitude in depicting landscapes and still lives or the portraits of adults. We need but consult the history of family life, education and economics to realize that children and childhood as we use the terms today are a late-invention.[1]

What is this peculiar realm we call "childhood," and what are we doing by establishing a special world with children's rooms and children's toys, children's clothes, and children's books, music, language, caretakers, doctors, of playing children so segregated from the actual lives of working men and women? Clearly, some realm of the psyche called "childhood" is being personified by the child and carried by the child for the adult. How curiously similar this *daseinsbereich* [realm of being] is to the realm of the madhouse some centuries ago and even today, when the madman was considered a child, the ward of the state or under the parental eye of the doctor who cared for his "children," the insane, like for his family. Again, how extraordinary this confusion of the child with the insane, of childhood with insanity.[2]

The confusion between the real child and his childhood and the fantasy child that obfuscates our perception of child and childhood is classical to the history of depth psychology. You may remember that Freud at first believed that repressed memories causing neuroses were forgotten emotions and distorted scenes from actual childhood. Later he abandoned this child, realizing that a fantasy factor had been placed in childhood events that had never actually happened; a fantasy child was at work and not an actual occurrence in the life of the person. He was obliged then to separate child of fact from that of fantasy, outer child events from inner childhood. Nevertheless, he stuck to his belief that the job of therapy was the analysis of childhood. A statement of 1919 is typical:

> Strictly considered . . . analytic work deserves to be recognized as genuine psycho-analysis only when it has succeeded in removing the amnesia which conceals from the adult his knowledge of his childhood from its beginning (that is, from about the second to the fifth year). . . . The emphasis which is laid here upon the importance of the earliest experience does not imply any underestimation of the influences of later ones. But the later impressions of life speak loudly enough through the mouth of the patient, while it is the physician who has to raise his voice on behalf of the claims of childhood.[3]

What childhood did Freud mean? Actual children, as I pointed out here two years ago, were never analyzed by Freud. He did not analyze children. Was the "childhood" which the analyst had to recapture actual childhood? Here, Freud himself remains ambiguous, for the actual small young human we call "child" merges in Freud with a Rousseauian, even Orphic-Neoplatonic child who is "psychologically a different thing than an adult. . . ."[4] "Childhood has its own ways of seeing, thinking and feeling; nothing is more foolish than to try to substitute our ways."[5] The difference lies in the child's special way of reminiscing: ". . . a child catches hold on . . . phylogenetic experience where his own experience fails him. He fills in the gaps in individual truth with prehistorical truth; he replaces occurrences in his own life by occurrences in the life of his ancestors. I fully agree with Jung in recognizing the existence of this phylogenetic inheritance. . . ."[6]

The actual child itself was not altogether actual because its experiences consisted in the confabulations of "pre-historic" occurrences, i.e., non-temporal, mythical, archetypal. And childhood thus refers in Freud partly to *a state of reminiscence*, like the Platonic or Augustinian *memoria*, an imaginal realm which provides the actual child with "its own ways of seeing, thinking, and feeling" (Rousseau). This realm, this mode of imaginal existence, is to be found, according to popular and depth psychology, in primitive, savage, madman, artist, genius, and the archeological past; the childhood of persons becomes merged with the childhood of peoples.[7]

But the child and the childhood are not actual. These are terms for a mode of existence and perception and emotion which we still today insist belongs to actual children, so that we construct a world for them following our need to place this fantasy somewhere in actuality. We do not know what children are in themselves, "unadulterated" by our need for carriers of the imaginal realm, of "beginnings" (i.e., "primitivity," "creation") and of the archetype of the child. We cannot know what children are until we have understood more of the working of the fantasy child, the archetypal child in the subjective psyche.

Freud gave to the child image and to the fantasy of childhood a group of startling attributes which you may remember: child had no super-ego (conscience) like the adult; no free associations like the adult but confabulated reminiscences. The child's parents and problems were external, rather than internal as with the adult, so that the child had no symbolically transferred psychic life.[8] How close to the mental life of "madness," of artist, and how close to what we call "primitive"—this absence of personal conscience, this mixture of behavior and ritual, or memory and myth.

But more startling than the attributes Freud enunciated are those which we may draw from his ideas. First, Freud gave the child *primacy*: nothing was more important in our lives than those early years and that style of thought and emotion of imaginal existence called "childhood." Second, Freud gave the child *body*: it had passions, sexual desires, lusts to kill; it feared, sacrificed, rejected; it hated and longed and it was composed of erogenous zones, pre-occupied with feces, genitals, and deserved the name polymorphous perverse. Third, Freud gave the child *pathology*: it lived in our repressions and fixations; it was at the bottom of our psychic disorders;[9] it was our suffering.

These are startling attributes indeed if they be compared with the child of Dickens, for Dorrit and Nell, Oliver and David had little passion and little body, and no sexuality at all, especially in view of little Hans and little Anna and other children of psychoanalytic literature. Perversity, when it entered in Dickens at all, came from adults, from industry, education and society; pathology was in deathbed scenes that claimed children back to paradise. Against Dickens we can see Freud's vision most sharply, even if in both the child as fact and the child as image were still not disentangled.

Jung's essay "The Psychology of the Child Archetype" in 1940 moved the matter much further; actual child is abandoned and with it the fantasy of empiricism, the notion that our apperception of the factor in our subjectivity results from empirical observation of actual childhood. Jung writes:

> It may not be superfluous to point out that lay prejudice is always inclined to identify the child motif with the concrete experience "child," as though the

real child were the cause and pre-condition of the existence of the child motif. In psychological reality, however, the empirical idea "child" is only the means . . . by which to express a psychic fact that cannot be formulated more exactly. Hence by the same token the mythological idea of the child is emphatically not a copy of the empirical child . . . not—and this is the point—a human child.[10]

What accuracy can our studies of the human child have so long as we have not recognized enough the archetypal child in our subjectivity affecting our vision? So let us leave the child and childhood to one side and pursue what Jung calls the "child motif" and the "childhood aspect of the collective psyche."

Our question now becomes what is the child *motif* which projects so vividly and draws such fantasies onto itself? Jung answers:

> The "child" is all that is abandoned and exposed and at the same time divinely powerful; the insignificant, dubious beginning and the triumphal end. The "eternal child" in man is an indescribable experience, an incongruity, a handicap, and a divine prerogative; an imponderable that determines the ultimate worth or worthlessness of a personality.[11]

Jung elaborates these general and special features: futurity, divine heroic invincibility, hermaphroditism, beginning and end, and the motif of abandonment from which my theme is drawn. Jung's elaborations of 1940 should be taken as an addition to those in his previous works where the child motif is related to archaic mythical thinking and the mother archetype[12] and to paradisiacal blissfulness.[13] Some of the aspects that Jung discusses Freud had already described in his language-style. The idea of the creative child occurs in Freud's equation child = penis, and the rejected child in his equation child = feces. " 'Feces', 'child', and 'penis' thus form a unity, an unconscious concept (*sit venia verbo*)—the concept, namely, of a little thing that can become separated from one's body."[(14)]

To these features I would add two others from our Western tradition, the first specifically Christian, the second specifically Classical. In the Christian tradition (Legasse) "child" refers also to the simple, the naive, the poor and the common—the orphans—of society and of the psyche, as it did in the language of the Gospels, where child meant outcast, the pre-condition for salvation, and was later placed in association with the feelings of the heart opposed to the learning of the mind. In the Classical tradition the child appears in those configurations of masculine psychology represented specifically by Zeus, Hermes and Dionysos, their imagery, mythemes and cults. The child motif there may be kept distinct from the child-and-mother motifs and also the child-hero motifs that have distinctly different psychological import.

Our theme follows Jung literally when he says: "The child motif represents something not only that existed in the distant past but something that exists *now* . . . not just a vestige but a system functioning in the present whose purpose is to compensate or correct, in a meaningful manner, the inevitable onesidedness and extravagances of the conscious mind."[15] If, according to Freud, the essence of the psychoanalytic method is to alter something, and if the child, according to Jung, is that which acts as psychological corrector, our reflections require that we bring the child back from his abandonment even while we speak of him. Then the general theme may become specifically focussed in the private subjectivity of each and may act to alter the onesidedness of consciousness in regard to the child.

ABANDONMENT IN DREAMS

We find the abandoned child first of all in dreams, where we ourselves or a child of ours or one unknown, is neglected, forgotten, crying, in danger or need, and the like. The child makes its presence known through dreams; although abandoned, we can still hear it, feel its call.

In modern dreams we find the child endangered by: drowning, animals, road traffic, being left behind in a car trunk (the "chest" motif), or a pram or supermarket cart (the "basket" motif); kidnappers, robbers, members of the family, incompetents; illness, crippling, secret infections, mental retardation and brain damage (the idiot child); or a wider less specific catastrophe such as war, flood or fire. Sometimes, one wakens in the night with the sensation of having heard a child crying.

Usually the dreamer's response to the motif of abandonment is acute worry, a guilty responsibility: "I should not have let it happen; I must do something to protect the child; I am a bad parent." If it is an infant in the dream, we believe we must keep the sense of this "child" with us all the time, feed it every three hours with thoughtful attention, carry it on our backs like a papoose. We tend to take the child as a moral lesson.

But guilt puts the burden of altering something (Freud) and correcting something (Jung) altogether upon the ego as doer. After all, the dreamer is not only in charge of the child; he also *is* the child. Consequently the emotions of worry, guilt and responsibility, morally virtuous as they may be and even partly corrective of neglect, may also prevent other emotions of fright, loss and helplessness. Sometimes the more we worry over the child the less the child really reaches us. So, as long as we take up any dream mainly from the position of the responsible ego, by reacting to it with guilt and the energetics of seeing matters straight, improving by doing, by changing attitudes, extracting from dreams moral lessons for the ethically responsible ego, we reinforce that ego. We thereby emphasize the parent-child cleavage: the ego becomes the responsible parent, which only further removes us from the emotions of the child.

Crucial in all dream integration—integration, not interpretation, for we are speaking now of integrity with the dream, standing with it and in it, befriending it in all its parts, participating in its whole story—is the emotional experience of *all* its parts. Gestalt therapy attempts to drive this home by demanding that the dreamer feel himself into all the parts: the distraught parent, but also the wild dogs, the flooding river, the secret infection, and the exposed child. It is as important to collapse with the child's crying, and to hate savagely the childish, as it is to go home from the analytical hour resolved to take better care of the new and tender parts that need help to grow.

As interpretation and ego responsibility may strengthen the parent at the expense of the child, so too may amplification not reach the child who is abandoned. An amplification of the child in the river, wandering lost in the forest or attempting a task beyond his strength, in terms of fairytales and myths and initiation rites, may stain the motif accurately so that we see certain aspects clearly—mainly heroic new consciousness emerging— but the staining technique of amplification to bring out the objective meaning also may obliterate the subjective reality of dereliction. Amplification often takes us away from the misery by placing it on a general level. For many psychic events this extension of awareness through amplification is just what is needed, but for precisely this motif it would seem contraindicated because the forsaken child can best be refound by moving closer to subjective misery and noting its precise locus.

Both responsibility and amplification are insufficient methods for this motif. As activities of the reasoned, mature person they distance us yet further from the child.

ABANDONMENT IN MARRIAGE

Because every home established, every nest, niche of habit offers the abandoned child a sanctuary, marriage unavoidably evokes the child. Sometimes an early marriage is obviously intended to find a basket for the child that was inacceptable in the parental house. The pattern may continue long afterwards: husband and wife in tacit agreement taking such care of the abandoned child left from their parental homes that they cannot find the child appropriate to themselves.

Being at home, coming home, heading for home—these are emotions which refer to the child's needs. They indicate abandonment. These emotions transform the actual home, its walls and roof, into a picture-book fantasy with psychic walls and psychic roof in which we place our vulnerability and in which we may be safely exposed to the polymorphous perverse fragmentation of our demands. At home, we are not only mother who embraces and father who captains, but also a little child. What is rejected everywhere else must be allowed here at home.

This reality, which some psychotherapists have called "the inner child of the past" and others "neurotic interaction in marriage" is as important in the fantasies which are enacted in a marriage as are the various patterns of the conjunction described by Jung. What prevents the aspirations of the conjunction are the fierce incest demands of the child, whose desires for union are of another order than the marriage quaternio[16] and whose image of "contained" and "container"[17] is wholly in terms of his anxious dereliction. Where else can he go? This is his home too, and more important to him than wife and husband are mother and father, nursing and protection, omnipotence and idealizations.

A purpose of marriage has been defined in terms of procreating and caring for children. But there is also the archetypal child who is constellated by marriage and whose need for care would wreck the actual marriage by insisting that it rehearse archetypal patterns that are 'pre'-marital (uninitiated, infantile, incestuous). Then there occur those struggles between the actual children and the psychic child of the parents as to whom will be abandoned. Then divorce threatens not only the actual children, but the abandoned child of the parents that found containment in marriage.

The concentration of abandonment in marriage because there is no other home for it makes marriage the principal scene for enacting the child archetype (not the conjunctio). In marriage we find the idealizations of the child: marriage as alpha and omega of life, hermaphroditism lived as "role-sharing," futurity lived as the planning of hopes and fears, and defensive vulnerability. The couple's attempts to contain the child (not each other) produce a familiar pattern alternating between emotionalism and none at all, marriage stiffened into a social norm. Lost in the oscillation is the imagination which the child can bring. Imagination is blown off in affects or concretizes into plans and habits that keep the child cribbed. If we may speak of a "marriage therapy" then it would be based not on the "neurotic interaction" of the *couple*, but on the child as central factor in marriage, and the child's imagination, i.e., the cultivation of the imaginal psyche, the peculiar fantasy life that plays between your child and mine.

BAPTISING THE CHILD

Usually we feel something fundamentally wrong in regard to the child, which wrong we then place into or onto the child. Societies have to do something with children in order to make right this wrong. We do not take children as they are given; they must be removed out of childhood. We initiate, educate, circumcise, innoculate, baptise. And if in the Romantic manner we idealize the child—and idealizations are always a sign of distance—calling the child a *speculum naturae*, we do not altogether trust this nature. Even the child Immanuel (Isaiah 7:14–16) has first to eat butter and honey before he can distinguish between good and evil. The child *per se* makes us uneasy, ambivalent; we are anxious about the human propensities concentrated by the child symbol. It evokes too much of what has been left out or is unknown, becoming easily associated with primitive, mad and mystical.

When one looks at the early controversies over infant baptism one wonders just what psychological content was so exercising these excellent

Patristic minds. Their energy spent on the child is comparable to that of ours spent on childhood in modern psychology. At first, though, they (Tertullian, Cyprian) did not urge early baptism, and Gregory of Nazianzus preferred some degree of mind, about the age of three, before baptism. But Augustine was adamant. Because man was born in original sin he brought it with him into the world, as Augustine himself had done from his pagan past. Only baptism could wash this from the child. Augustine was sharp about the child's need of salvation, writing: "Those who plead for the mimesis of children ought not love their ignorance, but their innocence."[18] And what is innocent? "It is the weakness of the faculties of the child that is innocent, not the soul."[19] How Freudian: the child cannot perform with its still-too-young faculties, those latent perversities that are in the soul. The soul carried not mere general sin, but the specific sin of pre-Christian, un–Christian impulses of polytheistic paganism, which Freud was later to discover and baptise "polymorphously perverse," and which Jung was later more comprehensively to describe as the archetypes. Baptism could redeem the soul from childhood, from that imaginal world of a multitude of archetypal forms, gods and goddesses, their cults and the unchristian practices they substantiated.

Inasmuch as the child is not a vestige but a system functioning now, and inasmuch as a sacrament is not a vestige of a one-time historical happening but continues now, then the baptism of the child is *always going on*. We are continually baptising the child, lustrating the psyche's "childhood," its "beginnings," its reminiscing, with the apotropaic rites of our Augustinian culture, cleansing the soul of its polytheistic imaginal possibility which is carried emblematically by the child, thereby taking the child of the psyche a "prisoner for Christ" (Gregory of Nazianzus, "In Praise of Basil"), much as the early church replaced the infants of the hero cults and pagan pantheon with the Jesus child.

This Christening goes on whenever we connect to the child motifs in our dreams and feelings using only Christian models. Then we regard the polymorphic potential of our inherent polytheism as fundamentally in need of updating by transformation into unity. Thus we prevent the child from performing its function of that which alters. We correct it, rather than let it correct us.

REGRESSION, REPRESSION

Baptism served two functions for which we have modern names: it prevented regression; it offered repression. Our most immediate experience of the child today is through these experiences.

What depth psychology has come to call regression is nothing other than a return to the child. Since this is so, we might inquire more fundamentally into psychology's notion of maturity, which has regression as its counterpart, and into psychology's idea of development, which requires that the child be abandoned. Regression is the unavoidable shadow of linear styles of thinking. A developmental model will be plagued by its counter-movement, atavism; and reversion will be seen, not as a return through likeness to imaginal reality along Neoplatonic lines (Proclus, Plotinus), but as a regression to a worse condition. Psychology presents "going back" as "going down," a devolution to prior and inferior patterns. Maturity and regression become incompatible. For regression we lose respect, forgetting the need of living things to "go back" to "beginnings."

Regression is made tolerable in theory today only in terms of a "regression in the service of the ego" (E. Kris, *Psychoanalytic Explorations in Art*, 1952). Even in Jung, regression is mainly compensatory, a *reculer pour mieux sauter*. In Maslow, Erikson, Piaget, Gesell, as well as in Freudian ego psychology, if we do not advance along certain well-researched paths from stage to stage we become fixated in "childhood" and show regressed behavior, styles called puerile and infantile. Behind every forward step into "reality" there is the threatening shadow of the child—hedonistic or mystical depending upon how we regard the reversion to primordiality. This child we propitiate with sentimentality, superstition and kitsch, with indulgent holidays and treats, and with psychotherapy which partly owes its existence and earns its living from the regressive pull of the child.

Our model of maturity tends to make regression attractive. At a distance we idealize the angelic state of childhood and its creativity. By abandoning the child we place it in arcadia, borne by the sea, cradled, rocking softly at water level among reeds and rushes, nourished by nymphs who delight in its whims, shepherds, kindly old caretakers who welcome the childish, the regressed. Then of course the counter-movement sets in again; the here constellates; from the abandoned child the great leap forward, the draining of the Zuyder Zee with which Freud compared the work of psycho-analysis.[20]

Because the major content of repression is the child, the contemporary revolution on behalf of the repressed—black or poor, feminine or natural or undeveloped—becomes unavoidably the revolution of the child. The formulations become immature, a touch pathetic, the behavior regressed, and the ambition invincible and vulnerable at the same time. Hermaphroditism of the archetype also plays its role in the revolution, as does that peculiar mixture of beginning and end: hope exemplified in apocalyptic destruction. Our theme thus touches upon psychology's relation to the times and its struggle with the child, all of which suggests that it might be profitable to reflect the statements of [Herbert] Marcuse, [R. D.] Laing, and [Norman O.] Brown concerning the contemporary revolution of the repressed in the light of archetypal psychology, i.e., as expressions of the cult of the child.

Preferable to the division into child and adult and the consequent patterns of abandonment which we have been sketching, would be a psychology less given over to the child, its woes and romanticism. We might then have a psychology descriptive of man, an aspect of whom is perennially child, carrying his incurable weakness and nurse to it, enacting the child neither by development nor by abandonment, but bearing the child, the child contained. Our subjective experience might then be mirrored by a psychology both more exact in its description and more sophisticatedly classical, where the child is contained within the man who carries in his face and mien the shame of the childish, its unchanging psychopathology —untranscended, untransformed—and the invincible high hopes together with the vulnerability of these hopes, who bears his abandonment in dignity, and whose freedom comes from the imaginal redeemed from the amnesia of childhood.

9 · THE ORPHAN ARCHETYPE

. . . .

ROSE-EMILY ROTHENBERG

This essay defines the archetype of abandonment, the orphan, and traces it authoritatively through myth, story, fairy tale, literature, and, perhaps most important, through the author's personal experience. This is a well-crafted treatment of the theme of abandonment that details the "inner orphan's" predicament. Ms. Rothenberg, a Jungian analyst, speaks from the depths when she says, "It is only when one is truly alone that the creative potential that is carried deep inside has the space and room to emerge into the light of day." This selection was originally published in the journal Psychological Perspectives, *1983.*

I was named Rose-Emily for my mother. Before I was born, my mother confided to her closest friend that she thought she was going to die. Six days after I was born, while she was still in the hospital, she developed an infection and died.

A year and a half later my father remarried. My first childhood memory is of standing in the dining room with my father, his wife, and my two sisters. My father said to us, "This is not your real mother, this is your stepmother." My fourteen-year-old sister said nothing. But my other sister, eighteen months older than me, kicked and screamed and yelled, "No, it isn't true." I just stood there silently. I felt an enormous fear, knowing that I would have to please this mother at all costs or she would leave me too.

Many years later, I tried to imagine what I must have felt when my mother left me after only six days. I imagined falling into a great black abyss with nothing there to hold me. Everything was unbelievably still. I felt abandoned, as if I had been dropped into this abyss and left alone. I have often been comforted by thinking of God creating the world in six days. I had my mother for six days: it was just enough time to get me started.

The first dream I can remember has lived vividly within me. I was about four at the time.

> I was standing in the center of my childhood house. Behind me stood a dead tree with bare branches and no leaves. From my forearm, black snakes were being born.

I have told several analysts this dream and each has listened attentively, but none has attempted to interpret it. I have contemplated it as I lived with it. The tree is often a symbol of the eternal spirit that sheds its leaves, dying in order to live. The dead tree in my dream seemed to carry the soul of my real mother, and the snakes born out of my arm represented my psyche's reaction to her death.

Snakes convey powerful energies. These energies can be used as poison or panacea. Snakes exemplify both the most inferior and the most superior in man: destruction or divine wisdom. Snakes symbolize the most primitive level of life as well as rebirth and resurrection. They can also represent the incarnation of the dead, and, perhaps, in the dream were a container for my mother's spirit.

Giving birth to snakes was my orphan dilemma. I could remain in the unconscious and succumb to its poisons, or I could use its healing powers to engage life.

Many years later, I had a dream in which Jung appeared.

> I was going to visit Jung, as he was soon to die. I wanted to talk with him about my progress in training to become an analyst. He said to me, "You need to integrate the two pains in your life. That is what you need to work on."

Even in the dream I knew he meant I needed to understand and integrate the death of my mother and the coming of my stepmother, and what it meant to be an orphan.

The term orphan was used by the alchemists as the name of a unique stone, a gem similar to our modern solitaire that was found in the Emperor's crown. The alchemists equated the orphan stone with the *lapis philosophorum*, the Philosopher's Stone. This stone represents the totality, or the "one"; it corresponds to the psychological idea of the Self. The lapis is the stone of the wise, the gem of the individuation process. In one text it was known as the homeless orphan who is slain at the beginning of the alchemical process for purposes of transformation. This graphically depicts what befalls the literal orphan after the initial, brutal separation is forced upon him. He, too, is "slain" before the transformation process permits him to discover the meaning of this unique event in his life.

The lapis or stone is also known as something that is both worthless and precious, a set of opposites familiar to the orphan. He often feels as if he is either the most "inferior one" or the most "superior one."

The Biblical image of the stone rejected by the builders that becomes the chief cornerstone of a building (Psalms 118:22) also calls up the orphan archetype. The stone that Jung carved at his tower in Bollingen was such a stone. In *Memories, Dreams, Reflections* Jung told of a mistake that was made in the dimensions of the cornerstone. Jung's mason wanted to send it back. Jung immediately felt it was "his" stone and insisted on keeping it. A Latin verse suddenly came to him, a verse which referred to the lapis as despised and rejected, and he chiseled it into the stone:

Here stands the mean, uncomely stone.
'Tis very cheap in price!
The more it is despised by fools
The more loved by the wise.

On the third side of the stone, the one facing the lake, he "let the stone speak for itself" and carved these quotations from alchemy (translated from the Latin inscription):

> I am an orphan, alone; nevertheless I am found everywhere. I am one, but opposed to myself. I am youth and old man at one and the same time. I have known neither father nor mother, because I have had to be fetched out of the deep like a fish, or fell like a white stone from heaven. In woods and mountains I roam, but I am hidden in the innermost soul of man. I am moral for everyone, yet I am not touched by the cycle of aeons.

The orphan archetype is frequently illustrated in a surprisingly large number of mythical and legendary figures, suggesting the intimate connection between being an orphan and being a hero. They range from the Mesopotamian hero named Sargon to the Biblical figures of Moses and Joshua Ben Nun; from a host of Greek deities (Oedipus, Aesculapius, and Dionysus) to the Syrian queen, Semiramis; and from the founder of Rome, Romulus, to the English king, Arthur, and the knight Tristan. All shared the fate of having been separated from their mothers and raised by others.

As many mythological examples indicate, the orphan archetype is inextricably connected with the hero, but it has also been constellated in the psyches of mortals who are about to embark on the hero's journey. For example, the orphan image has an appeal for the young person who undertakes his rite of passage, leaving the security and protection of the family. He undergoes a psychic loss of his parents and subsequent feelings of loneliness and isolation that recall the infant's physical separation from the mother. The adolescent who loses a parent is doubly affected by this symbolic and actual loss, and may suffer significantly.

In *Symbols of Transformation*, Jung wrote that adolescents, whose home conditions are difficult and whose unknown future lies ahead, may daydream that they are the adopted child whose real parents are royal and who will return someday to claim them. Their true identity will then be dramatically revealed. Another variation of the orphan daydream incorporated the fact that because the literal orphan doesn't have the usual family ties, he is free to devote himself to discovering life's mysteries, partaking in whatever romantic adventures he may fancy, and accomplishing numerous feats along the way.

The fantasy of being adopted is by no means limited to adolescents. Many children at an earlier age have recurrent daydreams about being an orphan. Regardless of the age, the frequency of this fantasy may indicate an attempt on the part of the psyche to establish the idea of one's uniqueness and inherent urge to undertake his own individual journey in life in order to fulfill his destiny.

Although these orphan fantasies are based, for the most part, on ancient folk beliefs, they also have their origins in some long-standing social practices. In the ancient world, children were sometimes cruelly abandoned and exposed because of the social stigma attached to birth defects, religious taboos, illegitimacy, and economic necessity. When parents wanted to preserve an opportunity for survival, they wrapped their child up in a blanket and left him in a well-populated area where he would easily be discovered. In contrast, some unwanted children were left in desolate regions where death from exposure or wild animals was unavoidable.

The orphan as an archetype has found its way into many narratives. The familiar stories of Harold Grey's *Orphan Annie*, Johanna Spyri's *Heidi*, and Frances Hodson Burnett's *The Little Princess* (or *Sara Crew*) are all well-known orphan stories.

Equally famous are the children created by Charles Dickens. In "The Dickens Child: From Infantilism To Wholeness," John McNeary discussed each of the Dickens characters, their initial stages of abandonment, their being misunderstood and ill-treated, and, finally, their archetypal journey toward discovering their true identity. McNeary wrote that the orphan child reaches his goal "only after terrible trials and near destruction, for the light carried by the child is always in danger of being swallowed up in the darkness."

Two of the most noble American literary wanderers are Melville's Ishmael, the biblical narrator of *Moby Dick*, and Ahab, the captain of his ship, the *Pequod*.

In *Melville's Moby Dick: A Jungian Commentary*, Edward Edinger wrote: "Ishmael is the rejected orphan who through no fault of his own has been cruelly cast out and condemned to wander beyond the pale. Ishmael is, therefore, the prototype of the alienated man, the outsider who feels he has no place in the nature of things."

Beyond alchemy, mythology and literature is the raw reality of the literal orphan. Many authors themselves were orphaned before the age of six: Edgar Allan Poe, the Brontës, George Sand, Jonathan Swift, Rousseau, Tolstoy, Baudelaire, Hawthorne, Byron, Dante, and others. The characters in their books often reflect the experience of their early loss.

To examine the psychological complexes that the orphan suffers, we need first to look at the significant primary relationship from which the orphan child emerges, and from which he has been abandoned. In his book *The Child*, Erich Neumann wrote: "Once we appreciate the positive significance of the child's total dependency on the primal relationship, we cannot be surprised by the catastrophic effects that ensue when that relationship is disturbed or destroyed."

Persons who are not orphans, such as adopted children and children of divorced parents, also may encounter the psychological trauma of loss.

Even when both parents are present, feelings of abandonment can be experienced by the child who feels he is not listened to or heard by his mother. When the child is not accepted for his reality, the authenticity of his own feelings is not experienced. Alice Miller, in *Prisoners of Childhood*, noted that this creates a feeling of emptiness, futility and homelessness on the part of the child. One doesn't have to be an actual orphan to experience the feelings of orphanhood, but these feelings are more intense in the literal orphan.

At a very early age, the mother represents the Self. A living connection to the mother who carries this important life-giving projection is crucial to the newborn's sense of security and self-worth. The mother also carries a link to the maternal past that goes all the way back to the earth. When there has been damage to this fundamental primary relationship, or when the infant's new life is cut off at birth, his ego is prematurely thrown back onto itself and reduced to its own resources. The infant then experiences abandonment.

As I conceive it, three dominant psychological complexes frequently result from such a catastrophe. They are basic to the psychological profile of the orphan. First, there is a profound sense of unworthiness. Maternal warmth gives one a sense of worth at a primary level. When that love is taken away, one feels rejected, that he has done something wrong or has been found totally unacceptable. Neumann conveyed it this way: "The child is cast out of the natural order of things and comes to doubt the justification of his own existence."

This feeling of unworthiness is commingled with the second most prominent feature in orphan psychology, the feeling of guilt. This is an archaic guilt, not to be confused with the more conscious guilt one feels when leaving the parents, but more closely akin to the guilt for becoming more conscious or for being alive. Neumann said: "The experience of not being loved is identical with being abnormal, sick, leprous and above all condemned. Instead of blaming the world or man, the orphan feels guilty." Since the Self has not been constellated, the orphan feels that the Self (the mother) has turned away, and that this is a higher judgment for which the orphan must carry the guilt.

The search for the missing parent, or for what she represents, is foremost in the life of the orphan. Born of his insatiable need to fill the gap created by his mother's death, he looks for the mother everywhere. In his article, "Paracelsus as a Spiritual Phenomenon," Jung wrote: "The more remote and unreal the personal mother is, the more deeply will the son's yearning for her clutch his soul, awakening that primordial and eternal image of the mother for whose sake everything that embraces, protects, nourishes, and helps assumes material form from the Alma Mater of the university to the personification of cities, countries, sciences, and ideals." This endless search for the mother can lead one into many troublesome predicaments.

The orphan usually feels he has a wound that cannot be healed and thus indulges in self-pity. He expects others to feel sorry for him and take him under their protective wing. He feels that he is the "injured one" and needs all the care he can possibly get. This state of mind brings on a dependency problem of considerable magnitude. Because the orphan has lost his connection to the original source of life-giving sustenance, he clings to the person who offers him the security for which he has longed, as if his very survival depended on it. To this end he will hold on to whatever object, person or form of behavior that, to him, represents security (sex, money, etc.) until he finds the object no longer carries the same meaning for him, i.e., it no longer carries the projection of the mother. At this point, the orphan must simply discard the object of the projection or turn away, often harboring hostile feelings toward the one that did not fulfill his needs or expectations.

Because the orphan does not have enough of "himself," he feels his worthiness only when he is in the presence of another person. Being with others becomes vital, but it only serves to give him the illusion of security. If a mutual dependency develops, they both may become entangled in an unconscious symbiotic bond. Neither can leave this bond of union until the contents of their involvement can be made conscious.

This condition of dependency puts the orphan in the "innocent child position" and constellates the parent in the other person; the orphan then becomes the child-victim to the other person's induced authority. He feels that "if I'm the good little child, maybe they will mother me." His helpless-victim identity elicits the compensatory witch-bully archetype on the other side. Sometimes it happens the other way around. The orphan may begin to behave exactly like the witch or the bully, and assume his/her characteristics and behavior patterns. Living out either of these roles—the victim or the oppressor—suggests that he is possessed by the negative side of the parent-child archetype. When he identifies with or is possessed by either side, he abdicates his independent functioning.

This overly dependent state of affairs between two people creates an unproductive and consequently perilous psychological condition for both individuals involved. In order to avoid the suffocation such a situation inevitably creates, one or the other will be forced to leave. This sets into motion one of the most obsessive of all the orphan's complexes, the fear of being left. This includes the ever-present concern about the possibility of "being left out" and conversely, the need to be included constantly.

The orphan has an immense fear of being left or abandoned, especially by a person who has carried great significance for him. He will go to untold lengths to prevent this from happening. The fear may be quite pervasive in his life. He might even leave the other person first, in spite of his desire to stay in the relationship, just to avoid the repeated experience of being left. He might, on the other hand, engage in lying, cheating or withholding information (even from himself) if it in any way suggests the wisdom of a parting or a separation. Participating in such a subterfuge, he betrays himself as well as the other person and sacrifices important life values along the way. He falls victim to the dark forces that he attempted to conceal. Until the orphan becomes conscious of his overly dependent attitude and its eventual consequences, he may constellate his original fate of being left over and over again.

The third most significant psychic legacy facing the orphan is a profound pull toward death. The archetypal image of the orphan includes the link of life and death. The orphan is the survivor of the death experience, but is bound by strong ties of affection and loyalty to his parent in the next world. The dead mother exerts a profound attraction for her orphan child, and the mother's absence or death portends the child's own death. In fact, some part of the unborn psyche may die with the mother and doesn't get born. One experiences it as something missing, something having been left behind in the womb.

Having lived through the shared death experience and come to life again and survived, the orphan may feel especially favored by God. Since someone or something spared his life, he assumes he must be very special to have deserved this special blessing. An inflation of no small proportions, and symptoms of narcissism and egocentricity, are often born out of this inflated attitude. Conversely, a negative inflation which takes the form of the "heroic sufferer" with an inferiority complex can just as easily develop. Feelings of guilt and unworthiness are basic ingredients in such an inferiority complex.

The pull toward death has an allure for the orphan. It is equivalent to the pull of the great unconscious. It is both feared and dreaded, yet alluring and captivating. One rationalized: "If my [mother] did it, why can't I?" At one level, this tension between life and death is experienced when one is at the gateway to every rebirth or creative venture. The urge to refuse the task and not to surpass one's present state is an ever-present dilemma. For the orphan, the inevitable state of chaos preceding each new birth is a painful reminder of his initial traumatic experience of chaos. Because his new life was cut off at birth, the orphan may turn away from life. He may also fall into a state of dependency the minute he stands on the brink of the unknown. Without a conscious connection to this experience of fear and an understanding of its roots, he can easily get stuck at this crucial moment of transcendence and not go beyond it.

Another death experience that befalls the orphan is the "anniversary syndrome." There is a strong tendency in the orphan to relive his childhood trauma at a specific time, such as when the orphan reaches the chronological age of the mother when she died, or when the orphan-daughter is about to deliver a child.

A good example of this may be found in a 1928 article by Marie Bonaparte, an analysand, friend, and colleague of Freud's. It was titled in English translation, "The Identification of a Girl with Her Dead Mother." Marie's mother died of tuberculosis when she was one month old. At four years of age, Marie became ill with tuberculosis and wasn't expected to live through the night. Although she fully recovered from her illness, symptoms of it recurred a few years before she reached the age of twenty-one, her mother's age when she died. In spite of total assurances that she was healthy, she was convinced she still had tuberculosis and went from one doctor to the next, finally committing herself to a complete rest. Soon after she passed her twenty-first birthday, she felt completely cured. Another interesting detail in the article was that she had an opal ring that her mother purchased when she was newly married and that Marie felt must have been a bad omen, foretelling her coming death. During the time Marie was pregnant, she looked for this ring, and it had mysteriously disappeared. After she decided not to have any more children, she miraculously found the ring in her dresser drawer. She did not realize that the connection to these events in her life was related to her unconscious identification with her mother's death, until it came out in her analysis with Freud. She later wrote about her phobias and visions, and her feeling of having lived through her child-hood years with guilt and fear of retaliation for having caused her mother's death.

When there has been a trauma or a deep injury, there is a compensatory effort on the part of the psyche to achieve a balance. Whenever there is a loss or a void, nature will attempt to fill it. In the case of an orphan, when a person as significant as the mother is lost or absent, a substitute mother will usually be found. Following the initial trauma of the death of the real mother, this often is the second most difficult trial for the orphan to un-dergo.

If the orphan has not become fully conscious of, or integrated the dark aspects of his fate, the unconscious aspects will usually be projected. This leaves the substitute mother to carry the dark side of the archetype, re-gardless of whether it "fits" her. Because the actual mother is absent, the orphan frequently has the fantasy that the true mother must have been the perfect, ideal, all-giving mother. This leaves the living "mother" to carry its opposite, the dark and demonic side. Since the stepmother is not the "real thing," nor the stepchild her "real child," both she and the child are left to endure the "second-best" psychology in this dual mother–child con-stellation.

A study conducted by John Birtchnell in England in 1980 on early parent death and mental illness revealed an interesting point vis-à-vis the negative mother surrogate. The research indicated that it was not the early parent death that predisposed one to subsequent mental illness, but rather the quality of the mother replacement that was the critical factor in one's future mental status. The circumstances that surround the orphan after death have a profound effect upon his psychic well-being. Consciously dealing with and talking about the issues and feelings that inevitably arise can help the child integrate the experience.

The attitudes and behavior of the surviving parent significantly affect the ability of the orphan to integrate the loss and his feelings of grief. If the child is forced to live out the role of the lost wife and mother, the orphan will lose touch with his childhood and his appropriate place in the family structure. If the surviving parent becomes emotionally dependent upon him, the orphan may be left with, among other problems, the difficulty in making a normal separation from the parent when the appropriate time comes for him to leave home.

Having a mother surrogate instead of one's natural mother elicits the dual-mother archetype implicit in the orphan's fate. Within this archetype are two strongly constellated opposites, which may be called "negative-stepmother-witch" and the "positive-mother-spirit." The negative stepmother may be potentially destructive to the orphan, and the positive mother spirit, potentially healing.

There is a popular fairy tale with these opposites of the negative stepmother on the one hand, and her fairy godmother on the other. Her living experience of both mothers provided the catalyst for her reaping good fortune. The fairy tale is Cinderella. As the tale is well known, I will limit my amplification to the section of the story where the fairy godmother's appearance helps pave the way for Cinderella's transformation from her status as the servant into a beautiful woman who goes to the ball and meets the prince.

In the seventeenth and eighteenth centuries, many tales arose in Scotland, China, Germany and Italy with the basic Cinderella theme. However, they revealed some interesting variations on the fairy-godmother motif. Several examples in Opie's *The Classic Fairy Tales* illustrate the healing presence of the fairy-godmother spirit.

In one version Cinderella's (or Rashin Coatie, in this tale) mother had died and left her a red calf that, upon request, gave her anything she wanted. When her evil stepmother discovered this, she had the calf butchered. But the red calf told her: "Pick me up, bone by bone, and put me under the grey stone." The spirit of her mother resided in the red calf, and it was from her mother's spirit that she received her fine clothes for the ball.

In another version, the cinder-maid, Aschenputtel, remained faithful to her dead mother's memory. Her father gave her a hazel twig, and she planted it upon her mother's grave. When a great tree grew out of it, a bird perched upon the tree and granted her every wish. In yet another version, Cinderella planted a seedling date tree brought to her by her father. In four days it grew to the size of a woman, and in the tree was a fairy who granted her wishes.

In a Chinese version, Cinderella caught a tame fish that grew to enormous size, ten feet long. The fish would place his head on the embankment beside her. When the stepmother found out about it, she killed and ate the fish. A man came out of the sky and informed Cinderella that the bones of the fish had been buried under the dung hill, and if she collected them and kept them in her room, she need only pray to them to obtain whatever she wished.

In these Cinderella tales, the benevolent creatures represent the numinous spirit of the real mother and also the instincts. Developing a close affinity to one's instincts means relating to one's own earth and to the mother they represent. The animals offer Cinderella a vital connection to the nourishing aspects of the Great Mother that can rescue her from her menial existence and from the grasp of the Terrible Mother. She then can become the princess. Another example of this phenomenon appeared in the myths of the heroes mentioned earlier. In many of the legends, animals and "people of the earth" (peasants, farmers, gardeners, etc.) provided for the care of the hero infants.

The support of the unconscious, and in this instance, the connection to the positive mother spirit, is a vital factor in healing the orphan's wounds. The mother spirit comes when one's attitude is open and receptive to its intervention.

The basic theme of Paracelsus, the alchemical philosopher and pioneer of empirical psychology, was the authenticity of one's own experience of nature against the authority of tradition. Paracelsus' mother died when he was very young, and the loss of his mother was said to have left a great deal of unsatisfied longing in him. Jung wrote that Paracelsus was nurtured within himself and derived his knowledge from the innate spirit that is the *lumen naturae*, the "light of nature." Just as it is naturally presented in animals, so also it dwells within man, who brought it into the world with himself. Paracelsus felt it was "man's mentor," and "though men die, the mentor goes on teaching."

In order for the orphan to begin to relate to this light within himself and to come to a conscious relation to his individual fate, he first needs to be released from an all-consuming identification with it. He needs to experience himself as a separate autonomous being in his own right. In order to assimilate the meaning of his myth and extract the value from his traumatic experience, the orphan has to expose himself to the feelings he has regarding his weaknesses and to understand these complexes that have resulted from his original loss. Mourning the loss of the loved one has to be fully experienced.

The orphan needs to accept his reality and not deny his feelings of need. To come to full terms with his reality, he cannot avoid the pain involved in re-experiencing his fate and its effects upon him. By allowing himself to feel the hurt, the anger, the pain, and the sadness, he begins to sacrifice his dependent expectations. By making this sacrifice, he begins to assume more responsibility for himself. If one takes up the task of living his own life, he will be more apt to lose his bitter resentment for not getting what he sees other people have, and what he feels he has been missing. This heroic task cultivates a greater ability in the orphan to hold on to the positive life-giving sustenance as opposed to falling back into the abyss, the dark pull of the underworld. The more he enters life, the more he releases death's hold on him.

The ultimate solution for the orphan's dilemma is a reconnection with the natural mother at her archetypal source. When one makes a connection with the unconscious, he receives the longed-for maternal sustenance. The personification of the Great Mother is the nourishing aspect of the unconscious, and one can get in touch with this aspect in many ways. Some examples are writing poems, working with art materials, or doing active imagination with the one who represents the inner sources of comfort and concern. By so doing, one activates a reciprocal connection between the ego and the unconscious. Without the support of the unconscious, the ego is likely to feel orphaned and abandoned by the Self, and without the ego's reciprocal involvement, the Self is likely to feel equally abandoned by the ego.

When one begins to separate from his identification with his orphan fate, he can begin to conceptualize the "inner orphan" inside himself that needs his, the ego's, care and protection. The orphan needs to protect his "inner orphan" from external demands and, in turn, to develop his own individual state of autonomy and independence that was intended for him by virtue of his orphanhood. It is only when one is truly alone that the creative potential that is carried deep inside has the space and room to emerge into the light of day. In *Psychology And Religion: West and East*, Jung said: "It is . . . only in the state of complete abandonment and loneliness that we experience the helpful powers of our own natures."

I have not escaped from my identity as an orphan. In my life, its drama continues to be played out. When I was 35, my mother's age when she died, I developed a serious illness. When my own son was born, my husband was critically ill and my infant son and I faced the possibility of his loss. I have always felt my mother in times of great need. Her presence has helped me continue.

The container in which many of the legendary hero-orphans were placed after their abandonment came to me in a dream.

> I was in my childhood bedroom, looking at an art book, and came upon a picture of a beautifully carved wooden cradle of a unique egg-shaped design. It had wooden slats about a half-inch apart and when it was closed, held the baby inside. The title of the painting was "Cradle for a Deathly Ill Infant."

Soon after this dream, a profound and healing thought came to me. My feelings of guilt about my mother's death and my anger at being abandoned were inextricably intertwined and made me feel inadequate and unworthy. Now I saw this in a completely different light. I saw myself as a seed floating around in space waiting to be born. The gods, knowing of my mother's approaching death, were looking for an available seed who was capable and worthy of surviving when the mother died. And they chose *me!*

10 · THE SOUL CHILD

· · · · · · ·

M A R I O N   W O O D M A N

This is an impassioned piece for the inner "abandoned one": "That child who is our very soul cries out from underneath the rubble of our lives, often from the core of our worst complex, begging us to say, 'You are not alone. I love you.' "

As you will undoubtedly notice when you read this essay, Canadian Jungian analyst Marion Woodman has a way with words. They overflow from her as amazing succor, giving nurture to many who hunger for psychological insight and who have had the good fortune to come into contact with her work. Her writings are highly relevant to contemporary lives. This chapter is an excerpt from her book The Pregnant Virgin.

I have found that individuals tend to repeat the pattern of their own actual birth every time life requires them to move onto a new level of awareness. As they entered the world, so they continue to re-enter at each new spiral of growth. If, for example, their birth was straightforward, they tend to handle passovers with courage and natural trust. If their birth was difficult, they become extremely fearful, manifest symptoms of suffocating, become claustrophobic (psychically and physically). If they were premature, they tend to be always a little ahead of themselves. If they were held back, the rebirth process may be very slow. If they were breech-birth, they tend to go through life "ass-backwards." If they were born by Caesarian section, they may avoid confrontations. If their mother was heavily drugged, they may come up to the point of passover with lots of energy, then, suddenly, for no apparent reason, stop, or move into a regression, and then wait for someone else to do something. Often this is the point where addictions reappear—binging, starving, drinking, sleeping, overworking—anything to avoid facing the reality of moving into a challenging world.

Many delightful babies appear in dreams, and just as many little tyrants who need firm and loving discipline. One child, however, is noticeably different from the others. This is the abandoned one, who may appear in bullrushes, in straw in a barn, in a tree, almost always in some forgotten or out-of-the-way place. This child will be radiant with light, robust, intelligent, sensitive. Often it is able to talk minutes after it is born. It has Presence. It is the Divine Child, bringing with it the "hard and bitter agony" of the new dispensation—the agony of Eliot's Magi. With its birth, the old gods have to go.

Since the natural gradient of the psyche is toward wholeness, the Self will attempt to push the neglected part forward for recognition. It contains energy of the highest value, the gold in the dung. In the Bible it is the stone that was rejected that becomes the cornerstone.[1] It manifests either in a sudden or subtle change in personality, or, conversely, in a fanaticism which the existing ego adapts in order to try to keep the new and threatening energy out. If the ego fails to go through the psychic birth canal, neurotic symptoms manifest physically and psychically. The suffering may be intense, but it is based on worshipping false gods. It is not the genuine suffering that accompanies efforts to incorporate the new life. The neurotic is always one phase behind where his reality is. When he should be moving into maturity, he hangs onto youthful folly. Never congruent with himself or others, he is never where he seems to be. What he cannot do is live in the *now*.

Many people are being dragged toward wholeness in their daily lives, but because they do not understand initiation rites, they cannot make sense of what is happening to them. They put on a happy face all day, and return to their apartment and cry all night. Perhaps their beloved has gone off with someone else; perhaps they are coping with a fatal illness; perhaps a loved one has died. Perhaps, and this is worst of all, everything has begun to go wrong for no apparent reason. If they have no concept of rites of passage, they experience themselves as victims, powerless to resist an overwhelming Fate. Their meaningless suffering drives them to escape through food, alcohol, drugs, sex. Or they take up arms against the gods and cry out, "Why me?"

They are being presented with the possibility of rebirth into a different life. Through failures, symptoms, inferiority feelings and overwhelming problems, they are being prodded to renounce life attachments that have become redundant. The possibility of rebirth constellates with the breakdown of what has gone before. That is why Jung emphasized the positive purpose of neurosis.[2] But because they do not understand, people cling to the familiar, refuse to make the necessary sacrifices, resist their own growth. Unable to give up their habitual lives, they are unable to receive new life.

Unless cultural rituals support the leap from one level of consciousness to another, there are no containing walls within which the process can happen. Without an understanding of myth or religion, without an understanding of the relationship between destruction and creation and rebirth, the individual suffers the mysteries of life as meaningless mayhem—alone. To ease the meaningless suffering, addictions may develop that are an attempt to repress the confusing demands of the growth process which cultural structures no longer clarify or contain.

The burning question when one enters analysis is "Who am I?" The immediate problem, however, as soon as powerful emotions begin to surface, is often a psyche/soma split. While women tend to talk about their bodies more than men, both sexes in our culture are grievously unrelated to their own body experience. Women say, "I don't like this body"; men say, "It hurts." Their use of the third-person neuter pronoun in referring to their body makes quite clear their sense of alienation. They may talk about "my heart," "my kidneys," "my feet," but their body as a whole is depersonalized. Repeatedly they say, "I don't feel anything below the neck. I experience feelings in my head, but nothing in my heart." Their lack of emotional response to a powerful dream image reflects the split. And yet, when they engage in active imagination with that dream image located in their body, their muscles release undulations of repressed grief. The body has become the whipping post. If the person is anxious, the body is starved, gorged, drugged, intoxicated, forced to vomit, driven into exhaustion or driven to frenzied reactions against self-destruction. When this magnificent animal attempts to send up warning signals, it is silenced with pills.

Many people can listen to their cat more intelligently than they can listen to their own despised body. Because they attend to their pet in a cherishing way, it returns their love. Their body, however, may have to let out an earth-shattering scream in order to be heard at all. Before symptoms manifest, quieter screams appear in dreams: a forsaken baby elephant, a starving kitten, a dog with a leg ripped out. Almost always the wounded animal is either gently or fiercely attempting to attract the attention of the dreamer, who may or may not respond. In fairytales it is the friendly animal who often carries the hero or heroine to the goal because the animal is the instinct that knows how to obey the goddess when reason fails.

It is possible that the scream that comes from the forsaken body, the scream that manifests in a symptom, is the cry of the soul that can find no other way to be heard. If we have lived behind a mask all our lives, sooner or later—if we are lucky—that mask will be smashed. Then we will have to look in our mirror at our own reality. Perhaps we will be appalled. Perhaps we will look into the terrified eyes of our own tiny child, that child who has never known love and who now beseeches us to respond. This child is alone, forsaken before we left the womb, or at birth, or when we began to please our parents and learned to put on our best performance in order to be accepted. As life progresses, we may continue to abandon our child by pleasing others—teachers, professors, bosses, friends and partners, even analysts. That child who is our very *soul* cries out from under the rubble of our lives, often from the core of our worst complex, begging us to say, "You are not alone. I love you."

The following is a recurring childhood dream which continued to haunt a fifty-year-old woman until it was worked through in analysis:

I am four or five years old. I'm with my mother in a crowded building, probably a department store. My mother is wearing dark clothes, a coat and a hat in brown or black, and throughout I see only her back. As we leave the building, I am slowed down by the crowd, and my mother, unknowing, moves ahead and disappears among the people. I try to call to her, but she doesn't hear me, nor does anyone else. I'm very frightened, not only at being lost but at my mother's not noticing we've been separated.

I come out of the building onto a long flight of broad steps, rather like those outside the National Gallery in London, but higher. The steps lead down into a large square, empty of any objects, but with similar steps leading to buildings on the other sides. The square, the steps and the buildings are very clean and white. From my vantage point I look around the square, hoping to see my mother. She is nowhere to be seen. I am alone on the steps. There are other people in the square, but they are unaware of me. I know nothing I do will make them notice me.

I am panic-stricken and overwhelmed with a sense of loss, of having been abandoned. It's as though I've ceased to exist for my mother, that she won't bother to come back for me, may even have forgotten about me, that in fact I can't make anyone aware that I exist.

For a moment, and at the same time, I'm an adult observer across the square who sees the small child standing alone at the top of the steps, trying to call out. This is also I, a grown woman who feels enormous pity for this child, longs to comfort and reassure her, but is unable to reach her. Something—the unconsciousness of the other people or the child's own panic—prevents communication between the child and the adult who cares and understands.

The woman associated this dream with Edvard Munch's painting *The Scream*, which evoked in her a similar panic. "The background is dark and

The Scream (1895), Edvard Munch. (*Bettmann Archive*.)

murky," she said, "while in my dream the environment is very clear, white and hard-edged, dotted with dark, ill-defined but equally hard-edged figures. The screamer is trying to escape from his environment; the child on the steps is trying to connect with hers." Many men and women are trapped in lives of quiet desperation until they turn to help that child within.

11 · LOVE AND THE FEAR OF ABANDONMENT

· · · · · · · ·

M.   SCOTT   PECK

This selection, an excerpt from M. Scott Peck's enormously popular book The Road Less Traveled, *looks at the nature of destructive love, the kind that produces fear and uncertainty in the child's emotional environment and that results in a major deficit for the child within the adult. "To the child," says psychiatrist Peck, "abandonment by its parents is the equivalent of death." He suggests that the parental threat of abandonment sacrifices loving involvement for control over the child. It is one of the most indecent, cruel interactions between parent and child, producing existential angst and poor self-concept, with devastating results for the inner child.*

It is not that the homes of unself-disciplined children are lacking in parental discipline. More often than not these children are punished frequently and severely throughout their childhood—slapped, punched, kicked, beaten and whipped by their parents for even minor infractions. But this discipline is meaningless—because it is undisciplined discipline.

One reason that it is meaningless is that the parents themselves are unself-disciplined, and therefore serve as undisciplined role models for their children. They are the "Do as I say, not as I do" parents. They may frequently get drunk in front of their children. They may fight with each other in front of the children without restraint, dignity, or rationality. They may be slovenly. They make promises they don't keep. Their own lives are frequently and obviously in disorder and disarray, and their attempts to order the lives of their children seem therefore to make little sense to these children.

If father beats up mother regularly, what sense does it make to a boy when his mother beats him up because he beat up his sister? Does it make sense when he's told that he must learn to control his temper? Since we do not have the benefit of comparison when we are young, our parents are godlike figures to our childish eyes. When parents do things a certain way, it seems to the young child the way to do them, the way they should be done. If a child sees his parents day in and day out behaving with self-discipline, restraint, dignity and a capacity to order their own lives, then the child will come to feel in the deepest fibers of his being that this is the way to live. If a child sees his parents day in and day out living without self-restraint or self-discipline, then he will come in the deepest fibers of being to believe that this is the way to live.

Yet even more important than role modeling is love. For even in chaotic and disordered homes genuine love is occasionally present, and from such homes may come self-disciplined children. And not infrequently parents who are professional people—doctors, lawyers, club women and philanthropists—who lead lives of strict orderliness and decorum but yet lack love, send children into the world who are as undisciplined and disorganized as any child from an impoverished and chaotic home.

Ultimately love is everything. . . .

When we love something it is of value to us, and when something is of value to us we spend time with it, time enjoying it and time taking care of it. Observe a teenager in love with his car and note the time he will spend admiring it, polishing it, repairing it, tuning it. Or an older person with a beloved rose garden, and the time spent pruning and mulching and fertilizing and studying it. So it is when we love children; we spend time admiring them and caring for them. We give them our time.

Good discipline requires time. When we have no time to give our children, or no time that we are willing to give, we don't even observe them closely enough to become aware of when their need for our disciplinary assistance is expressed subtly. If their need for discipline is so gross as to impinge upon our consciousness, we may still ignore the need on the grounds that it's easier to let them have their own way—"I just don't have the energy to deal with them today." Or, finally, if we are impelled into action by their misdeeds and our irritation, we will impose discipline, often brutally, out of anger rather than deliberation, without examining the problem or even taking the time to consider which form of discipline is the most appropriate to that particular problem.

The parents who devote time to their children even when it is not demanded by glaring misdeeds will perceive in them subtle needs for discipline, to which they will respond with gentle urging or reprimand or structure or praise, administered with thoughtfulness and care. They will observe how their children eat cake, how they study, when they tell subtle falsehoods, when they run away from problems rather than face them. They will take the time to make these minor corrections and adjustments, listening to their children, responding to them, tightening a little here, loosening a little there, giving them little lectures, little stories, little hugs and kisses, little admonishments, little pats on the back.

So it is that the quality of discipline afforded by loving parents is superior to the discipline of unloving parents. But this is just the beginning. In taking the time to observe and to think about their children's needs, loving parents will frequently agonize over the decisions to be made, and will, in a very real sense, suffer along with their children. The children are not blind to this. They perceive it when their parents are willing to suffer with them, and although they may not respond with immediate gratitude, they will learn also to suffer. "If my parents are willing to suffer with me," they will tell themselves, "then suffering must not be so bad, and I should be willing to suffer with myself." This is the beginning of self-discipline.

The time and the quality of the time that their parents devote to them indicate to children the degree to which they are valued by their parents. Some basically unloving parents, in an attempt to cover up their lack of caring, make frequent professions of love to their children, repetitively and mechanically telling them how much they are valued, but not devoting significant time of high quality to them. Their children are never totally deceived by such hollow words. Consciously they may cling to them, wanting to believe that they are loved, but unconsciously they know that their parents' words do not match up with their deeds.

On the other hand, children who are truly loved, although in moments of pique they may consciously feel or proclaim that they are being neglected, unconsciously know themselves to be valued. This knowledge is worth more than any gold. For when children know that they are valued, when they truly feel valued in the deepest parts of themselves, then they feel valuable.

The feeling of being valuable—"I am a valuable person"—is essential to mental health and is a cornerstone of self-discipline. It is a direct product of parental love. Such a conviction must be gained in childhood; it is extremely difficult to acquire it during adulthood. Conversely, when children have learned through the love of their parents to feel valuable, it is almost impossible for the vicissitudes of adulthood to destroy their spirit.

This feeling of being valuable is a cornerstone of self-discipline because when one considers oneself valuable one will take care of oneself in all ways that are necessary. Self-discipline is self-caring. For instance—since we are discussing the process of delaying gratification, of scheduling and ordering time—let us examine the matter of time. If we feel ourselves valuable, then we will feel our time to be valuable, and if we feel our time to be valuable, then we will want to use it well. The financial analyst who procrastinated did not value her time. If she had, she would not have allowed herself to spend most of her day so unhappily and unproductively. It was not without consequence for her that throughout her childhood she was "farmed out" during all school vacations to live with paid foster parents although her parents could have taken care of her perfectly well had they wanted to. They did not value her. They did not want to care for her. So she grew up feeling herself to be of little value, not worth caring for; therefore she did not care for herself. She did not feel that she was worth disciplining herself. Despite the fact that she was an intelligent and competent woman she required the most elementary instruction in self-discipline because she lacked a realistic assessment of her own worth and the value of her own time. Once she was able to perceive her time as being valuable, it naturally followed that she wanted to organize it and protect it and make maximum use of it.

As the result of the experience of consistent parental love and caring throughout childhood, such fortunate children will enter adulthood not only with a deep internal sense of their own value but also with a deep internal sense of security. All children are terrified of abandonment, and with good reason. This fear of abandonment begins around the age of six months, as soon as the child is able to perceive itself as an individual, separate from its parents. For with this perception of itself as an individual comes the realization that as an individual it is quite helpless, totally dependent and totally at the mercy of its parents for all forms of sustenance and means of survival. To the child, abandonment by its parents is the equivalent of death. Most parents, even when they are otherwise relatively ignorant or callous, are instinctively sensitive to their children's fear of abandonment and will therefore, day in and day out, hundreds and thousands of times, offer their children needed reassurance: "You know Mommy and Daddy aren't going to leave you behind"; "Of course Mommy and Daddy will come back to get you"; "Mommy and Daddy aren't going to forget about you." If these words are matched by deeds, month in and month out, year in and year out, by the time of adolescence the child will have lost the fear of abandonment and in its place will have a deep inner feeling that the world is a safe place in which to be and protection will be there when it is needed. With this internal sense of the consistent safety of the world, such a child is free to delay gratification of one kind or another, secure in the knowledge that the opportunity for gratification, like home and parents, is always there, available when needed.

But many are not so fortunate. A substantial number of children actually are abandoned by their parents during childhood, by death, by desertion, by sheer negligence, or, as in the case of the financial analyst, by a simple lack of caring. Others, while not abandoned in fact, fail to receive from their parents the reassurance that they will not be abandoned. There are some parents, for instance, who in their desire to enforce discipline as easily and quickly as possible, will actually use the threat of abandonment, overtly or subtly, to achieve this end. The message they give to their children is: "If you don't do exactly what I want you to do I won't love you any more, and you can figure out for yourself what that might mean." It means, of course, abandonment and death. These parents sacrifice love in their need for control and domination over their children, and their reward is children who are excessively fearful of the future. So it is that these children, abandoned either psychologically or in actuality, enter adulthood lacking any deep sense that the world is a safe and protective place. To the contrary, they perceive the world as dangerous and frightening, and they are not about to forsake any gratification or security in the present for the promise of greater gratification or security in the future, since for them the future seems dubious indeed.

In summary, for children to develop the capacity to delay gratification, it is necessary for them to have self-disciplined role models, a sense of self-worth, and a degree of trust in the safety of their existence. These "possessions" are ideally acquired through the self-discipline and consistent, genuine caring of their parents; they are the most precious gifts of themselves that mothers and fathers can bequeath. When these gifts have not been proffered by one's parents, it is possible to acquire them from other sources, but in that case the process of their acquisition is invariably an uphill struggle, often of lifelong duration and often unsuccessful.

12 · THE ONES WHO WALK AWAY FROM OMELAS

· · · · · · ·

URSULA K. LEGUIN

It's fitting to end this section on abandonment with a story of the scapegoat, an idea that turns on the moral dilemma of sacrifice: one tortured soul exchanged for the happiness of an entire community. This is analogous to the moral problem of the internal community: Can the inner child and its needs be abandoned in order to assure the survival and contentment of the adult personality?

Like Ms. LeGuin, I first encountered this motif in Dostoyevsky's Brothers Karamazov, *where Alyosha, the younger brother, is given the moral challenge of establishing a utopian society, heaven on earth, which can happen only if he is willing to sacrifice the life of one human infant. Would he do it?*

Consider your own moral effort: Would you sacrifice (have you abandoned) the inner child for the promise of perfection? LeGuin asks "Would you walk away from Omelas?" She has such a wonderful flair for the morally perverse in this tale that her talents wring the feelings right out of you.

This story originally appeared as part of the author's collection of stories, The Wind's Twelve Quarters. *Ms. LeGuin is a widely read and honored writer of fiction.*

· · · · · · ·

*T*he central idea of this psychomyth, the scapegoat, turns up in Dostoyevsky's Brothers Karamazov, and several people have asked me, rather suspiciously, why I gave the credit to William James. The fact is, I haven't been able to re-read Dostoyevsky, much as I loved him, since I was twenty-five, and I'd simply forgotten he used the idea. But when I met it in James's "The Moral Philosopher and the Moral Life," it was with a shock of recognition. Here is how James puts it:

> Or if the hypothesis were offered us of a world in which Messrs. Fourier's and Bellay's and Morris's utopias should all be outdone, and millions kept permanently happy on the one simple condition that a certain lost soul on the far-off edge of things should lead a life of lonely torment, what except a specifical and independent sort of emotion can it be which would make us immediately feel, even though an impulse arose within us

to clutch at the happiness so offered, how hideous a thing would be its enjoyment when deliberately accepted as the fruit of such a bargain?

The dilemma of the American conscience can hardly be better stated. Dostoyevsky was a great artist, and a radical one, but his early social radicalism reversed itself, leaving him a violent reactionary. Whereas the American James, who seems so mild, so naively gentlemanly—look how he says "us," assuming all his readers are as decent as himself!—was, and remained, and remains, a genuinely radical thinker. Directly after the "lost soul" passage he goes on,

> *All the higher, more penetrating ideals are revolutionary. They present themselves far less in the guise of effects of past experience than in that of probable causes of future experience, factors to which the environment and the lessons it has so far taught us must learn to bend.*

The application of those two sentences to this story, and to science fiction, and to all thinking about the future, is quite direct. Ideals as "the probable cause of future experience"—that is a subtle and exhilarating remark!

Of course I didn't read James and sit down and say, Now I'll write a story about that "lost soul." It seldom works that simply. I sat down and started a story, just because I felt like it, with nothing but the word "Omelas" in mind. It came from a road sign: Salem (Oregon) backwards. Don't you read road signs backwards? POTS. WOLS nerdlihc. ocsicnarF naS . . . Salem equals schelomo equals salaam equals Peace. Melas. O melas. Omelas. Homme helas. "Where do you get your ideas from, Ms. LeGuin?" From forgetting Dostoyevsky and reading road signs backwards, naturally. Where else?

With a clamor of bells that set the swallows soaring, the Festival of Summer came to the city Omelas, bright-towered by the sea. The rigging of the boats in the harbor sparkled with flags. In the streets between houses with red roofs and painted walls, between old moss-grown gardens and under avenues of trees, past great parks and public buildings, processions moved. Some were decorous: old people in long stiff robes of mauve and grey, grave master workmen, quiet, merry women carrying their babies and chatting as they walked. In other streets the music beat faster, a shimmering of gong and tambourine, and the people went dancing, the procession was a dance. Children dodged in and out, their high calls rising like the swallows' crossing flights over the music and the singing. All the processions wound toward the north side of the city, where on the great water-meadow called the Green Fields boys and girls, naked in the bright air, with mud-stained feet and ankles and long, lithe arms, exercised their restive horses before the race. The horses wore no gear at all but a halter without bit. Their manes were braided with streamers of silver, gold, and green. They flared their nostrils and pranced and boasted to one another; they were vastly excited, the horse being the only animal who has adopted our ceremonies as his own. Far off to the north and west the mountains stood up half encircling Omelas on her bay. The air of morning was so clear that the snow still crowning the Eighteen Peaks burned with white-gold fire across the miles of sunlit air, under the dark blue of the sky. There was just enough wind to make the banners that marked the racecourse snap and flutter now and then. In the silence of the broad green meadows one could hear the music winding through the city streets, farther and nearer and ever approaching, a cheerful faint sweetness of the air that from time to time trembled and gathered together and broke out into the great joyous clanging of the bells.

Joyous! How is one to tell about joy? How describe the citizens of Omelas?

They were not simple folk, you see, though they were happy. But we do not say the words much any more. All smiles have become archaic. Given a description such as this one tends to make certain assumptions. Given a description such as this one tends to look next for the King, mounted on a splendid stallion and surrounded by his noble knights, or perhaps in a golden litter borne by great-muscled slaves. But there was no king. They did not use swords, or keep slaves. They were not barbarians. I do not know the rules and laws of their society, but I suspect that they were singularly few. As they did without monarchy and slavery, so they also got along without the stock exchange, the advertisement, the secret police, and the bomb. Yet I repeat that these were not simple folk, not dulcet shepherds, noble savages, bland utopians. They were not less complex than us. The trouble is that we have a bad habit, encouraged by pedants and sophisticates, of considering happiness as something rather stupid. Only pain is intellectual, only evil interesting. This is the treason of the artist: a refusal to admit the banality of evil and the terrible boredom of pain. If you can't lick 'em, join 'em. If it hurts, repeat it. But to praise despair is to condemn delight, to embrace violence is to lose hold of everything else. We have almost lost hold; we can no longer describe a happy man, nor make any celebration of joy. How can I tell you about the people of Omelas? They were not naive and happy children—though their children were, in fact, happy. They were mature, intelligent, passionate adults whose lives were not wretched. O miracle! but I wish I could describe it better. I wish I could convince you. Omelas sounds in my words like a city in a fairy tale, long ago and far away, once upon a time. Perhaps it would be best if you imagined it as your own fancy bids, assuming it will rise to the occasion, for certainly I cannot suit you all. For instance, how about technology? I think that there would be no cars or helicopters in and above the streets; this follows from the fact that the people of Omelas are happy people. Happiness is based on a just discrimination of what is necessary, what is neither necessary nor destructive, and what is destructive. In the middle category, however—that of the unnecessary but undestructive, that of comfort, luxury, exuberance, etc.—they could perfectly well have central heating, subway trains, washing machines, and all kinds of marvelous devices not yet invented here, floating light-sources, fuelless power, a cure for the common cold. Or they could have none of that: it doesn't matter. As you like it. I incline to think that people from towns up and down the coast have been coming in to Omelas during the last days before the Festival on very fast little trains and double-decked trams, and that the train station of Omelas is actually the handsomest building in town, though plainer than the magnificent Farmers' Market. But even granted trains, I fear that Omelas so far strikes some of you as goody-goody. Smiles, bells, parades, horses, bleh. If so, please add an orgy. If an orgy would help, don't hesitate. Let us not, however, have temples from which issue beautiful nude priests and priestesses already half in ecstasy and ready to copulate with any man or woman, lover or stranger, who desires union with the deep godhead of the blood, although that was my first idea. But really it would be better not to have any temples in Omelas—at least, not manned temples. Religion, yes, clergy, no. Surely the beautiful nudes can just wander about, offering themselves like divine souffles to the hunger of the needy and the rapture of the flesh. Let them join the processions. Let tambourines be struck above the copulations, and the glory of desire be proclaimed upon the gongs, and (a not unimportant point) let the offspring of these delightful rituals be beloved and looked after by all. One thing I know there is none of in Omelas is guilt. But what else should there be? I thought at first there were no drugs, but that is puritanical. For those who like it, the faint insistent sweetness of *drooz* may perfume the ways of the city, *drooz* which first brings a great lightness and brilliance to the mind and limbs, and then after some hours a dreamy languor, and wonderful visions at last of the very arcane and inmost secrets of the Universe, as well as exciting the pleasure of sex beyond all belief; and it is not habit-forming. For more modest tastes I think there ought to be beer. What else, what else belongs in the joyous city? The sense of victory, surely the celebration of courage. But as we did without clergy, let us do without soldiers. The joy built upon successful slaughter is not the right kind of joy; it will not do; it is fearful and it is trivial. A boundless and generous contentment, a magnanimous triumph felt not against some outer enemy but in communion with the finest and fairest in the souls of all men everywhere and the splendor of the world's summer: this is what swells the hearts of the people of Omelas, and the victory they celebrate is that of life. I really don't think many of them need to take *drooz*.

Most of the processions have reached the Green Fields by now. A marvelous smell of cooking goes forth from the red and blue tents of the provisioners. The faces of small children are amiably sticky; in the benign grey beard of a man a couple of crumbs of rich pastry are entangled. The youths and girls have mounted their horses and are beginning to group around the starting line of the course. An old woman, small, fat, and laughing, is passing out flowers from a basket, and tall young men wear flowers in their shining hair. A child of nine or ten sits at the edge of the crowd, alone, playing on a wooden flute. People pause to listen, and they smile, but they do not speak to him, for he never ceases playing and never sees them, his dark eyes wholly rapt in the sweet, thin magic of the tune.

He finishes, and slowly lowers his hands holding the wooden flute.

As if that little private silence were the signal, all at once a trumpet sounds from the pavilion near the starting line: imperious, melancholy, piercing. The horses rear on their slender legs, and some of them neigh in answer. Sober-faced, the young riders stroke the horses' necks and soothe them, whispering, "Quiet, quiet, there my beauty, my hope. . . ." They begin to form in rank along the starting line. The crowds along the race-course are like a field of grass and flowers in the wind. The Festival of Summer has begun.

Do you believe? Do you accept the festival, the city, the joy? No? Then let me describe one more thing.

In a basement under one of the beautiful public buildings of Omelas, or perhaps in the cellar of one of its spacious private homes, there is a room. It has one locked door, and no window. A little light seeps in dustily between the cracks in the boards, secondhand from a cobwebbed window some-where across the cellar. In one corner of the little room a couple of mops, with stiff, clotted, foul-smelling heads, stand near a rusty bucket. The floor is dirt, a little damp to the touch, as cellar dirt usually is. The room is about three paces long and two wide: a mere broom closet or disused tool room. In the room, a child is sitting. It could be a boy or a girl. It looks about six, but actually is nearly ten. It is feeble-minded. Perhaps it was born defective, or perhaps it has become inbecile through fear, malnutrition, and neglect. It picks its nose and occasionally fumbles vaguely with its toes or genitals, as it sits hunched in the corner farthest from the bucket and the two mops. It is afraid of the mops. It finds them horrible. It shuts its eyes, but it knows the mops are still standing there; and the door is locked; and nobody will come. The door is always locked; and nobody ever comes, except that sometimes—the child has no understanding of time or interval—sometimes the door rattles terribly and opens, and a person, or several people, are there. One of them may come in and kick the child to make it stand up. The others never come close, but peer in at it with frightened, disgusted eyes. The food bowl and the water jug are hastily filled, the door is locked, the eyes disappear. The people at the door never say anything, but the child, who has not always lived in the tool room, and can remember sunlight and its mother's voice, sometimes speaks. "I will be good," it says. "Please let me out. I will be good!" They never answer. The child used to scream for help at night, and cry a good deal, but now it only makes a kind of whining, "eh-haa, eh-haa," and it speaks less and less often. It is so thin there are no calves to its legs; its belly protrudes; it lives on a half-bowl of corn meal and grease a day. It is naked. Its buttocks and thighs are a mass of festered sores, as it sits in its own excrement continually.

They all know it is there, the people of Omelas. Some of them have come to see it, others are merely content to know it is there. They all know that it has to be there. Some of them understand why, and some do not, but they all understand that their happiness, the beauty of their city, the tenderness of their friendships, the health of their children, the wisdom of their scholars, the skill of their makers, even the abundance of their harvest and the kindly weathers of their skies, depend wholly on this child's abominable misery.

This is usually explained to children when they are between eight and twelve, whenever they seem capable of understanding; and most of those who come to see the child are young people, though often enough an adult comes, or comes back, to see the child. No matter how well the matter has been explained to them, these young spectators are always shocked and sickened at the sight. They feel disgust, which they had thought themselves superior to. They feel anger, outrage, impotence, despite all the explanations. They would like to do something for the child. But there is nothing they can do. If the child were brought up into the sunlight out of that vile place, if it were cleaned and fed and comforted, that would be a good thing, indeed; but if it were done, in that day and hour all the prosperity and beauty and delight of Omelas would wither and be destroyed. Those are the terms. To exchange all the goodness and grace of every life in Omelas for that single, small improvement: to throw away the happiness of thousands for the chance of happiness of one: that would be to let guilt within the walls indeed.

The terms are strict and absolute; there may not even be a kind word spoken to the child.

Often the young people go home in tears, or in a tearless rage, when they have seen the child and faced this terrible paradox. They may brood over it for weeks or years. But as time goes on they begin to realize that even if the child could be released, it would not get much good of its freedom: a little vague pleasure of warmth and food, no doubt, but little more. It is too degraded and imbecile to know any real joy. It has been afraid too long ever to be free of fear. Its habits are too uncouth for it to respond to humane treatment. Indeed, after so long it would probably be wretched without walls about it to protect it, and darkness for its eyes, and its own excrement to sit in. Their tears at the bitter injustice dry when they begin to perceive the terrible justice of reality, and to accept it. Yet it is their tears and anger, the trying of their generosity and the acceptance of their helplessness, which are perhaps the true source of the splendor of their lives. Theirs is no vapid, irresponsible happiness. They know that they, like the child, are not free. They know compassion. It is the existence of the child, and their knowledge of its existence, that makes possible the nobility of their architecture, the poignancy of their music, the profundity of their science. It is because of the child that they are so gentle with children. They know that if the wretched one were not there snivelling in the dark, the other one, the flute-player, could make no joyful music as the young riders line up in their beauty for the race in the sunlight of the first morning of summer.

Now do you believe them? Are they not more credible? But there is one more thing to tell, and this is quite incredible.

At times one of the adolescent girls or boys who go to see the child does not go home to weep or rage, does not, in fact, go home at all. Sometimes also a man or woman much older falls silent for a day or two, and then leaves home. These people go out into the street, and walk down the street alone. They keep walking, and walk straight out of the city of Omelas, through the beautiful gates. They keep walking across the farm-lands of Omelas. Each one goes alone, youth or girl, man or woman. Night falls; the traveler must pass down village streets, between the houses with yellow-lit windows, and on out into the darkness of the fields. Each alone, they go west or north, toward the mountains. They go on. They leave Omelas, they leave Omelas, they walk ahead into the darkness, and they do not come back. The place they go toward is a place even less imaginable to most of us than the city of happiness. I cannot describe it at all. But they seem to know where they are going, the ones who walk away from Omelas.

PART 3

. . . .

Eternal Youth and Narcissism: The Child's Dilemma

INTRODUCTION

· · · · · · ·

Only to a child is pure happiness possible.
Later it is always tainted with the knowledge that it will not last.

—CHINESE PROVERB

There are special circumstances in the life of a child that can have lifelong
debilitating consequences. One such minefield is crossed early in life, when
the developing childhood Self begins to separate from the mother or from
both parents. This is the narcissistic problem, expressed in the symbol of
the *puer aeternus*, the archetype of eternal youth. It is a difficulty that can
split the child between attempts to please the parents or to follow the child's
developing sense of Self. Narcissism has been called the psychological disturbance of our time. Part 3 is devoted to the problem of the narcissistic
relationship to the Self and its consequences for the inner child.

This problem can generally be attributed to defective parental love: the
parents, caught in their own impoverished sense of Self, and unable to
separate the child from the parental ego, create a bind for the developing
Self in the child. The parent's incapacity to see or to meet the child's needs
creates in the child an "as if" Self, one that will please the parents. The
nascent real Self of the child is thus split off or hidden and becomes, in
effect, the lost inner child.

Those wounds resulting from faulty separation eventually create a complex set of disturbances in the adult personality, which fall under the general
term narcissistic disorders, named from the Greek mythological story of
Narcissus. At the heart of that great story is the idea of seeing one's own
reflection—whether it is in the surface of a pond or in the mirroring face
of one's mother—and becoming transfixed there, unable to separate and
relate to others. In the myth, Narcissus becomes fixated with his own
reflection in a pool and, unable to move from the spot, dies of malnutrition.
The story symbolically suggests that the individual child can become fixated
at one stage of development, looking to consolidate a sense of his or her
true Self but unable to fully accomplish the task of separation for fear of
primal rejection by the parent. This unresolved circumstance can later doom
the child to a life of restriction, cut off from the Self (the inner child) and
unable to deal with the disturbing side of life.

This "child's dilemma" is a perpetuation of what Joel Covitz calls, in the opening essay of this section, the "family curse." As a result of the narcissistic wounds that parents themselves have sustained as children, they are unable to validate their own child's true Self. In turn, they *unconsciously perpetrate* the same fate on their children, demanding perfection and leaving the children feeling inadequate and impaired, believing they can only be loved if they fit the parents' image of perfection. The pain of not being seen, known, loved, and cared for *as one is* causes the child to develop a protective set of behaviors to control the anxiety of the situation.

This, then, is the inner child's dilemma: *"How can I identify with my true childhood Self and avoid the pain of primal rejection?"* For the undeveloped ego of a child, this often means choosing to identify with the false, "as if" Self in order to gain caring attention. The roots of the narcissistic disorders lie here, in the child's resulting fear that no one will love him as he is. The true Self, or inner child, is rejected as inferior or disgusting. As protection from these feelings, the narcissist builds a facade of grandiosity, making the inner child a prisoner of the dilemma.

In the adult, this problem makes it very difficult for an individual to relate to others or to the spiritual reality of the Self. The inner child, thoroughly hidden, is unavailable to the adult. The narcissistic personality is vulnerable to the least failure and craves admiration and adulation to support the false Self, which is maintained with the sacrifice of the inner child. The child in the adult is tormented by feelings of envy and rage, inner despair, isolation, and depression.

In the second essay in this section, "The Search for the True Self," Alice Miller says that "It is one of the turning points in analysis when the narcissistically disturbed patient comes to the emotional insight that all the love he has captured with so much effort and self-denial was not meant for him as he really was, that the admiration for his beauty and achievements was aimed at this beauty and these achievements, and not the child himself."

The narcissistic character as an adult may long for the paradise of childhood and, as Marie-Louise von Franz suggests in the third essay, *"Puer Aeternus,"* may adopt a provisional lifestyle, in which life is not quite "for real"—there is always something missing. In identifying with the *puer aeternus*, the narcissistically injured person can lose the inner child's capacity for life and waste inner riches. "You feel that such a person has a tremendous wealth and capacity," says von Franz, "but there is no possibility of finding a means of realization."

To be identified with the *puer aeternus* archetype is to lock into the child's dilemma, to indulge in a perpetual fantasy of youth, and deny the experience of real loss and transition that is so essential to development and growth. Only with good fortune and perseverance can one work this through as an adult. However, the *puer* finds it difficult to get into the world of the adult, seeing it as empty and meaningless. "He has not found a bridge by which he could take over what we would call the true life [the inner child] into adult life," says von Franz.

Jeffrey Satinover, in his essay "The Childhood Self and the Origins of *Puer* Psychology," complements both Miller and von Franz as he elaborates on the theme of the *puer aeternus* as a symbol of the narcissistic relation to the Self. Satinover suggests that a child can become addicted to the grandiose fantasies of the childhood Self as a result of parental disruption of the child's assertiveness, thus avoiding those frustrations that diminish his sense of specialness.

This has come to be known in the popular literature as the Peter Pan syndrome—a never-never-land resolution that says "I won't grow up," and "adults are untrustworthy." It can leave the growing individual adrift in life, bent on preserving the fantasy of the inner child, and granting no substance to the rest of life. The *puer* has a fear of aging, of never regaining the inner child, and, as Helen Luke suggests in the final chapter in this section, a need to move beyond one's limitations, which is often literalized in an irresistible attraction to actual aircraft and flight.

Jung saw the *puer aeternus* as referring to the child archetype, suggesting that its recurring fascination arises from our projection of our inability to renew ourselves. Hence the *puer* does not have an altogether negative connotation. It can embody some of the most positive attributes of the inner child: spontaneity of thought, creativity for problem-solving and original expression, a capacity to risk detachment from one's origins, to exist in a perpetually evolving state, to visualize new beginnings, to seek out opportunities, and to delight others with charm. James Hillman suggests in his book *The Dream and the Underworld* that as long as we are not caught in an identification with the archetype, the *puer aeternus* can endow us with a sense of destiny and meaning.

13 · NARCISSISM: THE DISTURBANCE OF OUR TIME

· · · · · · ·

JOEL COVITZ

This essay sets the tone for Part 3 by giving the general context of the narcissistic dilemma: We live in a time when parenting seems in danger of becoming a lost art. Children's healthy needs and rights are often not understood and frequently are stifled and denied, folded back onto the immature ego of the child with disastrous results. Joel Covitz, a Jungian analyst in Boston, considers this parental negligence to be psychological child abuse. "Parents have tremendous power," he says, and the injuries to the soul of the child have lifelong consequences, of which the other essays in this section speak at length. This chapter is an excerpt from Covitz's 1986 book, Emotional Child Abuse: The Family Curse, *which is a useful handbook on healthy parenting styles.*

Each age seems to have its characteristic disturbances. Freud found hysteria a prominent complaint; today's therapist is more likely to see patients who are depressed or compulsive, who feel that their lives lack affection, attention, and fulfilling relationships.

When we examine the roots of narcissistic disturbances, it becomes clear that most of them are connected to childhood. Simply stated, a child whose early, healthy narcissistic needs (for attention, affection and respect, as well as for food and shelter) are not met has trouble developing strength, independence and self-esteem. Parents who repeatedly fail to meet these early needs are abusing their children psychologically and emotionally. In almost every case, this is the opposite of what the parents intend; they want to be nurturing and helpful, but it doesn't work out that way. In some cases, they simply don't know how to go about parenting. In others, the parents are so needy themselves—because their early narcissistic needs weren't met—that they cannot meet their child's needs. Until these parents can break this chain of abuse, the effect on their children will be devastating and this destructive pattern will likely be repeated in future generations.

The incidence of physical child abuse in our society raises serious questions about the culture in which we live. Battered children who arrive in hospital emergency rooms bearing the wounds of their parents' anger and frustration will carry those scars for years. But children who are emotionally and psychologically abused also carry scars—harder to see at first, but no less crippling and difficult to heal.

One reason, of course, that the problem is so difficult to solve is that these children are generally unable to fight back in any effective way. As Maria Montessori points out in *The Child in the Family*, "No social problem is as universal as the oppression of the child. . . . No slave was ever so much the property of his master as in the case of the child."[1] Our society regards children as the parents' property. Parents have tremendous power, and children have few effective means of protest against abuse while they are still young. But eventually the price of that abuse will be exacted on the next generation. In her book *Prisoners of Childhood*, Alice Miller writes, ". . . in twenty years' time these children will be adults who will have to pay it all back to their own children."[2]

When a child's narcissistic needs are frustrated, he will usually manifest this frustration in anger toward the parents or in depression. But as the child grows older and gets more "socialized," he tends to repress the anger and tries to behave in a manner that will win or keep his parents' affection (sometimes an impossible task). The repressed rage and hurt must ultimately come out in some form, whether it be a failure to thrive, a poor self-image, self-destructive tendencies, or an adoption of the same mechanisms of defense used by the parents: tyranny, promiscuity, inadequacy. Whatever the adaptive behavior, the underlying frustration does not go away by itself. Only when a child can dig through his own defenses and get to the roots of the problem can he come to terms with his parents' abusive behavior. Almost always, shadows of that parental behavior can be recognized in his own. It is impossible to break the family's chain of abuse completely, to cut oneself off entirely from one's emotional heritage (in its good or bad aspect). But an understanding of the basis for that abusive behavior can help parents and children alike to modify it—with the goal being a step forward for each generation.

There are no secrets from a child's unconscious, although parents sometimes act as though their conscious words and deeds are the only messages they transmit to their children. Much of parents' communication with their children is nonverbal. Subliminally transferred from parent to child, all of the messages will be perceived by the child's unconscious, and he or she will have a fairly accurate perception of the parent's personality. As Jung says in *The Development of Personality*,

> Children are so deeply involved in the psychological attitude of their parents that it is no wonder that most of the disturbances in childhood can be traced back to a disturbed psychic atmosphere in the home. . . . There can be no doubt that it is of the utmost value for parents to view their symptoms in the light of their own problems and conflicts. It is their duty as parents to do so. Their responsibility in this respect carries with it the obligation to do everything

in their power not to lead a life that could harm the children. Generally far too little stress is laid upon how important the conduct of the parents is for the child, because it is not always words that count, but deeds. Parents should always be conscious of the fact that they themselves are the principle cause of neurosis in their children.[3]

But it must be remembered that the parents alone are not responsible for the family curse. As Jung also wrote, "It is not so much the parents as their ancestors—the grandparents and great-grandparents—who are the true progenitors."[4]

A child can be set up to repeat a parent's inadequacies. For example, Katherine's mother had always considered herself intelligent but not beautiful. Instead of trying to deal with this situation, however, she transmitted to her children the idea that only intelligence was important—not attractiveness or social ease or friendships. Her sons and daughter grew up intellectually accomplished but socially inept. Katherine was taught not to value her clothes or appearance. She was always clean, but she described herself as the kind of child whose kneesocks were always falling down, whose hair was out of place. All of her clothes were handed down from her cousins. Makeup was scorned in the household. The children grew up thinking that they were intelligent but ugly, which was not actually the case. Katherine in particular had trouble adjusting socially. She was a victim of the family curse.

Breaking free completely from one's family curse is almost impossible. But parents *can* become aware of the manifestations of this curse in their children, and can work to change the conditions that foster it. They have an opportunity to change whatever they are able to change in order to make their lives more healthy. And as Jung says, "Nature has no use for the plea that one 'did not know.' "[5]

THE ROOTS OF THE PROBLEM

How can so much go wrong so early in a child's life? The basic reasons are twofold: the inadequate personality development of the parents, who nearly always suffered abuse themselves as children, and the frustrations parents feel trying to bring up children in a culture that undervalues parenting.

Our children are victims of the increasingly prevalent view that parenting is a messy, frustrating job that gets in the way of one's growth and life, rather than enriching it. The lack of a creative, functioning culture of child-rearing becomes more grievous when we observe the breakdown in family life today. Children of divorce, of abandonment; children, some under ten years old, who run away from home to live in the streets rather than face abusive parents; children who vehemently resolve never to have children of their own; children who become parents while they are still teenagers; children who hate themselves and lash out at others—all are victims, not only of abusive parents, but of a culture that has devalued the art of parenting.

To ask a young woman who is raising two toddlers, "But what are you *doing* with your life?" is to tell this mother that what she is doing—the job of parenting—is not worthy of respect. When a culture removes status from the role of mother or father, the self-esteem from assuming that role is lessened. It is as if society is punishing parents rather than respecting them for tackling a tremendously important task. Only jobs in the "real world" seem to earn such respect. One such young woman, whose situation reflects that of thousands, decided to go back to work when her child was two months old, even though the cost of day-care and other expenses cut into her salary so much that she actually netted less than a dollar an hour. When asked the reason for the choice, she replied, "I don't want my self-esteem to come from my husband telling me I prepared a good dinner for the family."

The desire for self-esteem, and indeed the desire to be a working parent, is not a negative one at all. But it is unfortunate that our culture no longer encourages people to feel self-esteem for the work involved in raising a family. John Bowlby expresses a more encouraging approach with regard to parenting:

> A child needs to feel he is an object of pleasure and pride to his mother; a mother needs to feel an expansion of her own personality in the personality of her child: each needs to feel closely identified with the other. The mothering of a child is not something which can be arranged by rote; it is a live human relationship which alters the characters of both partners.
>
> . . . Continuity is necessary for the growth of a mother. Just as a baby needs to feel that he belongs to his mother, a mother needs to feel that she belongs to her child, and it is only when she has the satisfaction of this feeling that it is easy for her to devote herself to him. The provision of constant attention . . . is possible only for a woman who derives profound satisfaction from seeing her child grow from babyhood, through the many phases of childhood, to become an independent man or woman, and knows that it is her care which made this possible.[6]

But our culture, instead of encouraging *both* parents to develop this "profound satisfaction," makes parents frustrated with the demands the child makes for "constant attention."

For this reason, many couples choose not to have children. They feel that they should have children only if they want them, and they view child-rearing only as an unwanted burden. If this is their view, then their choice is presumably beneficial both to them and to their unborn children. But what does this imply about our culture? And what are the possible reasons for this decision?

The reasons a person decides not to have children are usually related fairly directly to his or her own childhood experiences. The primary reason for the rejection of parenting is that children are being brought up on such negative, dysfunctional households that they instinctively do not want to recreate such environments for any future generation. Many of these children have experienced first-hand what it means to have parents who do not want them. One patient told me she had decided not to have children because she wouldn't be able to stand it if her children rejected her the way she had rejected her mother, and the way her mother had rejected her grandmother.

People who choose not to have children usually have held this resolve for as long as they can remember. These people found childhood a disaster for themselves, and they feel no desire to take part in the continuation of the life cycle. In light of their experiences, they may be making an understandable choice. But the increasing number of such choices provides a sad commentary on family life today. In an age of individualism, the choice not to be a parent is a person's right—but it may also be a tragic error.

EVALUATING THE PARTICULAR SITUATION

To determine the nature and extent of emotional abuse, each family must be examined in light of its own particular situation. The family as an institution is one thing; the individual family is another. Every element of the parent-child relationship is affected by this specificity. When we look at any family, we are looking at its unique combination of hopes, education, assets and aspirations. The child is aware of and makes allowances for the particular situation in which he is raised. There is a vast difference, for instance, in a rich parent who brings up his child "poor" and a parent who really has no money to offer.

Keith's father, who was a college professor, said to him, "When I was your age, I had to work my way through college. I had to earn the money for all of my schooling, and I expect you to do the same." Keith saw the flaw in his father's reasoning. Because Keith's grandfather had died when Keith's father was six, he was forced to go to work when he was still in his early teens and had grown up in the lower middle class. But by the time Keith was ready for college, his father was part of the upper middle class where parents generally help pay for a child's education. Keith's father functioned as though he were still stuck at a lower socioeconomic level; he refused to be aware of the special needs and expectations of his family. He failed to understand or realize that developing the ability to deal with the family situation as it is—not simply as one experienced it in the past, or as one might like it to be—is an essential part of the art of parenthood.

DEVELOPMENT OF THE GENUINE SELF

Narcissus, as the Greek myth goes, stared endlessly at his own reflection. He had no desire to develop his genuine self; he was in love with what has been called "the false self," the self that wants to deal only with the beautiful, pleasant, happy side of life. This fixation cut him off from a full range of life experiences and emotional responses such as envy, jealousy, and anger.

This reluctance to come to terms with the disturbing side of life is characteristic of the narcissistically disturbed individual. There is a portion of life which is not conscious, but that is hidden and unavailable. This unknown side can be called the shadow, as these unknown qualities, be they good or bad, remain obscure or in the dark.

As Jung points out, "Childhood is not only important because it is the starting point for possible crippling of instinct, but also because this is the time when, terrifying or encouraging, those far-seeing dreams and images come from the soul of the child, which prepares his whole destiny."[7]

The parents' responsibility at this time is extensive. The genuine self is a treasure which each of us is in the process of discovering. Abusive behavior on the part of the parents can inhibit the development of the genuine self of the child.

14 · THE SEARCH FOR
THE TRUE SELF

· · · · · · · ·

ALICE MILLER

This chapter is drawn from the celebrated work of Swiss psychoanalyst Alice Miller, an exceptionally readable writer, who since 1981 has provided American readers with a primer on narcissistic disturbances and a searing indictment of modern child-rearing practices. She has become, for many, the patroness saint of the inner child.

First with Prisoners of Childhood *(renamed* The Drama of the Gifted Child *in subsequent editions), she outlined the inner child's narcissistic dilemma. The selection reprinted below comprises the core chapter of that book. Then, in* For Your Own Good, *she defined the "poisonous pedagogy" behind cruelty to children and described at length the lives of three exemplary children (including Adolf Hitler) whose inner child was tormented and crushed by destructive parenting. In* Thou Shalt Not Be Aware, *she broke with traditional psychoanalytic drive theory to indict society itself for its betrayal of the child. (An excerpt from that book is included in Part 4 of this collection.)*

In the introduction to The Drama of the Gifted Child, *Dr. Miller confesses that she is telling the story of her own inner child's abuse and suffering, which, she has discovered, is a mirror for many people. "I realized," she says, "that I could not change in the slightest my parents' and teachers' past, which had made them blind. But at the same time I felt that I could and must attempt to point out to today's young parents—and especially to future parents—the danger of misusing their power, that I must sensitize them to this danger and make it easier for them to hear the signals of the child inside them, as well as of children everywhere."*

INTRODUCTION

Experience has taught us that we have only one enduring weapon in our struggle against mental illness: the emotional discovery and emotional acceptance of the truth in the individual and unique history of our childhood. Is it possible then, with the help of psychoanalysis, to free ourselves altogether from illusions? History demonstrates that they sneak in everywhere, that every life is full of them—perhaps because the truth often would be unbearable. And yet, for many people the truth is so essential that they must pay dearly for its loss with grave illness. On the path of analysis we try, in a long process, to discover our own personal truth. This truth always causes much pain before giving us a new sphere of freedom—unless we content ourselves with already conceptualized, intellectual wisdom based on other people's painful experiences, for example that of Sigmund Freud. But then we shall remain in the sphere of illusion and self-deception.

There is one taboo that has withstood all the recent efforts at demystification: the idealization of mother love. The usual run of biographies illustrates this very clearly. In reading the biographies of famous artists, for example, one gains the impression that their lives began at puberty. Before that, we are told, they had a "happy," "contented," or "untroubled" childhood, or one that was "full of deprivation" or "very stimulating." But what a particular childhood really was like does not seem to interest these biographers—as if the roots of a whole life were not hidden and entwined in its childhood. I should like to illustrate this with a simple example.

Henry Moore described in his memoirs how, as a small boy, he massaged his mother's back with an oil to soothe her rheumatism. Reading this suddenly threw light for me on Moore's sculptures: the great, reclining women with the tiny heads—I now could see in them the mother through the small boy's eyes, with the head high above, in diminishing perspective, and the back close before him and enormously enlarged. This may be irrelevent for many art critics, but for me it demonstrates how strongly a child's experiences may endure in his unconscious and what possibilities of expression they may awaken in the adult who is free to give them rein. Now, Moore's memory was not harmful and so could survive intact. But every childhood's conflictual experiences remain hidden and locked in darkness, and the key to our understanding of the life that follows is hidden away with them.

THE POOR RICH CHILD

Sometimes I ask myself whether it will ever be possible for us to grasp the extent of the loneliness and desertion to which we were exposed as children, and hence intrapsychically still are exposed as adults. Here I do not mean to speak, primarily, of cases of obvious desertion by, or separation from, the parents, though this, of course, can have traumatic results. Nor am I thinking of children who were obviously uncared for or totally neglected, and who were always aware of this or at least grew up with the knowledge that it was so.

Apart from these extreme cases, there are large numbers of people who suffer from narcissistic disorders, who often had sensitive and caring parents from whom they received much encouragement; yet, these people are suffering from severe depressions. They enter analysis in the belief, with which they grew up, that their childhood was happy and protected.

Quite often we are faced here with gifted patients who have been praised and admired for their talents and their achievements. Almost all of these analysands were toilet-trained in the first year of their infancy, and many of them, at the age of one and a half to five, had helped capably to take care of their younger siblings. According to prevailing, general attitudes, these people—the pride of their parents—should have had a strong and stable sense of self-assurance. But exactly the opposite is the case. In everything they undertake they do well and often excellently; they are admired and envied; they are successful whenever they care to be—but all to no avail. Behind all this lurks depression, the feeling of emptiness and self-alienation, and a sense that their life has no meaning. These dark feelings will come to the fore as soon as the drug of grandiosity fails, as soon as they are not "on top," not definitely the "superstar," or whenever they suddenly get the feeling they failed to live up to some kind of ideal image and measure they feel they must adhere to. Then they are plagued by anxiety or deep feelings of guilt and shame. What are the reasons for such narcissistic disturbances in these gifted people?

In the very first interview they will let the listener know that they have had understanding parents, or at least one such, and if ever they lacked understanding, they felt that the fault lay with them and with their inability to express themselves appropriately. They recount their earliest memories without any sympathy for the child they once were, and this is the more striking since these patients not only have a pronounced introspective ability, but are also able to empathize well with other people. Their relationship to their own childhood's emotional world, however, is characterized by lack of respect, compulsion to control, manipulation, and a demand for achievement. Very often they show disdain and irony, even derision and cynicism. In general, there is a complete absence of real emotional understanding or serious appreciation of their own childhood vicissitudes, and no conception of their true needs—beyond the need for achievement. The internalization of the original drama has been so complete that the illusion of a good childhood can be maintained.

In order to lay the groundwork for a description of these patients' psychic climate, I first will formulate some basic assumptions, which will provide us with a starting point and are close to the work of D. W. Winnicott, Margaret Mahler, and Heinz Kohut.

- The child has a primary need to be regarded and respected as the person he really is at any given time, and as the center—the central actor—in his own activity. In contradistinction to drive wishes, we are speaking here of a need that is narcissistic, but nevertheless legitimate, and whose fulfillment is essential for the development of a healthy self-esteem.

- When we speak here of "the person he really is at any given time," we mean emotions, sensations, and their expression from the first day onward. Mahler (1968) writes: "The infant's inner sensations form the core of the self. They appear to remain the central, the crystallization point of the 'feeling of the self' around which a 'sense of identity' will become established."[1]

- In an atmosphere of respect and tolerance for his feelings, the child, in the phase of separation, will be able to give up symbiosis with the mother and accomplish the steps toward individuation and autonomy.

- If they are to furnish these prerequisites for a healthy narcissism, the parents themselves ought to have grown up in such an atmosphere.

- Parents who did not experience this climate as children are themselves narcissistically deprived; throughout their lives they are looking for what their own parents could not give them at the correct time—the presence of a person who is completely aware of them and takes them seriously, who admires and follows them.

- This search, of course, can never succeed fully since it is related to a situation that belongs irrevocably to the past, namely to the time when the self was first being formed.

- Nevertheless, a person with this unsatisfied and unconscious (because repressed) need is compelled to attempt its gratification through substitute means.

- The most appropriate objects for gratification are a parent's *own children*. A newborn baby is completely dependent on his parents, and since their caring is essential for his existence, he does all he can to avoid losing them. From the first day onward, he will muster all his resources to this end, like a small plant that turns toward the sun to survive.[2]

So far, I have stayed in the realm of more or less well-known facts. The following thoughts are derived more from observations made in the course of analyses I have conducted or supervised and also from interviews with candidates for the psychoanalytic profession. In my work with all these people, I found that every one has a childhood history that seems significant to me.

- There was a *mother* who at the core was emotionally insecure, and who depended for her narcissistic equilibrium on the child behaving, or acting, in a particular way. This mother was able to hide her insecurity from the child and everyone else behind a hard, authoritarian, and even totalitarian facade. [*By "mother" I here understand the person closest to the child during the first years of life. This need not be the biological mother nor even a woman. In the course of the past twenty years, quite often the fathers have assumed this mothering function.]

- This child had an amazing ability to perceive and respond intuitively, that is, unconsciously, to this need of the mother, or of both parents, for him to take on the role that had unconsciously been assigned to him.

- This role secured "love" for the child—that is, his parents' narcissistic cathexis. He could sense he was needed and this, he felt, guaranteed him a measure of existential security.

This ability is then extended and perfected. Later, these children not only become mothers (confidants, comforters, advisers, supporters) of their own mothers, but also take over the responsibility for their siblings and eventually develop a special sensitivity to unconscious signals manifesting the needs of others. No wonder that they often choose the psychoanalytic profession later on. Who else, without this previous history, would muster sufficient interest to spend the whole day trying to discover what is happening in the other person's unconscious? But the development and perfecting of this differentiated sensorium—which once assisted the child in surviving and now enables the adult to pursue his strange profession—also contains the roots of his narcissistic disturbance.

THE LOST WORLD OF FEELINGS

The phenomonology of narcissistic disturbance is well-known today. On the basis of my experience, I would think that its etiology is to be found in the infant's early emotional adaptation. In any case, the child's narcissistic needs for respect, echoing, understanding, sympathy, and mirroring suffer a very special fate, as a result of this early adaptation.

One serious consequence of this early adaptation is the impossibility of consciously experiencing certain feelings of his own (such as jealousy, envy, anger, loneliness, impotence, anxiety) either in childhood or later in adulthood. This is all the more tragic since we are here concerned with lively people who are especially capable of differentiated feelings. This is noticeable at those times in their analyses when they describe childhood experiences that were free of conflict. Usually these concern experiences with nature, which they could enjoy without hurting the mother or making her feel insecure, without reducing her power or endangering her equilibrium. But it is remarkable how these attentive, lively, and sensitive children who can, for example, remember exactly how they discovered the sunlight in bright grass at the age of four, yet at eight might be unable to "notice anything" or to show curiousity about the pregnant mother or, similarly, were "not at all" jealous at the birth of a sibling. Again, at the age of two, one of them could be left alone while soldiers forced their way into the house and searched it, and she had "been good," suffering this quietly and without crying. They have all developed the art of not experiencing feelings, for a child can only experience his feelings when there is someone there who accepts him fully, understands and supports him. If that is missing, if the child must risk losing the mother's love, or that of her substitute, then he cannot experience these feelings secretly "just for himself" but fails to experience them at all. But nevertheless . . . something remains.

Throughout their later life, these people unconsciously create situations in which these rudimentary feelings may awaken but without the original connection ever becoming clear. The point of this "play," as Jurgen Habermas (1970) called it, can only be deciphered in analysis, when the analyst joins the cast and the intense emotions experienced in the analysis are successfully related to their original situation. Freud described this in 1914 in his work "Recollection, Repetition, and Working Through."

Take, for an example, the feeling of being abandoned—not that of the adult, who feels lonely and therefore takes tablets or drugs, goes to the movies, visits friends, or telephones "unnecessarily," in order to bridge the gap somehow. No, I mean the original feeling in the small infant, who had none of these chances of distraction and whose communication, verbal or preverbal, did not reach the mother. This was not the case because his mother was bad, but because she herself was narcissistically deprived, dependent on a specific echo from a child that was so essential to her, for she herself was a child in search of an object that could be available to her. However paradoxical this may seem, a child is at the mother's disposal. A child cannot run away from her as her own mother once did. A child can be so brought up that it becomes what she wants it to be. A child can be made to show respect, she can impose her own feelings on him, see herself mirrored in her love and admiration, and feel strong in his presence, but when he becomes too much she can abandon that child to a stranger. The mother can feel herself the center of attention, for her child's eyes follow her everywhere. When a woman had to suppress and repress all these needs in relation to her own mother, they rise from the depth of her unconscious and seek gratification through her own child, however well-educated and well-intentioned she may be, and however much she is aware of what a child needs. The child feels this clearly and very soon forgoes the expression of his own distress. Later, when these feelings of being deserted begin to emerge in the analysis of the adult, they are accompanied by such intensity of pain and despair that it is quite clear that these people could not have survived so much pain. That would have only been possible in an empathetic, attentive environment, and this they lacked. The same holds true for emotions connected with the Oedipal drama and the entire drive development of the child. All this had to be warded off. But to say that it was absent would be a denial of the empirical evidence we have gained in analysis.

Several sorts of mechanisms can be recognized in the defense against early feelings of abandonment. In addition to simple denial there is reversal ("I am breaking down under the constant responsibility because the others need me ceaselessly"), changing passive suffering into active behavior ("I must quit women as soon as I feel that I am essential to them"), projection onto other objects, and introjection of the threat of the loss of love ("I must always be good and measure up to the norm, then there is no risk; I constantly feel that the demands are too great, but I cannot change that, I must always achieve more than others"). Intellectualization is very commonly met, since it is a defense mechanism of great reliability.

All these defense mechanisms are accompanied by repression of the original situation and the emotions belonging to it, which can only come to the surface after years of analysis.

Accommodations to parental needs often (but not always) lead to the "as-if personality" (Winnicott has described it as the "false self"). This person develops in such a way that he reveals only what is expected of him, and fuses so completely with what he reveals that—until he comes to analysis—one could scarcely have guessed how much more there is to him, behind this "masked view of himself."[3] He cannot develop and differentiate his "true self," because he is unable to live it. It remains in a "state of noncommunication," as Winnicott has expressed it. Understandably, these patients complain of a sense of emptiness, futility, or homelessness, for the emptiness is real. A process of emptying, impoverishment, and partial killing of his potential actually took place when all that was alive and spontaneous in him was cut off. In childhood these people have often had dreams in which they experienced themselves as partly dead. I should like to give three examples:

> My younger siblings are standing on a bridge and throw a box into the river. I know that I am lying in it, dead, and yet I hear my heart beating; at this moment I always wake [a recurrent dream].

This dream combines her unconscious aggression (envy and jealousy) against the younger siblings, for whom the patient was always a caring "mother," with "killing" her own feelings, wishes, and demands, by means of reaction formation. Another patient dreamed:

> I see a great meadow, on which there is a white coffin. I am afraid that my mother is in it, but I open the lid and, luckily, it is not my mother but me.

If this patient had been able as a child to express his disappointment with his mother—to experience his rage and anger—he could have stayed alive. But that would have led to the loss of his mother's love, and that, for a child, is the same as object loss and death. So he "killed" his anger and with it a part of himself in order to preserve his self-object, the mother. A young girl used to dream:

> I am lying on my bed. I am dead. My parents are talking and looking at me, but they don't realize that I am dead.

The difficulties inherent in experiencing and developing one's own emotions lead to bond permanence, which prevents individuation, in which both parties have an interest. The parents have found in their child's "false self" the confirmation they were looking for, a substitute for their own missing structures; the child, who has been unable to build up his own structures, is first consciously and then unconsciously (through the introject) dependent on his parents. He cannot rely on his own emotions, has not come to experience them through trial and error, has no sense of his real needs, and is alienated from himself in the highest degree. Under these circumstances he cannot separate from his parents, and even as an adult he is still dependent on affirmation from his partner, from groups, or especially from his own children. The heirs of the parents are the introjects, from whom the "true self" must remain concealed, and so loneliness in the parental home is later followed by isolation within the self. Narcissistic cathexis of her child by the mother does not exclude emotional devotion. On the contrary, she loves the child, as her self-object, excessively, though not in the manner he needs, and always on the condition that he presents his "false self." This is no obstacle to the development of intellectual abilities, but it is one to the unfolding of an authentic emotional life.

IN SEARCH OF THE TRUE SELF

How can psychoanalysis be of help here? The harmony depicted in Kathchen von Hollbronn (Heinrich von Kleist's romantic heroine in the drama of the same name, 1810) is probably only possible in fantasy, and particularly understandable arising from the longing of such a narcissistically tormented person as Kleist. The simplicity of Shakespeare's Falstaff—of whom Freud is reported to have said that he embodied the sadness of healthy narcissism—is neither possible nor desirable for these patients. The paradise of pre-ambivalent harmony, for which so many patients hope, is unattainable. But the experience of one's own truth, and the postambivalent knowledge of it, makes it possible to return to one's own world of feelings at an adult level—without paradise, but with the ability to mourn.

It is one of the turning points in analysis when the narcissistically disturbed patient comes to the emotional insight that all the love he has captured with so much effort and self-denial was not meant for him as he really was, that the admiration for his beauty and achievements was aimed at this beauty and these achievements, and not at the child himself. In analysis, the small and lonely child that is hidden behind his achievements wakes up and asks: "What would have happened if I had appeared before you, bad, ugly, angry, jealous, lazy, dirty, smelly? Where would your love have been then? And I was all these things as well. Does this mean that it was not really me whom you loved, but only what I pretended to be? The well-behaved, reliable, empathetic, understanding, and convenient child, who in fact was never a child at all? What became of my childhood? Have I not been cheated out of it? I can never return to it. I can never make up for it. From the beginning I have been a little adult. My abilities—were they simply misused?"

These questions are accompanied by much grief and pain, but the result always is a new authority that is being established in the analysand (like a heritage of the mother who never existed)—a new empathy with his own fate, born out of mourning. At this point one patient dreamed that he killed a child thirty years ago and no one had helped him to save it. (Thirty years earlier, precisely in the Oedipal phase, those around him had noticed that this child became totally reserved, polite, and good, and no longer showed any emotional reactions.)

Now the patient does not make light of manifestations of his self any more, does not laugh or jeer at them, even if he still unconsciously passes them over or ignores them in the same subtle way that his parents dealt with the child before he had any words to express his needs. Then fantasies of grandeur will be revived, too, which had been deprecated, and so split off. And now we can see their relation to the frustrated and repressed needs for attention, respect, understanding, for echoing and mirroring. At the center of these fantasies there is always a wish that the patient could never have accepted before. For example: I am in the center, my parents are taking notice of me and are ignoring their own wishes (fantasy: I am the princess attended by my servants); my parents understand when I try to express my feelings and do not laugh at me (fantasy: I am a famous artist, and everyone takes me seriously, even those who don't understand me); my parents are rich in talents and courage and not dependent on my achievements; they do not need my comfort nor my smile (they are king and queen). This would mean for the child: I can be sad or happy whenever anything makes me sad or happy; I don't have to look cheerful for someone else, and I don't have to suppress my distress or anxiety to fit other people's needs. I can be angry and no one will die or get a headache because of it. I can rage and smash things without losing parents. In D. W. Winnicott's words: "I can destroy the object and it will still survive."[4]

Once these grandiose fantasies (often accompanied by obsessional or perverse phenomena) have been experienced and understood as the alienated form of these real and legitimate needs, the split can be overcome and integration can follow. What is the chronological course?

1) In the majority of cases, it is not difficult to point out to the patient early in his analysis the way he has dealt with his feelings and needs, and that this was a question of survival for him. It is a great relief to him that things he was accustomed to choke off can be recognized and taken seriously. The psychoanalyst can use the material the patient presents to show him how he treats his feelings with ridicule and irony, tries to persuade himself they do not exist, belittles them, and either does not become aware of them at all or only after several days when they have already passed. Gradually, the patient himself realizes how he is forced to look for distraction when he is moved, upset, or sad. (When a six-year-old's mother died, his aunt told him: "You must be brave; don't cry; now go to your room and play nicely.") There are still many situations where he sees himself as other people see him, constantly asking himself what impression he is making, and how he ought to be reacting or what feelings he ought to have. But on the whole he feels much freer in this initial period and thanks to the analyst as his auxiliary ego, he can be more aware of himself when his immediate feelings are experienced within the session and taken seriously. He is very grateful for this possibility, too.

2) This will, of course, change. In addition to this first function, which will continue for a long time, the analyst must take on a second as soon as the transference neurosis has developed: that of being the transference figure. Feelings out of various periods of childhood come to the surface then. This is the most difficult stage in analysis, when there is most acting out. The patient begins to be articulate and breaks with his former compliant attitudes, but because of his early experience he cannot believe this is possible without mortal danger. The compulsion to repeat leads him to provoke situations where his fear of object loss, rejection, and isolation has a basis in present reality, situations into which he drags the analyst with him (as a rejecting or demanding mother, for example), so that afterward he can enjoy the relief of having taken the risk and been true to himself. This can begin quite harmlessly. The patient is surprised by feelings that he would rather not have recognized, but now it is too late, awareness of his own impulses has already been aroused and there is no going back. Now the analysand must (and also is allowed to!) experience himself in a way he had never before thought possible.

Whereas this patient had always despised miserliness, he suddenly catches himself reckoning up the two minutes lost to his session through a telephone call. Whereas he had previously never made demands of others, now he is suddenly furious that his analyst again is going on vacation. Or he is annoyed to see other people waiting outside the consulting room. What can this be? Surely not jealousy. That is an emotion he does not recognize! and yet . . . "What are they doing here? Do others besides me come here?" He had not realized that before. At first it is mortifying to see that he is not only good, understanding, tolerant, controlled and, above all, adult, for this was always the basis of his self-respect. But another, weightier mortification is added to the first when this analysand discovers the introjects within himself, and that he has been their prisoner. For his anger, demands, and avarice do not at first appear in a tamed adult form, but in the childish-archaic one in which they were repressed. The patient is horrified when he realizes that he is capable of screaming with rage in the same way that he so hated in his father, or that only yesterday, he has checked and controlled his child, "practically," he says, "in my mother's clothes!" This revival of the introjects, and learning to come to terms with them, with the help of the transference, forms the major part of the analysis. What cannot be recalled is unconsciously reenacted and thus indirectly discovered. The more he is able to admit and experience these early feelings, the stronger and more coherent the patient will feel. This in turn enables him to expose himself to emotions that well up out of his earliest childhood and to experience the helplessness and ambivalence of that period.

There is a big difference between having ambivalent feelings toward someone as an adult and, after working back through much of one's previous history, suddenly experiencing one's self as a two-year-old who is being fed by the maid in the kitchen and thinking in despair: "Why does mother go out every evening? Why does she not take pleasure in me? What is wrong with me that she prefers to go to other people? What can I do to make her stay at home? Just don't cry, just don't cry." The child could not have thought in these words at the time, but in the session on the couch, this man was both an adult and a two-year-old child, and could cry bitterly. It was not only a cathartic crying, but rather the integration of his earlier longing for his mother, which until now he had always denied. In the following weeks the patient went through all the torments of his ambivalence toward his mother, who was a successful pediatrician. Her previously "frozen" portrait melted into the picture of a woman with lovable aspects but who had not been able to give her child any continuity in their relationship. "I hated these beasts who were constantly sick and always taking my mother away from me. I hated my mother because she preferred being with them to being with me." In the transference, clinging tendencies and feelings of helplessness were mingled with long dammed-up rage against the love object who had not been available to him. As a result, the patient could rid himself of a perversion that had tormented him for a long time; its point was now easy to understand. His relationships to women now lost their marked characteristics of narcissistic cathexis, and his compulsion first to conquer and then to desert them disappeared completely.

At this stage in the analysis the patient experienced his early feelings of helplessness, of anger, and of being at the mercy of the loved object in a manner that he could not previously have remembered. One can only remember what had been consciously experienced. But the emotional world of a child with a narcissistic disturbance is itself the result of a selection, which has eliminated the most important elements. These early feelings, joined with the pain of not being able to understand what is going on that is part of the earliest period of childhood, are then consciously experienced for the first time during analysis.

The true self has been in "a state of noncommunication," as Winnicott said, because it had to be protected. The patient never needs to hide anything else so thoroughly, so deeply, and for so long a time as he has hidden his true self. Thus it is like a miracle each time to see how much individuality has survived behind such dissimulation, denial, and self-alienation, and can reappear as soon as the work of mourning brings freedom from the introjects. Nevertheless, it would be wrong to understand Winnicott's words to mean that there is a fully developed true self hidden behind the false self. If that were so, there would be no narcissistic disturbance but a conscious self-protection. The important point is that the child does not know what he is hiding. A patient expressed this in the following way:

> I lived in a glass house into which my mother could look at any time. In a glass house, however, you cannot conceal anything without giving yourself away, except by hiding it under the ground. And then you cannot see it yourself either.

An adult can only be fully aware of his feelings if he has internalized an affectionate and empathetic self-object. People with narcissistic disturbances are missing out on this. Therefore they are never overtaken by un-expected emotions, and will only admit those feelings that are accepted and approved by their inner censor, which is their parents' heir. Depression and a sense of inner emptiness is the price they must pay for this control. To return to Winnicott's concept, the true self cannot communicate because it has remained unconscious, and therefore undeveloped, in its inner prison. The company of prison warders does not encourage lively development. It is only after it is liberated in analysis that the self begins to articulate, to grow, to develop its creativity. Where there had only been fearful emptiness or equally frightening grandiose fantasies, there now is unfolding an un-expected wealth of vitality. This is not a homecoming since this home has never existed. It is the discovery of home.

3) The phase of separation begins when the analysand has reliably acquired the ability to mourn and can face feelings from his childhood, without the constant need for the analyst.

15 · PUER AETERNUS

· · · · · · ·

MARIE-LOUISE VON FRANZ

This is an excerpt from the classic study of the adult struggle with the paradise of childhood, Puer Aeternus. *Dr. von Franz's original lectures from the Jung Institute in Zurich have spawned an entire generation of thought on the subject of the* puer *and the narcissistic character disorders. This is a special case of the inner child motif—a very troublesome one—that is always an "agent of destiny," according to Jung. Everyone who comes into contact with these ideas about this special archetype is moved by them. Von Franz is a founder of the C. G. Jung Institute, an author, analyst, and world-famous researcher on dreams.*

Puer aeternus is the name of a god of antiquity. The words themselves come from Ovid's *Metamorphoses*[1] and are there applied to the child-god in the Eleusinian mysteries. Ovid speaks of the child-god Iacchus, addressing him as *puer aeternus* and praising him in his role in these mysteries. In later times, the child-god was identified with Dionysus and the god Eros. He is the divine youth who is born in the night in this typical mother-cult mystery of Eleusis, and who is a redeemer. He is a god of life, death, and resurrection—the god of divine youth, corresponding to such oriental gods as Tammuz, Attis, and Adonis. The title *puer aeternus* therefore means "eternal youth," but we also use it to indicate a certain type of young man who has an outstanding mother complex and who therefore behaves in certain typical ways, which I would like to characterize as follows.

In general, the man who is identified with the archetype of the *puer aeternus* remains too long in adolescent psychology; that is, all those characteristics that are normal in a youth of seventeen or eighteen are continued into later life, coupled in most cases with too great a dependence on the mother. The two typical disturbances of a man who has an outstanding mother complex are, as Jung points out,[2] homosexuality and Don Juanism. In the latter case, the image of a mother—the image of the perfect woman who will give everything to a man and who is without any shortcomings —is sought in every woman. He is looking for a mother goddess, so that each time he is fascinated by a woman he has later to discover that she is an ordinary human being. Having lived with her sexually, the whole fascination vanishes and he turns away disappointed, only to project the image anew onto one woman after another. He eternally longs for the maternal woman who will enfold him in her arms and satisfy his every need. This is often accompanied by the romantic attitude of the adolescent.

Generally, great difficulty is experienced in adaptation to the social situation. In some cases, there is a kind of asocial individualism: being something special, one has no need to adapt, for that would be impossible for such a hidden genius, and so on. In addition, an arrogant attitude arises toward other people, due to both an inferiority complex and false feelings of superiority. Such people usually have great difficulty in finding the right kind of job, for whatever they find is never quite right or quite what they wanted. There is always "a hair in the soup." The woman is never quite the right woman; she is nice as a girl friend, but. . . . There is always a "but" which prevents marriage or any kind of commitment.

This all leads to a form of neurosis which H. G. Baynes has described as the "provisional life"; that is, the strange attitude and feeling that the woman is *not yet* what is really wanted, and there is always the fantasy that sometime in the future the real thing will come about. If this attitude is prolonged, it means a constant inner refusal to commit oneself to the moment. Accompanying this neurosis is often, to a smaller or greater extent, a savior or Messiah complex, with the secret thought that one day one will be able to save the world; that the last word in philosophy, or religion, or politics, or art, or something else, will be found. This can progress to a typical pathological megalomania, or there may be minor traces of it in the idea that one's time "has not yet come." The one situation dreaded throughout by such a type of man is to be bound to anything whatsoever. There is a terrific fear of being pinned down, of entering space and time completely, and of being the specific human being that one is. There is always the fear of being caught in a situation from which it may be impossible to slip out again. Every just-so situation is hell. At the same time, there is something highly symbolic—namely, a fascination for dangerous sports, particularly flying and mountaineering—so as to get as high as possible, the symbolism of which is to get away from the mother; i.e., from the earth, from ordinary life. If this type of complex is very pronounced, many such men die at a young age in airplane crashes and mountaineering accidents. It is an exteriorized spiritual longing which expresses itself in this form.

A dramatic representation of what flying really means to the *puer* is given in John Magee's poem. Soon after the poem was written, Magee died in an airplane accident.

HIGH FLIGHT

Oh! I have slipped the surly bonds of Earth
*   And danced the skies on laughter-silvered wings;*
Sunward I've climbed, and joined the tumbling mirth
*   Of sun-split clouds,—and done a hundred things*

You have not dreamed of—wheeled and soared and swung
    High in the sunlit silence. Hov'ring there,
I've chased the shouting wind along, and flung
    My eager craft through footless halls of air . . .

Up, up the long delirious, burning blue
    I've topped the wind-swept heights with easy grace,
Where never lark, or even eagle flew—
    And, while with silent, lifting mind I've trod
    The high untrespassed sanctity of space,
Put out my hand and touched the face of God.[3]

Pueri generally do not like sports which require patience and long training, for the *puer aeternus*—in the negative sense of the word—is usually very impatient by disposition. I know a young man, a classical example of the *puer aeternus*, who did a tremendous amount of mountaineering but so much hated carrying a rucksack that he preferred to train himself even to sleep in the rain or snow outdoors. He would make himself a hole in the snow and wrap himself up in a silk raincoat and, with a kind of yoga breathing, was able to sleep out-of-doors. He also trained himself to go practically without food, simply to avoid carrying any weight. He roamed about for years all over mountains in Europe and other continents, sleeping under trees or in the snow. In a way, he led a very heroic existence, just in order not to be bound to go to a hut or carry a rucksack. You might say that this was symbolic, for such a young man in real life does not want to be burdened with any kind of weight; the one thing he absolutely refuses is responsibility for anything, or to carry the weight of the situation.

In general, the positive quality of such youths is a certain kind of spirituality which comes from a relatively close contact with the collective unconscious. Many have the charm of youth and the stirring quality of a drink of champagne. *Pueri aeterni* are generally very agreeable to talk with; they usually have interesting subjects to talk about and have an invigorating effect upon the listener; they ask deep questions and go straight for the truth; usually they are searching for genuine religion, a search that is typical for people in their late teens. Usually the youthful charm of the *puer aeternus* is prolonged through later stages of life.

However, there is another type of *puer* that does not display the charm of eternal youth, nor does the archetype of the divine youth shine through him. On the contrary, he lives in a continual sleepy daze and that, too, is a typical adolescent characteristic: the sleepy, undisciplined, long-legged youth who merely hangs around, his mind wandering indiscriminately, so that sometimes one feels inclined to pour a bucket of cold water over his head. The sleepy daze is only an outer aspect, however, and if you can penetrate it, you will find that a lively fantasy life is being cherished within.

The above is a short summary of the main characteristics of certain young men who are caught up in the mother complex and, with it, are identified with the archetype of the *puer*. I have given a mainly negative picture of these people because that is what they look like if viewed superficially, but, as you will see, we have not explained exactly what is the matter. The question to which my words are directed is why the problem of this type, of the mother-bound young man, has become so pronounced in our time. As you know, homosexuality—I do not think Don Juanism is so widely spread—is increasing more and more; even teenagers are involved, and it seems to me that the problem of the *puer aeternus* is becoming increasingly actual. Undoubtedly, mothers have always tried to keep their sons in nest, and some sons have always had difficulty in getting free and have rather preferred to continue to enjoy the pleasures of the nest; still one does not quite see why this in itself, a natural problem, should become such a serious time problem. I think that is the important and deeper question we have to put to ourselves because the rest is more or less self-evident. A man who has a mother complex will always have to contend with his tendencies toward becoming a *puer aeternus*. What cure is there? you might ask. If a man discovers that he has a mother complex, which is something that happened to him—something he did not cause himself—what can he do about it? In *Symbols of Transformation*, Dr. Jung spoke of one cure—work—and having said that, he hesitated for a moment and thought, "Is it really as simple as all that? Is that the only cure? Can I put it that way?" But work is the one disagreeable word which no *puer aeternus* likes to hear, and Dr. Jung came to the conclusion that it was the right answer. My experience also has been that it is through work that a man can pull himself out of this kind of youthful neurosis. There are, however, some misunderstandings in this connection, for the *puer aeternus* can work, as can all primitives or people with weak ego complexes, when fascinated or in a state of great enthusiasm. Then he can work twenty-four hours at a stretch or even longer, until he breaks down. But what he cannot do is to work on a dreary, rainy morning when work is boring and one has to kick oneself into it; that is the one thing the *puer aeternus* usually cannot manage and will use any kind of excuse to avoid. Analysis of a *puer aeternus* sooner or later always comes up against this problem. It is only when the ego has become sufficiently strengthened that the problem can be overcome, and the possibility of sticking to the work is given. Naturally, though one knows the goal, every individual case is different. Personally, I have not found that it is much good just preaching to people that they should work, for they simply get angry and walk off.

As far as I have seen, the unconscious generally tried to produce a compromise—namely, to indicate the direction in which there might be some enthusiasm or where the psychological energy would flow naturally, for it is, of course, easier to train oneself to work in a direction supported by one's instinct. That is not quite so hard as working completely uphill in opposition to your own flow of energy. Therefore, it is usually advisable to wait a while, find out where the natural flow of interest and energy lies and then try to get the man to work *there*. But in every field of work there always comes the time when routine must be faced. All work, even creative work, contains a certain amount of boring routine, which is where the *puer aeternus* escapes and comes to the conclusion again that "this is not it!" In such moments, if one is supported by the unconscious, dreams generally occur which show that one should push on through the obstacle. If that succeeds, then the battle is won.

In a letter Jung says about the *puer*: "I consider the *puer aeternus* attitude an unavoidable evil. *Identity* with the *puer* signifies a psychological puerility that could do nothing better than outgrow itself. It always leads to eternal blows of fate which show the need for another attitude. But reason accomplishes nothing, because the *puer aeternus* is always an agent of destiny."[4]

When the child motif turns up, it represents a bit of spontaneity, and the great problem—in each case an ethical individual one—is to decide whether it is now an infantile shadow which must be cut off and repressed, or something creative that is moving toward a future possibility of life. The child is always behind and ahead of us. Behind us, it is the infantile shadow which we leave behind, and infantility which must be sacrificed— that which always pulls us backwards into being infantile and dependent, being lazy, playful, escaping problems, responsibility and life. On the other hand, if the child appears ahead of us it means renewal, the possibility of eternal youth, of spontaneity and of new possibilities—the life flows toward the creative future. The great problem always is to make up one's mind in every situation whether there is now an infantile impulse which only pulls backwards, or an impulse which seems infantile to one's own consciousness but which really should be accepted and lived because it leads forward.

Sometimes, the answer to this dilemma is quite obvious, for the context of the dreams may show very clearly which is meant. Let us say a *puer aeternus* type of man dreams about a little boy; then we can tell from the story of the dream if the apparition of the child has a fatal effect, in which case I treat it as the infantile shadow still pulling backwards. If the same figure appears positively, however, then you can say that it is something which looks very childish and silly but which must be accepted because there is a possibility of life in it. If it were always like that, then the analysis of this kind of problem would be very simple. Unfortunately, like all products of the unconscious, the destructive side and the constructive side, the pull backward and the pull forward, are very closely intertwined and are completely enmeshed in each other. That is why if such figures appear, it is very difficult to decide between them; sometimes it is practically impossible.

If you look at the *puer aeternus* in the negative sense, you can say that he does not want to outgrow his youth or youthful stage, but the growth goes on all the same, until it destroys him; he is killed by the very factor in his soul through which he could have outgrown his problem. If you have to contend with such a problem in actual life, then you see how people refuse to grow, become mature and tackle the problem, and more and more a destructive unconscious piles up. Then you have to say, "For God's sake, do something, for the thing is growing against you and you will be hit over the head by it." But the moment may come . . . when it is too late, for the destructive growth has sucked up all the energy.

The luxuriant growth is also an image of a rich fantasy life, of an inner creative richness. Very often, you find in the *puer aeternus* such a rich fantasy life, but that wealth of fantasy is dammed back and cannot flow into life because the *puer* refuses to accept reality as it is, and thereby piles up life. He dams up his inner life. In actuality, for instance, he gets up at 10:30 A.M., hangs around till lunch time with a cigarette in his mouth, giving way to his emotions and fantasies. In the afternoon he means to do some work but first he goes out with friends and then with a girl, and the evening is spent in long discussion about the meaning of life. He then goes to bed at one, and the next day is a repetition of the one before. In that way, the capacity for life and the inner riches are wasted, for they cannot get into something meaningful but slowly overgrow the real personality. The individual walks about in a cloud of fantasies, fantasies which in themselves are interesting and full of rich possibilities, full of unlived life. You feel that such a person has a tremendous wealth and capacity, but there is no possibility of finding a means of realization. Then the tree—the inner wealth —becomes negative, and in the end kills the personality. That is why the tree is frequently linked up with the negative mother symbol, for the mother complex has that danger; because of it, the process of individuation can become negative in this sense.

The child has a naive view of life, and if you recall your own childhood, you remember you were intensely alive. The child, if it is not already neurotic, is constantly interested in something. Whatever else from which the child may suffer, it does not suffer from remoteness from life, normally—only if it is thoroughly poisoned by the neuroses of its parents. Otherwise, it is fully alive, and that is why people, thinking back to their own childhood, long to have that naive vitality which they have lost in becoming a grown-up. The child is an inner possibility, the possibility of renewal. But how does that get into the actual life of an adult?

16 · THE CHILDHOOD SELF AND THE ORIGINS OF PUER PSYCHOLOGY

· · · · · · ·

JEFFREY SATINOVER

Jeffrey Satinover's contribution takes up where the preceding essay by von Franz leaves off. He departs by specifically locating the origins of puer *psychology in the early development of the child and by directly demonstrating the commonality between* puer aeternus *psychology and the variety of narcissistic difficulties. Satinover, a psychiatrist and Jungian analyst, understands the sources of the* puer *dilemma to be at either extreme of parental care—neglect or overindulgence—during the child's earliest experiences of the emerging Self. The parents of narcissistically injured* puer aeterni *fail to recognize the "twin needs of the child: for an acceptance of his [or her] grandeur and specialness, unrealistic though it may be, and for the moderate frustrations of reality, painful though these may be." He suggests that parents who deny their children either the healthy inflations or the common pains of reality have an unresolved* puer *dilemma of their own, that they are too consumed by reactions to their own inner child's needs to respond to the child's Self. This piece is excerpted from a larger discussion originally published in the journal* Quadrant *in 1980.*

What events lead to the *puer*? To answer we need first make a rough sketch of how the Self constellates and of what the consequences of this proper constellation are in the emerging personality. The constellation of the Self in childhood has a definite effect on the ego, similar to later, more conscious experiences of the Self: it catalyzes a coalescing of ego fragments to form a functional unity. This coming-together is marked by greatly improved functioning, just as later in life, a loss of the sense of identity is accompanied by a severe decrease in the capacities of the ego as it returns to a state analogous to the one prevailing in childhood before the appearance of the Self.

An example: A woman recalled having awakened one afternoon from a nap at the age of two and a half with the realization of who she was and with a sudden knowledge that *she* could decide for herself whether or not to take a nap. She called her parents into her room and announced to them that from that day hence she was no longer taking afternoon naps.

This early, abrupt kind of experience of identity is marked by specific feelings. These are of a certain specialness and importance, even of grandeur or god-likeness, of omniscience and omnipotence. These feelings themselves suggest that it is, indeed, the Self which, under the surface, has been constellated.

At the core of later adult identity is, therefore, what we might call a necessary inflation. The child, as part of the normal constellation of the Self, needs to experience a grandiose enlargement of his sense of who he is. Thus, the two and a half year-old could order his parents into his room with the voice of the Self and assert authority over them.

This is the way that the Self is experienced in childhood. The "childhood Self," as I will from now on refer to it, remains at the core of the later experience of identity by providing, beyond all rational argument and relativisms in the face of social and physical reality, a deep belief in one's ultimate worth and value. This early experience of the Self provides the basis, too, of later healthy introversion. That is, the child who has deeply experienced this sense of unity and grandeur knows that, in times of frustration and failure, he can always look inward and touch a sense of worthiness. This act of turning to himself, and so learning to depend on himself, becomes a habit.

In the normal course of development the effect of the childhood Self on the child's identity becomes greatly modified. At the time of its constellation he experiences himself as far more potent than he actually is. This is the time in childhood when imagination is at its peak; where the child can play at being a king or queen, a warrior, a homemaker, a parent, an explorer, a villain, all with equal ease. It is as if, in imagination, the full range of what it means to be human—the image of the Anthropos—is available to the child. No human capacity is too great or too demeaning to be embraced in the life of fantasy and play. However, the child is faced with the task of increasing adaptation to mundane reality, and in this his capacities are as undeveloped as the imaginative capacities of the childhood Self are rich.

As the child is impelled into reality by his grandiose fantasies, the inevitable result is frustration. This frustration is a necessary and good thing. If the child experiences it slowly, piece by piece, the fantasies of who he is, generated by the Self, will be slowly modified and made smaller. Simultaneously, the capacities and functions of the ego, through exercise, will grow larger and more efficient. Late in adolescence, ideally, a point will be reached where the idealizations of himself and the pressure to grandeur exerted by the Self will have shrunk to the point where they match his increasing abilities.

At this point a new, adult, and more extraverted process can begin. The young adult still has a deep inner sense of his specialness and worth, the heritage of the childhood Self, but his fantasies of who he is are more limited. The sense of specialness lends to his goals and desires a barely conscious sense of numinosity, making them consistently worth pursuing. But now, instead of the frustration he experienced earlier, when his fantasies were greater than his capacities, he experiences validation of his image of himself. Now his idea of who he is, of his talents and limitations, correspond to his actual abilities. He learns that he is indeed who he has come to hope he is and he gains a renewed sense of satisfaction from this verification. In this way he achieves and reinforces a stable identity.

There are two ways this process can go wrong and produce the *puer* later in life. First, the constellation of the Self can be consistently obstructed; second, having been constellated, the Self can be protected from the limitations of reality which modify and reduce the grandiose sense of identity it generates.

Puer psychology in the man is sometimes traced (von Franz, *Puer Aeternus*) to early experiences of a mother who attacks a boy's emerging masculinity. A classical psychoanalytic view of the same development would trace it to excessive fears of castration by the father (this fear being proportional to the attachment to the mother). Each of these views is similar in locating the origin of *puer* psychology rather later (age 3–5) than I do, by attributing a sexual character to it, and in providing an explanation that lends itself more readily to masculine psychology. However, *puers* are to be found no less commonly among women than men. This, plus the fact that *puers* of each gender tend toward a more or less blurred sexual identity, suggests that the origin of the *puer* is earlier, before identity becomes further differentiated along gender lines.

I would say that the *puer* may result from a parental milieu which, in a roughly eighteen-month- to a two-year-old child, habitually disrupts any sign of *assertiveness*, of action or fantasies that carry not the hallmark of masculinity, but of specialness and grandeur. This kind of assertiveness is equally present, at certain ages, in both boys and girls. Disrupting it will generate later disturbances of identity on top of which problems with masculinity and femininity will be overlaid. The kind of disruption I have in mind is akin to the habit we all share in greater or lesser degree, of attacking inflations we sense in others (and, indeed, the origin of this habit is in our own early experiences of having it done to us).

The disruption of the childhood Self, as it constellates, will return the child again and again to a preceding state we call fragmentation, unless he can find a haven where his inflation is accepted—with a grandparent, another adult friend, or with a therapist.

If the disruption remains uncountered, the child will come to internalize the parental disapproval of the childhood Self, and the child will then himself later take over the role of undermining his idealizations of himself. If it persists into adulthood, this internal criticism will return whenever a new idea, an enthusiasm, a spirit of hope or a self-gratifying fantasy arises. Every hopeful response to the question, "Who am I?" will be stopped with, "Oh, that's just an inflation." In the child, as part of the innate urge to development, the Self will attempt to constellate. Thus, an internal vicious circle is established; each constellation of the Self, bringing with it a tide of grandiose fantasies, is followed by a tide of self-criticism and re-fragmentation.

This cycling between states of grandeur in which the Self is constellated, and states of despair in which the Self is fragmented, is a typical feature of *puer* psychology and the source of the *puer's* exquisite sensitivity. If he does not himself deliver the blow that ushers in fragmentation, the least criticism from another will do it.

The persistence of a state of fragmentation, though sometimes induced by external events, is not dependent upon them. The Self will reconstellate, in its own time. Thus, apologies and reasonable explanations which appeal to the ego have little effect. A person suffering from such a fragmentation will remain depressed, sullen, or angry regardless of attempts to undo the damage, often to the chagrin, frustration, and guilt of the one who seemed to have caused it.

When reconstellated in the *puer*, the Self is in its childhood form and thus especially liable to refragmentation. It has not been tempered by the immersion in reality, and it reacts as it does in a child. This sensitivity accounts for the essential similarity between children of insufficiently supportive parents and those of excessively supportive ones. In the latter instance, the Self is allowed to constellate, but it remains insulated from the frustrations of real life that make identity less grandiose but more cohesive. In this case, the grandiose fantasies are not only accepted, they are pushed. The parents overstimulate the child's sense of specialness and press him to behave and to accomplish beyond his age. Precociousness becomes the currency he exchanges for love and admiration.

Such a child can, in effect, become addicted to the childhood Self. He will later devote much of his life to seeking experiences which maintain or re-establish the grandiose constellation, while avoiding frustrations that diminish his sense of specialness.

Puers from each kind of upbringing strike others as being narcissistic: the introversion of each is engaged in a ceaseless effort to maintain the experience of the childhood Self, and each will choose external circumstances—drugs, brief affairs, intense physical or mental activities—that enhance this experience. Both will appear inordinately sensitive, and both are liable to radical and sudden shifts in self-esteem.

There is another source which also can yield *puer* psychology. This third source is the presence of great talent. A gift, in proportion to its strength, can generate varying degrees of *puer* psychology, and thus, in the course of self-exploration, one can set off on a relatively fruitless search for the roots of one's neurosis in the relationship to one's parents. On the other hand, the fantasy of being gifted is one of the most frequent self-definitions generated by the childhood Self, leading to the self-serving redefinition of one's flaws as the necessary price of genius. Since this latter problem may occur as easily in a genuinely gifted individual as in a relatively ungifted one, the matter is confusing. It is important to distinguish between an objective assessment of ability, and the need to consider oneself especially able.

Talent produces *puer* psychology in the following way. As in the ungifted, the constellated childhood Self produces fantasies of omnipotence and grandeur in the gifted child; however, he meets with far fewer frustrations in his attempt to realize these fantasies than does the ungifted child. So, for instance, the magical, childish way to play an instrument with little or no practice is, for the musically gifted child, nearly possible. The protean diversity of the Self, the Anthropos, is more than just a rich inflation for the multigifted child. In fact he comes close to being able to do everything.

As a result, the gifted child meets with less pressure to modify his grandiose self-image than does the ungifted child. His capacities meet his fantasies, and he is confirmed in a view of himself, not in late adolescence, but very early on, when that view retains much of its original splendor. His parents, in their astonishment and pride, reflect back to him a true view of himself, and not the artificial inflation of the excessively supportive parent.

Thus, the development of the gifted child resembles the development of the child in an overly supportive environment. He is prey to the essential *puer* feature of unstable identity, because he rests upon a less modified Self than does the normal child, and his sense of identity is consequently more labile. Naturally, the gifted child staves off fragmentation and maintains a high in the fashion he is most adept: by the exercise of his talents. It is, therefore, in this area that he is most sensitive to criticism and why, so commonly, criticism of a creative individual's products ushers in fragmentation of his identity.

PUER PSYCHOLOGY IN THE ADULT

Some of the characteristic features of the *puer* syndrome can be related to the preceding model. The most general feature of this model is that in the *puer*, the sense of identity is closely tied to the cycles of the Self, and relatively little of it is derived from or capable of verification by achievements of the ego in the physical or social worlds. There are two broad categories we can examine from this point of view. One is the area of goals and achievements; the other is the area of personal relationships. In both these areas there are two basic sources for *puer* characteristics. That is, some characteristics stem directly from the states of fragmentation or inflation, while other characteristics stem from defenses against experiencing either state.

Within the area of goals and achievements we can look at two things: problems in setting and reaching realistic goals, and fantasies of specialness. A characteristic feature of the *puer* is the pressure of intense, recurrent fantasies of grandeur. These fantasies are the translation in consciousness of, and a way of defining identity, based on the childhood Self. Depending on the degree of modification by experience, the fantasies correspond more or less to the pure image of the Self.

The most common fantasies today can be placed on a scale of decreasing grandeur: 1) Messianic fantasies in which personal identity is equivalent to Self. 2) Fantasies of being spiritually chosen, or of having great spiritual accomplishment. 3) Fantasies of being a genius, or of being gifted and especially creative. 4) The wish for great fame or power. 5) The wish for great wealth. 6) The wish for professional success.

Keeping in mind that the core of each fantasy remains the Self, we see that as the pressure exerted by the childhood Self decreases, and realistic capacities increase, a point is reached where the fantasies become realistic. Where the point is reached depends, of course, upon the individual's actual ability. In the course of a successful analysis, the fantasies of grandeur will follow some such descent.

It is often overlooked that these fantasies are not only gratifying; they are painful. The *puer* experiences these fantasies as a call to action, and to the degree that he has a genuine appreciation of reality and its limitations the failure to live up to the call will be experienced as an inner reproach that itself reinduces fragmentation and a sense of worthlessness. He often "knows" that his fantasies are unrealistic, but the *puer* is unable to experience satisfaction from anything less. Thus he is either forced to greater and greater efforts (often of an exhibitive nature where the feedback is large and immediate) or he splits off the pressure entirely and loses all motivation ("being laid-back"). He never gains any true satisfaction from the achievements he accomplishes since they never can match the demands of the childhood Self.

When the talents of such individuals are sufficient, they will commonly follow a meteoric rise in a profession that keeps them before the approving reflection of the public: thus today's plethora of superstars and the desperate struggle for fame, "becoming somebody." *Puers* commonly fantasize or dream of flying. I consider this the essential intrapsychic representation of the pressure to specialness and grandeur exerted by the childhood Self. Such dreams and fantasies (and more generally the experience or symbolic representation of "being high") are often interpreted as meaning that the individual is out of touch with reality. Conversely, they are interpreted as indications of a spiritual ascent. This interpretation is sometimes correct, if by "reality" we mean the outside world and its demands, but only secondarily. Rather, the motif of flying represents the way in which the sense of specialness raises a person beyond his limitations. Man's age-old dream of flying has always been the prototypical expression of the urge to escape the restraints of mundane existence. It is fitting that such dreams should have as their source the Self. Likewise, the motif of crashing is as common to *puer* fantasy as that of flying. The two types of dreams represent the polar states of the Self: constellation and fragmentation.

Therapeutically, it is crucial that the *puer* become familiar with the way these two states are intertwined and that by experiencing and understanding how behind every high is a sense of desperation, and behind every low a struggle for glory. Dreams often signal the appearance of this realization. For instance, "I am lifted up by a giant parachute drop machine, but without a parachute. When it gets to the top it drops me and I crash to the earth. There it picks me up again. This happens over and over."

A common feature of such dreams, as in this instance, is the mechanical nature of the cycling. This corresponds to an introspective feature of *puer* psychology that the individual at least partly aware of his nature will express: "I cannot help getting high, nor can I prevent the crash that follows." As a result, accusing such a person of being inflated, when he is, rarely has a beneficial effect. Rather, it exacerbates the underlying feeling of frustration, isolation and helplessness in the face of what he already knows is a problem.

Because of the widespread existence of occult and spiritual groups of every sort, the messianic fantasy—being a guru of greater or lesser following—has become much more acceptable, and commonplace, than it once was. This ambition, and the somewhat lesser of being perfectly enlightened, are common in the *puer* and commonly acted on concretely. Why is this so?

Here again, the rarely mentioned fact is that the grandeur of the idea of perfect spiritual attainment exerts a powerful fascination on the *puer*. By taking on the role of master or disciple he acquires an identity that carries with it the numinosity of the Self in its most undiluted concrete form. Furthermore, the general sense that spiritual attainment can lift one out of the mundane world, particularly since it finds support in certain hermetic approaches to the spirit, relieves the constellated childhood Self of daily frustrations, and preserves it in its original, unmodified form. The tenacity with which the *puer* clings to such cults stems from the price he would pay in sacrificing this attachment: fragmentation of his identity.

In her book on the *puer* [see the previous essay], Dr. Marie-Louise von Franz remarks that the *puer* is often engaged in a quest for spirituality of the sort typical of late adolescence. I would add to her observation the following: in later adolescence the spiritual quest often quietly drops away. This happens at the point where the decreasing pressure to specialness and increasing realistic capacities meet. It can be seen that adolescent spirituality often screens a search for identity which is not being consciously acknowledged as such (though years later the person can smilingly admit that, indeed, that's what it was). When identity is found, the spiritual interests can safely be dropped. The same is true for the older *puer* personality. The intense spiritual interests often mask the missing identity. When the personal identity has been successfully forged, the spiritual quest for meaning may drop away.

Of course, this is not always the case. There are individuals whose actual gift is that of spirit. In them, resolution of the *puer* structure will yield a personal identity formed around a complex and realistic orientation towards pressing spiritual questions—Jung would have been such a person. But the spirituality of such individuals is highly modified from the ideal generated by the childhood Self. Because of the conflict with reality, it lacks the degree of intense, covert personal grandeur of *puer* spirituality, and further, it is not attracted to perfected, closed systems with guaranteed results. For such individuals, spirit and meaning are always great open questions; they are led onward by doubt rather than belief; by what they don't know than by what they do. The missing identity makes it impossible for the *puer/puella* to maintain this sort of openness. The lack of internal certainty creates a narcissistic dependency on what is perceived as external truths.

An interesting question in this regard is why Jungian psychology is so attractive to the *puer*, especially when Jung himself conceived of his work as addressed primarily to the questions of later life. The answer, I believe, is this: Jungian psychology holds out the possibility of a close relation to the Self and to the archetypes, and it is this that the *puer* seeks. However, the *puer* seeks it for different reasons, and seeks a different sort of close relation to the Self, than that which concerned Jung. Whereas Jung sought to work out an *objective* relationship between the Self and an ego which sensed an already established personal identity (by objective I mean, precisely, as an object of awareness), the *puer* seeks the Self as subject in order to acquire a personal identity. Jung and his early students found themselves in the way of individuation out of necessity; the *puer* seeks individuation because of its appeal.

Another fantasy related to the wish for individuation and common today to the *puer* is that of being creative. As before, I want to make a clear distinction between creativity *per se*, and the need to consider oneself creative, which may be present in both creative and relatively uncreative individuals. The fantasy of being creative belongs to the constellated childhood Self.

Being creative was not always the hallmark of personal identity that it has become today. During the Middle Ages, much of the most creative work was anonymous (as in the illuminated manuscripts of the monks), or collective (as in the great cathedrals which often required three generations of stonemasons to complete). "Creativity," as the word itself implies, was the prerogative of God. Psychologically, therefore, it now appears as a fantasy generated by the Self.

During the Renaissance, the identification of individuals as creators burgeoned, hence the rise of the "Renaissance Man" and the great concern during the Renaissance with cataloging the signs of genius. The Romantics, harkening back to the Renaissance in the way that the Renaissance harkened back to the Greeks, disseminated the cult of genius more widely with the poets as, in Shelley's phrase, "the unacknowledged legislators of mankind." We, inheriting the Romantic tradition and making of it a popular product, now require creative writing, creative footwear, creative marriages, and creative divorces. Ironically, the fantasy of being creative can be a great obstacle to actually being so. The pressure that this fantasy places on the *puer* is often what inhibits or weakens his expressive capabilities. This leads us to the more general topic of ambition.

In spite of their great ambitions, spiritual, creative, fame-seeking or otherwise, many *puers* are described as lazy. "Laziness" is not exactly accurate. It is true that *puers* have typical sorts of work disturbances, but I do not believe these disturbances derive from an unwillingness to work. That is, they are not disturbances of the ego, or the will. Indeed, many *puers* know quite well that they have high ambitions but find themselves unable to properly pursue them. The painful tension between ambitions and the incapacity to fulfill them is in my experience the single most common presenting complaint.

And, some *puers* are overworkers who are unable to stop working or enjoy the fruits of their labor. Such individuals seek analysis less frequently because they gain, for a time at least, sufficient satisfaction from the image of themselves as hard-working to obscure the underlying emptyness.

The inability to work coupled with great ambition is a source of distress to many *puers*. They will often come into analysis having failed at work of a creative sort: they have writer's block, or stage fright, or, commonly are unable to complete their Ph.D. theses. Frequently they engage in what appear to be deliberately self-destructive behaviors: they will have dropped out of school in the semester before graduation; they will have failed to study for a final exam or a professional school admissions test (though having performed excellently in all the preceding work or requirements); they put off important tasks until the last minute even though the task may involve no more than a phone call, or they procrastinate on a large project so long that they must do the whole thing in a rush and thereby guarantee an impressive accomplishment but a mediocre product.

More commonly, *puers* will simply not finish projects that they have already begun, either by ceasing work altogether, or by continuing to re-work what they have done, so that it is never finished. In these and similar instances, the problem can be traced to the pressures exerted by the constellated childhood Self. The problem is the fear of failure, and more specifically the fear of a failure where, by definition, failure is guaranteed. The *puer* will commonly acknowledge that fear and that it paralyzes him or causes him to undo what he has already done. This is most easily seen in cases of stage fright where the fear and paralysis is acute, intense and evident. It is less easily seen in long-term projects such as a thesis. In all cases, what is less accessible to consciousness is the fact that the project must fail no matter how great the actual success. This stems from the fact that no success can live up to the core fantasy of the childhood Self.

This core is the archetype of the divine child. The individual narcissistically bound to this image for identity can experience satisfaction from a concrete achievement only if it matches the grandeur of this archetypal image. It must have the qualities of greatness, absolute uniqueness, of being the best, and more than anything else it must be prodigiously precocious.

This latter quality explains the enormous fascination of child prodigies, and also explains why even a great success yields no permanent satisfaction for the *puer*: being an adult, no accomplishment is precocious unless he stays artifically young or equates his accomplishments with those of old age (hence the premature striving after the wisdom of those who are much older).

The *puer* lives with a constant, vague sense of having failed since he never quite lives up to the archetypal demand. Projected onto his surroundings, he therefore sees the world around him as similarly having failed. The time of glory was earlier, in his childhood or in the younger days of the culture. Nothing in the present, his present or his society's present, no new accomplishment can ever make up for the defect and so the past is tinged with nostalgia. This attitude strongly affects *puer* aesthetics, which runs to camp tastes and antiquarianism. The yearning backwards is not so much a yearning for the mother nor for the *mundus imaginalis* (the imaginal world), as it has variously been explained, but for the Self and for the time of life when the Self had not yet met up with reality.

The beginning of a project is marked by fantasies of its grandeur and specialness, and particularly by fantasies of the grandeur and specialness of the creator. The project is thus embarked upon with a strong sense of identity whose source is the reconstellated childhood Self. But as the project drags on, the enthusiasm fades; completion nears and it begins to look like simply another book, or thesis, or piece of music like thousands of others. With the dawning of this realization the reestablished sense of identity begins to crumble and depression sets in. The project is either abandoned for a new one that reconstellates the Self or the fragmentation is staved off by endless revisions according to an impossibly high set of standards.

Alternatively, as completion approaches, methods are devised to snatch a grandiose defeat from the jaws of banal victory. To barely pass the admissions test, but without studying at all, comes closer to preserving prodigality than does an excellent performance as a result of strenuous effort. One prefers to be known, and to know oneself, as brilliant if erratic, than as a successful drudge. The *puer* prefers his fantasied potentials to his actual capacities because the former preserves more of the flavor of the childhood Self than the latter.

We need now to return to the time in early childhood when the original constellation of the Self is determined. You will recall that one of the important functions of the parents, usually at this age the mother, is to provide a reflection of the child's emerging Self. By reflecting back to the child his specialness and grandeur, the parent helps to sustain a kind of necessary inflation. This inflation will motivate the child to move into an ever-expanding world where, by suffering tolerable defeats, the inflation will be modified and personal identity sustained more and more by the capacities of the ego.

In situations where this reflection fails—either by its absence or its excess—the interaction of the childhood Self with the world fails to take place and normal development is interrupted. The individual then experiences, into adulthood, a constant pressure to return to the state of the constellated childhood Self so that development can proceed anew. The manifestations of *puer* psychology are therefore not so much pathological, but the expression in adulthood of a normal, long-deferred process that stems from the archetypally determined pathway of development. The reason that this process often does not simply take over and bring about a self-cure is that the individual has internalized from his childhood experiences a faulty introversion—one that either automatically attacks the Self as soon as it is constellated, or protects it from modification when frustration is sensed.

The core of *puer* relationships is this: the *puer* seeks relationships that provide him the kind of reflection he is unable to perform for himself. What appears as extraversion in the *puer* is not that at all. In effect, the *puer* does not relate to objects (in the analytic sense); he relates instead to a missing part of himself which he either sees in another or makes another perform. Objects function for the *puer* primarily as an indirect means of introversion.

A type of *puer* relationship consists in an individual, in order to maintain an identity based on the childhood Self, seeking an admirer or admirers who will reflect back to him his specialness and grandeur. While the most common situation is in friendship or marriage, this also occurs in psychoanalysis.

RECONSTELLATING THE SELF

We can now turn to the final question of this essay: what can we do about all this? I believe there is a concrete and practical approach that can be taken, it is an approach that can be used in day to day relationships, and in therapy as well. The *puer* development is a consequence of the parental response to the constellating Self of the child. We can ask ourselves, now, why does the parent fail to recognize the twin needs of the child; for an acceptance of his grandeur and specialness, unrealistic though it may be, and for the moderate frustrations of reality, painful though these may be? The answer should be clear: the parent fails to understand this, cannot understand it, because he . . . is, due to his own unresolved *puer* psychology, too reactive to his own inner states to recognize and respond to the child's Self.

The pattern of interaction in *puer-puella* dyads, a pattern that repeats, for each, the inappropriate childhood constellation, must be interfered with. The way to do this, in general, is to switch attention from the content of the interaction to the process.

Concretely, this means that the partners must avoid acting out the irritation, anger or rage that they are impelled to by the precipitating fragmentation of their own Self. Instead, they need to look inward and ask what feeling is arousing this anger? Generally, the remark that triggers the irritation has had the effect of making one feel small, worthless, wounded. The response of the tip of the tongue is a response to this inner state, and not truly a response to the other person. The fact of the way one feels—worthless—can be simply and neutrally communicated, in a nonaccusatory way.

The straightforward offering of feelings accomplishes a number of things. First, it is an act of intimacy, even when the feelings are negative. The fact that one is willing to expose his vulnerability to his partner reveals an attitude of trust which stops his further fragmentation. It is therefore an implicit form of the reflection he requires. Second, the fact that one is able to talk neutrally about pain he is experiencing means that there is a part—the part that observes and comments—which is outside the cycle of inflation and fragmentation. Third, one partner perceives the other thus relatively at ease with painful feelings, willing to accept them and not shattered as a result. He therefore experiences less of the implicit accusation that he is at fault for the partner's feelings, and is in this way further stabilized.

In general, the goal to be worked for in personal relationships, as in therapy, is the *creation of a third point of view* which is neither split off from the cycles of inflation and fragmentation, nor completely immersed in either the constellated or fragmented Self. This outside point of view is the nucleus around which a new identity, no longer dependent on the cycles of the Self, will be created.

If the defenses of the self are worked through and the individual receives the appropriate reflection, the Self will reconstellate. Proper reflection means that the divine child is being accepted by another and so eventually by oneself. As a result of the ensuing frustration, also properly reflected, the Self will be modified in the fashion that didn't occur in childhood.

17 · THE LITTLE PRINCE

· · · · · · · ·

HELEN M. LUKE

The narcissistic need to be raised beyond and above one's limitations, a fantasy the two previous authors suggest is a characteristic problem of the puer aeternus, *is often literalized in an irresistible attraction to aircraft and flying. Jungian counselor Helen M. Luke's sensitive treatment sums up the puer's flight fantasy. She illustrates the problem by telling us the story of the famous inner child figure in* The Little Prince, *and of the adult to whom this child belongs, the author/flyer Antoine de Saint-Exupéry. This is a cautionary tale, warning us of the dangers of overidentification with the inner child archetype.*

The psychological treatment of the story of The Little Prince *was originally taken up by Marie-Louise von Franz in her lectures on the* puer aeternus, *presented in 1959–60 at the C. G. Jung Institute, Zurich. Mrs. Luke's work builds on that precedent, while exhibiting her gift as a storyteller. This essay is a chapter from her book* The Inner Story.

Two famous books have been written in the twentieth century about the "eternal boy," as different from each other as they can be, except in their essential theme of the boy who refuses to grow up. James Barrie's *Peter Pan*, written in 1902, is an entrancing fairy-tale play for children, a fantasy of pirates, fairies, Indians, a loving mother, adventurous children who learn to fly, and the hero boy who can face death as "a great adventure" but who will not live in the human adult world. *The Little Prince*, by Antoine de Saint-Exupéry,[1] written almost forty years later, is not really addressed to children at all, in spite of the words of the dedication, but is a book about the child in adults, an infinitely sad story of the sterility of the world and the lost wisdom and beauty of childhood. It is the tragedy of those people of our times, of whom Saint-Exupéry was one, whose eyes are open to the inner world of dream and image, who know the child's wisdom of innocence and folly and the emptiness of collective values, but who fail to bridge the gap between their inner vision and the harshness of outer reality. These people are split apart to the point of suicide, sometimes actual physical suicide, conscious or unconscious, but certainly to the suicide of one value or the other.

From the beginning it is plain that the book is concerned with the experience of an actual child. A little boy is not separated from humanity in this way, living in a remote and empty place with three volcanoes, one extinct, and sadly watching the beauty of the sunsets. Already the feeling of the tragic end is there. Childhood is sunrise, not sunset, whether we speak of the human child or of the archetypal child in the unconscious of an adult. The child who appears in our dreams speaks of new beginnings, or hints at the wholeness of the end, when sun and moon shine together. Compare the atmosphere of the Little Prince's planet with the Never-Never Land of Peter Pan and the lost boys. (If anyone knows Peter Pan only through Walt Disney's cartoon, let him banish that travesty of the story from his mind.) The Never-Never Land is also remote from the everyday world but vigorously alive with the sparkling fantasy of the child. The boys fly in the air, they live underground, they fight the evil pirates among whom, delightfully, is the "lovable" Smee, they have Indians and fairies for friends, they vanquish wolves, and Peter is rescued from the rising water of the blue lagoon by a bird. When Wendy comes among them the boys turn her at once into a mother, and through her they are finally brought back into the real world, and all, except Peter himself, accept the necessity of growing up, of meeting the dreary world of school and work and responsibility. There is sadness, for most will lose, one knows, their contact with the bright world of childhood and its wisdom, but only so can there be any hope of final wholeness. In Peter there is a hint of the archetype— living in the trees alone but visited each year by Wendy. It is all in a light vein, with tinges of sentimentality, but nevertheless we may see in Wendy a hint of the function of the *anima*, connecting the conscious with the unconscious world of fantasy.

It is interesting to compare with this the symbol of the feminine in *The Little Prince*. In the human boy it is love and care of the mother that connects him (if she is a true mother) with the world and pushes him out of the nest when the right time comes. The *arrested* child in a man may be awakened from his disconnected state by the dawning of an uneasy perception that all is not well with his own feeling life, however "beautiful," and so he is driven to attempt to connect with the world of men. The Little Prince's single rose (his potential relatedness) shows herself as very vain and not altogether truthful, so the boy rejects her and starts on the journey that leads to the earth.

His first experiences are not encouraging. He comes to several other tiny, isolated planets, on each of which a man as lonely as himself lives in his private world, pursuing his empty goal of power or wealth or knowledge or pleasure. On the last one he meets the lamplighter, with whom he feels some kinship—the ordinary man, not imprisoned by an obsession with his own importance, but nevertheless still alone, bound by his daily task and never looking beyond it, lighting and extinguishing his lamp with the setting and rising of the sun every few minutes on his tiny, tiny world, with no time for rest, no eyes for beauty. In his first glimpses of mankind the Little

Prince has seen only the polar opposite of the simplicity of the child—that is, the obsession with goals.

The Little Prince now finally reaches the earth itself. He is still alone in the desert, but being on earth he is confronted immediately with the life of instinct. He comes upon the snake, the most earthbound of all, the furthest from human consciousness, who warns him that the world of men and women will prove just as lonely as his planet and reminds him that the bite of the snake can bring death and release. He will not bite the child now for snakes do not harm the completely innocent; only when the Little Prince wishes to return to his planet and comes back to this place will the snake bite him and so release him from the earth. There is an undertone of the cynicism of the devil in this. The snake has no belief in the success of the child's attempt to meet the grown-up world. At the very outset the Little Prince assures himself of a line of retreat from his venture. How unchildlike! He is fatally uncommitted, one feels. He has an insurance policy.

Now the Little Prince crosses the desert looking for men and grows more and more unhappy, until he comes one day to a garden of roses. For the first time he knows that *his* rose on *his* planet is not unique in the universe, and he lies down and cries. His rose for the moment becomes a "nothing but"—that well-known state of mind, the polar opposite of possessive pride. It is at the moment of the breakdown that he meets the fox.

Now the fox is a kind of Mercurius or Hermes symbol in the inner world. He is cunning and wise, the trickster and the guide—an image carrying, even today, the numinous intuition of the tie between the hunter and the hunted. *The Running Foxes*, by Joyce Stranger, is a very beautiful and true story on this theme. It seems proven that an old fox will even invite the hunt to pursue him. It is this animal, the ruthless hunter, the constantly hunted, who teaches the Little Prince what it means to have a friend and what the real nature of uniqueness is.

The fox asks the Prince to *tame* him, and in answer to the boy's questioning he says that to tame and be tamed means "to establish ties"—in other words, to have relationship and responsibility. He teaches the Little Prince that to be unique does not consist of possessing the only rose in all the world—uniqueness comes when love is awakened between oneself and another, be the other fox or rose or person. It is, as we all know, an immensely powerful delusion of the ego, this identification of our personal worthiness with the possession of some special ability or virtue or achievement. The fox reveals the profound paradox that each person's uniqueness is born solely through his or her capacity to "establish ties," conscious ties between self and "other" (whether that other be an outer or an inner reality), and through a willingness to sacrifice the unconscious ties of possession.

The fox now instructs the Little Prince how to tame another. He tells him that with infinite patience he must sit near to him without words and move a little closer every day. It is also good to observe "the proper rites," which, he explains, means always coming at the same time every day, thus infusing the simple act with the power of ritual—a very sound piece of advice, particularly when it is a question of "taming" our inner images.

Now the fox comes to the heart of his message—the strange paradox that is an essential element in the establishing of a tie is the acceptance of parting—even of final parting. The uniqueness of the tie is not lost; indeed, it finds its greatest fulfillment in the inevitable separation, for out of the pain of this experience accepted (accepted daily, not only in the moments of outer loss), meaning is born where before there was no meaning. The gold of the wheat fields, hitherto unnoticed and meaningless to the fox, is now forever alive with beauty because of the gold of his friend's hair. Every wheat field is now unique because of the uniqueness of the Little Prince. The mark of a love that is purged of possessiveness and has become a tie between two who consent to be *separate* is that it does not exclude (so that everything outside it becomes merged in a dreary mass). On the contrary, it begets an intuition of the uniqueness and meaning of every person, every experience we encounter. All of this does not mean that the grief of parting is any less. "I shall cry," said the fox.

The fox's last message is this: "What is essential is invisible to the eye. . . . It is the time you have *wasted* for your rose that makes the rose so important. . . . You become responsible, forever, for what you have tamed" (p. 87). That the Little Prince, deeply as he has understood the fox's lesson, has still missed the essential point becomes clear at once. Here is the passage that reveals this misunderstanding, which was indeed that of Saint-Exupéry himself. He is looking at the bed of hundreds of roses and he says:

> You are not at all like my rose. As yet you are nothing. No one has tamed you, and you have tamed no one. You are like my fox when I first knew him. He was only a fox like a hundred thousand other foxes. But I have made him my friend and now he is unique in all the world.
>
> You are beautiful, but you are empty. One could not die for you. To be sure, an ordinary passerby would think that my rose looked just like you— the rose that belongs to me. But in herself alone she is more important than all the hundreds of you other roses: because it is she that I have watered; because it is she that I have put under the glass globe; because it is she that I have sheltered behind the screen; because it is for her that I have killed the caterpillars (except the two or three that we saved to become butterflies); because it is she that I have listened to, when she grumbled, or boasted, or even sometimes when she said nothing. Because she is *my* rose (pp. 86–87).

It is true, but it is not the whole truth. He realizes his responsibility for the rose he has tamed on his planet, accepts its imperfections, and begins to know love. But he does not see that, just as his responsibility to the fox involved accepting his own and the fox's sadness when the moment of parting came, so his responsibility to this rose meant also the acceptance of parting so that the beauty of the rose could live *in* the world, not only on his private planet. So he looks at the hundred roses not with the joy of recognizing the image of the beloved in each one of them, as the fox looked at the wheat fields, but with an almost contemptuous pity.

He passes on to meet the world of men—sees crowds going aimlessly to and fro in trains, talks to a merchant who has invented pills to quench thirst in order to save people from wasting time looking for water. (How very apt an image of our predicament today!) One could imagine that at this point the little fox might have said, "Look beyond what the eye sees and the ear hears and see the human being behind that false mask and take the trouble to tame him. The red glow of his cheeks, even the red paint on the railway engine, could remind you of your rose and give these people and things beauty and meaning. It is thus that you must carry the responsibility to your rose." But the Little Prince misses the point, misses his chance—he thinks only of the beauty of *his* rose, her need of him, and so he makes the final refusal to involve himself in life on this earth, and in clinging to his rose he most tragically betrays her. He starts on his regressive journey to the snake who will give him death—not the death that is acceptance of life and of fate, but the death which is refusal of life and of responsibility. Jung has said that the "threat of the snake" points to the danger of newly acquired consciousness being swallowed again by the instinctive psyche. This is precisely what happens to the Little Prince.

Before the final tragedy he meets the airman mending his crashed plane and asks him for a sheep to take back with him to his planet. The drawings the airman makes are rejected. The sheep is too old, or too sickly; finally the drawing of a box is accepted, in which the sheep lies unseen and can be imagined by the Little Prince in any form he pleases. This would be a delight in a little boy, but not in a man identified with the child. Surely it is again a dangerous misunderstanding of the fox's words, "What is essential is not visible to the eye," which certainly does not mean that you may turn a real sheep into a private image of what you would like it to be, but that behind the outer apparance of the sheep, be it sickly or old, there is an essential uniqueness that may be found if you will "tame" it. This is the fatal misunderstanding of the infantile personality, whereby the imagination, the intuition of ultimate truths, may be used to distort present reality instead of to fill it with meaning.

The man, led by the boy, finds a well in the desert. They do not just imagine it—they know that the water of life is there under the arid surface, for the beauty of the desert lies in the fact of the well. Here the man learns deep wisdom from the eternal child, but, instead of taking that wisdom to the meeting and taming of life itself, he will not risk it among men and thinks to preserve it remote and alone in the sky, so that he must spend his life with his eyes on the stars and in a continual torment as to whether or not it still lives. For the Little Prince had taken something back with him from the earth—the sheep that may eat the rose. The man had forgotten to add a strap to the muzzle he had drawn to control the sheep; the unconscious had seen to that, for we cannot ever ensure the safety of anything. The child, by coming to earth, had experienced the opposites; he could not return unscathed to his infantile paradise. He wanted to preserve only that which he wished from his journey, but willy-nilly he took with him that unconscious instinctual urge that could eat the weeds on his planet but could equally well devour his roses and leave him more horribly alone than before. So the man who has refused to hear the *whole* message of the fox, and who tries to preserve the beauty of his inner life isolated from and untarnished by the world, must live with a gnawing doubt forever in his heart. Has the sheep destroyed the rose? It is a doubt that haunts us all whenever we turn even briefly from the fox's message.

So the book ends with the same image with which it began. The actual child's drawing of the boa constrictor with the elephant inside it is full of imagination and promise that the dull adult cannot see, but the image has passed through the separation of the opposites to the opportunity of consciousness, only to end in a regression in which one opposite may be swallowed again in the belly of the other—the tender uniqueness of the rose devoured by the sheeplike collectivity from which the Little Prince sought to fly. The man lives now with his eyes on the stars, seeing their beauty and filled with an insatiable longing, for he has known and loved the child within. But the earth under his feet he has rejected with contempt, and wholeness must forever elude him in this life. It is a moving and beautifully told story, with the impact of a tragic truth, but a feeling of sadness and hopelessness pervades the whole book.

So it was in the life of Saint-Exupéry himself—a man of potential genius who never broke his identification with the eternal child. Someone who knew him well wrote of him that he had in equal degree "real and profound mysticism, great appetite for pleasures of the senses and total irresponsibility in daily life." Also, it was said that he was "an extremist in all things. He could not bear contradiction." These are the marks of this identification. It is interesting that some psychologists have said that a large proportion of airmen are of this kind, particularly, perhaps, the dare-devil pilots—fighter pilots of the war, test pilots.

Saint-Exupéry was rarely happy except when flying. It was an essential need of his nature—almost as though he were constantly trying to reach his Little Prince, alone and sad on his planet. In the air he felt free of all the deadening smallness and meanness of the ordinary man, of whom he writes with such withering contempt. Even his greatest admirers admit this contemptuous attitude in him. He was a pilot of great skill but caused everyone the greatest anxiety by what was known as his "absent-mindedness." He would forget to let down his undercarriage; lost in his inner dream, he would fly off course and suddenly return to reality to find himself in danger, and so on. There is an unconscious courting of death in such men—a yearning for the bite of the snake that can restore them to the lost child. Finally he did meet death in the air, living out the symbol. His plane was lost over France on the last mission permitted to him in the war. No trace of it was ever found. It just disappeared as the Little Prince's body had disappeared.

He had been, as usual in the case of such personalities, his mother's special favorite, and he adored her all his life. Barrie, too, had this devotion to his mother. In *Peter Pan* the father, Mr. Darling, is shown as stupid, even pettily cruel. Saint-Exupéry's marriage was a stormy, irresponsible affair, as one would expect, of violent quarrels, separations, and equally passionate reconciliations. When separated from his wife he would write movingly of his responsibility for his "poor Consuelo." He genuinely felt it, but he could not live it. He could never live responsibly because he had rejected one-half of the fox's wisdom, and so his delicate perception of real values remained "in the air," constantly threatened by the "sheep." The sheep, double-sided like all archetypal images, is the symbol of both innocence and of the collective stupidity that he so bitterly despised.

The images of his unconscious—the King, the Wise Man, the Practical Worker, the Lover of Play, the Servant—remained forever on their lonely planets, possessive and meaningless to the end. For the child, who could have brought all of them to earth, if he had heeded the message of the fox, had chosen to return to his planet. Thus the man could not grow to that true meeting of opposites in which the inner child remains vividly alive but "tamed," related to outer reality. Saint-Exupéry had genius, and he did *not* evade his responsibility to express it. But inevitably his genius did not mature. Perhaps only in *The Little Prince* did it truly come to earth, for in it he describes his own tragedy with power and truth. Many have acclaimed *The Wisdom of the Sands* as his greatest book. He thought so himself. Beautiful as so many of the sayings in it are, it remains somehow remote from humanity and therefore tinged with unreality and sentimentality. In it the king of a desert kingdom speaks all his thoughts about life and its meaning. It is significant that near the beginning of the book the king goes up onto a high tower and *looking down* on men he pities them and resolves to heal them. He then claims to have "embellished the soul of my people." The king is concerned with "people," not individuals. He is alone with his rose to the end. The book's French title is *La Citadelle*—the tower, the fortress, the safe place from which the king looks down on the world.

One such boy-man came for analysis many years ago. His quickness of understanding, his intuitive awareness of the unconscious and eager enthusiasm were full of promise. But he was not seventeen; he was near thirty and had no notion of what it meant to accept the responsibility of manhood. Such men often have very great charm, carrying as they do the image of the eternal promise of youth. Older women will forgive them again and again their enormities! This man was continually in and out of jobs, and it was his wife, older than himself, who earned their basic living. As with Saint-Exupéry, partings and reconciliations succeeded each other with bewildering speed. He was not a flier but courted death through reckless driving of cars. When his license was revoked it never occurred to him to stop driving—the risk just made it a bigger thrill! The taking of wild risks in the outer world is a compensation for the inner refusal to risk the infantile psyche in a meeting with the responsibilities of a man. He made endless good resolutions, with complete sincerity, but they broke down at the touch of reality and the necessity for discipline. Yet how much he knew of a wisdom closed to the dull and respectable! He died violently in an accident.

He had returned to his snake, refused to leave his infantile paradise and expose his rose to this world.

The *puer aeternus* personality is rarely met in such extreme form. But for every one of us there is a warning in the images of Saint-Exupéry's story. We need to become conscious of the partial ways in which we identify with and so banish to a lonely planet our inner child. For whatever we identify with is lost to us as a reality. If we will hold to the child's value of innocence and folly while at the same time fully accepting the realities of space and time; if we will endure the separations through which possessiveness and the demand to be "special" are dissolved; then our feet will be firmly planted on the earth while we watch the stars in their courses. Only then, having emerged from the easy paradise of unconscious child-ishness, we may "tame" and "be tamed" by the Child within, who brings true uniqueness and ultimate wholeness. This lovely image comes to us in our dreams, grave and gay, wise and innocent, the promise of the beginning and the fullness of the end. "Unless ye become as little children [become as, not identify with] ye shall not enter the Kingdom of Heaven" (Matt. 18:3).

We turn now to some words of Jung: "The child is the beginning and the end. . . . The child symbolizes the pre-conscious and the post-conscious nature of man—his wholeness. . . . The child is all that is abandoned and exposed and at the same time divinely powerful; the insignificant, dubious beginning and the triumphant end. The 'eternal child' in man is an inde-scribable experience—an imponderable that determines the ultimate worth or worthlessness of a personality."[2]

· · · · · · ·

PART 4

THE
WOUNDED
CHILD
WITHIN

INTRODUCTION

. . . .

> The violation of the natural weakness and
> simplicity of the young child not ready
> for autonomy can turn into a protective
> infantilism that lasts through one's life.
> These wounds may be redeemed through
> the natural simplicity of loving; indeed,
> they may offer the gateway through which
> love may enter.
>
> —JEAN HOUSTON, *The Search for the Beloved*

Today, in our socially conscious age of information, we are surrounded by images of the abused child. This outer wounded child has been propelled into our awareness through the innumerable stories of child victims that surface daily in all strata of our society. These incidents, ranging from minor neglect and accidental injury to the morally reprehensible exploitation and sexual abuse of young people, are pathetic manifestations of a social and mental epidemic.

The anxiety that results from mistreatment often leads children to become compliant and, for safety's sake, to identify with a false self in their outer personalities. These fears also can give rise to an inflated grandiosity (as we saw in the problem of the *puer aeternus*), in which smugness and superiority mask deeper feelings of injury and unworthiness. In either case, the authentic and vulnerable childhood Self is disowned and aliveness is diminished. To identify with vulnerability is to feel a pain so frightening to the child's fragile developing ego identity that it seems to threaten its very existence.

Those childhood injuries to the soul create a child within the adult who longs for understanding, love, respect, and possibly justice. Rediscovery of the inner child is often painful, because it returns to consciousness the memories and emotions of childhood wounds. Typically, these wounding experiences have taken place in the family. Reconnecting to the wounded child brings us into contact with our parents, whom we tried to please and satisfy. We must also face our angry, sad, and injured Self. Redeeming this inner problem child means, at the very least, reparenting him or her in ways we have longed to be loved, cared for, and nourished.

To heal the wounded child within, we as adults also must learn to understand our parents' suffering. Because we have internalized these damaged parents as well, we must waive harsh judgment or vindictiveness. If we are to stop abusive family patterns and not transmit them to the next generation, then the internalized parental image also must be recognized as wounded. Such compassionate awareness is a developing phenomenon in the lives of those courageous adults who are overcoming their shame and pain in order to acknowledge and heal the wounded child within.

The wounded inner child is the emergent symbol for this compassionate awareness. It represents the obstructed potential of the inner child. It is the inner victim who has suffered the thousands of hurts and who has been buried inside for protection from further humiliation and injury. This authentic being within us—our vulnerable childhood Self—is caught in an unfortunate web of reactive, self-protective behaviors, and is often debilitated by a confusion of feelings of anxiety, hopelessness, hurt, and rage.

The essays in this section are organized around the theme of injury to the child within; each chapter contains a distinct psychological model and sensibility about the wounding and the healing of the inner child.

Charles L. Whitfield's opening essay, "How Can We Heal Our Child Within?" stems from the 12-step recovery model adopted by self-help groups for people who identify themselves as adult children of dysfunctional families, who may themselves be recovering from alcoholism, chemical dependency, or co-dependency. In this model, the child within and the wounded child are the same. The child within is the real or true Self that suffers displacement by a false or co-dependent self. According to this model, the false self is a mechanism of denial and defense in the personality that suppresses and impairs the true Self, stifling the expression of the child within. The wounding described by this model is a thorough co-optation of the inner child.

Hal Stone and Sidra Winkelman postulate a psychological model in which the wounded child is disowned by the conscious personality very early in life, during the first five years. "This child cannot exist in our civilized societies," they say, "without the protection of a very strong protector/controller" element in the personality that buries the child so that it will not be hurt. The primary qualities of woundedness in the inner child described in this model are vulnerability and a dissociation from the other parts of the total person. Healing, according to the authors, is a full integration of the inner child into conscious awareness, so that an aware ego can properly take care of the child.

Alexander Lowen relates the personal discovery of woundedness and betrayal he made in his therapy with the famous psychiatrist Wilhelm Reich. His story gives us a somatically based model of the wounded inner child, whose unexpressed pain and hurt are locked in the musculature of the adult's body. "The truth about our childhood," says Alice Miller, "is stored up in our body," and that aptly sums up Lowen's bioenergetic model of the wounded child within.

Alice Miller's article "Advocating for the Child" describes a model of injury based on actual child abuse. Her focus is on outer children—and by implication, on the wounded child within—the ones who suffer through cruel and unconscious abuse by parental and authority figures. "Only when we realize how powerless a child is in the face of parental expectations," she says, ". . . will we grasp the cruelty of parents' threats to withdraw their love if the child fails to meet these impossible demands. And this cruelty is perpetuated in the child."

Robert M. Stein's depth psychology model explicitly relates outer abuse to inner wounding: "Depth psychology assumes that the external and internal worlds reflect each other. . . . We need to ask what lies within the compulsive need to abuse and sexually molest the outer child." In contradistinction to Alice Miller's literalized model, Stein's wounded child within suffers from polarizations in the individual and in the culture, splittings of attitudes and beliefs that deny the natural, elemental being of the child and that cut off the child from its grounding in instinct.

Finally, Susanne Short gives us, through the lens of Jungian psychology, the pathos of the wounded child who is drowned in the depravity of parental self-involvement. This is a tragedy we witness every day around us, which goes unacknowledged because in such defective parenting there is no verification of the child's reality through healthy bystanding or mirroring. In effect, the inner experience of the child is ignored. As Short implies, there are only whispers and murmurs as clues, and the child doesn't even know what hit him.

18 · HOW CAN WE HEAL OUR CHILD WITHIN?

· · · · · · · ·

CHARLES L. WHITFIELD

People working in the recovery process in the field of chemical dependency, especially those involved in the growing movement known as Adult Children of Alcoholics, use the inner child language to refer to that part of us that is our real Self. People who grew up in alcoholic or otherwise dysfunctional families most likely have had their real Self denied. In response, many have developed an identification with a false or co-dependent self. Hence, the need to intervene in the denial process and to heal and recover the child within.

Recovery of the real Self is a major focus of therapist/author Charles L. Whitfield's work. This selection is from his book Healing the Child Within, *a best seller that has become a source book on the recovery model for working with the inner child. Recently, Dr. Whitfield published a companion workbook,* A Gift to Myself.

To rediscover our True or Real Self and heal our Child Within, we can begin a *process* that involves the following four actions.

1. Discover and practice being our *Real Self* or Child Within.
2. Identify our ongoing physical, mental-emotional and spiritual *needs*. Practice *getting* these needs *met* with safe and supportive people.
3. Identify, re-experience and *grieve* the pain of our ungrieved *losses* or traumas in the presence of safe and supporting people.
4. Identify and work through our *core issues* (described below).

These actions are closely related, although not listed in any particular order. Working on them, and thereby healing our Child Within, generally occurs in a circular fashion, with work and discovery in one area a link to another area.

STAGES IN THE PROCESS OF RECOVERY

Survival

To get to the point of recovery, we must survive. Survivors are by necessity co-dependents. We use many coping skills and ego defenses to do this. Children of alcoholics and from other troubled or dysfunctional families survive by dodging, hiding, negotiating, taking care of others, pretending, denying and learning and adapting to stay alive using any method that works. They learn other often unhealthy ego defense mechanisms, as described by Anna Freud[1] and summarized by Valliant.[2] These include: intellectualization, repression, disassociation, displacement and reaction formation (all of which if overused can be considered to be neurotic) and projection, passive-aggressive behavior, acting out, hypochondriasis, grandiosity and denial (all of which if overused can be considered immature and at times psychotic).

While these defenses are functional in our dysfunctional family, they tend to work poorly for us as adults. When we attempt to participate in a healthy relationship, they tend not to further our best interests. Using them stifles and stunts our Child Within and promotes and reinforces our false or co-dependent self.

Ginny was a 21-year-old who grew up in an alcoholic family. At the beginning of her recovery, she wrote the following poem. It exemplifies some of the pain of the survival stage.

AFRAID OF NIGHT

Like the child waiting in the night
For warm hands and arms to wrap
Themselves around her loneliness:
To spend herself in tears of sudden safety—
And of love.

I, too, in the dark aloneness of self unloved,
Unanchored, abandoned, and denied,
Still summon with silent child cries
the ancient hope—
The old sure magic of wantedness.

The child still lives in me
With that eager hurt of innocence bewildered
And betrayed. Ah, that painful paradox.

To sense the rescue,
And know there is none.
But driven by old dreams, pale yet powerful,
Remembrances of the soft dear touch of love,
I wait.
One waits. One always waits.
It is forgotten—that nameless need
The years have beaten from my wasted heart.
But like some unshaped primeval force,
It beckons, crowds my reality,
Blunts stiff reason.

And I am grotesque with helpless wanting,
Turning my mind inwards, backwards.
Dull, too, is pain with young memories
That weaken and defy,
Submit then die.
I do not live;
I wait in such unhope.

Ginny tells us about her pain, numbness, isolation and hopelessness. Yet, she also reflects one ray of potential hope in the line "The child still lives in me."

Part of recovery is to *discover* ourselves, our Child, and how we use these ineffective means of relating to ourselves, to others and to the universe. This can be most productively accomplished during the working stages of recovery.

While it is clear that we are surviving, it is also true that we experience a good deal of pain and suffering. Or we become numb. Or we alternate between suffering and numbness. Slowly we become aware that these very skills and defenses that allowed us to survive as mistreated infants, children and adolescents, do not work well when we try to have healthy, intimate relationships as adults. It is the frustration of this mistreatment, this suffering of co-dependence and this failure in our relationships that do not work for us, that push and at times even force us to begin looking elsewhere than these ineffective methods. Looking elsewhere can trigger our recovery.

Gravitz and Bowden describe recovery in their ACoA patients as occurring in six stages: 1) Survival; 2) Emergent Awareness; 3) Core Issues; 4) Transformations; 5) Integration; and 6) Genesis (or spirituality).[3] These stages parallel the four stages of growth and transformation described by Ferguson[4] and the three stages of the classical mythological hero or heroine's journey as described by Campbell[5] and by others.

We can clarify and summarize the similarities of each approach as follows:

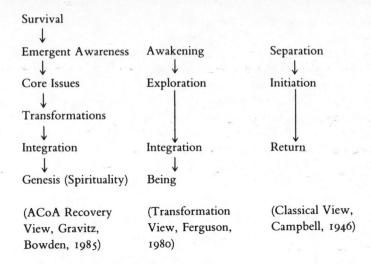

Survival
↓
Emergent Awareness	Awakening	Separation
↓	↓	↓
Core Issues	Exploration	Initiation
↓		
Transformations		
↓		
Integration	Integration	Return
↓	↓	
Genesis (Spirituality)	Being	

| (ACoA Recovery View, Gravitz, Bowden, 1985) | (Transformation View, Ferguson, 1980) | (Classical View, Campbell, 1946) |

Each stage is useful in healing our Child Within. Each stage is often recognized only in retrospect. When we are *in* the stage, we do not always realize that we are there. This is one reason why it is helpful to have a sponsor, guide, counselor or therapist during recovery.

Awakening (Emergent Awareness)

Awakening is the first glimpse that "things" or "reality" are not what we thought. Awakening is an ongoing process throughout recovery. To begin, we generally require an *entry point* or trigger—anything that shakes up our old understanding or belief system of reality, of the way we thought things were.[6]

Because our True Self is so hidden, and because our false or co-dependent self is so prominent, awakening may not come easily. Nonetheless, it often happens. I have witnessed this process in hundreds of children of trauma. The entry point or trigger may range across a wide spectrum. It may start with hearing or reading someone describe their own recovery or own True Self, or being "sick and tired" of our suffering, or beginning to work seriously on another life problem in counseling or therapy. For others, it may be attending a self-help meeting or an educational experience, reading a book or hearing about it from a friend.

At this time, we often begin to experience confusion, fear, enthusiasm, excitement, sadness, numbness and anger. These mean that we are beginning to *feel* again. We begin to get in touch with who we really are—our Child Within, our Real Self. At this point, some people will give up—will go no further. They find it easier and more "comfortable" to retreat back into their false or co-dependent self (i.e., into a relapse of co-dependence) because these feelings are frightening.

Those who are recovering alcoholic, other drug dependent, or dependent upon other unproductive behavior, such as overeating or compulsive gambling, may begin to experience a relapse. Or they may precipitate another form of shame-based compulsive behavior, such as spending money that they do not have. But this awakening can be an opportunity to take a risk or a plunge to discover our whole self, our aliveness and even eventually our happiness.

Beginning to Deal with Core Issues

An *issue* is any conflict, concern or potential problem, whether conscious or unconscious, that is incomplete for us or needs action or change.

There are at least 14 *core issues* in the recovery of our Child Within that we can work through. Eight of these have been described by clinicians and authors, including Gravitz and Bowden,[7] Cermak and Brown,[8] and Fischer.[9] These core issues are: control, trust, feelings, being over responsible, neglecting our own needs, all-or-nothing thinking and behaving, high tolerance for inappropriate behavior and low self-esteem. To these I have added being real, grieving our ungrieved losses, fear of abandonment, difficulty resolving conflict, and difficulty giving and receiving love.

As problems, concerns, conflicts or patterns come up in our life, we can bring them up with selected safe and supportive people. At first it may not be clear just which of these core issues—or perhaps more than one of them—is involved for us. Core issues do not present themselves to us as an "issue." Rather, they present at first as problems in everyday life. However, with persistent considering and describing how we feel, it will generally become clear which issue or issues are involved. This knowledge will be helpful in gradually getting free of our confusion, discontent, and unconscious negative life patterns (repetition compulsions).

Transforming

Through various ways, including being real, self-reflection, therapy groups, self-help groups and counseling, many people are transforming their lives to become more free, whole and fulfilling.

Transformation is a changing of form, a forming over, a restructuring. Ultimately it is a shift from living our life to get somewhere to living our life as an expression of our being. When we transform, we transform our awareness or consciousness. We switch from one domain of reality and being to another. Through such change, we grow and transcend to higher, more empowering, more peaceful and more creative levels of being. At the same time that we experience more personal power and more possibility and choice, we also begin to take more responsibility for making our lives work.

In the transforming stage of recovery we work to *expose* the vulnerable parts of our Child Within and almost paradoxically at the same time claim the power that is inherently there, *within* our Child. We transform the burdensome and often dysfunctional parts of our lives into positive and more functional ones. For example, when we identify, work through and change our core issues, we may make some of the following transformations.

Making such changes in our lives may not come easily. We have to work at it by risking and telling our story to close people who are safe and supportive. However, when we transform, we generally don't just one day feel a low self-esteem, wish we felt better about ourself, and the next morning awaken with a healthy self-esteem. Rather, there are specific steps in this kind of life-changing work.

After becoming aware of core issues, we now work with them. Becoming more aware, we act on what we experience, calling things for what they are. We learn to respect our own internal monitoring system—our senses and reactions. Ignoring or neglecting this crucial part of us is now a thing of the past. We are open to our feelings, senses and reactions, all an important part of our Real Self.

19 · THE VULNERABLE
INNER CHILD

· · · · · · ·

HAL STONE AND SIDRA WINKELMAN

Stone and Winkelman are the co-creators of a process called the Voice Dialogue Method, which is based on the idea that each individual contains a multiplicity of selves, or subpersonalities. The selves are in varying degrees of relationship to one another and to what the authors term the protector/controller, which is different from what is commonly thought of as the ego.

Stone and Winkelman suggest that certain troublesome selves become disowned and, therefore, live as unintegrated energy patterns in the unconscious. Dialoguing with these disowned selves, recognizing and objectifying them, enables the aware ego to understand and work with them creatively.

Voice Dialogue is a powerful means of gaining direct access to these subpersonalities or inner voices by engaging each in a dialogue without the interference of a protector/controller. With the assistance of a facilitator, the subpersonality can be addressed directly as an individual entity and as a part of the total personality. This process puts the subject into an altered state of consciousness, which is similar to hypnosis. Eventually, more and more of the subpersonalities can be brought into awareness. "Our task," Stone and Winkelman say, "is to become aware of this fragmentation of selves so that we can make valid choices in our lives."

A key subpersonality is the abandoned inner child. "Perhaps the most universally disowned self in our civilized world is the vulnerable child," say the authors. This chapter demonstrates how the inner child manifests in the Voice Dialogue process. It has been excerpted from the authors' two books, Embracing Our Selves: The Voice Dialogue Manual, *and* Embracing Each Other.

The children of our inner world know how to "be," while the rest of our personality knows how to "do" and how to "act." In working with these patterns we are given the opportunity to learn how to "be" with them; otherwise, they cannot emerge. When dealing with the inner child, the dictum is: "There's nowhere to go and there's nothing to do."

The loss of the inner child is one of the most profound tragedies of the "growing up" process. With its loss we lose so much of the magic and mystery of living, the delight and intimacy of relationship. So much of the destructiveness we express to each other is a function of our lack of connection to our sensitivities, our fears, our own magic. How different the world would be if our political figures could say: "I feel very bad. You really hurt my feelings when you said that." Or: "I want to apologize to my colleagues for my remarks yesterday. My feelings were hurt and I was angry and I am sorry."

If the inner child is operating in our lives autonomously and without protection, we can be fairly sure that we will end up as some kind of victim. The child, however wonderful, cannot drive our cars any more successfully than any other single energy pattern. It, too, needs balancing. But as long as the protector/controller is in charge of the personality, the child will remain buried and therefore inaccessible.

As we become more aware of the inner child, our aware ego gradually becomes the parent to our child. We can then take responsibility to use the energy of the inner child in our lives and provide it with appropriate protection when needed.

When the aware ego becomes more effective, we can begin to relax, knowing that the fundamental integrity of the system is in good hands. Let us look now at how the inner child manifests in the Voice Dialogue process.

VULNERABILITY—A PRIMARY DISOWNED SELF

Perhaps the most universally disowned self in our civilized world is the vulnerable child. Yet this child may be our most precious subpersonality, the one closest to our essence, the one that enables us to be truly intimate, to fully experience others, and to love. Unfortunately, it usually disappears by the age of five. This child cannot exist in our civilized societies without the protection of a very strong protector/controller. The only way a protector/controller can handle the vulnerable child is to disown it. It is usually so completely disowned that the protector/controller no longer even worries about it.

What is this child like? The most striking quality is its ability to be deeply intimate with another person. The facilitator can feel a physical warmth and a fullness radiating from this child. It is as though the space between the two people is alive and vibrating. When the vulnerable child withdraws (as it does at the slightest provocation), this warmth and fullness disappears, leaving behind a slight chill. This experience is somewhat similar to the special feelings that might occur with a small child or with a dog in a moment of deep affection and mutual trust. This ability to be fully "with" another human being is most precious.

However, being fully with another brings its share of discomfort as well as pleasure. The vulnerable child is tuned in energetically—it is aware of *everything* that is happening. Words will not fool it for a moment. As you speak, the child will know if there is any change whatsoever in your energetic connection to it. An outside thought may have intruded—you may be wondering what time it is, you may suddenly decide you're hungry—and the child will know you have withdrawn. It is exquisitely sensitive and reacts immediately to any abandonment it perceives. It may not know why the withdrawal has happened, but it will know that one has occurred.

Getting in touch with this subpersonality can open us to the most embarrassing feelings of rejection, such as experiencing a sense of abandonment when a spouse leaves the bed in the morning to go to the bathroom. However, when made conscious, this subpersonality can often tell us who is to be trusted and who is not. It usually recognizes the people who have disowned their vulnerable child and who can, therefore, hurt others, either accidentally or deliberately.

The first dialogue with a vulnerable child may simply involve sitting quietly and encouraging it to come forth. It is often preverbal and may sit quietly or cry. In its initial emergence, it might curl up in a foetal position, cover its head, and weep with great wrenching sobs. Another might be very tentative, checking out the facilitator's ability to sense its presence or absence. Above all, no vulnerable child will appear unless the facilitator can be trusted not to hurt it. It has invariably been hurt in the past and is fearful of being hurt again. This was dramatically illustrated by the vulnerable child of a Jewish woman who had managed to stay alive in Europe through World War II.

CHILD: It hurts to think of everything that she's been through. I had to go away when she was very, very young (crying). It's too painful to exist. It just feels like a skin full of tears.

FACILITATOR (with concern): Do you want to go away now?

CHILD: No, it feels good to have you here with me. I always go into hiding, but it even hurts worse when I'm alone. I need someone to be with me and let me be sad.

The pain of the vulnerable child is a deep pain that requires respect and empathy. The child will know if you are feeling aloof or rational and it will not emerge. It sometimes demands that a facilitator actually search for it. With Natalie, a therapist, the vulnerable child emerged in a most surprising fashion. Natalie began the session by expressing her discomfort at hugging the facilitator. Actually, this was Natalie's rational voice, as it turned out later, but it certainly sounded like an aware ego at first.

RATIONAL NATALIE: I've been thinking a great deal about this business of hugging you at the end of our sessions and it's not comfortable for me. It seems to me that it's a way of discharging anxiety and it works against the therapy. Also, I don't feel I have free choice in the situation.

FACILITATOR (equally rational to protect her own vulnerable child): Well, why don't we forget about hugging and see how that works? I can certainly see your point about the discharge of anxiety and tension and it's not comfortable for me if it feels compulsive.

At this point, the facilitator noticed a change, a sense of sadness in Natalie.

FACILITATOR: Wait a minute. Let me talk to the part of you that wants me to hug her.

VULNERABLE CHILD (bursts into tears): I was afraid you wouldn't know I was here. She's so sensible—I was afraid she'd hurt your feelings and you wouldn't think of looking for me. I *want* you to hug me. I like it. I *want* you to pay attention to me. (A fresh outburst of tears.)

FACILITATOR: I'd love to pay attention to you. Tell me about yourself.

CHILD: I'm very little, about four years old, and I'm cute. But I'm scared. And I'm hiding. I'm hiding in the closet. And I'm hoping that someone will come looking for me but (more sobbing) nobody comes, nobody ever comes. I really want someone to come and look for *me* and pay attention to *me*. She's acted grown up and sensible ever since she was little and nobody has ever thought to look for me. Nobody ever misses me. I need people to notice I'm gone, and to care.

This dialogue is a most touching portrait of the vulnerable child. It wants to be missed, sought after, and valued although the protector/controller and other rational subpersonalities do not want it to exist at all.

Men have even greater difficulty than women in agreeing to contact their vulnerable children because it is socially unacceptable for men to be vulnerable. Their children, too, are often in hiding. They have been found hidden in closets, under the kitchen sink, in a cave, up in a tree house, in the woods, in a barn, or in an attic. Sometimes the facilitator can make an initial contact by asking for the part that runs away from people or stays hidden.

FACILITATOR: I know that Mike is very efficient and successful, but I'd like to talk to the part of him that's a little more sensitive and needs to keep away from people; maybe it even needs to hide.

CHILD: I certainly do need to hide. When he was little, I used to go out into the woods when someone hurt my feelings. I'd wait and wait for someone to come looking for me. I was really scared that if they found Mike, they'd hurt my feelings again, but I really wanted them to notice that he was gone and to come looking. And do you know what? They never did. And then I'd really feel bad.

Once Mike knows how his feelings have been hurt, he can speak to his wife about this issue. If he doesn't know, he withdraws into a cold parental subpersonality, and his wife's vulnerable child is hurt by his withdrawal so she becomes even more rejecting to protect herself.

The vulnerable child helps us to remove ourselves from painful situations if they cannot be changed. The vulnerable child will also pull us out of an unrewarding relationship or a thankless job, once we listen to it. For instance, Frank was in a relationship with a younger woman who was fond of him but clearly let him know that she didn't love him enough to see their relationship move toward marriage as he hoped it would. Frank had disowned his vulnerable child so completely that at first we could only talk to it through the protector/controller. However, the protector/controller finally agreed to let us consult directly with the child.

FACILITATOR: Would you please tell us how you feel about Frank's relationship with Claire?

CHILD: I don't like it at all. I get hurt all the time. He keeps thinking that she's going to learn to love him but I know she's not. She's just sticking around for what she can get. He's nice and he does things for her so she stays around. I know that she doesn't love him and it makes me feel bad. But he doesn't care how I feel.

FACILITATOR: If you were running Frank's life, what would you do?

CHILD: I'd get away from her. It makes me feel too lonely when he's with her. It's much worse than being alone.

As we have said before, the vulnerable child often sees emotional matters clearly and can give good advice. Frank had to decide what to do with this information. He also consulted other subpersonalities, but in the end he followed his vulnerable child's advice—he confronted the situation and, with tact and diplomacy, ended the relationship.

In contrast with its ability to end an unrewarding relationship, the integration of the vulnerable child into a relationship encourages unparalleled intimacy and depth, as we will see in Suzanne's experience.

Suzanne had been raised by a very cold and rejecting mother. Her vulnerable child was disowned quite early in life and replaced with charm, sophistication, and a whimsical, delightful wit. Suzanne was irresistible to men but very lonely. She was shocked to realize she had vulnerable feelings and her child felt worthless.

CHILD: But what good can I do her? I just get hurt and frightened.

FACILITATOR: I know it feels awfully good to be with you and you have lots to tell both Suzanne and myself. You're delicious.

CHILD: I don't know about that (but she smiles because the energetic contact is good).

FACILITATOR: Tell me, why did you have to hide?

CHILD: Her mother (she starts to cry)—her mother is very mean and she made me cry all the time. She always told Suzanne that she was ugly and stupid and that she didn't want Suzanne in the first place. Do you know that she still tells Suzanne that she never wanted her? (She cries for a while as the impact of this revelation is absorbed.)

FACILITATOR: Well, I can certainly see why you wanted to hide. Tell me more about yourself.

CHILD: I'm really sensitive and lots of things hurt my feelings. Suzanne keeps getting into these relationships where another part of her laughs and I feel bad. Like with Eric. He has lots of girlfriends and he likes them all to think he's terrific but he never really loves them. He just collects them. It hurts my feelings but she just gets sophisticated and laughs.

FACILITATOR: That sounds as though it must be difficult for you. Tell me, how do you like being here now?

CHILD (shyly): I really like it. I trust it and it feels good.

Suzanne embraced her vulnerable child quickly. She enjoyed the special opening of her heart energy that it brought and she wanted to seek it elsewhere. She had a great deal of strength, above-average looks, and the intelligence and social skills to protect her vulnerable child. She used everything she had quite consciously. She calmly and objectively confronted Eric with her child's observations and ended her romantic involvement with him, but not her friendship.

Her next relationship, begun shortly after her introduction to this vulnerable child, was like none she had ever before experienced. She found herself communicating her feelings and reactions immediately and actually discussed her past and her mother with her new partner. She verbalized each "little" hurt and fear as it arose, and the man did likewise. For each, it was a depth of sharing never before experienced. It took real courage, but Suzanne was a determined woman who learned quickly and her bravery inspired equal intimacy in her partner. As each risk was rewarded with deeper mutual understanding and love, they became less fearful and more daring in this mutual exploration of their complex humanity. Although this was not always easy or pleasant, it was deeply satisfying to each of them. With the information provided by their vulnerable children, they were able to deal practically with pain in the relationship and protect the delicious energetic interchange—that warm pulsating energy that vibrates between people when they are truly open and trusting.

A warning—this is not to say that all is forever perfect. Circumstances beyond the control of the aware ego sometimes cause the vulnerable child to withdraw from a relationship. But once this warmth has been experienced it is something to strive for and return to, and most of us are willing to experience much discomfort in order to do so.

We would like to give you one final example of an excerpt from a Voice Dialogue session with the vulnerable child. In this instance, the facilitator asked questions that would allow the subject's awareness level to witness the requirements of the vulnerable child.

FACILITATOR: We've been talking so far about how lonely things are for you and how much you feel left out in Peter's life. Is there anything that Peter could do that might be helpful to you?

CHILD: I don't know what he could do. He always runs away from me.

FACILITATOR: Well, I know that—but Peter is listening to our conversation and he might learn a thing or two about you. I can't guarantee it, but Peter could learn how to be a proper parent to you. I know that he's never done it before, but it could happen.

CHILD: I'd like that. I'd feel better if he'd take care of me. It's especially when I get scared that I need him, and I get scared a lot. I wish he would just learn to be with me and not run away all the time. If he would just talk to me I'd feel so much better.

FACILITATOR: So one of the things he could do for you is just learn to be with you.

CHILD: And maybe he could save more money. I get scared when there's no money. He likes to do things with money that are scary to me. I hate the stock market. I hate the feeling that he could lose it all. He likes to gamble.

FACILITATOR: So now we have another thing that would make you feel better. You need the feeling of financial security. Is there anything else?

CHILD: He could let me out more. Nobody knows about me. Everyone thinks Peter is strong and tough. That's what everyone sees. No one ever sees me. That makes me feel lonely. Even Margaret (his wife) doesn't know about me. He never tells her about my feelings.

As a child grows up, it is common for parents to reject its vulnerability because life demands strength. Additionally, parents usually have no conscious relationship to their own vulnerability. So it is that we, as adults, reject our own inner child, further perpetuating this ancestral disowning process. Through dialogue work, we can hear the child's voice and gradually take over the responsibility of child-rearing from the protector/controller.

We have seen individuals do very interesting things as they begin tuning in to the needs of their inner child. Cynthia built a large doll house and furnished it, and then made it clear to her children that it was *her* doll house. John constructed an imaginary home for the child where he would visit him regularly. Ann took her special pillow to sleep on when she went on business trips. Sam started reading spy novels rather than purely redemptive literature. Lianne got a job to help her child feel more secure about money. A multitude of different activities can support the needs of the child.

Once the reality of the child has been established, journal writing becomes an excellent tool for working with it. Prior to making this connection, the question will be: Who is doing the writing? If an aware ego has not separated from the protector/controller, then the protector/controller itself may be doing the writing.

Dialoguing with the inner child is very satisfying and very revealing. One excellent approach to this kind of writing is to use the nondominant hand for the child and the dominant hand for the primary self. This same principle can apply to any primary/disowned self system while doing dialogue work in a journal format.[1] For an aware ego to properly take care of the child, it must have the power energy available to it. Without the protection of the heavyweights, the child will not be safe, and generally it knows this. What we aim at here is an aware ego related to the energies of the heavyweights on the one side, and the vulnerability, playfulness, and magic on the other. This is true empowerment. Learning to be powerful and knowing how to consciously use our heavyweights is generally an important step in attaining this empowerment.

THE VULNERABLE CHILD AND INTIMACY

The entire development of personality or primary selves is aimed at protecting one's vulnerability. When we fall in love, the actual act of falling in love allows the vulnerable child, the carrier of this vulnerability, to surface and to make an intense contact with another human being without the usual protection of these primary selves. This ability to be vulnerable with one another, to allow the emergence of every feeling, thought and reaction and to cherish all of them, makes the process of falling in love a wonderful experience. *It is one's vulnerability which makes intimacy in relationship possible and, conversely, it is this same vulnerability and apparent lack of power which the protective primary selves most fear in relationship.*

Just as it is the inclusion of vulnerability in relationship that allows intimacy, so it is the disowning of this vulnerability that later destroys intimacy. When we disown our vulnerable child, we do not attend to it properly. Since it is imperative for this child to receive adequate care, it will look elsewhere and bond in to the people around us requiring them to provide the care that is otherwise lacking. We will not be aware of this process because we do not know about our vulnerability. So, in an entirely unconscious fashion, we are automatically drawn into powerful parent/child bondings over and over again.

Caring for this inner child through an aware ego gives a feeling of real strength. It represents real empowerment. When the aware ego is caring for the vulnerable child, there is no longer the need to rely solely upon the automatic protective devices provided by the primary selves even though this has given a sense of security in the past. Nor is there the need to rely upon others to assume responsibility for this child. *It is important to know that each one of us is ultimately responsible for parenting the vulnerable child within. When we are caring adequately for our own vulnerability, we are in a position to relate deeply and effectively to others.* When we do not care adequately for our own vulnerable child, it will seek this care elsewhere and bond in deeply and unconsciously to the parental side of others. This idea that we need to love our own child first before we can relate to others in a conscious fashion is similar to the old adage that we must love ourselves before we will be able to love another.

How can we take care of our inner children? The most important step in caring for the inner child is to recognize its presence and to develop an awareness of its particular personality, its needs and its reactions. Once we know about the child and its needs and feelings, we are in a position to do something about them. We must learn to separate far enough from our vulnerable selves to realistically evaluate situations in which they have been activated and then to speak up for them in an objective fashion rather than to put them in a position of taking care of themselves. This ability to be objective, or to use impersonal energies, in considering and then in putting forth the requirements and reactions of the vulnerable child is a true position of empowerment. It is the most powerful way in which to move into a truly intimate connection with another person and to avoid the pitfalls of bonding patterns—or to gently extricate ourselves once these bondings have been constellated.

The discovery of the inner child is really the discovery of a portal to the soul. A spirituality that is not grounded in understanding, experience, and an appreciation of the inner child can move people away from their simple humanity too easily. The inner child keeps us human. It never grows up, it only becomes more sensitive and trusting as we learn how to give it the time, care, and parenting it so richly deserves.

20 · WHY ARE YOU SO ANGRY WITH ME?

· · · · · · ·

ALEXANDER LOWEN

This chapter is a personal account of Alexander Lowen's experience in therapy with Wilhelm Reich, the originator of psychotherapeutic work with the body. The powerful inner child experience that Lowen recounts here clearly has had a profound effect on his own creative development as an innovative therapist and teacher. This piece is an excerpt from the author's book Bioenergetics, *which describes the methodology of the same name that he devised, based on Reich's groundbreaking work, in collaboration with John Pierrakos.*

I began my personal therapy with Reich in the spring of 1942. During the preceding year I had been a fairly frequent visitor at Reich's laboratory. He showed me some of the work he had been doing with bio preparations and cancerous tissue. Then, one day, he said to me, "Lowen, if you are interested in this work, there is only one way to get into it, and that is by going into therapy." His statement startled me, for I had not contemplated this move. I told him, "I am interested, but what I want is to become famous." Reich took this remark seriously, for he replied, "I will make you famous." Over the years I have regarded Reich's statement as a prophecy. It was the push I needed to overcome my resistance and to launch me into my lifework.

My first therapeutic session with Reich was an experience I will never forget. I went with the naive assumption that there was nothing wrong with me. It was to be purely a training analysis. I lay down on the bed wearing a pair of bathing trunks. Reich did not use a couch since this was a body-oriented therapy. I was told to bend my knees, relax, and breathe with my mouth open and my jaw relaxed. I followed these instructions and waited to see what would happen. After some time Reich said, "Lowen, you're not breathing." I answered, "Of course I'm breathing; otherwise I'd be dead." He then remarked, "Your chest isn't moving. Feel my chest." I placed my hand on his chest and noticed that it was rising and falling with each breath. Mine clearly was not.

I lay back again and resumed breathing, this time with my chest moving outward on inspiration and inward on expiration. Nothing happened. My breathing proceeded easily and deeply. After a while Reich said, "Lowen, drop your head back and open your eyes wide." I did as I was told and . . . a scream burst forth from my throat.

It was a beautiful day in early spring, and the windows of the room opened onto the street. To avoid any embarrassment with his neighbors, Reich asked me to straighten my head, which stopped the scream. I resumed my deep breathing. Strangely, the scream had not disturbed me. I was not connected to it emotionally. I did not feel any fear. After I had breathed again for a while, Reich asked me to repeat the procedure: Put my head back and open my eyes wide. Again the scream came out. I hesitate to say that I screamed because I did not seem to do it. The scream happened to me. Again I was detached from it, but I left the session with the feeling that I was not as right as I thought. There were other "things" (images, emotions) in my personality that were hidden from consciousness, and I knew then that they would have to come out.

At that time Reich called his therapy Character Analytic Vegetotherapy. Character analysis had been his great contribution to psychoanalytic theory, one for which he was highly regarded by all analysts. Vegetotherapy referred to the mobilization of feeling through breathing and other body techniques that activated the vegetative centers (the ganglia of the autonomic nervous system) and liberated "vegetative" energies.

For Reich, then, the first step in the therapeutic procedure was to get the patient to breathe easily and deeply. The second was to mobilize whatever emotional expression was most evident in the patient's face or manner. In my case this expression was fear. We have seen what a powerful effect this procedure had on me.

Succeeding sessions followed the same general pattern. I would lie on the bed and breathe as freely as I could, trying to allow a deep expiration to occur. I was directed to give in to my body and not control any expression or impulse that emerged. A number of things happened that gradually brought me into contact with early memories and experiences. At first the deeper breathing to which I was not accustomed produced strong, tingling sensations in my hands which, on two occasions, developed into a severe carpopedal spasm, severely cramping the hands. This reaction disappeared as my body accommodated to the increased energy the deeper breathing produced. Tremors developed in my legs when I moved my knees gently together and apart, and in my lips when I followed an impulse to reach out with them.

Several breakthroughs of feelings and associated memories followed. On one occasion, as I was lying on the bed breathing, my body started to rock involuntarily. The rocking increased until I sat up. Then, without my seeming to do so, I got off the bed, turned to face it, and started to pound it with both fists. As I was doing this, my father's face appeared on the bedsheet, and I suddenly knew I was hitting him for a spanking he had given me when I was a young boy. Some years later I asked my father about this incident. He said it was the only spanking he had ever given me.

He explained that I had come home very late and my mother was upset and worried. He had spanked me so that I would not do that again. The interesting part of this experience, as of the scream, was its completely spontaneous and involuntary nature. I was moved to strike the bed as I was to scream, not by any conscious thought but by a force within that had taken over and possessed me.

On another occasion, while on the bed breathing, I began to get an erection. I had an impulse to touch my penis, but I inhibited it. Then I recalled an interesting episode out of my childhood. I saw myself as a boy of five walking through the apartment where I lived, urinating on the floor. My parents were out. I knew I was doing it to get back at my father, who had scolded me the day before for holding my penis.

It took about nine months of therapy for me to find out what had caused the scream in the first session. I had not screamed since then. As time went on, I thought I had the distinct impression that there was an image I was afraid to see. Contemplating the ceiling from my position on the bed, I sensed it would appear one day. Then it did, and it was my mother's face looking down at me with an expression of intense anger in her eyes. I knew immediately that this was the face that had frightened me. I relived the experience as if it were occurring in the present. I was a baby about nine months of age, lying in a carriage outside the door of my home. I had been crying loudly for my mother. She was obviously busy in the house, and my persistent crying had upset her. She came out, furious at me. Lying there on Reich's bed at the age of thirty-three, I looked at her image and, using words I could not have known as a baby, I said, "Why are you so angry with me? I am only crying because I want you."

In those days Reich used another technique to implement the therapy. At the beginning of each session he asked his patients to tell him all the negative thoughts they had about him. He believed that all patients had a negative transference to him as well as a positive one, and he did not trust the positive unless negative thoughts and ideas were expressed first. I found this extremely difficult to do. Having made a commitment to Reich and the therapy, I had banished all negative thoughts from my mind. I felt that I had nothing to complain about. Reich had been very generous with me, and I had no doubt about his sincerity, his integrity, or the validity of his concepts. Characteristically, I was determined to make the therapy succeed, and it was not until it almost failed that I opened up my feelings to Reich.

Following the experience of fear when I saw my mother's face, I went through a long stretch of several months during which I made no progress. I was seeing Reich three times a week then, but I was blocked because I couldn't tell Reich my feeling about him. I wanted him to take a fatherly interest in me, not merely a therapeutic one, but knowing this was an unreasonable request, I couldn't express it. Struggling inwardly with the problem, I got nowhere. Reich seemed unaware of my conflict. As hard as I tried, I couldn't let my breathing become deeper and fuller, it just didn't work.

I had been in therapy for about a year when this impasse developed.

When it seemed to go on indefinitely, Reich suggested I quit. "Lowen," he said, "you are unable to give in to your feelings. Why don't you give up?" His words were a sentence of doom. To give up meant the failure of all my dreams. I broke down and cried deeply. It was the first time I had sobbed since I was a child. I could no longer hold back my feelings. I told Reich what I wanted from him, and he listened sympathetically.

I do not know if Reich had intended to end the therapy or whether his suggestion that I terminate treatment was a maneuver to break through my resistance, but I had the strong impression that he meant it. In either case, his action produced the desired result. I began to move again in the therapy.

For Reich the goal of therapy was the development by the patient of the capacity to give in fully to the spontaneous and involuntary movements of the body that were part of the respiratory process. Thus the emphasis was on letting the breathing take place fully and deeply. If this was done, the respiratory waves produced an undulating movement of the body that Reich called the orgasm reflex.

My therapy with Reich was resumed in the fall of 1945 with sessions once a week. Within a short time the orgasm reflex came through consistently. There were several reasons for this positive development. During the year's leave of absence from therapy, striving to please Reich and gain sexual health was in abeyance, and I was able to assimilate and integrate my previous work with Reich. At this time, too, I saw my first patient as a Reichian therapist, which gave my spirit a tremendous boost. I felt I had come home and was aware of feeling very secure about my life. Surrender to my body, which also meant a surrender to Reich, became very easy. In a few months it was obvious to both of us that my therapy had come to a successful conclusion by his criteria. Years later I realized, however, that I had not resolved many of my major personality problems. My fear of asking for what I wanted even if it was unreasonable had not been fully discussed. My fear of failure and my need to succeed had not been worked through. My inability to cry unless I was pushed to the wall had not been explored. These problems were finally resolved many years later through bioenergetics.

I do not wish to say that the therapy with Reich was ineffective. If it did not fully resolve all my problems, it made me more aware of them. More important, however, it opened a way for me to self-realization and helped me advance toward that goal. It deepened and strengthened my commitment to the body as the basis of the personality. And it gave me a positive identification with my sexuality, which has proved to be the cornerstone of my life.

21 · ADVOCATING
FOR THE CHILD

· · · · · · · ·

ALICE MILLER

Psychoanalyst and author Alice Miller is a staunch advocate of enlightened witnesses taking action on behalf of children whom they see being abused. Adults who have a connection to the inner child need to act, she says, on behalf of children at risk. "Had just one person understood what was happening and come to my defense," she says in the introduction to The Drama of the Gifted Child, *"it might have changed my entire life. . . . In our society, with its hostility toward children, such people are still hard to find, but their number is growing daily." In addition, as a therapist, she challenges psychotherapy to work out a new vision of its role in the light of the new knowledge of the inner child's truth and of what we now know about the destructive socialization of the child. This excerpt is from Dr. Miller's third book,* Thou Shalt Not Be Aware.

More than eighty years ago Freud claimed he had "established" that his patients' memories of being sexually molested as children by adults were not memories of real events at all but merely fantasies. How was he able to establish this? Only since I have become more familiar with the circumstances surrounding sexual abuse has it struck me that Freud's conclusion, which provides an important premise for his drive theory and has been repeated in good faith countless times since by students in examinations, "establishes" something that he can only have conjectured; for it can be established with the aid of witnesses that a certain act took place, but we can never be certain that something did *not* take place if both parties to the act have an interest in keeping it secret. This is usually the case with sexual abuse, for even the victim cannot bear the truth because of the accompanying feelings of fear, shame, and guilt.

I cannot emphasize enough the importance of this point, for whether it is understood or not will determine whether the patient in society, like the child in the family, is left alone with his or her trauma or finds the necessary understanding in the therapist, i.e., understanding for the fact that reality is more tragic than all fantasies, which do indeed contain certain aspects of the trauma experienced but essentially serve to conceal the unbearable truth. A particular difficulty—indeed, an actual hindrance—on the path to remembering in therapy comes about as a result of the mechanism of warding off, once required for survival, and which can manifest itself in fantasies and imagery from fairy tales or in chronic perversions. Perversion, addiction, and self-destructive enactments—like fantasies—take on the function of concealment. They organize present suffering in exact accordance with the pattern of the past and in this way guarantee that the earlier, unbearable suffering remains repressed.

There are now, to be sure, numerous techniques that allow feelings from early childhood to come to the surface in a short period of time and that provide temporary relief. These techniques can be learned, but they cannot be called therapy if a sufficient degree of adequate support is not provided at the same time. The application of learned techniques can have such detrimental effects that the patient remains locked in a depression or in the chaos of awakened feelings. Results of this kind are not rare even if the therapist possesses technical skill and has a well-meaning and concerned attitude but shows tendencies that are both pedagogical and sparing of the parents in his or her therapeutic approach.

Thus, therapists' adequate support must be reinforced by their knowledge *and* emotional experience. I have made every effort to call attention to that aspect of knowledge having to do with the actual situation of the child in our society because I think it is a necessary (although not sufficient) condition if therapy is to be successful. When it is lacking, even the best method will be of no avail, and if the treatment fails, it is not necessarily the method that is at fault. But theoretical understanding alone is still not enough. Only therapists who have had the opportunity to experience and work through their own traumatic past will be able to accompany patients on the path to truth about themselves and not hinder them on their way. Such therapists will not confuse their patients, make them anxious, or educate, instruct, misuse, or seduce them, for they no longer have to fear the eruption in themselves of feelings that were stifled long ago, and they know from experience the healing power of these feelings.

But this expanding knowledge will scarcely emanate from authoritative institutions such as universities and institutes. Once the survivors of abuse (sexual and non-sexual) feel truly supported by society and by their therapists so that they are able to find their own voice, therapists will learn more from them than from any teacher. As a result, therapists will find it easier to relinquish many of these misguided beliefs that are based on the pedagogical principles of earlier centuries.

Only liberation from pedagogical tendencies will bring about crucial insights into the child's actual situation. These insights can be summarized in the following points:

1. The child is always innocent.

2. Each child needs among other things: care, protection, security, warmth, skin contact, touching, caressing, and tenderness.

3. These needs are seldom sufficiently fulfilled; in fact, they are often exploited by adults for their own ends (trauma of child abuse).

4. Child abuse has lifelong effects.

5. Society takes the side of the adult and blames the child for what has been done to him or her.

6. The victimization of the child has historically been denied and is still being denied, even today.

7. This denial has made it possible for society to ignore the devastating effects of the victimization of the child for such a long time.

8. The child, when betrayed by society, has no choice but to repress the trauma and to idealize the abuser.

9. Repression leads to neuroses, psychoses, psychosomatic disorders, and delinquency.

10. In neuroses, the child's needs are repressed and/or denied; instead, feelings of guilt are experienced.

11. In psychoses, the mistreatment is transformed into a disguised illusory version (madness).

12. In psychosomatic disorders, the pain of mistreatment is felt but the actual origins are concealed.

13. In delinquency, the confusion, seduction, and mistreatment of childhood are acted out again and again.

14. The therapeutic process can be successful only if it is based on uncovering the truth about the patient's childhood instead of denying that reality.

15. The psychoanalytic theory of "infantile sexuality" actually protects the parent and reinforces society's blindness.

16. Fantasies always serve to conceal or minimize unbearable childhood reality for the sake of the child's survival; therefore, the so-called invented trauma is a less harmful version of the real, repressed one.

17. The fantasies expressed in literature, art, fairy tales, and dreams often unconsciously convey early childhood experiences in a symbolic way.

18. This symbolic testimony is tolerated in our culture thanks to society's chronic ignorance of the truth concerning childhood; if the import of these fantasies were understood, they would be rejected.

19. A past crime cannot be undone by our understanding of the perpetrator's blindness and unfulfilled needs.

20. New crimes, however, can be prevented, if the victims begin to see and be aware of what has been done to them.

21. Therefore, the reports of victims will be able to bring about more awareness, consciousness, and sense of responsibility in society at large.

Thanks to these honest reports of childhood experiences, other men and women will be encouraged to confront their own childhood, take it seriously, and talk about it. In so doing, they in turn will provide information to others about what so many human beings have had to undergo at the beginning of life without even knowing about it in later years and without anyone else knowing about it either. Earlier, it simply was not possible to be aware of these matters and there were virtually no published reports by the victims that did not idealize the perpetrators. But now such reports are available and will continue to appear, presumably in growing numbers. I do not believe this process can be reversed.

I have not founded a psychoanalytic school or an institute nor have I established any groups, and I am not in a position to provide names and addresses of therapists. My intention has been to describe the unstated commandment that forbids us to see the true situation of children in our society. Once their plight has become visible, it will be easier to offer therapeutic help through existing channels, and the danger that therapeutic practices will be used to subjugate people (in sects, for instance) will be reduced. Research in the field will also be of more use to therapists than before, once researchers have accepted the truth, which is no less true because it is painful and which for that reason has healing and transforming powers.

The truth about our childhood is stored up in our body, and although we can repress it, we can never alter it. Our intellect can be deceived, our feelings manipulated, our perceptions confused, and our body tricked with medication. But someday the body will present its bill, for it is as incorruptible as a child who, still whole in spirit, will accept no compromises or excuses, and it will not stop tormenting us until we stop evading the truth.

22 · ON INCEST AND CHILD ABUSE

· · · · · · ·

R O B E R T   M .   S T E I N

This short essay revolves around Jungian analyst Robert M. Stein's belief that "The way I treat my inner child is the way I am going to treat my outer child." The near epidemic of child abuse in our culture today reveals a terrible disconnection from the inner child, individually and collectively. Stein's rigorous yet sensitive approach to the subject makes him a leader in understanding the phenomenon of abuse and what we can do to change it. He challenges Alice Miller's view of the "always innocent" child, suggesting that such a literal idealization of the outer child misses the truth and can be a dangerous way to fall into an unconscious collusion with the anger of the wounded inner child. The debate developing between these two outspoken contributors is a provocative one.

This paper was originally published in the journal Voices *in 1986, then revised for the journal* Spring *the following year.*

Actual child abuse always reflects a lack of connection to and respect for the internal or psychic child. As an archetype, the image of the child is associated with a newly developing aspect of the psyche which is still very much contained in nature. As Kerenyi puts it, being at home in the primeval world is an essential quality of the child archetype.[1] The attitude toward the child which we seem to have inherited from Victorian times, if not much earlier, is that the psyche of a newborn infant is a *tabula rasa* (clean slate), and that the child's development depends entirely on how we educate and shape it. Treating the child as an object to be molded instead of relating to it as an intelligent soul capable of intentionality and choice is the main psychological root of child abuse. Studies of abusive parents show that the majority claim to have been abused themselves as children. Abuse has been perpetuated internally by a loveless, critical superego that has no understanding or respect for the inner child.

Depth psychology assumes that the external and internal worlds reflect each other. If the prevailing epidemic of incest and child abuse reflects our collective attitude toward the child within, then we need to ask what lies within the compulsive need to abuse and sexually molest the outer child.

The way I treat my inner child is the way I am going to treat my outer child. Why would I want to abuse my inner child? How do I abuse it? If my child is getting out of hand, I want to stop it and that may result in abuse. For example, my child enjoys just playing and being, it doesn't much like schedules and the pressure which I put on it to work, to write this paper, to do anything that isn't fun. I abuse my child primarily by rarely letting it have its way and by putting it down for being so lazy and unproductive. And when it becomes withdrawn and depressed, I do everything possible at first to get it moving, to get it busy doing something worthwhile. The more ego-directed and collective are our attitudes and goals, the more trouble we are likely to have with the inner child, because the archetypal child contains knowledge about its own developmental needs which is often in opposition to our ego orientation. And, those of us who are not clever enough to manipulate and control the child verbally often resort to abusive physical measures to keep it in its place.

Paradoxically, an adult's compulsive need for sexual intimacy may initially have arisen out of deep feelings of compassion for the neglected, abused child. What I am suggesting is that the other side of this hate for the troublesome child is a deep love and compassion for this vulnerable, neglected, abandoned and abused aspect of the soul. The soul's need for union is often expressed in images of sexual intimacy. When an adult suffers from a deep spirit/flesh, mind/body, love/sex split, he or she will often fall under the compulsive power of the sexual drive to literalize those images. Healing does not lie in attempting to overcome these "perverse" desires, but in being able to experience fully the incestuous desires emotionally and imaginally. In this way the sexual drive is gradually transformed, and the child (inner and outer) can be loved, honored, and respected as a unique being.

The image of the child as innocent, helpless, unprotected and lacking a sexual drive seems to be more rooted in the archetype of the innocent divine maiden (Kore) than in the empirical realities of childhood. Persephone, the innocent maiden Goddess who is raped and carried off to the underworld by Hades, represents a charming, seductive soul-quality which certainly belongs to the child. This innocent, vulnerable, virginal quality of the soul which is so easily violated—and even invites violation from the dark underworld forces—belongs to the soul's need to be penetrated and deepened. This psychological penetration from below, often experienced as rape, needs to be recognized as a psychological process essential to soul-making or the process will tend to be lived in a literal way, i.e., through identification with the innocent victim or through attachment to others upon whom the archetype is projected. Perhaps the current epidemic of child abuse and sexual molestation is also in part owing to the fact that the Kore archetype has been projected on our children, who then tend to live out this projection for us.

I believe Alice Miller, in her book *Prisoners of Childhood*,[2] describes the child identified with the Kore projection and who is, as a consequence, repeatedly violated because it has no access to the ground of its instinctual being. No healthy young animal would allow itself to be close to anyone it sensed as abusive; nor would it tolerate for an instant anyone taking advantage of its trust and vulnerability. Why should a healthy child be any less capable of protecting itself? My three-year-old granddaughter, who is as vulnerable and seductive as a playful kitten, is also as determined, independent and powerful as a tiger when she wants her way. Miller's image of the child as "always innocent" and her rejection of Freud's theories of infantile sexuality as a projection of the Victorian patriarchal attitude toward children[3] seem to me rather a regression to the pre-Freudian, Victorian idealized projection on the child.

Freud destroyed the Victorian image of the child as innocent, pure, helpless and asexual in his seminal work *Three Contributions to the Theory of Sex*.[4] In making us aware of the crucial importance to psychological development of the sexual drive in infancy and childhood, Freud paradoxically established that the sexual instinct and probably other basic human instincts contain an intelligence and intentionality that go beyond the mere physical survival of the species. Thus, when a child is blocked or cut off from its sexual instincts as a consequence of an Oedipal complex, or what I have termed the incest wound, it loses touch with an instinctual power and intelligence that could protect it from abuse and manipulation.

Freud dropped his trauma theory, not because he believed that these childhood memories were of seductions that had not occurred, but because he realized that whether or not these sexual memories were literally true was less important psychologically than the psychic reality of the images. In my book *Incest and Human Love*,[5] I argue that psychologically the incest taboo functions to stimulate the sexual imagination and the formation of the image of marriage as a Sacred Union, the *hieros gamos*; to humanize and transform sexuality; to make us aware of our incompletion and to stimulate our desire to attain completion, first through union with another, but ultimately through an internal union. I also argued that *contained within the polarity of the incest archetype is both the desire and the inhibition, and that the tension between these opposites is essential to psychological development*. I proposed that the repression of either the desire or the inhibition causes a split in the child's psyche between love/sex, mind/body, spirit/flesh, and I used the term *incest wound* to describe these developmental splits. The depth of the incest wound is determined by the severity of the psychic split between love and sex, mind and body, desire and inhibition. In my view, the wounds to the soul from the repression of sexuality can be as damaging as actual sexual contact between parent and child. The current myopic focus on the literal violation of the incest taboo is unfortunate because it has diverted attention away from the deeper and more relevant psychological issues. Alice Miller's anti-psychological literalism suggests that she has fallen into an identification with her own angry, neglected, deprived inner child. Unfortunately, *nothing is more damaging to the child and its rich imaginal life than literalism*.

Is there perhaps a connection between the exploitation and abuse of children in Victorian times and the onset of the industrial age? And is there perhaps a similar connection between the onset of our modern computer age and the epidemic of child abuse? Are we, like our Victorian ancestors, perhaps inflated with our new-found power to understand and manipulate the natural forces of the universe? Are we perhaps identified with what Jung would call the all-knowing Old Wise Man or senex archetype?

Identification with an archetype always leads to inflation, onesidedness and literalism. Cut off from the renewing vitality of the child archetype, the senex becomes progressively narrow, arid and rigid. The greater the internal split between senex and child archetypes, the more desperate is the need of the senex to unite with those qualities of innocent wonder, openness, vulnerability and virginal freshness which the child carries. But the child also needs the stabilizing strength, ancient spiritual wisdom, limits and depths of the senex. Thus, Senex and Child are a polarity that functions creatively for psychological development only when forming a complementary whole rather than an oppositional split. This sort of split is probably a major factor responsible for the compulsive need of so many adults for sexual intimacy with children. As for the child who may be living out this projection of the innocent, virginal Kore archetype, not only has it been deprived of its instinctual power to protect itself from such abuse, but also it is in the grips of an archetypal power needing to unite with its other half.

The current hysteria about incest and sexual molestation intensifies the fear of sensuality and sexuality between parent and child instead of inspiring us to find a new, creative relationship to the incest mystery. I have suggested that the primary function of the incest prohibition is to stimulate the sexual imagination and to bring instincts into the service of love, kinship and creativity. This means that essential to the psychological health and maturation of the child is that it experience an erotic flow and connection to parents and siblings without fear, guilt or violation.

Let me end these reflections with a few quotes from a superb original paper, "Oedipal Love in the Countertransference," by Harold Searles. He proposed that the mutual experience of romantic and erotic feelings between analyst and analysand is an essential aspect of the resolution of the Oedipus complex in analysis:[6]

> I have found, time after time, that in the course of the work with every one of my patients who has progressed to, or very far toward, a thorough-going analytic cure, I have experienced romantic and erotic desires to marry, and fantasies of being married to the patient.[7]

He indicates that he has experienced the same phenomenon occurring with both sexes.[8] Searles offers further evidence to support his concepts through his experience as a husband and parent:

> Toward my daughter, now eight years of age, I have experienced innumerable fantasies and feelings of romantic-love kind, thoroughly complementary to the

romantically adoring, seductive behavior she has shown toward her father often times ever since she was about two or three years of age. I used at times to feel somewhat worried when she would play the supremely confident coquette with me, and I would feel enthralled by her charms; but then I came to the conviction, some time ago, that such moments of relatedness could only be nourishing for her developing personality as well as delightful to me. If a little girl cannot feel herself able to win the heart of her father, who has known her so well and for so long, and who is tied to her by mutual blood ties, I reasoned, then how can the young woman who comes later have deep confidence in the power of her womanliness.[9]

23 · THE WHISPERING
OF THE WALLS

. . . .

S U S A N N E   S H O R T

Jungian analyst Susanne Short brings us into the intensely dramatic world of D. H. Lawrence's "Rocking Horse Winner" to show us the crushing effects of unconscious destructive love on the inner and outer life of the child. This original paper focuses on the unspoken word in family life, which for the child is "insidious and harmful and can drive one to madness, because there is no evidence of what is really happening." Unfortunately, some children suffer this fate inconsolably.

Jung understood such a parent-child predicament as having a limited solution: "What has been spoiled by a father," he said, "can only be made good by a father, just as what has been spoiled by the mother can only be repaired by a mother" (C. G. Jung, CW, vol. 14, para. 182). This harsh subject is softened considerably in this warm, compassionate treatment by Ms. Short, who sees the inner child as that portion of our soul that experiences distress and suffers. "Unless we listen to the child within us," she says, "we are like parents who do not hear their own children."

"Whispering of the Walls" was originally published as part of a larger piece in the journal Psychological Perspectives, *Fall,* 1989, *a special issue devoted to the child.*

"The whispering of the walls" comes from a story by D. H. Lawrence. It refers to what is unspoken in the family, particularly what is palpable but unarticulated in the lives of the parents, and how it affects the child. Jung felt that "nothing influences children more than the silent facts in the background" of the home.[1] One of the silent facts was the "unlived life of the parents," as he called it: the part of life affected by circumstance that had prevented the parents from pursuing their own fulfillment, or the part of life they had shirked, either consciously or unconsciously. Another was the denial of their own needs for love or power. He especially thought that parents' troubles in love relationships had a great effect on how children were able to negotiate their own love lives. And the final silent fact was the parents' quiet expectation that the child fulfill their narcissistic needs. In other words, in one way or another, the child is forced to live out the shadow side of the parents.

These subtle forms of cruelty often pass for good parenting and hardly give us a clue to what has gone wrong in the psychic development of the child. Lawrence's short story, "The Rocking Horse Winner," illustrates this subtle wounding. It is a story analysts might well hear in their consulting rooms:

> There was a woman who was beautiful, who started with all the advantages, yet she had no luck. She married for love, and the love turned to dust. She had bonny children, yet she felt they had been thrust upon her, and she could not love them. They looked at her coldly, as if they were finding fault with her. And hurriedly she felt she must cover up some fault in herself. Yet what it was that she must cover up she never knew. Nevertheless, when her children were present, she always felt the center of her heart go hard. This troubled her, and in her manner she was all the more gentle and anxious for her children, as if she loved them very much. Only she herself knew that at the center of her heart was a hard little place that could not feel love, no, not for anybody. Everybody else said of her: "She is such a good mother. She adores her children." Only she herself, and her children themselves, knew it was not so. They read it in each other's eyes.
>
> There were a boy and two little girls. They lived in a pleasant house, with a garden, and they had discreet servants, and felt themselves superior to anyone in the neighborhood.
>
> Although they lived in style, they felt always an anxiety in the house. There was never enough money.
>
> And so the house came to be haunted by the unspoken phrase: There must be more money! There must be more money! The children could hear it all the time, though nobody said it aloud. They heard it at Christmas, when the expensive and splendid toys filled the nursery. Behind the shining modern rocking-horse, a voice would start whispering: There must be more money! There must be more money! And the children would stop playing, to listen for a moment. They would look into each other's eyes, to see if they had all heard. There must be more money! There must be more money!
>
> Yet nobody ever said it aloud. The whisper was everywhere, and therefore no one spoke it.[2]

The story focuses on the boy, Paul, who goes mad trying to make his mother happy so that she will be free to love him. Paul thinks that if he can just get enough money for his mother, she will be happy. (It is not uncommon for children to resort to magical thinking when they cannot understand what is going on in the world around them.) With the help of the family gardener who bets on race horses, Paul begins to win money by knowing which horse will win a race. The gardener tells him the names of the horses in a race; Paul gets on his rocking horse and rides until the right name comes to him—by riding himself into a trance, he eventually gets the name of the horse from the unconscious; the gardener puts a bet on the horse and they both make money. All of this takes place in secret. The boy then gives the money to his uncle to give to his mother anonymously. But no matter how much money Paul gives her, it is never enough. Finally, he exhausts himself riding his horse, becomes ill and dies, but not before winning for his mother the last amount of 80,000 pounds. In one of the final lines in the story, Paul's uncle says to the mother, "You are 80,000 pounds to the good and a poor son to the bad."

Many children sacrifice themselves to their parents' needs. They kill themselves trying to make their parents happy and trying to live up to their parents' and society's expectations of them. As Jung has said, they live the unlived life of the parents rather than their own, and they don't even know they are doing it. In the past few years we have all become aware of the increasing child and adolescent suicide rate in the affluent suburbs of our cities. Suicidal children are typically superachievers. The youngest I have heard of was 10 years old. Many school systems now teach a suicide prevention course. Such young people come to analysis depressed and cut off from their own feelings, without any notion of who they are. Usually the one feeling available to them is a sense of emptiness, or what Jungians would call a "hopeless loss of soul." They feel emotionally abandoned, as if they are nothing more than a product of parents' and society's expectations, as I have said.

In order to understand your own childhood, it is important to know what the house whispered when you were a child, or what it continues to whisper. It can whisper, *There's not enough money.* (In America's imperial cities where money is abundant, this is an often-heard whisper, even among the rich.) The house can whisper, *There's no one in charge here.* Or, *You're not good enough, you're not as pretty as your sister, you're not as smart as your brother, you'll never amount to anything, you must distinguish yourself or have a worthy career.* Or, *It's not perfect enough, what you are doing is not good enough for someone as gifted as you are, you really could do better* (a comment which makes any child's giftedness a curse).

One of the natural jobs of childhood is to develop an ego. When you are a child and following this natural path, it is tragic to hear in the silence that something is wrong with you or that something vaguely sensed is expected of you. T. S. Eliot has said: "It is the conversation not overheard, not intended to be heard, with the sidewise looks, that brings death to the heart of a child."[3] "These are the things that hang in the air," Jung wrote, "and are vaguely felt by the child, the oppressive atmosphere of foreboding, that seeps into the child's soul like a poisonous vapor[4] . . . through the thickest walls of silence, through the whitened sepulcher of deceit, complacency, and evasion."[5]

Even though unspoken, the messages are heard in the psyche of the child as clearly as any spoken word. In fact, the more hidden something is, the more powerful it becomes. The unspoken word is insidious and harmful and can drive one to madness, because there is no evidence of what is really happening. (Analysts often hear patients say of their childhoods, "There was absolutely no evidence for what I was experiencing.") The spoken word wounds and angers, causes children either to rebel or capitulate, but it is the whisper of the house that drives them to neurosis because they are never sure where it comes from, who says it, or what exactly it means. Whispered messages come out of the woodwork, so to speak, to eat away at the child's confidence, sense of well-being, and sense of being loved. Instead of being a safe, secure place for the child, the home then becomes a container that does not contain, a container that does not reflect back to the child who he is or what she feels. According to Jung, the child picks up only the unresolved conflicts of the parents.

A child needs to have its mysterious feelings made conscious, to hear someone confirm that the unspoken message is, in fact, true. If someone had said to Paul, "It sounds as if the walls are whispering. . . . What is really happening is that your mother isn't happy because she can never be satisfied with what she has. . . . But your parents don't talk about this, so you feel you have to do something to make her happy and therefore free her to love you"—then Paul would have known what the real suffering was: that his mother could not love him no matter what he did or how he tried. *His* suffering, then, would have been legitimated and it would not have made him sick.

Jung says that neurosis is the avoidance of legitimate suffering. By *suffering* here I mean conscious suffering. It seems odd to be in favor of a child suffering, but, paradoxically, conscious legitimate suffering is what saves a child. When a child is not allowed to experience feelings of sadness, anger, loss, and frustration, his or her real feelings become neurotic and distorted; in adulthood, that child will unconsciously arrange life to repeat these same repressions of feeling. Child psychologist Bruno Bettelheim laments that children are not being allowed legitimate suffering. He states that even the books children read in school show life as nothing but a succession of pleasures. Nobody is really angry, nobody truly suffers, there are no real emotions. Bettelheim is recognizing the same problem Jung has described.

Paul's mother avoided legitimate suffering. If she had been able to talk with someone and say, "I love my children, but when I'm with them my heart goes hard, and I think I should cover up some fault in myself," she would have come to understand the underlying problem. Not only did she need to speak about her experience, she needed to know what her real suffering was. When a child seeks love, attention, or confirmation from an unloving parent, we know that that is what the parent also needs: Paul's mother sought the same thing he did—love and attention—which apparently she had never gotten.

How can we hope to extricate ourselves from this morass? It may seem as if our lives are very determined and restricted by the potency of the family's influence. But does a child's fate lie totally within the boundaries of the family?

Jung's statement in 1928 that "parents should always be conscious of the fact that they themselves are the principal cause of neurosis in their children"[6] is very disquieting. His notion that "the things which have the most powerful effect on children don't necessarily come from the conscious state of the parents but from their unconscious background"[7] is frightening because we can control our conscious lives more or less, but the unconscious is uncontrollable. It is important to recognize that although Jung's view here is true to some extent, it ignores the fact that the *child* has a nature of his or her own, which may or may not include a predisposition to embody the neurosis of the family. There is a fascinating body of psychological research based on the work of Manfred Bleuler, whose 30-year investigation of the *healthy* children of *schizophrenic* parents illustrates this point. The role of the child's own personality in the generation of his or her psychology and fate as the symptom-bearer in the family must not be overlooked. Psychological difficulties are ultimately the result of both family dynamics and the child's unique constitutional variables. We have learned since 1928 that a child is an individual, and that the theory of parent–child fusion can be overdone. In fact, even Jung softened his views over the years.

The child, no matter how young, is a person in his or her own right —not a blank slate, a *tabula rasa*, for adults to "write on," as some philosophers have thought. Certainly, a very small infant is a person in formation, but he or she is nonetheless an individual.

A child brings something special and unique to the context of the relationship with parents. When children are born a part of what they will become is born in them; they have within them the "raw materials" they will need to grow and mature. They will unfold not only physically but psychically as well. The adults' task is not to violate the essence of the child but to trust what is within the child. Gertrude Stein once said that it wasn't what Paris gave you, but what it didn't take away. This holds true for children. The issue is not so much what parents give to them as what they *don't take away*. We can apply this idea to ourselves: we need to understand what we have been allowed to keep, what was not taken away from us, and what was taken away so that we can replace it. Jung said: "If parents because of their own insecurity cannot accept sufficiently the basic nature of the child, then its personality becomes damaged. If it is beyond the normal bruising of life the child becomes estranged from his center of being and feels forced to abandon his natural pattern of unfoldment."[8]

How is this natural pattern of unfoldment facilitated? We know of the importance of mirroring: when there is a significant person in a child's world who is well trusted or well loved and who can interpret to the child what the child is experiencing, then that child will experience his or her reality as a true reality. To prevent the walls from whispering, the adult must speak out the whispers. A child feels what he or she feels, but the language and conceptual equipment to interpret these feelings are not fully developed. Ideally, the job of the responsible adult who is equipped with rational thinking processes and undistorted perception is to observe and reflect what the child is feeling.

Mirroring is self-affirming and reveals to the child who he/she is and what he/she is becoming. It is important to distinguish between *praise* and *mirroring*. Praise tends to be evaluative; it implies judgment, and can create the need for constant reassurance. Mirroring, however, affirms the *self.* For example, if I praise you, I am telling you what I feel or think about you. If I *mirror* you, I am reflecting to you what *you* feel or think about *yourself.* If there is no verification of the child's own reality, the child can feel disoriented. Lack of verification creates the feeling of non-being. Then a child can feel that it is his or her own fault that something bad is happening.

Remember, for instance, the D. H. Lawrence story. What was so tragic was that the whispers were never concretized into speaking, into real communication within the family. They remained the whisperings of the walls. To undo the damage that such murmurings can cause we need to make real whatever is the message of the family.

Children need to have all of their true feelings confirmed and mirrored in order to develop faith in and allegiance to their own experiences. When a child realizes that her parents will never confirm what she senses, she gives up and develops a false persona that covers a very fragile foundation. If she is not allowed to be herself and experience her own feelings, then she will become someone else. This is true for most of us. We have become our mothers or our fathers or the fantasy of what the good little child is or what the bad little child is. Sometimes we hide ourselves so well that eventually even we no longer recognize our own disguises. Wearing these disguises, we stray far from our original connection to the self. Only in the discomfort of our depressions or anxieties are we forced to seek out a reconciliation. It is in the vague feeling of being "homesick even when we are at home"[9] that we begin to search for answers in the dark caves of infancy.

Jung has said: "In the adult there lurks a child—an eternal child, something that is always becoming, is never completed, and that calls for increasing care, attention, and education. This is the part of the human personality that wishes to develop and become whole."[10] Our highly developed ego-consciousness strongly resists this inner child. Such resistance makes the task of discovering the inner child a critical one. What are its qualities? Jung has several responses. The inner child is "something that existed not only in the past but exists now"; that "is not only a picture of certain forgotten things in childhood but a preconscious aspect of the collective psyche. . . . The idea of child is a means to express a psychic fact that cannot be formulated more exactly. . . . It is a system functioning to compensate a one-sidedness of conscious mind . . . consciousness needs compensating through the still existing state of childhood."[11]

The part of our psyches that experiences distress and suffering is the part containing the inner child. Unless we make ourselves aware of this child within, we will sometimes behave unconsciously from that part of ourselves. Many of us have repressed or ignored childhood experiences and our inner child. When we are blinded in this way, we are limiting our consciousness and our ability to experience life. Unless we listen to the child within us, we are like parents who do not hear their own children.

PART 5

. . . .

RECOVERING
THE CHILD

INTRODUCTION

· · · · · · ·

Return to the beginning;
Become a child again.

—TAO TE CHING

People get absolutely intolerable when they
have a creative idea in their womb and
can't bring it out. So one has to help them
bring the child out.

—MARIE-LOUISE VON FRANZ

The essays in this section need little general introduction, for the theme they have in common is self-evident: They have been selected for their practical and direct approach to the task of realizing the inner child, and each discusses how to recover the child's special gifts and embrace its vitality.

Lucia Capacchione has created a series of exercises to help you understand and love your child within, based on her discovery of the linkage between self-expression with the non-dominant hand and the inner child. Here we have included material for getting to know your inner child, for healing your vulnerable child, and for meeting your playful child.

In their straightforward essay, Joyce C. Mills and Richard J. Crowley describe techniques for contacting the child within, as well as approaches to the inner child used by two master therapists, the preeminent psychoanalyst C. G. Jung and the dean of hypnotherapists, Milton Erickson.

In "Liberating Your Lost Inner Child," popular therapist and teacher John Bradshaw describes a process he calls "shame reduction" for reclaiming the inner child and the authentic Self.

With clarity of voice and spirit, author John Loudon's essay answers the difficult question of how to become like a child and yet put away the things of childhood.

Psychologist and author Nathaniel Branden has created some very practical sentence-completion exercises for awakening the awareness of the child-self and facilitating its integration. This is a powerful tool of auto-suggestion for recovering the child.

Jean Houston's article "Recalling the Child" asks you to befriend the child you once were and connect this child to your Higher Self, to evoke what she calls your "extended sense of being," to know the living presence of the child within.

In "Replaying the Movies of Your Childhood," Adelaide Bry has assembled a series of visualization techniques for reconnecting with the child and for learning to trust your deepest nature.

The interview excerpt "Killing the Dragon" comes from the late, great visionary mythologist Joseph Campbell, and speaks to getting in touch with the child that lies within us.

Finally, in a cogent, challenging, and rewarding essay, Jungian analyst Robert M. Stein discusses the redemption of the neglected inner child in relationships, marriage, and psychotherapy.

24 · THE POWER OF YOUR OTHER HAND

· · · · · · · ·

LUCIA CAPACCHIONE

Consultant and workshop leader Lucia Capacchione has a great enthusiasm for the life of the inner child. Her work reads like a coursebook for "Inner Child 101." Through her own healing process, she has discovered a way to unlock the child inside. She also generously acknowledges the work of several other of our contributors and describes how to integrate some of their practical techniques, along with her own, into a full-out crash program for the recovery of the inner child. This selection is excerpted from Capacchione's book of the same title.

Child abuse is a downward spiral, a tragic affliction handed down from one generation to the next. It has always existed, but we've heard more about it in recent years through media coverage. It may have gotten worse or it may simply be that we are willing to bring it out in the open now. And we are shocked at what we find: psychological torment, physical and sexual abuse in families and in schools, child pornography, and kidnapping. More and more children are escaping into gangs, drugs, and sometimes even suicide.

Since the beginning of modern psychotherapy, the issue of childhood trauma has been a central factor in many methods of treatment. More recently, in the writings of psychoanalyst Alice Miller, we learn how society breeds psychopathology and violence in the home, school, and other institutions. In childhood, most of us were abused to one degree or another. Those of us who have worked as therapists with adults, adolescents, or children will attest to the grim fact that many people prefer to deny the deplorable treatment they received in their early years—the neglect, coercion, or outright violation—in favor of a fantasy memory of "happy childhood." As long as the denial continues, there is no way to "work through" the abuse, so it is passed down to the next generation.

Denial has been a key issue in the families of alcoholics/addicts/obsessive-compulsives. The denial of family problems was so great that, in the case of adult children of alcoholics, it isn't until many years after leaving home that the truth is allowed to surface, sometimes overwhelming the individual with pain, grief, and rage. The problem in the U.S. has reached staggering proportions. In his book, *Healing the Child Within: Discovery and Recovery for Adult Children of Dysfunctional Families*, Charles Whitfield, M.D., writes that new self-help groups for adult children of alcoholics were forming in the late '80s at the rate of one per day. These are non-professional, no-fee organizations patterned after the highly successful twelve-step program of Alcoholics Anonymous and Alanon. As a participant in these programs, I can personally attest to their effectiveness. They have given hope to the hopeless and strength to the helpless.

In the fields of psychotherapy, social work, and education, more and more professionals are addressing the problem of child abuse. And in counseling work with adults, the theme of healing the Inner Child is being presented in books, workshops, seminars, and professional training programs. If Whitfield is correct in his estimation that 80 to 95% of the population did not receive adequate parenting, then healing the Inner Child becomes a task for most of us.

Starting in the '60s and '70s, Hugh Missildine (*Your Child of the Past*) and Eric Berne (*Transactional Analysis*) introduced the concept of the Inner Child. In the '80s, Miller, Whitfield, and Stone and Winkelman have continued with books and therapeutic techniques for finding and healing the Child Within. These experts are all in agreement that there is still a Child living in all of us, a Child who continues to need parenting. But we must become our own parents. We must provide the understanding, compassion and guidance of a parent for our own Inner Child.

The Inner Child consists of all our childlike feelings, instincts, intuitions, spontaneity, and vitality. It is naturally open and trusting unless it learns to shut down for self-protection. It is emotional and expressive until condemned for being what it is—a child. It is playful until it is crushed for being childish. This Inner Child is creative until ridiculed for its expression. It is magical until it is punished for using its imagination. We can bury it, distort it, handicap it, make it sick, but we can't get rid of it.

By the time most of us reach adulthood, our natural, healthy childlike traits are so wounded they are nearly dead. Or they are distorted beyond recognition. Alcoholism, drug addiction, sexual obsession, eating disorders, compulsive spending, and gambling are some of the misguided attempts to return to childhood. The behavior that results is inappropriate childishness rather than true child-likeness.

Hal Stone and Sidra Winkelman write poignantly about

the loss of the Inner Child . . . one of the most profound tragedies of the "growing-up" process. We lose so much of the magic and mystery of living. We lose so much of the delight and intimacy of relationship. So much of the destructiveness that we bring to each other as human beings is a function of our lack of connection to our sensitivities, our fears, our own magic . . . perhaps the most universally disowned self in our civilized world is the Vulnerable Child. Yet this Vulnerable Child may be our most precious sub-personality—the closest to our essence—the one that enables us to become truly intimate, to fully experience others, and to love.

But there is hope. The Child doesn't die. It's still in there and it can be contacted and revived. As Charles Whitfield puts it:

Our Child Within flows naturally from the time we are born to the time we die and during all of our times and transitions in between. We don't have to do anything . . . it just is. If we simply let it be, it will express itself with no particular effort on our part. Indeed, any effort is usually in denying our awareness and expression of it.

And where does this Child live? In our feelings, hunches, likes and dislikes, our wishes and dreams, our fantasies and wildest imaginings. The exercises in this chapter are designed to help you find, understand, and love that Child Within: the Vulnerable Child, the Playful Child, the Magical Child, and all the other subtle nuances of feeling which this part of you contains. You will learn techniques for recovery from the abuses of childhood.

First, you'll have an opportunity to spend some time getting acquainted with your Inner Child. You will discover who that aspect of yourself really is, what it likes and doesn't like, how it feels, and what it needs. You will also have a chance to accept and nurture your Inner Child in a mutually beneficial way. You may even come home to the joy of the Inner Child.

Getting to Know Your Inner Child

1. Picture a place you feel would be comfortable for your Inner Child, such as:

> near a lake, river or ocean
> in a meadow
> in a garden
> in a beautiful room.

2. Now invite your Inner Child to come into the picture. See this child in your mind's eye and ask yourself, Is it a boy or girl? How old? What does the child look like?

3. Now, start writing out a dialogue. Writing with your dominant hand, greet the child, introduce yourself and ask his or her name. Let your Inner Child respond by writing with the *other hand*.

4. Tell the child you want to get to know his or her feelings, needs, likes and dislikes. Then continue the conversation. The Nurturing Parent writes with the dominant hand, the Inner Child with the non-dominant hand.

5. Complete your conversation by asking the Inner Child for one special thing it wants from you. Work out something that is mutually agree-

able, that satisfies the Child's needs as well as those of the Nurturing Parent, who is responsible for following through. Make sure you are willing to keep the agreement made to the Child. If not, don't make any promises, otherwise you will disappoint the Child and cause further hurt.

6. Thank the Child for coming out. If you are willing to meet again, agree on a place and time.

The next exercise will enable you to meet your Vulnerable Child. Since the Vulnerable Child does not fit with the "adult" image, this might be the disowned part of you. It is probably buried pretty deep. But as we have seen, letting it write with your dominant hand will give it a chance to come out more easily. It may take a little more time, but it will be well worth it, as you will discover for yourself. The energy and vitality that results from these dialogues is quite remarkable.

Healing Your Vulnerable Child

1. Visualize a very safe place, an environment that is sheltered and soothing, such as a cozy little room with soft furniture, or some other space that feels warm and inviting.

2. Picture your Vulnerable Child in detail: age, gender, appearance, place in the room or environment you've created.

3. Greet and invite the Child to be with you. Write out your conversation, using both hands. The Nurturing Self writes with your dominant hand, the Vulnerable Child with the non-dominant.

4. Ask your Vulnerable Child the following questions:
   Who are you?
   How do you feel?
   Why do you feel this way?
   What can I do to help you?

5. Tell your Vulnerable Child exactly what you will do to follow through, and meet its needs. If you can't, don't make any promises. This will betray your Child's trust and only make matters worse.

6. If you want to visit with your Vulnerable Child again, agree on a place and time. Then thank your Child for coming out and say good-bye for now.

Notice in your everyday life when your Vulnerable Child is present. This usually happens when you experience fatigue, sickness, fear, sadness, shyness, disappointment. Observe what you do with these feelings. Do you allow yourself to truly feel them? Do you block them out with food, drugs, alcohol, extra work, oversocializing, TV?

Just as it is possible to establish a rapport with the Vulnerable Child who lives in us today, it is also possible to heal the Child of the Past. One of my students who healed his Vulnerable Child of the Past is Tom, a

Dear Vulnerable Child, I'm so glad I found you again.
Is there anything you'd like to say to me today?

YES. I WANT YOU TO STAY WITH ME.
AND TAKE ME WITH YOU WHEREVER
YOU GO. PLEASE LISTEN TO MY
FEELINGS AND TAKE CARE OF
ME. DON'T LET THOSE OTHER
ONES DROWN ME OUT OR
BE MEAN TO ME. DON'T LET
THEM TALK YOU INTO TRYING
TO LEAVE ME OUT 'CAUSE
YOU CAN'T LEAVE ME OUT..
I'M YOUR VERY OWN
CHILD AND I LIVE INSIDE
YOU. AND I'LL NEVER
GROW UP AND GO
AWAY. I'LL ALWAYS BE HERE,

distinguished-looking middle-aged medical doctor and counselor. He attended my weekly journal-keeping class for himself, but also to learn methods to use with his patients, especially those who were hospitalized.

When Tom came to my class he thought he was right-handed. As it turned out, he was actually a switch-over (a natural lefty forced into right-handedness). There is no question in my mind that such coercion to conform to the "majority hand" does deep psychological damage to the individual's Vulnerable Child. But the wound can be healed in adulthood, as we will see in Tom's case.

When Tom was given permission to write with his left hand, he re-experienced a situation with an early teacher. While writing, he actually relived some painful events and later told a grim story. In his early childhood, a teacher had forced little Tom (through physical abuse and threats) into right-handedness. He had attempted to fight back, but the teacher won out. He saw the teacher as a witch and was able to feel the rage and frustration he had been forced to repress as a child in the adult's world. Later, he was able to forgive her by changing her from a witch into a woman (a human being who was doing the best she could). By doing this, Tom healed the childhood trauma of being forced to switch from his natural hand.

A few weeks after Tom started to write with his left hand, class members remarked that he smiled more and seemed far more relaxed. Several years later, this is how he described his left handwriting:

> My left handwriting is more graceful and is actually more legible than writing done with my right hand. If I have time, I write any personal expression with my left hand. My right-hand writing is unpleasing to me now.

Tom's story had a happy ending: healing his Vulnerable Inner Child. Forced to renounce his left-handedness by a grown-up who was stronger and held authority, Little Tom was denied his natural style of expression. Big Tom finally rescued Little Tom by putting a pen in his natural hand and allowing him to speak.

The next exercise will enable you to revisit and heal a situation that may have overwhelmed you when you were a child. You will be collapsing time, so to speak, and bringing the past into the present moment. You will deal with a concrete situation, with specific feelings and reactions that were buried at the time. You will become your own counselor. This exercise can empower you to take responsibility for yourself instead of blaming your parents or others from your childhood. If there are still feelings alive in you from past situations, then the Inner Child is still alive. And *you*, the adult, are now its parent. It's up to you to give the Child that kindness and understanding it needs, instead of demanding that others do it for you.

Healing Your Child of the Past

1. Go back to a time in your childhood when you were frightened, sad, lonely, or felt some very strong emotion that you couldn't express at the time.

2. Imagine that the adult of the present visits this Child of the past and sits down to talk with it. Be the Child's counselor.

3. Have a conversation with the Inner Child of the past. As a counselor, let the Child tell you about itself, what happened, and what it needs. Let the counselor write with your dominant hand; invite the Inner Child of the Past to write with your *other hand*. Ask the Inner Child the following questions:

> What's your name or nickname?
> How old are you?
> Tell me about yourself. What happened to you?
> How do you feel?
> Why do you feel that way?
> What do you need now? How can I help you?

Observe your feelings in everyday life. Watch to see if this Child of the past comes out.

The next exercise is intended to help you meet your Playful Child. This is the part of you that is genuinely fun-loving, spontaneous, and exuberant. It can be silly, have a sense of humor, and experience joy in being alive. The Playful Child is very present in the body and *in the moment*. It enjoys pleasurable sensations: beautiful colors, delicious tastes, the feel of an ocean breeze, moving the body in ways that are enjoyable, a hot bath on a cold day. The Playful Child doesn't do things because they're supposed to be "good for you." It does them because they feel good.

So send your "stuffy" grown-up on a brief vacation (the part of you that's all work and no play), and invite the Playful Child that lives inside of you to come outside.

Playful Child

1. Imagine an environment where your Playful Child would enjoy meeting with you, such as:
   a playroom
   a playground
   a zoo
   an amusement park or carnival
   the beach
   recreation center

2. Now invite the Child to come out and be with you. Let the Playful Child draw a picture of itself with your non-dominant hand. Ask the Child to tell you its name and print it on the picture.

3. Writing with your dominant hand (as your adult self), have a conversation with your Playful Child (who writes through your non-dominant hand). Ask the Child all about itself.

What do you like? What don't you like?
Where do you like to play?
What kind of things do you like to do when you play?
Who do you like to play with?
What do you like to eat and drink?
What are your favorite places to eat?
Where do you like to go on vacation?
What kind of clothes do you like to wear?
What are your favorite colors?
What is your favorite room? Favorite place?

4. Ask your Playful Child how it feels about its place in your life at this time. Does it feel wanted and included? Does it feel ignored and left out?

5. Ask your Playful Child for one thing it wants from you. If you are willing to do it, tell the Child exactly how you will meet its request. Be specific. If you are not going to follow through, don't make promises. This will only disappoint the Child and weaken the trust between you.

6. Thank your Playful Child for coming out to talk with you and agree to meet again if you are willing to do that.

Later on, be aware of the Playful Child when it wants to come out in your everyday life. It may want some time to take a hot bath or pick a bunch of flowers or bike ride to the store instead of driving.

25 · CONTACTING THE CHILD WITHIN

· · · · · · ·

JOYCE C. MILLS AND RICHARD J. CROWLEY

Through their work with children in therapeutic settings, child therapists Joyce C. Mills and Richard J. Crowley have discovered the crucial ability to utilize an inner child awareness when communicating with children. A most interesting feature of this essay is the description and comparison of the two masters, Milton Erikson and Carl Jung, and the ways they both worked from their relationship to the inner child. This chapter is excerpted from the authors' book Therapeutic Metaphors for Children and the Child Within.

For those of us who work with children, "Return to the beginning, become a child again" can truly be a helpful passage to remember. We have found it invaluable to return to our own *child within* by recapturing pleasant memories and playful fantasies, or by observing children playing at parks, beaches, and schoolyards. This enables us to revivify those remembered or observed spontaneous moments and utilize them later as important therapeutic tools.

Volumes of material are available on the theory of what contributes to an effective therapeutic relationship with children.[1] There is general agreement on the need for providing a safe environment in which the qualities of rapport, respect, and cooperation can be fostered. For us, *contacting the child within* is the pivotal element in building these many dimensions of the therapeutic relationship. Indeed, it may even be the single most critical element in ultimately reaching the child. At times we as therapists have found that our own limitations and feelings of frustrations have occurred when we momentarily forgot to allow ourselves to "enter the world of the child within."

THROUGH A CHILD'S EYES

A colleague of mine called one day and asked if I would be able to see a client of his immediately—a mother with her four-year-old son, Mark. My colleague explained that Mark had been repeatedly sexually abused by his father, as reported by the mother. The mother was currently involved in a custody battle, trying to convince the courts of the father's abusive behavior. The child had been questioned and tested by many court-appointed therapists over the last few months. However, the process of decision-making was still in abeyance. In the meantime Mark's behavior and emotional status continued to deteriorate rapidly. The mother reported that he was awakening in the middle of the night with uncontrollable screams, and that he was extremely fearful during the day, manifesting numerous tearful outbursts.

I agreed to see the child and his mother the following morning. When this lovely mother walked into my office, she was carrying an entire armload of files and case material already amassed on her young son. Mark, a small, ash-blond boy with bright blue eyes and a hesitant smile, held onto the pocket of his mother's jeans with his tiny hand. Although the mother looked overwhelmed with emotion and distress, she bravely sat down on the couch and began ruffling through her files as efficiently as she could. Mark sat close to her, his fingers still looped through one of her pockets. I noticed his eyes scanning the many shelves of toys, games, stuffed animals, puppets, pictures, and drawing materials that were all around him.

Did I want to read the previous therapist's report first? Or did I want to glance through the extensive court report? For the first several minutes of this encounter I followed along with the mother's wishes, all the while peripherally observing little Mark. I glanced through the therapist's file, letting my eyes scan the key words. It seemed that there were endless psychodynamic explanations for what had occurred between the father and his child. I flipped through hefty court proceedings, and again a blur of suggestions and recommendations presented themselves. An inner awareness of feeling uncomfortable and distracted began to emerge in me. It felt as if 5,000 facts were all jumping up and down in the room, vying for my attention. The more "information" I took in, the further removed from the child I felt.

Meanwhile this little four-year-old boy before me, whom this barrage of information concerned, was sitting silently and sadly next to his mother. He moved very little, but his eyes continued to wander curiously about the room. Even though my review of the "pertinent information" was occurring within a short time-period of the session, I realized nonetheless that I could no longer continue in this manner. I became quickly aware that I had allowed this seemingly relevant material to interfere with the most essential element in the treatment of this child: making contact with Mark in *his own world*.

I put all the materials aside, explaining to the mother that it was important for me to just play with Mark for awhile so that we could get to know each other. I then went over to Mark, took his hand in mine, and with an uplifting tone in my voice said, "I've noticed you've been looking around this room, and I'll bet you'd like to get an even closer look." His eyes brightened as he nodded yes and began to move off the couch. As this shift took place, I noticed that my sense of discomfort and disconnection began to lessen.

As Mark looked around the room, I crouched down next to him and tried to look around the room through his eyes, not through the eyes of an adult therapist. I repeated the words he used to describe the toys and the games he saw. I also matched his childlike tonality and pronunciations, not only for the sake of making it sound like I was talking his language, but more for myself—to feel how my own four-year-old child within would feel being in yet another office with another therapist after such traumatic life experiences.

As therapists, we are trained to be cornered with such issues as objectivity and transference. However, we cannot really be objective about something until we know what it is the person is experiencing. This child had been objectively assessed to the point of accruing a combined psychological and court file that nearly outweighed him! Clearly there was an abundance of objectivity present in this case. Therefore, I felt strongly that it was vital for me to do just the opposite—to put aside temporarily all objectivity and really identify with Mark by allowing myself to feel my own child within. I knew I had to sense some of Mark's world before all the objective information would have any helpful meaning to me in terms of intervening.

Although Mark had been described by previous therapists as extremely reticent and unresponsive, in this first session he was able to begin giving expression to the many struggles in his life via artwork and storytelling. This occurred only after we had spent some thirty minutes mutually exploring the room and getting to know each other in the special way that only "children" can.

There are also times when we have searched for ways to help parents suspend their adult viewpoints in favor of the very real world of their child's problem. This suspension automatically requires parents to make at least a minimal connection to their own child within, for by agreeing to see the situation from their child's point of view they are actually seeing it from behind the lens of their own childhood life experiences. From this vantage point two important gains occur: 1) they can feel a greater empathy for what their own child is experiencing, and 2) they are simultaneously accessing a potential wealth of resources learned decades ago but not normally available to them from their adult perspectives.

THE MONSTERS AND THE CUPCAKE

Daniele was a delightful eight-year-old girl who came to therapy with her mother for numerous complaints, including nervousness and chronic sleeping problems. For several years, Daniele had been afraid to go to sleep at night because she believed there were monsters in her bedroom. Her mother had rationally explained that monsters do not exist and that there was nothing to fear, but Daniele insisted that they did exist and tried desperately to convince her mother of this "fact." Daniele's initial fear of the monsters crystallized even more adversely when she was unable to convince anyone of their reality to her.

During the first session, I inquired about the monsters and learned what they looked like, if they made noise, if they made physical contact with the little girl, and so forth. Daniele became animated and excited as she responded to questions which acknowledged the reality of her world. Her mother appeared perplexed while Daniele and I interacted. She called me aside to tell me that she was irritated by my supporting Daniele's belief in monsters when she had spent painstaking years trying to dismiss such ideas in her child. I told the mother that before she could direct Daniele toward her way of thinking, she first needed to enter Daniele's reality, acknowledge her fears, and *then* lead her to other choices. I suggested that she herself just pretend she was an eight-year-old child terrified by monsters, and that she might learn something important as I continued working with Daniele. In the remaining time a metaphor was created which reframed Daniele's monsters and allowed her to create solutions that deflated her fears.

Daniele shook her head, "No" when I asked if she had ever heard the "Untold Story of the Monsters and the Cupcake." Looking at her mother, I asked, "And you?" I received a shrug of her shoulders and a reply, "No."

Daniele was then told how monsters were really make-believe disguises for unhappy children who had no friends. Originally, these unhappy children, now disguised as monsters, tried to make friends in many ways, but the other children ignored them. Nobody would ever pay them the attention they truly wanted. The children became so sad that they just went off by themselves and felt bad. Then one day they finally figured out that they needed to create lots of attention in order to get the other children to like them. So they dressed up in a strange, strange fashion and behaved in a strange, strange way. They returned to the other children expecting to be greeted as friends. Instead the other children ran away scared and frightened, thinking that they had just seen monsters!

Now the unhappy children in the monster costumes were very confused and even frightened themselves. Since Daniele had seen the movie *ET*, she was asked at this time to remember how frightened Elliott and ET were when they first met in Elliott's backyard, and how Elliott had given ET a gift to become friends. "Reeses Pieces!" proudly interjected Daniele. "Yes, that's right," the therapist acknowledged enthusiastically. "Now, Daniele, I would like you to go home and give your monsters a gift that will change them into being friendly."

It was about this time that Daniele excused herself to go to the bathroom. Her mother looked at me with a smile on her face and commented, "You know, I could visualize everything you were saying and it made sense in some sort of crazy way. I had forgotten how I used to listen to stories on the radio when I was young and how I would imagine all sorts of exciting things. Thanks for reminding me."

The next week her mother reported that Daniele had made a cupcake especially for the monsters and had put it in front of the bedroom closet door where the monsters "lived." With one night's exception, Daniele slept soundly all that week.

During the course of the next three weeks, Daniele occasionally regressed into her fears before going to bed at night. It was her mother who then reminded Daniele about the cupcake, Elliott and ET, and Reeses Pieces. To her delight, Daniele's mother found herself becoming a storyteller lulling her daughter into sleep.

JUNG AND THE CHILD WITHIN

In his autobiographical work, *Memories, Dreams & Reflections*, Jung beautifully recalls his unexpected encounter with his own child within and the oddly enduring impact it had on his life. The chapter entitled "Confrontation with the Unconscious" describes a series of dreams which had left Jung feeling disoriented and "under constant inner pressure." So intense was his emotional disquiet that he suspected he had a "psychic disturbance." In the hope of finding the root cause of the problem, he began to search through his childhood memories. The search, however, led him only to an acknowledgment of his own ignorance and to a resolve to "simply do whatever occurs to me." The result was an activation of a vivid and moving image which became a memorable turning point in his life:

> The first thing that came to the surface was a childhood memory from perhaps my tenth or eleventh year. At that time I had had a spell of playing passionately with building blocks. I distinctly recalled how I built little houses and castles, using bottles to form the sides of gates and vaults. Somewhat later I had used ordinary stones, with mud for mortar. These structures had fascinated me for a long time. To my astonishment, this memory was accompanied by a good deal of emotion. "Aha," I said to myself, "there is still life in these things. The small boy is still around, and possesses a creative life which I lack. But how can I make my way to it?" For as a grown man it seemed impossible to me that I should be able to bridge the distance from the present back to my eleventh year. Yet if I wanted to reestablish contact with that period, I had no choice but to return to it and take up once more that child's life with his childish games. This moment was a turning point in my fate, but I gave in only after endless resistance and with a sense of resignation. For it was a painfully humiliating experience to realize that there was nothing to be done except play childish games.[2] [See also G. Frantz and C. G. Jung in this volume.]

Jung indeed "gave in" and began collecting the stones and materials needed to sculpt and build his creation—an entire village complete with castle and church. He worked on his "building game" without fail every day after lunch, and then again in the evenings after his last session. Although he continued to question what he was doing and why he was doing it, he also simply trusted the yearning and proceeded on a vague inner sense of value:

> In the course of this activity my thought clarified, and I was able to grasp the fantasies whose presence in myself I dimly felt. Naturally, I thought about the significance of what I was doing, and asked myself, "Now, really, what are you about? You are building a small town, and doing it as if it were a rite!" *I had no answer to my question, only the inner certainty that I was on the way to discovering my own myth. For the building game was only a beginning.*³ [Italics added]

Jung's contact with his own inner child played a crucial part in releasing the extraordinary creative energies that culminated in his theory of the archetypes and the collective unconscious.

Jung described many different archetypal figures—mother, father, child, hero, villain, temptress, trickster, and so forth. Pertinent to this chapter is his lucid discussion of the unique importance of the child archetype—the child within—in a chapter entitled, "The Psychology of the Child Archetype."⁴ For Jung the child archetype was a living symbol of future potentialities that brings balance, unity, and vitality to the conscious personality. Through the inner child, opposite qualities within the personality are synthesized and new possibilities are freed:

> The child-motif represents not only something that existed in the distant past but also something that exists now; that is to say, it is not just a vestige but a system functioning in the present. . . . The "child" paves the way for a future change of personality. In the individuation process, it anticipates the figure that comes from the synthesis of conscious and unconscious elements in the personality. It is therefore a *unifying symbol* which unites the opposites.⁵

In another chapter entitled "The Special Phenomenology of the Child Archetype," Jung states even more strongly:

> It [the child-motif] is a personification of vital forces quite outside the limited range of our conscious mind; of ways and possibilities of which our one-sided conscious mind knows nothing. . . . It represents the strongest most ineluctable urge in every being, namely the urge to realize itself.⁶

For Jung the child archetype was far more than a concept or a theory. It was a living force that helped to guide and sustain his adult personality. Indeed, he continued to draw upon his special contact with the inner child as builder at difficult times throughout his personal and professional life.

ERICKSON AND THE CHILD WITHIN

Milton Erickson also had a natural respect for childhood qualities, probably borne out of the mischievous and playful characteristics of his own adult personality. One delightful story well illustrates his willingness (albeit un-conscious) to contact his inner child in order to help him solve an "adult" problem:

> There was a chapter that I just couldn't write for a certain paper. I couldn't figure out how to portray the illogic of one of my patients. I went into a trance wondering if I'd work on that case or another case, and I found out later that I had spent the time reading a whole bunch of comic books. I had used up the entire time reading a bunch of comic books.
>
> The next opportunity I got to work on the paper, I was perfectly content to do it in a waking state. I came to the difficult section I hadn't been able to portray, and, that's right, Huey, Dewey, Louie, and Donald Duck paraphrased that very situation, that particular type of logic! My unconscious mind had sent me to the box of comic books and had me search through them until I had found the exact paraphrasing that I had wanted to use.[7]

Erickson tells yet another charming story that again demonstrates his connection to his own child within. A two-year-old child was waiting with her mother in an airport. Erickson was also waiting for a flight, and to occupy time he engaged in his favorite pastime of observing human be-havior. The little girl was restless and the mother was tired. The child spotted a toy in a nearby counter and quickly glanced back at the mother, who was absorbed in reading a newspaper. Methodically and repetitiously the child interrupted the mother by jumping up and down and racing about. Finally, the exasperated mother got up to give the child some exercise, and, of course, the child led the mother straight to the toy counter. Without uttering a single verbal request, the child had managed to get exactly what she wanted. Erickson provides an appreciative summary which reflects his perception and respect of the world as viewed through the eyes of a child:

> And so that two-year-old, with all the wisdom of its infancy uncomplicated by the false learnings that society and convention force upon us, reacted to its own understanding: "I want that toy; Mother often says no; maybe the best thing to do is to annoy her and give her a chance to quiet me down." I don't think the child thought all that out very clearly, but I watched the entire episode wondering just exactly how that child was going to get the toy. I thought—but then I'm an adult—that the child would simply take the mother and lead her right over. But the child was a lot brighter than I was—she knew the right technique![8]

We as therapists can learn from the personal experiences of both Jung and Erickson who, in their individual ways, sustained a nourishing and creatively rejuvenating contact with their own child within.

26 · LIBERATING
YOUR LOST
INNER CHILD

. . . .

JOHN BRADSHAW

Counselor and workshop leader John Bradshaw's ability to synthesize ideas into a truly usable form is impressive. Many people have experienced this quality in his highly acclaimed showcase presentations on the family for PBS television. This piece, a chapter from his book Healing the Shame That Binds You, *represents Bradshaw's current thinking on the inner child. The child within concept is a theme that has surfaced in his work from a variety of sources, but the 12-step alcoholism recovery movement remains his primary model and metaphor for healing and growth. His "lost inner child meditation," included here, is of special interest.*

> Probably I, too, would have remained trapped by this compulsion to protect the parents . . . had I not come in contact with the CHILD IN ME, who appeared late in my life, wanting to tell me her secret . . . filled with an adult's fear of the darkness. . . . But I could not close the door and leave the child alone until my death. . . . I made a decision that was to change my life profoundly . . . to put my trust in this nearly autistic being who had survived the isolation of decades.
>
> —ALICE MILLER, "Pictures of Childhood"

Bradshaw On: The Family describes three distinct phases of my own shame reduction and externalization process. The figure on page 226 gives you a visual picture of these phases.

The first phase is the recovery phase. Through the group's support and mirroring love, I recovered my own sense of worth. I risked coming out of hiding and showing my shame-based self. As I saw myself reflected in the non-shaming eyes of others, I felt good about myself. I reconnected with myself. I was no longer completely alone and beside myself. The group and significant others restored my sense of having an interpersonal bond.

The recovery process is a first-order change. What that means is that I changed one kind of behavior for another kind of behavior. I quit drinking and isolating. I shared my experiences, strength and hope. I started talking and sharing my feelings. I started to feel my feelings again. I shifted my dependency to the new family I had discovered. There was still a dependent and shame-based child in me who made the new group into my parents' safeguarding security.

My shame was reduced but still active. This was evidenced by the fact that I was still compulsive and having trouble with intimacy. I chose women who I felt needed me, confusing love with pity. I set up rescuing-type relationships where others became dependent upon me and saw me as all-powerful. I started working 12-hour days, including Saturday. I smoked more and started eating lots of sugar. Indeed I had stopped a life-threatening disease called alcoholism; I had reduced my shame; I felt better about myself, but I was still compulsive and driven. I was not yet free.

In order to get free I had to do my family-of-origin work. I still needed to grow up and truly leave home.

Fritz Perls once said, "The goal of life is to move from environmental support to self-support." The goal of life is to achieve undependence. Undependence is grounded in a healthy sense of shame. We are responsible for our own lives.

Our source relationships were bathed in poor modeling and abandonment. This created our shame-based identity. Because we had no authentic self, we clung to our caregivers in a fantasy bond or built walls around us where no one could hurt us. These earliest imprints colored all our subsequent relationships.

I once heard Werner Erhard, the founder of *est*, say, "Until we resolve our source relationships, we are never really in another relationship." Leaving home means breaking our source relationships. And since we carry much of our shame as a result of those relationships, leaving home is a powerful way of reducing shame.

LEAVING HOME

What does leaving home involve? How do we do it?

Leaving home is the second phase of the journey to wholeness. I call it the Uncovery Phase. What it involves is making contact with the hurt and lonely inner child who was abandoned long ago. This child is that part of us that houses our blocked emotional energy. This energy is especially

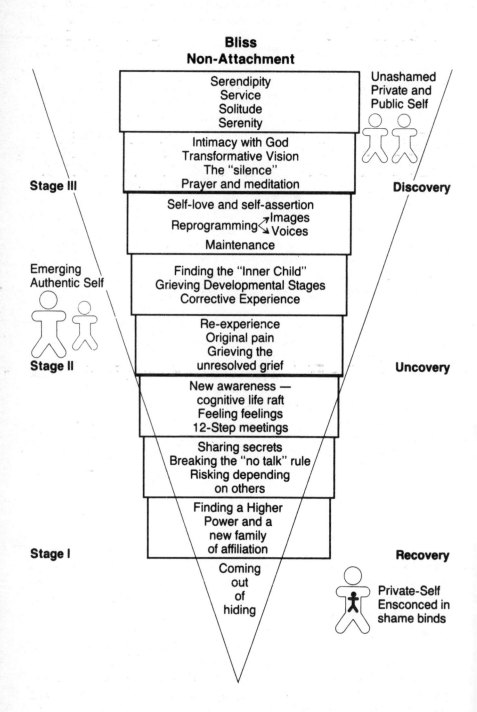

Bliss
Non-Attachment

Serendipity
Service
Solitude
Serenity

Unashamed
Private and
Public Self

Intimacy with God
Transformative Vision
The "silence"
Prayer and meditation

Stage III

Discovery

Self-love and self-assertion
Reprogramming ↗ Images
↘ Voices
Maintenance

Emerging
Authentic Self

Finding the "Inner Child"
Grieving Developmental Stages
Corrective Experience

Re-experience
Original pain
Grieving the
unresolved grief

Stage II

Uncovery

New awareness —
cognitive life raft
Feeling feelings
12-Step meetings

Sharing secrets
Breaking the "no talk" rule
Risking depending
on others

Finding a Higher
Power and a
new family
of affiliation

Stage I

Recovery

Coming
out
of
hiding

Private-Self
Ensconced in
shame binds

blocked when we have experienced severe abuse. In order to reconnect with the wounded and hurt child, we have to go back and re-experience the emotions that were blocked.

When we form emotional energy blocks, they seriously affect our ability to think and reason. Our mind is narrowed in its range of vision. We are contaminated in our judgement, perception and ability to reason about the concrete personal events in our life. (Such emotional blockage does not seem to impair abstract or speculative modes of thought.)

Once our practical judgement is shut down, the will, which is the executor of our personality, loses its ability to see alternatives, and is no longer grounded in reality. The emotionally shut-down person literally is filled with will, i.e., becomes will-full. Willfulness is characterized by grandiosity and unbridled attempts to control, and is the ultimate disaster caused by toxic shame. Willfulness is playing God; it's the self-will riot referred to in the 12-Step programs.

The only way to get our brains out of hock and cure our compulsivity is to go back and re-experience the emotions. The blocked emotions must be re-experienced as they first occurred. The unmet and unresolved dependency needs must be re-educated with new lessons and corrective experiences.

Our lost childhood must be grieved. Our compulsivities are the result of those old blocked feelings (our unresolved grief) being acted out over and over again. We either work these feelings out by re-experiencing them, or we act them out in our compulsivities. We can also act them in as in depression or suicide, or project them onto others as in the interpersonal strategies for transferring shame.

We must leave home and become our own person in order to cure our compulsivities. Even though I was in recovery, I had never left home. I had never uncovered the sources and set-up for my toxic shame. I had never done the "original pain" feeling work. I had never dealt with my family of origin.

ORIGINAL PAIN-FEELING WORK

Any shame-based person has been in a family of trauma. Children of trauma experience too much stimulus within a short period of time to be able to adequately master that stimulus. All the forms of the abandonment trauma stimulate grief emotions in children and then simultaneously block their release.

I watched a man and his young daughter in the airport recently. I was getting a haircut and he was sitting two chairs down. He constantly scolded the child, and at one point angrily told her that she was a lot of trouble, just like her mother. I assumed he was separated or divorced. As he walked out, he slapped her a couple of times. It was really painful to watch. As the child cried, he slapped her again. Then he dragged her into the ice cream parlor and bought her ice cream to shut her up. This child is learning at a very early age that she's not wanted, that it's all her fault, that she's not a person, that her feelings don't count and that she's responsible for other people's feelings. I can't imagine where she could find an ally who would sit down with her and validate her sadness and allow her to grieve.

In a healthy respectful family a child's feelings are validated. Trauma is bound to happen somewhere along the way in any normal childhood.

As Alice Miller has repeatedly written, "It is not the traumas we suffer in childhood which make us emotionally ill but the inability to express the trauma."

When a child is abandoned through neglect, abuse or enmeshment, there is outrage over the hurt and pain. Children need their pain validated. They need to be shown how to discharge their feelings. They need time to do the discharge work and they need support. Each abandoned child would not become shame-based if there was a nourishing ally who could validate his pain and give him time to resolve it by doing his grief work.

I think of a healthy family I know in which the father was severely injured in a home accident. The six-year-old son was playing outside when he heard an explosion. He was shocked to find his father bleeding and apparently crippled. The father directed him to call an ambulance. A neighbor kept him until his mother returned from work. The boy was in a state of shock. The mother took him to a child play-therapist. He was afraid to go into the basement of the house (where the heater was). He was angry with his mother for not being home and his father for going away (being taken to the hospital).

Over the next months the boy worked his feelings out in the context of symbiotic play. His mom and his dad were both happy that he was able to express his anger toward them. (Shame-based parents would have guilted him for expressing anger.) They gave him support as he worked through his fears of going into the basement where the new heater was. They shared their own feelings with the child.

VALIDATION

In order for grief to be resolved several factors must be present. The first factor is validation. Our childhood abandonment trauma must be validated as real or it cannot be resolved. Perhaps the most damaging consequence of being shame based is that *we don't know how depressed and angry we really are*. We don't *actually feel* our unresolved grief. Our false self and ego defenses keep us from experiencing it. Paradoxically, the very defenses which allowed us to survive our childhood trauma have now become barriers to our growth. Fritz Perls once said, "Nothing changes 'til it becomes what it is." We must uncover our frozen grief.

I remember my paternal grandmother ridiculing me because I was in hysterics over my dad going out to get drunk. He had just had a fight with my mom and left the house in anger, vowing to get drunk. I began to cry and was soon out of control. I was told that I was a "big sissy" and to get hold of myself. I've never forgotten this experience. Years later I still carried the unresolved grief.

SUPPORT

The greatest tragedy of all this is that we know grief can naturally be healed if we have support. Jane Middleton-Moz has said, "One of the things we know about grief resolution is that grief is one of the only problems in the world that will heal itself with support." (For a clear and concise discussion of unresolved grief read *After the Tears* by Jane Middleton-Moz and Lorie Dwinell.)

The reason people go into delayed grief is that there's nobody there to validate and support them. You cannot grieve alone. Millions of us adult children tried it. We went to sleep crying into our pillows or locked in the bathrooms.

Delayed grief is the core of what is called the post-traumatic stress syndrome. As soldiers come back from the war, they have common symptoms of unreality: panic, being numbed-out psychically, easily startled, depersonalization, needing to control, nightmares and sleeping disorders. These same symptoms are common for children from dysfunctional families. They are the symptoms of unresolved grief.

"GRIEF WORK" FEELINGS

After validation and support one needs to experience the feelings that were not allowed. This must be done in a safe non-shaming context. The feelings involved in "grief work" are anger, remorse, hurt, depression, sadness and loneliness. Grief resolution is a kind of "psychic work" that has to be done. It varies in duration depending upon the intensity of the trauma. One needs enough time to finish this work. In dysfunctional families, there is never enough time.

At our Center for Recovering Families in Houston we do four-and-one-half-day "original pain" workshops. We use the family system roles as a way for people to see how they lost their authentic selves and got stuck in a false self. As a person experiences how he got soul murdered, he begins his grieving. Often the therapy facilitator has to help him embrace the feelings because they are bound in shame. As a person connects with his true and authentic feelings, the shame is reduced. This work continues after the workshop. It may go on for a couple of years.

There are many other methods for doing this original pain work. It must be done if the grief is to be resolved and the re-enactments and compulsive lifestyle stopped.

CORRECTIVE EXPERIENCE

The unresolved grief work is a re-experiencing process, liberating and integrating your lost inner child. Since the neglect of our developmental dependency needs was a major source of toxic shame, it is important to reconnect. Each developmental stage was unique with its own special needs and dynamics. In infancy we needed a mirror of unconditional love. We needed to hear words (nonverbal to an infant) like "I'm so glad you're here. Welcome to the world. Welcome to our family and home. I'm so glad you're a boy or girl. I want to be near you, to hold you and love you. Your needs are okay with me. I'll give you all the time you need to get your needs met." These affirmations are adapted from Pam Levin's book *Cycles of Power*.

I like to set up small groups (six to eight people) and let one person sit in the center of the group. The person in the center directs the rest of the group as to how close he wants them to be. Some people want to be cradled and held. Some want only touching. Some who were stroke-deprived don't feel safe enough for such closeness. Each person sets his own boundary.

After the group is set, we play lullaby music and each person in the group communicates one of the verbal affirmations while touching, stroking or just sitting near the subject.

Those who have been neglected will start sobbing when they hear the words they needed to hear, but did not hear. If a person was a Lost Child, he will often sob intensely. These words touch the hole in his soul.

After the affirmation the group discusses their experience. I always try to have a mixed group so that a person hears male and female voices. Often a person will report that he especially loved hearing the male voice or the female voice, since he never heard it as a child. Sometimes if a person has been abused by a parent, he will not trust the voice that corresponds to that parent's sex. The group sharing, hearing the affirmations, being touched and supported, offers a corrective kind of experience.

I also suggest other ways people might get their infancy needs met as those needs are recycled in new experiences. They usually need a friend who will give them physical support (lots of touching), and who will feed them (take them out to eat). They need lots of skin satisfaction. They may need a nice warm bath, or wrap up in a blanket. They may want to try a body massage.

We go on to toddler needs, repeating the group process. Since the toddler needs to separate, we let the person sit near but separate from everyone. I usually do an age-regression type meditation, in which I ask the one in the middle to experience himself as a toddler. I give affirmations like, "It's okay to wander and explore. It's okay to test your limits. It's okay for you to do it and to do it your way. I'll be here. You don't have to hurry. I'll give you all the time you need. It's okay to practice holding on and letting go. I won't leave you."

Again the group shares after each person has heard these affirmations several times. Frequently people express deep emotions as they share. Often they remember an episode of abandonment that was long forgotten. Some get into more unresolved grief work.

We go through all the developmental stages through adolescence. Adolescence is important because many people went through painful abandonment and shaming incidents during adolescence. . . .

I usually ask each person to write a letter to his parent(s) telling them the things he needed that he didn't get.

Wayne Kritsberg has them write the letter with the non-dominant hand. Writing with the non-dominant hand helps create the feeling of being a child. Great emotion is discharged as the person reads his letter to the group. After the letter is read, I ask the group to give the person the affirmations that correspond to the unmet needs that he described in his letter to his parents.

Toward the close of the workshop I have each participant encounter his Lost Child. I cannot describe the power of this exercise. I have put it on several of my cassette tapes. There's no way to convey its power through the written word. I'll outline the meditation. You can put it on a tape recorder and listen to it. I recommend using Daniel Kobialka's "Going Home" as background music.

MEDITATION: EMBRACING YOUR LOST INNER CHILD

Sit in an upright position. Relax and focus your breathing . . . Spend a few minutes becoming mindful of breathing . . . Be aware of the air as you breathe it in and as you breathe it out . . . Notice the difference in the air as it comes in and as it goes out. Focus on that difference . . . (one minute). Now imagine that you're walking down a long flight of stairs. Walk down slowly as I count down from ten. Ten . . . (ten seconds) Nine . . . (ten seconds) Eight . . . (ten seconds), etc. When you reach the bottom of the stairs, turn left and walk down a long corridor with doors on your right and doors on your left. Each door has a colored symbol on it . . . (one minute). As you look toward the end of the corridor there is a force field of light . . . Walk through it and go back through time to a street where you lived before you were seven-years-old. Walk down that street to the house you lived in. Look at the house. Notice the roof, the color of the house and the windows and doors . . . See a small child come out the front door . . . How is the child dressed? What color are the child's shoes? Walk over to the child . . . Tell him that you are from his future . . . Tell him that you know better than anyone what he has been through . . . His suffering, his abandonment . . . his shame . . . Tell him that of all the people he will ever know you are the only one he will never lose. Now ask him if he is willing to go home with you . . . If not, tell him you will visit him tomorrow. If he is willing to go with you, take him by the hand and start walking away . . . As you walk away see your mom and dad come out on the porch. Wave goodbye to them. Look over your shoulder as you continue walking away and see them getting smaller and smaller until they are completely gone . . . Turn the corner and see your Higher Power and your much cherished friends waiting for you. Embrace all your friends and allow your Higher Power to come into your heart . . . Now walk away and promise your child you will meet him for five minutes each day. Pick an exact time. Commit to that time. Hold your child in your hand and let him shrink to the size of your hand. Place him in your heart . . . Now walk to some beautiful outdoor place . . . Stand in the middle of that place and reflect on the experience you just had . . . Get a sense of communion within yourself, with your Higher Power and with all things . . . Now look up in the sky; see the purple white clouds form the number five . . . See the five become a four . . . and be aware of your feet and legs . . . See the four become a three . . . Feel the life in your stomach and in your arms. See the three become a two; feel the life in your hands, your face, your whole body. Know that you are about to become fully awake—able to do all things with your fully awake mind—see the two become a one and be fully awake, remembering the experience. . . .

I encourage you to get an early photo of yourself. Preferably a photo of you before you were seven years old. I suggest you put it in your wallet or purse. Put the picture on your desk so that you can be reminded of this child that lives in you.

Much data supports that the child lives within us in a fully developed stage. This child is the most vital and spontaneous part of us and needs to be integrated into our life.

GETTING CHILD DEVELOPMENTAL NEEDS MET AS AN ADULT

We recycle our developmental needs all through our lives. Each time we start something new we trigger our infancy needs. After we are secure and trust our new environment, our toddler part wants to explore and experiment. Our own children trigger our needs as they go through their various developmental stages. We have an opportunity as an adult to care for us at each of these stages.

As adults we can create a context where we can get our needs met. I was neglected in fathering. I've created a group of men who serve as supporting friends who give me feedback. I've learned that as an adult I can make what I get from others serve my needs. Children never get enough. Adults learn as they mature to make what they get to be enough. So I can take an event of sharing in my group and make fathering out of it. If one of the members is especially nurturing to me, I can allow that to be fathering. I can also let other events in my life serve as fathering and mothering. I can also learn as an adult to get the things I specifically need. I can be good to myself and treat myself with nurturing respect and kindness.

THE UNIVERSAL QUEST FOR
THE INNER CHILD

It is important to note that the need to find the Inner Child is part of every human being's journey toward wholeness. No one had a perfect childhood. Everyone bears the unresolved unconscious issues of his family history.

The Inner Child journey is the hero's journey. Becoming a fully functioning person is a heroic task. There are trials and tribulations along the way. In Greek mythology, Oedipus kills his father, Orestes kills his mother. Leaving one's parents are obstacles one must encounter on the hero's journey. To kill our parents is a symbolic way to describe leaving home and growing up.

To find our Inner Child is the first leap over the abyss of grief that threatens us all. But finding the Inner Child is just the beginning. Because of his isolation, neglect and neediness, this child is egocentric, weak and frightened. He must be disciplined in order to release his *tremendous spiritual power*.

27 · BECOMING
A CHILD

· · · · · · · ·

J O H N   L O U D O N

The idea of becoming like a child as an adult is a paradox that many interpreters have tried to solve: how is it possible, asks John Loudon, to accomplish this most subtle task? Loudon's essay actually does much more than address this question. He gives a philosophical, spiritual, and religious context to the quest, emphasizing the lifelong process of development. "In a sense," he says, "becoming a child—achieving the levels, skills, orientations, and so on that we are called to—may be a task it takes a lifetime to accomplish."

This selection was originally published in the journal Parabola *(Volume IV, number 3), a special issue dedicated to the child. Loudon is a writer and editor in Northern California.*

> Verily, I say unto you, except ye be con-
> verted and become as little children, ye
> shall not enter into the kingdom of heaven.
>
> —MATTHEW 18:3–KJV

> When I was a child, I spake as a child, I
> understood as a child, I thought as a child;
> but when I became a man, I put away
> childish things.
>
> —I CORINTHIANS 13:11–KJV

Religious traditions, especially Christianity, seem to offer conflicting messages about childhood as an ideal state. On the one hand, the Gospels say that unless you change the direction of your life (*metanoia*) and become as a little child you cannot enter the kingdom of heaven. In the more mystical Gospel of John, Jesus says, "Except a man be born again, he cannot see the kingdom of God" (John 3:3-KJV). On the other hand, Jesus regularly rejects the rote passivity of childish religiosity, and Paul admonishes us to put away, as he did, the things of childhood. More significantly, all of the Gospels and Paul's proclamation are, in effect, stories climaxing with Jesus's passion, death, and resurrection and declaring that only by losing your life will you find it. What is this ideal that is something like childhood yet comes only with reaching maturity, with a dying to self and being born to a new life?

Obviously, two different views of childhood are involved here. For me, the paradox they represent seems another of those rich seeming-conflicts with which living traditions are rife and which invite deeper probing, a quest for understanding.

One line of resolution—the one most Christian exegetes and theologians tend to take—would be to study the seemingly contradictory passages with painstaking analysis (examining the language, the context, the function, the date, etc., of the passages) and to come up with a synthetic interpretation. Doubtless some such studies have been conducted already. But I am hesitant to remove the sting of contradiction too readily. There's a sense of challenge here worth taking up, and I sense that it is authentic and somehow central to what the New Testament wants to say.

So I propose a perhaps more fruitful, or at least novel, avenue into the truth at the heart of the paradox. It is to investigate the seeming ideal of childhood in the light of traditional and contemporary understandings of the stages of life. How does the demand to become like a child relate to traditional stages of growth and to the burgeoning research into the various dimensions and discernible steps in human development? Is the biblical injunction anomalous, or a coded saying reflecting early Christian debates, or does it contain accessible insight into human growth and potential, into the laws of our becoming and perfection?

The most universal distinctions between stages of life in traditional societies and religions are surely those exhibited by rites of passage. As an Apache woman forthrightly put it:

> We think of a woman's life as blocked out in parts. One is girlhood, one is young womanhood, one is middle age, and one is old age. The songs are supposed to carry her through them. The first songs describe the holy home and the ceremony. Later come the songs about the flowers and the growing things. These stand for her youth, and as the songs go through the seasons the girl is growing up and reaching old age.

There are rites for pregnancy, birth, childhood, initiation into adulthood, betrothal and marriage, initiation into priesthood, and for death as the final passage. What is particularly noteworthy about the stages these rites identify is that they are connected with growth, development. They are cumulative, with each transition adding a dimension or level to one's life. Thus, for instance, the initiations into adulthood generally involve the acquisition of special knowledge with a concomitant disillusionment from childish beliefs and a new burden of responsibility. In some traditions, these stages of life have been discriminated into distinct religious ideals, each with their attractions, perils, and responsibilities. In Hinduism, for instance, there are the four stages (*ashramas*) on the way of knowledge: student, householder (family, career), forest dweller (recluse, ascetic) and wanderer (holy man, *sannyasin*). While a relative perfection is attainable in each state, the clear teaching is that full development, full attainment of *moksha* (release from finitude) comes only with completion of the cycle. And in general the traditional divisions of the stages of life forcefully suggest that childhood is a stage that obviously must be passed beyond to reach full knowledge, life, being. Still—and this observation begins to adumbrate something of the answer to the posed dilemma—there are aspects of the final stage (simplicity, a certain dependency, contemplation, etc.) that in some ways bring the life full circle back to the world of childhood.

The psychology of human development is very much an independent, twentieth-century science, basing its conclusions on empirical evidence. Jean Piaget, the Swiss psychologist, pioneered developmental studies with his painstaking observations of children's intellectual and moral development and ingenious tests to determine stages of growth. He identifies four basic stages of child development up to age twelve, and each involves an expansion of the initial infantile worlds of self-centered feeling-action response into a wider world via language, socialization, thinking. Erik Erikson built on Piaget's foundational work (and Freud's) to identify eight stages through the whole of human life: four stages from infancy to adolescence, and then adolescence, early adulthood, middle age, and maturity. At each stage, we are faced with a new hope, new potentialities, and a new responsibility, and the basic success or failure with which each challenge is met affects the fulness of our development throughout life.

Thus, for instance, at the stage of infancy (roughly the first year of life), a fundamental sense of trust or mistrust is established and it pervades the rest of life. Hence, the "task" of infancy is for the child to develop a root sense of well-being and of being accepted, belonging, being at home in the universe. Subsequent tasks are the "achievement" of autonomy, initiative, industry, identity, intimacy, generativity (productivity in a quite broad sense), and integrity (a sense of satisfaction for a life whose parts add up to a well-lived whole). Failure in these psychosocial "accomplishments" produces a comparable devolution of human potentiality. Thus, for instance, if in middle age one doesn't achieve the "self-actualization" that the dynamism of human development calls for, one tends to "stagnation"—as Erikson puts it—marked by a retreat to childish indulgences and an arrested development of personality and personal relations.

Needless to say, the work of Piaget and Erikson is often technical and quite complex, and it has been integrated into a vast ongoing program of research and theorizing. What is most significant for present purposes is to know that fairly clear developmental stages in life can be scientifically determined and that these stages are not just an automatic sequence lived out by simply growing older. Rather there is a dynamism to the development—both inner drive and external demands—that propels us from stage to stage, while each stage involves fundamental tasks to be accomplished and dimensions of our humanity to be discovered and integrated in order for us to become whole persons. There is a sense then in which the self is a lifelong project, as long as we remember that it is a project that requires as much passivity as activity (to use Teilhard's terms)—both receptivity and taking hold, yin and yang.

Since our concern is with childhood as a kind of religious ideal, another aspect of developmental psychology deserves exploration: viz., the analysis of stages of moral and religious development. In the late fifties, Robert Havighurst and Robert Peck identified five character types through which people might develop: the amoral in infancy; the expedient in early childhood; the conforming (following an external norm) and the irrational-conscientious (following one's own internal norm) in later childhood; and the rational-altruistic (objective decision-making), of which adolescents are capable (though the capacity is rarely actualized). They discovered that adolescents and adults could be at any of the stages, although many remain in the second type.

Then in the last two decades Lawrence Kohlberg has devised tests for discerning six stages of sequentially related moral stances. In moral development, he finds that there are preconventional, conventional, and postconventional levels (adopting John Dewey's distinctions) of two stages each. Younger children (up to grade six) are mostly on the first level of trying to keep the rules that authority figures set: in stage one (ages six and seven), rules are obeyed in order to escape punishment; in stage two (eight and nine), the right course is identified with satisfying personal needs, such as acceptance, rewards, etc. Older children may advance to the second level: in stage three—the good-boy/nice girl orientation—one acts in ways that win approval from the group; at stage four—the law-and-order orientation—acting rightly means obeying the law, respecting authority, maintaining the social order. The third level involves autonomy and principle, and can be attained only when one has the capacity to make reasoned decisions (i.e., with the dawn of abstract thinking in adolescence); stage five is a social contract orientation, with principles of behavior gauged according to their contribution to the highest good (which could be contrary to the prevailing conventions of law and order); stage six requires moral judgements on the basis of universal (and universalizable) moral principles, and—according to Kohlberg—is rarely achieved. It is important to note that progress in moral development is dependent on psychological and intellectual development.

On the religious side, Lewis Sherrill early on (in *The Struggle of the Soul*, 1951) drew out the parallels between religious development and Erikson's stages of psychosocial development. He argued that the various critical junctures in life there was a struggle between reversion to an earlier simpler level of faith and commitment and the challenge to a higher phase of maturity. Such turning points occur on entering childhood from infancy, the coming of adulthood, and then middle age and old age.

More recently, James Fowler has developed tests and analyses based

on Kohlberg's work in order to differentiate six stages of faith development:
1. infant/undifferentiated faith—caught up in feeling and a sense of magic;
2. mythic/literal faith—dependence on the religious explanations of authority figures; 3. synthetic/conventional faith—sharing the meanings and values of the home, school, church, peers; 4. individuating/reflexive faith —deciding the meaning(s) of life for oneself; 5. polar/dialectic faith—a personal reappropriation of one's own tradition; 6. fully integrated faith— a stance that is at once completely personal and universal. For Fowler, as for other developmentalists, it is possible for one to stop at any stage or to revert to earlier stages. Thus, the achieving of mature faith is not so much a matter of finding the right things to believe as it is what John Dunne calls a "spiritual adventure," an odyssey of discovery with more ports of call than conventional faith. Development—psychological, moral, religious, even physiological—involves continuing demands, key break-throughs to new levels, and "our conversions," our *metanoias* at each stage are fragile attainments.

It is time to return to our original question. In what sense are we called to become like a child and yet put away the things of childhood? It seems from our quick survey of traditional and modern views of human development that childhood itself entails various stages and these form the foundation for subsequent stages all the way to death. Childhood is a period of life in which basic achievements must be made in order to allow full human development. And it seems clear that the struggles of growth in childhood continue through life; in a sense, becoming a child—achieving the levels, skills, orientations, and so on that we are called to—may be a task it takes a lifetime to accomplish.

But there is, I think, a richer way to grasp the paradox in developmental perspective. The various stages alluded to above can, as the Apache quotation suggests, be boiled down to the common ones of childhood, adolescence, adulthood, and maturity. In this scheme, as in the more elaborate analyses, each stage is double-edged: full of promise and peril, hope and despair. Childhood, both popularly and psychologically, represents a kind of ideal: at root, it seems to be the pure, and hence uncorrupted, potential of the young child that is so attractive. Seemingly without burdening responsibilities and compromising demands, the child appears to possess a wholeness, a simplicity, a spontaneity, an integrity that all our adult striving cannot seem to attain (or recover). The child has the glory of simply being, like a flower or an animal, without the necessity of doing anything, becoming anything in order to be fully what it is. This kind of idealization of childhood has been especially prominent in the West, particularly since the Renaissance and then the Romantics. It represents innocence, wonder, receptivity, freshness, noncalculation, the lack of narrow ambitions and purposes. At times the child seems peculiarly capable of living out the Hindu ideal of "acting without seeking the fruits of action" or the *wu-wei* ("non-action") of living with Tao.

However, appearances deceive, and much of our idealization of childhood involves adult projections of our own hopes and fears. For childhood, as Piaget and others show, is a time of intense and vital development—of becoming and doing, and not just being—and to the extent that its tasks remain unaccomplished the child's life becomes more and more problematic. For the young child lives in a world of immediacy (the real, the important is what is tasted, touched, seen, etc.), is dependent for meanings and values on others, is constitutionally self-centered, and lives in worlds of fantasy and magic that can relate little to how things actually happen. Thus child-hood religiosity—as Gordon Allport observed—is very dependent, full of magical beliefs and uncontrolled fantasy, and if carried into adult life (as it often is), it retards other aspects of development and is one of the things that gives religion, myth, contemplation, etc., a bad name.

In later childhood, one is socialized into conventional values and mean-ings. While this is necessary for an adequate sense of self-worth and basic orientation and for social order, all too many of us can become arrested at this stage of development and lead what Paul Tillich calls "heteronomous" lives, in which something external sets our priorities, establishes what is meaningful and worthwhile.

Thus, the dawning of adolescence is both liberating and daunting. The onset of doubts, distinctions, questioning, complications, anxieties (sex, death), responsibilities of learning and work, rebellions and reconciliations, sufferings, opens the path to autonomy and self-determination. It is vital to the choice of one's own meanings and values and the discovery of one's own identity. But the dangers are many, and we can be swept up by the strong tides that begin to ebb and flow. In many areas of our life, we tend to remain adolescents: our questioning can degenerate into a kind of func-tional nihilism, our challenges of authority rebellions without cause, our self-discovery an ego trip. It is all too easy to give up on the work of development, to either shun or become trapped in our "dark nights," and to retreat again and again—when crises come—to the hedonism, the ego-centricity, the simple-mindedness of childishness.

But if we give ourselves to the process of growth, if we take up the search for wholeness, the quest for understanding (rather than the vain longing for certainty), we are set on a path that leads not back to the childhood we may nostalgically idealize but forward toward an authentic fullness and integration. Without undertaking the quest, we remain children; without committing ourselves to real growth, we can remain prodigal sons who never come home. And so there are the challenges of adulthood, in which our youthful drives and needs are to be met in achieving intimacy, personal identity, creativity. And it is not that we simply grow up persons who love, have convictions and a sense of being and worth, make contri-butions to the world's store of meaning, beauty, value, life; it is rather that as we struggle with the "tasks" of adulthood we "make" ourselves. To the degree we retreat from the demands, the sacrifices, the stretching, to that degree we are less ourselves, and, instead, narrow selves, "hollow men," empty symbols. As Tillich said, there is a courage to being.

However, it is also possible to get caught up in the tasks of house-holding and to make of life nothing more than sets of conventional obligations, to endure the struggle without being transformed. It can easily seem that it is the tangible fruits of action that count, and one measures one's life by its external results (whereas, in the end, what seems to matter is what sort of self one is becoming in the course of all one's activities). This attitude too is a kind of reversion to the simple pain-pleasure principles and conventional behavior of childhood. It seems that in mid-life one needs somehow to maintain the potential ideals of childhood and the drives of adolescence.

Maturity, then, is an achievement of synthesis. It is not simply a chronological stage of life. As synthesis, it represents a kind of second childhood—a wholeness, a certain perfection and completeness, a joy in being —but an "achieved" childhood, in which initial ideals, even dreams, have been integrated into real living. One is full of wonder without being naive, reverent without being a dupe, humble without being a milquetoast. It involves a centeredness, an integrity, a wisdom, a compassion that come only from traveling the full route, the *via crucis* of the crises (as Erikson calls them) on life's way. There is objectivity, real knowing: it is the real mysteries one marvels at, the real graciousness at the heart of being that one trusts in.

This final stage of integration is one known to the great traditions of spirituality and philosophy. It is that of the elders of the tribe, the Russian *staretz* who culminates a long life of acquiring the spirit by becoming a spiritual guide, the true Master and guru, the genuine thinker who knows his field not only in its particulars but in its essences, the mature believer who has experienced the consolations and endured the dark nights to come out with tempered faith, the critic who can respond to literature with informed delight, "educated imagination" (Northrop Frye), the seeker who has found the path with heart and has learned how to will one thing. And the virtues of the child one is challenged to become turn out to be—and this seems to me Jesus's answer to our question—those of the beatitudes of the Sermon on the Mount: "Blessed are the poor in spirit, for theirs is the kingdom of heaven" (Matthew 5:3-KJV).

As one searches the literature of mysticism and spiritual guidance and the life stories of those who seem to have become mature selves, the goal seems common: an integration that embraces the fullness of human potentiality that is at the same time uncomplicated, wise, joyful, and even playful. One thinks of Gandhi, Merton, Einstein, John XXIII. Or someone closer to us in capacities and circumstances, like Dag Hammarskjold, whose *Markings* reveals a remarkable sensitivity to the rigors and rewards of full human development. He knew that "The longest journey / is the journey inwards," and experience something of the journey's final stage:

> There is a point at which everything becomes simple and there is no longer any question of choice, because all you have staked will be lost if you look back.

Maturity: among other things, the unclouded happiness of the child at play, who takes it for granted that he is at one with his playmates.

And the achieving of maturity should not be taken as journey's end. Rather it is a new beginning, in a sense *the* beginning, and it first dawns once we set forth on the quest and are determined to live it out. As John Dunne says in *The Reasons of the Heart*: "To enter upon the spiritual adventure is . . . to be 'born anew', to be 'born of the Spirit.' " And in the same book:

> The individual emerges in a life . . . whenever the deep aloneness . . . that is not ordinarily touched in love and work and communal life, becomes so intense that it begins to undermine ordinary human intercourse and makes it seem unsatisfactory, when it seems no longer possible to find fulfillment in love and work and communal life. When that happens, the spiritual adventure . . . can begin.

"Old men ought to be explorers," T. S. Eliot tells us, and all the stages on life's way are vital journeys too, on the way to that ultimate vocation—a voyage into the unknown not unlike the newborn child's venture into life.

28 · INTEGRATING
THE YOUNGER
SELF

· · · · · · ·

NATHANIEL BRANDEN

For a practical approach to realizing and reclaiming the inner child, psychologist Nathaniel Branden has packaged his materials very attractively. "We reject that child just as, perhaps, others once did," he says, "and our cruelty to that child can continue daily and indefinitely through our lifetime." As an antidote to this negative possibility, Branden recommends specific action steps such as sentence-completion work. This is hard-core how-to-ism from Branden's How to Raise Your Self-Esteem.

"As a girl, I so desperately wanted my mother to love me," says a thirty-seven-year-old female dentist. "I felt starved for simple touching or any kind of affection. Looking back, I'm appalled at how needy I seem to myself. I suppose that's why I don't like to look back. I don't like knowing that about myself, at least as I was then. Was that really me? I refuse to believe it. I like to think that girl died a long time ago and I'm somebody else."

When her husband leaves her, complaining that she seems incapable of either giving or receiving love, she is devastated and bewildered; she professes not to understand what he means.

"I don't like to remember myself as a young child," echoes a forty-six-year-old male computer programmer. "I was so terrified all the time. My father coming home drunk—hitting whoever came within his reach. Mother never protecting us. Me hiding; looking for places to hide; too scared half the time even to talk. It was sickening; that child was sickening. I don't feel any connection to him."

His children do not understand why Daddy seems incapable of playing with them. They know only that, emotionally, Daddy rarely seems there —as if they have no father.

"Mother was so sarcastic," says a thirty-one-year-old female nurse. "She had a tongue that could kill. When I was a small child, I couldn't handle that. I cried so much. I cringe when I think of myself at age three, four, five."

But any number of her patients have complained about her brusque manner and her occasional biting remarks. She knows she tends to be disliked but is mystified as to why.

"When I was twelve," says a fifty-one-year-old male lawyer, "there was a bully on our block who terrified me. He beat me up a few times, and after that, just seeing him, I would feel reduced to nothing. I don't like to remember that. I don't like to talk about it. In fact, I don't like to admit that a frightened little boy was me. Why couldn't he handle the situation better? I'd just as soon forget about the little bastard."

Although he is brilliant in his work, few of his clients are able to like him. They perceive him as insensitive and cruel. "He's a bully," more than one client has remarked.

There are many reasons why people feel that they cannot forgive the child they once were. Like the clients quoted above, they deny and disown that child. Translated into words, their attitude amounts to the following: I cannot forgive that I was so frightened by my mother; that I so desperately craved my father's approval; that I felt so unlovable; that I so hungered for attention and affection; that I was so confused by things; that I somehow sexually aroused my mother; that I did something, even if I have no idea what, to make my father molest me; that I was so awkward in gym class; that I was so intimidated by my teacher; that I hurt so much; that I wasn't popular at school; that I was timid; that I was shy; that I wasn't tougher; that I was afraid to disobey my parents; that I would do anything to be liked; that I was starved for kindness; that I was angry and hostile; that I was jealous of my younger brother; that I felt everyone understood more than I did; that I didn't know what to do when I was being ridiculed; that I didn't stand up to people; that my clothes were always the poorest and shabbiest of anyone's at school.

In effect, the child we once were can be experienced as a source of pain, rage, fear, embarrassment, or humiliation, to be repressed, disowned, repudiated, forgotten. We *reject* that child just as, perhaps, *others once did*— and our cruelty to that child can continue daily and indefinitely through our lifetime, in the theater of our own psyche where the child continues to exist as a subpersonality, a *child-self*.

Unaware of what we are doing, we may, as adults, profess to find evidence of being rejected everywhere in our current relationships, not realizing that the roots of our experience of rejection are internal rather than external. Our whole lives can be acts of nonstop self-repudiation, while we go on complaining that others do not love us.

When we learn to forgive the child we once were for what he or she didn't know, or couldn't do, or couldn't cope with, or felt or didn't feel; when we understand and accept that that child was struggling to survive the best way he or she could—then the adult-self is no longer in an adversarial relationship to the child-self. One part is not at war with another part. Our adult responses are more appropriate.

The child-self is the internal representation of the child we once were, the constellation of attitude, feelings, values, and perspective that were ours long ago, and that enjoys psychological immortality as a component of our total self. It is a *sub*self, a *sub*personality—a mind state that can be more or less dominant at any given time, and out of which we sometimes operate quite exclusively without necessarily being aware of doing so.

We can (implicitly) relate to our child-self consciously or unconsciously, benevolently or with hostility, compassionately or harshly. As I trust the exercises in this chapter will make clear, when related to consciously and positively a child-self can be assimilated and integrated into the total self. When related to unconsciously and/or negatively, a child-self is left in a kind of alienated oblivion. In the latter case, when the child-self is left unconscious, or is disowned and repudiated, we are fragmented; we do not feel whole; in some measure we feel self-alienated; and self-esteem is wounded.

Left unrecognized, not understood, or rejected and abandoned, a child-self can turn into a "troublemaker" that obstructs our evolution as well as our enjoyment of existence. The external expression of this phenomenon is that we will at times exhibit harmfully childish behavior, or fall into patterns of inappropriate dependency, or become narcissistic, or experience the world as belonging to "the grown-ups."

On the other hand, recognized, accepted, embraced, and thereby integrated, a child-self can be a magnificent resource that enriches our lives, with its potential for spontaneity, playfulness, and imaginativeness.

Before you can befriend and integrate a child-self, so that it exists in harmonious relationship to the rest of you, you must first make contact with that identity within your inner world. By way of introducing clients or students to their child-selves, I sometimes ask them to enter a fantasy, to imagine themselves walking along a country road and, in the distance, to see a small child sitting by a tree and, as they draw near, to see that that child is the self they once were. Then I ask them to sit down by the tree and enter into dialogue with the child. They are encouraged to speak aloud, to deepen the reality of the experience. What do they want and need to say to each other? Not uncommonly there are tears; sometimes there is joy. But there is almost always the realization that in some form the child still exists within the psyche (as a mind state) and has a contribution to make to the life of the adult—and a richer, fuller self emerges from the discovery. Often, there is the sad realization that they had mistakenly thought they needed to rid themselvees of that child in order to grow up.

When working with a client toward the goal of integrating a child-self, I will often suggest this simple exercise that you can easily do yourself. (If you have a friend who can read the following instructions to you, so much the better; or you can read them into a cassette recorder and then play them back; or simply read them until you master them before proceeding.)

Spend a few minutes looking at photographs of yourself as a young child (assuming you have some; otherwise, proceed without them). Then close your eyes and take several deep, relaxing breaths. Go inside and explore these questions: What did it feel like to be five years old? How do you imagine you experienced your body then? . . . What did it feel like to be sad? . . . What did it feel like to be excited? . . . What was it like living in your home? . . . How did you sit? Sit as you *imagine* a five-year-old sits. Pay attention to what you are feeling. Stay with the experience.

If you did nothing else but this one exercise every day for two or three weeks, you would begin to archive not only an enhanced awareness of your child-self, but also a higher level of integrating that you probably experience at present—because you would be taking the first step toward making the child-self *visible* and treating him or her *seriously*.

But sentence-completion work is a more advanced and powerful tool for awakening your awareness of your child-self and facilitating integration. As I've mentioned before, use a notebook, and write each of the incomplete sentences listed below at the top of a fresh page, then write six to ten endings for each, working as rapidly and as unself-critically as you can, *inventing* when need be to keep the momentum going.

When I was five years old . . .

When I was ten years old . . .

If I recall how the world seemed when I was very young . . .

If I recall how my body felt when I was very young . . .

If I recall how people seemed when I was very young . . .

With my friends I felt . . .

When I felt lonely I . . .

When I felt excited I . . .

If I recall how life seemed when I was very young . . .

If the child in me could speak, he/she might say . . .

One of the things I had to do as a child to survive was . . .

One of the ways I treat my child-self as my mother did is . . .

One of the ways I treat my child-self as my father did is . . .

When the child within feels ignored by me . . .

When the child within feels criticized by me . . .

One of the ways that child sometimes gets me into trouble is . . .

I suspect I am operating out of my child-self when I . . .

If that child were to feel accepted by me . . .

Sometimes, the hard thing about fully accepting the child within is . . .

If I were more forgiving of my child-self . . .

I would be kinder to the child within if I were to . . .

If I were to listen to the things that child needs to tell me . . .

If I fully accept that child as a valuable part of me . . .

I am becoming aware . . .

When I look at myself from this perspective . . .

I have had clients do this exercise several times, at intervals of about a month. They were asked not to look at how they ended the stems on previous occasions. Each time they generated some new endings that took them deeper. With no other work in this area they achieved extraordinary insights and integrations that resulted in self-healing and enhanced self-esteems.

I recommend that you experiment with this set of sentence completions and discover what it can accomplish for you. In doing this, it will become more real to you how such work can benefit your self-confidence, self-respect, and sense of wholeness.

Here is a more advanced way to work on the territory opened up in the above sentence stems. Do again the stem *When I was five years old . . .* followed by *One of the things my five-year-old-self needs from me and has never gotten is . . .* followed by *When my five-year-old-self tries to talk to me . . .* followed by *If I were willing to listen to my five-year-old self with acceptance and compassion . . .* followed by *If I refuse to be there for my five-year-old self . . .* followed by *At the thought of reaching back to help my five-year-old-self. . . .* Then do this same set for you six-, seven-, eight-, nine-, ten-, eleven-, and twelve-year-old selves. You will perform a miracle of self-healing.

Finally, when you feel you have established a good sense of your child-self as a psychological entity, which the sentence-completion work should give you, here is one more exercise to facilitate integration that is both simple and extraordinarily powerful.

Using whatever kind of imagery works for you—sight, hearing, kinesthetic feelings—generate the sense of your child-self standing in front of you. Then, without saying a word, imagine holding that child in your arms, embracing and gently stroking, so that you are in a nurturing relationship to him or her. Allow the child to respond or not to respond. Remain gentle and firm. Let the touch of your hands, your arms, and your chest communicate acceptance, compassion, respect.

I recall a client, Charlotte, who initially had difficulty with this exercise because, she said, her child-self was an amalgam of pain, rage and suspiciousness. "She keeps slipping away," Charlotte said. "She doesn't trust me—or anybody." I pointed out that, given little Charlotte's experiences, her response was perfectly natural. Then I went on, "Imagine that I came to you with a little girl and said, 'Here is someone I would like you to take care of. She's had some pretty bad experiences and is very distrustful of people. For one thing, an uncle attempted to molest her, and when she tried to tell her mother, her mother became angry at her. So she feels abandoned and betrayed. (Charlotte had had this experience at the age of six.) Her new home—and her new life—will be with you. You will probably have to help her learn to trust you and to realize that you are different from the other grown-ups she's encountered.' Later, you can talk to her— and listen, and let her tell you all the things she needs an adult to understand. But first, just hold her. Let her feel safety through the quality of your being, the quality of your presence. Can you do that?"

"Yes," Charlotte replied eagerly. "Up till now, I've been treating her like everyone else has. Pretending she didn't exist, wasn't there, because her pain frightened me. I think I've been blaming her, too, *almost as my mother did.*"

"Then close your eyes, create her in front of you, then take her in your arms and allow her to feel your nurturing. And what is that like for you? . . . And I wonder what you might like to say to her. . . . Take your time and explore that."

Later, Charlotte remarked, "All these years I've tried to be an adult by denying the child I once was. I was so ashamed and hurt and angry. But I truly felt like an adult for the first time when I took her in my arms and accepted her as part of me."

This is one of the ways we build self-esteem.

29 · RECALLING
THE CHILD

· · · · · · · ·

JEAN HOUSTON

Teacher and philosopher Jean Houston asks us in this exercise to return to the child and befriend it wholeheartedly. This is a very practical approach for evoking what Ms. Houston calls "an extended sense of being." It is recommended that you do this exercise with another person serving as guide. "Recalling the Child" is excerpted from the author's 1982 book, The Possible Human.

What would it be like if you, at your present age and knowing what you now know, could go back and become the great friend and guide of yourself as a child? Many who have explored this possibility with me report that the child in them seems to respond to this friendship in such a way that makes them feel their past life is enriched, although not necessarily changed. In their present adult state they feel the effects that come from experiencing an enriched earlier life, often feeling stronger, more secure and resilient, more creative, and even beginning to lose some disabling and neurotic behavior that may have started in childhood.

Remember, as you go back in your life to meet the child living within you, to choose to encounter that child at some time when he or she would have been receptive to the arrival of a sympathetic stranger. Very few children are capable of welcoming someone new in the midst of great emotional trauma. Once you and your child have become acquainted and accepting of one another, you can repeat the exercise on other occasions and approach more sensitive areas. You might want to meet your child as he or she goes to school for the first time, or when a tooth is lost, or when your child needs a push on a swing or someone to talk to in the dark.

In the second stage of this exercise you will contact the person you will become in the future, allowing the three of you—yourself now, yourself past and yourself future—to experience the renewal that is inherent in this meeting. It may be possible to go forward in time as well as backward. If we hold this perspective, future selves may be both willing and able to nurture and redeem our present existence. Certainly modern physics has suggested that time is not linear but rather is an omnipresent dimension of reality, and that it is only our experiential limitations which keep us locked into a serial view of this dimension.

PREPARATION

This exercise is best done with one person serving as a guide and reading the instructions. The guide will need a drum or gong to mark the passage across time. If this is not possible, the instructions and the drumming can be put on a tape.

THE EXERCISE

Stage One: Befriending Yourself as a Child

Sitting with your eyes closed, breathe deeply, following your breath in and out. For this exercise act *as if* the following were true: that there still exists in your being yourself as a child, a child who does not know that in some other time frame of its existence it has grown up.

As the drum (or gong) sounds, call upon this child to come forward from wherever it exists. You might even want to open your right hand so that it can be reached by your child. The child, who was yourself, may appear during the sounding of the drum or gong or it may appear at the ending of the sounds. In either case, as soon as you feel your child to be present, be attentive to the child. Some will want to do this with the active imagination, others will actually rock the child or walk around with it, and be very active during this exercise. Find the ways that seem appropriate for you.

You may feel that you actually feel in your right hand a little hand holding yours. Feel the needs and personality of this child. Hold your child in your arms if the child is willing. Talk with your child. Walk with it. Take it, if you like, to some place like the circus or the beach or the zoo, or let it take you somewhere. Play with this child who was you. Give it love, friendship, nurturing, and allow yourself to receive from the child, who may actually have as much if not more to offer you than you have to offer it. You have fifteen minutes to begin the friendship with yourself as a child.

If you go outside, you will be called back by the ringing of a bell.

The guide will then beat a drum or gong slowly thirty to sixty times.

At this point, depending on whether or not you want to go on to the next sequence in this exercise, you can do one of several things. If the exercise has been done in a group, you can meet with one or two others in a small circle, each of you with your child so that adults and "children" share their experiences. Allow your child to talk and act through you as well as sharing from your mature consciousness. In this kind of group sharing, the reality of the child is honored and so becomes clearer.

If you are doing this alone, make something with your child—a drawing or clay figure or poem—that will serve to remind you of this meeting and what you have learned. Work with your child as partner in this process.

When this process has been completed, you can tell your child goodbye, assuring it that you will come back and visit often if you plan to do so. If you choose to go on to the next sequence, in which you are befriended by your extended self, tell the child you will call it back in a few minutes.

Stage Two: Becoming Befriended by Your Extended Being

In this next sequence you become as a child to the extended version of yourself. This extended self is the *entelechy* of you—who you said you would be and could be if your potentials were fully realized. This Higher Self is the oak tree of which you at present are still the acorn. We are assuming that in some realm of the psyche this being already exists, just as the child that you were still persists.

Closing your eyes and following the path of your breathing in and out, become aware of the following: Your extended being is about to enter your present reality and be for you as you were for your child. This is the high being of yourself, full of wisdom and grace, free of meanness and pettiness, filled with empowering love, who has multiple ways of knowing, learning, sharing. This is you as Sage, you if you had a hundred more years to consciously work on yourself.

Now as you hear the sound of the gong or drum, this potential being is becoming real, for it truly is real. This richly extended self is coming to meet you from a dimension beyond space and time.

Sound the gong or drum slowly for ten to twenty times.

As this being comes and cares for you, allow yourself to be nourished, empowered and awakened. Let yourself receive and be refined by the gifts that your High Self has for you.

Allow about five to ten minutes for this experience.

Guided and cared for, loved, acknowledged, and evoked, call forward the child that was you. Hold the child in your arms, as you are being held by your own extended being. The three of you are now together, a trinity that is a perfect oneness. Let a continuum of love, encouragement, and empowerment flow among the three of you so that the child gives its freshness of vision to the extended one, while he or she quickens the child, and you give to both.

Allow about five minutes for this experience.

Release now the child and the extended self so that they may return to their own place of being, knowing that they can be called into your

reality frame whenever needed. Know also that each of these parts of yourself has access to the other, and that this communion and communication
is a high practice that must be nourished in order to be known.

And coming back now to regular reality, be still for a few minutes as
you open your eyes. Reflect upon what has been given to you and what
you have given. Sense the extension of yourself flowing through your body
as you begin to move around. Share this, if you wish, with another person
or by writing in your journal.

DISCUSSION

As I suggested earlier, an extended sense of being is evoked in this exercise.
Knowing the living presence of the child within and the promise of the
person you are becoming, you are free to draw on these beings, to see the
current reality through their eyes and so gain multiple perspectives that still
have the integrity of your own experience and your own nature.

While this seems to be true for most people, there is still the possibility
of a wide range of individual responses, ranging from poignancy to pathos
to falling-out-of-the-chair laughter. One woman who had no memory at
all of her father, who had died when she was three, found herself with her
two-year-old child being sung to by her father. Others have been surprised
to find the great resiliency and strength of their child.

You can extend the power and possibilities of this exercise by allowing
your child and your High Self each to have a bit of your day that is theirs,
a time in which you might play or listen to music—or pay your bills!—
guided by the particular knowing of this being. Some parents and teachers
have found that their child within has been most perceptive about the
children without, offering helpful advice and insights about the headstrong
nine-year-old or tearful adolescent. The High Self provides a different sense
of time, putting the drama and trauma, and even the tedium, of the moment
into a longer and larger perspective. As these beings become your allies,
you extend the horizons of the timebound self.

30 · REPLAYING THE MOVIES OF YOUR CHILDHOOD

. . . .

A D E L A I D E   B R Y

This chapter applies modern visualization techniques to the recovery of the inner child. It appeared originally as part of the author's extensively researched book, Visualization: Directing the Movies of Your Mind. *This is a whole new slant on the child within; with a wink and a nod, psychotherapist and author Adelaide Bry asks you to take a look at your child's actual experience with your adult sensibilities and discover the truth the child has known and carried all along.*

In preparing her book, the author says, she once asked during a visualization how could she present the incredible truth of visualization techniques in such "a way that will touch people deeply, help them move closer to wholeness and happiness, open them to this extraordinarily meaningful process." A lovely golden child suddenly appeared in the space before her and delivered its message: "Speak to the golden child in each and every one."

> I inform the patient . . . that he will see
> before him a recollection.
> And I pledge him to communicate this
> picture or idea to me.
>
> —SIGMUND FREUD

I challenge you to remember the way things *really* were when you were growing up.

For a start, who was the boss in your home—your mother or your father? When they were together, *how* were they together? Did one lead the other . . . were they partners . . . or did they each have equal—but separate—powers?

With these questions in mind, you're ready to direct the following movie-of-the-mind.

I. Parents-Running-Through-a-Field Script

Begin by closing your eyes and letting yourself relax. Breathe deeply from your abdomen and feel the sweet relaxation that flows through your body.

Now, in your mind's eye, see a lovely green meadow in springtime. When you can sense it very clearly—the grass, the trees surrounding it, the wildflowers, perhaps even the butterflies and the sound of the breeze blowing through the leaves—then see your mother and father running through this meadow.

Look at them closely and see the expressions on their faces and how their bodies move. Regardless of how far from real life the notion of them running in a field may be, let yourself go with the fantasy and watch them be there. Whether they look as they do today or as they did when you were a child makes no difference. The truth of the story is all that's important here.

As you watch them, ask yourself these questions. Are they both running or does one refuse to run? Who is running faster? Are they running very fast, at a medium pace, or dragging? What do their bodies look like as they run—stiff, relaxed, loose, tight? Take your time and just watch your movie unreel, noting everything that's happening.

This visualization lets you look at your parents in a new light, to see them in a way that may be very different from what you *believe* about them. You will probably find that your images of the way they run across a field are a parallel to the way they have moved through life. After you've done the exercise (and hopefully not before), here are some guidelines to help you interpret it.

It is more usual in our culture to see the father running faster than the mother, as it is more likely that the man was dominant in the family. If the mother runs faster, it indicates that she may have been the dominant parent.

When their legs move freely and they're relaxed as they run, it is a sign of a relatively relaxed home environment. While there may have been areas of conflict in your childhood, they probably weren't shattering ones.

Those who have done this exercise and have a lot of conflict with their parents often report that the parents run stiffly; in fact, mental rigidity and rigid legs seem to go together, in life as in fantasy. When a parent tended to self-pity and martyrdom, he or she also usually had stiff limbs in the visualization.

A young woman who was having trouble getting away from her mother's control told me that she saw her parents running in a brilliant golden field with large white clouds hovering overhead. They ran together up a long steep hill, her father running with his fists clenched; then her mother suddenly sprinted ahead, as though she were determined to win a race. As she told the story of her movie, the young woman recognized how it paralleled her real situation. "My mother ran us all with her angry determination," she noted bitterly. She fell silent for a moment and then began to cry. "I also see the most tremendous courage in her face."

That one session proved to be a breakthrough for her. She saw her mother as she really was, angry, determined—and also courageous. Putting her mother into perspective helped her to put herself into perspective. She began to see that she could run her own life.

A patient of mine saw his mother begin by running alongside his father. Then, with no warning, she turned and ran in the opposite direction, upon which his father immediately followed. This triggered a flow of recollections which were very different from the way he had previously remembered his father. It also led to a new insight about his own marriage. Like his father, he was the pacifier in the marriage relationship, often at the expense of his feelings and deeper needs.

This particular technique is the creation of Akhter Ahsen, a Pakistani psychologist who came to the United States ten years ago with a theory he called "psycheye." I met Akhter soon after he arrived in Philadelphia, and began for the first time in my life to consider the value of pictures, rather than words, to reach the truth about a person's past. "Words are not experience," he told me then. "They merely talk about experience." Since that first meeting with Akhter, who has become one of the country's top experts in this field, my fascination with pictures of the mind has continued.

The parents-in-a-field visualization was one of those he used, and the one I first used with myself. In creating my mother and father running through a field, I saw my mother, who had arthritis and walked awkwardly, pulling my father's arm and almost dragging him through that field. It was enough to convince me of the validity of Akhter's system. Although I had chosen to deny it, my mother ran our household with an iron hand!

PLAYING DETECTIVE IN YOUR CHILDHOOD HOME

Freud, the master himself, used visualization for a while and then stopped in favor of other analytic tools. If he had continued, the whole picture of psychotherapy during the past fifty years might have been different.

What happens with many people who go into therapy is that they simply repeat to the therapist words they have been repeating over and over again in their minds. Talking about feelings is not the same as experiencing the feelings themselves. As a result, today there are many psychotherapists working with pictures-in-the-mind, either as a primary therapy technique or as an adjunct, to get their patients out of entrenched mind patterns about their childhoods.

When a patient replays the movies of his childhood, if only for a few seconds, it actually catapults him out of old, often paralyzing, thoughts into seeing the old situation in a brand-new way. Bringing these old memories into consciousness has the power to heal old wounds and bring people closer to wholeness.

In my own practice I see repeatedly that, no matter how miserable my patients may be, they cling to their distortions about what may have happened when they were growing up. The most effective way I've found to break through this is to invite them to play detective in their own homes.

I suggest that they see themselves lying in bed as a child and take in everything that's going on around them—the cracks in the ceiling, the feel of their bedspread, the smell of the house, the muffled sounds of their parents talking in another room.

After you've digested the experience of your parents running through a meadow, I suggest that you explore your own similar images from childhood. Not only can I promise that they'll be fascinating, you may also find a wonderful feeling of release in them.

II. A Script for Replaying Your Childhood

Pick any time or place in your life and see yourself there. When the movie begins to unreel, pay particular attention to the details or where you are. Really feeling yourself in that place sets the stage for the drama to unfold.

The most important things to notice during this movie are your thoughts and judgments. Be aware of them as they come—"I was right, he was wrong"; "I am bad, she was good"; "I never did anything right"; etc.—and then let them gently float out of your mind. Each one of these negative impulses simply reinforces old thoughts and prevents your movie from unreeling freely.

It is possible that you will see unhappy movies, and even fearful ones. Just as you would do when you watch a scary movie in a movie theater, simply watch it and feel whatever feelings it brings up, knowing that they will pass. When you are willing to look at the uncomfortable picture, it often changes into something happier by itself.

Dr. Robet Leichtman, a Baltimore psychiatrist who works with inner pictures, suggests that when you see a frightening figure—human or animal—on your private movie screen, you should offer it some food.

He tells the story of a patient who saw a huge bear appear before her the moment after she had been visualizing her mother and father. She became frightened by the picture, and felt she might be crushed. When Dr. Leichtman suggested that she spread honey on the ground for the bear, her picture changed instantly, first to a panda, and then to a playful fox terrier.

At that instant she thought of her father, who had always frightened her. To her surprise, her next thought was of a man who needed love and tenderness. With that recognition her relationship with her father, which had always been guarded, began to change and she was able to feel her love for him. In return he let himself show the love for her that he had withheld out of fear of rejection. This lovely true story reminds us, again, that hidden behind our fears are often warmth, tenderness, and love. When people shut down what I call their "feeling systems," they cut themselves off from all emotion.

Dr. Peter Brill, a free-spirited psychiatrist at the University of Pennsylvania, shared with me this story in which he used movies-of-the-mind to help a man he worked with get in touch with his feelings. Peter does "transition workshops" for men and women whose personal or career lives are in flux.

This particular person, a forty-five-year-old widower, simply could not express emotion; his face was humorless and deadpan. He told Peter that his father had left his mother when he was three, and then died. He was brought up by his mother and grandmother, and said that he had always felt "frozen."

As part of the workshop program, the participants were instructed to think of a high or low moment in their childhoods and then to focus on whatever moment first came to their minds. The man remembered going to school for the first time, and his unbelievable fear. Then he suddenly remembered his Teddy bear, which he hadn't thought of in years.

At Peter's suggestion, he drew the Teddy bear on a large piece of child's construction paper. The memories then came rushing in. He remembered how his mother and grandmother had made fun of him for wanting the toy, and how humiliated he had felt. He specifically remembered that deeply upsetting moment when he put his Teddy bear in the closet for good. Through this replay of an important incident of his childhood, a flood of tears was released. He was then able to begin to connect with other feelings and to talk about them.

In explaining to me what happens in a case like this, Peter told me he believes that the important events in most of our lives are primarily visual experiences, and are retained in our memories as images. Like others who are now working with this remarkable tool, he has discovered that people get to these events much better through their stored inner images than by talking about them.

AN IMAGE WORTH A THOUSAND WORDS

Psychosynthesis, created by Italian psychiatrist Dr. Roberto Assagioli, is a most remarkable system using pictures in the mind's eye along with other techniques for psychotherapy, self-awareness, and growth.

An example of how this very effective system works can be seen through the true story of a woman who identified her main problem in life as a dominating husband. When she was asked to visualize the way she felt about the relationship, she immediately saw herself as a baby robin being held in someone's hand. The baby bird could not get away and was being crushed.

The therapist suggested that she see the hand opening. When she did, the bird flew away to a nearby branch, where it settled down and then refused to move. Try as she might to see the bird fly off the branch, it continued to hang on. From this image, she saw clearly that it was she who allowed herself to be dominated by her husband because it gave her a sense of security. And from this new recognition emerged another: that she alone was responsible for her situation and that she had the freedom to be dominated or not dominated as she chose. When she stopped blaming her husband for her predicament, she was able to see the other options in her life.

Robert Gerard, a Los Angeles psychotherapist who works with imagery, uses a visualization script he calls "the door." The patient is asked to picture a door in a wall or at the entrance to a house and on the door imagine a word. That word can be suggested by the patient: anxiety, depression, love, hate, hope, for example. Then the patient opens the door and reports what he sees on the other side. In the spontaneous movie that follows, he will usually see an actual scene from childhood which is associated with the word—parents fighting, perhaps, or himself in a schoolroom being the target of ridicule.

What happens here is different from simply *remembering* a childhood incident which had been particularly upsetting, because the word on that door helps us to expand the way we now see the original event. We also see it more objectively than when we just remember, since remembering often has a possessive, holding-on quality about it.

For example, my brother had an amateur radio station, and I remember that he sometimes used to hold my fingers to the wires to give me a light electric shock (out of sight of my parents, naturally). Every time I thought back to that, I was filled with the original emotion of fear and anger. When I used Robert Gerard's technique and saw the word "fear" on that door, and then went through it to watch an incident when my brother gave me a shock, my images forced me to let go of what I remembered. For the first time, I saw the fear in *my brother's* eyes while he was doing it, which was an incredible revelation for me. I then looked at myself and saw clearly that I had invited his attack by my teasing and defiance. Bringing my memory in line with the truth, I could never again blithely recite the lines, "When I was a little girl, my brother used to grab my hands and give me an electric shock with wires." It was a story that had once served me wonderfully when I saw myself as a victim, but which now I could accept as only a fraction of the truth.

III. A Script for Getting to the Truth

Right at this moment, surely, you have an old or current anger or resentment which runs through your mind. Either it continually preoccupies you, or it pops up just at the moment when you want nothing more than to have a good night's rest. To help yourself move through and let go of it, try this:

Picture the word that is most applicable to the problem you now have, and see it clearly in huge block letters marked on a door. Pick the door carefully and note the details of it. Perhaps it is an ornately carved antique door or it is a very simple wooden or painted door. Now see the word you've chosen standing out clearly on that door.

Very gently open that door and look in front of you, to the left and to the right to see what is there, just as you would if you went into a room you had never been in before.

If you see a person, begin to talk with that person about your problem. If you see nothing but a vast horizon, continue on and see another door, and go through that one until you can find a person or an animal with whom you can talk about your problem or a place where you can be alone with it.

Give yourself time to be with the problem. Then give yourself time to see what the truth about the situation is. Old memories and people associated with them may come onto your screen. See how they relate to it. See them as they are, even if it's different from the way you think they are.

Now open your eyes and put your left brain to work by deliberately figuring out what the images are saying to you. You can now take those insights into your life and put them to work for you. What they've told you is what you need to know.

Dare to ask yourself "Who Am I?" and expect a response that will be deeply satisfying. Dr. Roberto Assagioli has said: "You can trust your deepest being and learn to live from that place. The real you knows all that you need to know, knows the future, will lead you." Dr. Assagioli, as have many others who have followed him, saw visualization as the channel to the higher self—the esssential core of one's being, the spark of one's uniqueness, the connection to all of life—which is the source of both our individuality and our universality. It is from this place that life takes on the richness, the meaning, and the pleasure that most of us long for.

31 · KILLING THE
DRAGON

· · · · · · ·

JOSEPH CAMPBELL

With the death of the great mythologist Joseph Campbell in 1987, a surge of interest in his work seemed to be met synchronistically with the release of books, television programs, and video. Considering how widely he ranged in his speculations and ideas about the universal nature of mythological motifs, Campbell had curiously little to say about the child or the inner child. However, what he did say was clear, terse, and to the point, as you will see below. The question is quite evident: "How might we as individuals get in touch with the child that lies within us?"

Here is an excerpt from the interviews Campbell gave on the national public radio program "New Dimensions," in dialogue with host Michael Toms. These transcripts are available in book form, published as An Open Life: Joseph Campbell in Conversation *with Michael Toms.*

We've been talking about the Eastern guru, but we also have gurus in the West. I think of people in the human potential movement, for example: there are people who have taken on the role of guru.

They themselves are following an Oriental model, I would say. But it must be *really* flattering to say, "Are you enlightened? I am! So listen! I don't take any guff." One of the typical things in the Orient is that any criticism disqualifies you for the guru's instruction. Well, in heaven's name, is that appropriate for a Western mind? It's simply a transferring of your submission to the childhood father onto a father for your adulthood, which means you're not growing up.

Similarly, in psychoanalysis there's the whole idea of transference. What do you transfer to the analyst? You transfer all the parental systems of relationships, so you're still bound; you're still a submissive and dependent person.

When you talk about maturity in adulthood, I think of what Jesus said, "You must become as a little child to enter the kingdom of heaven." Let's juxtapose that with adulthood and maturity. How do those two come together?

I think what he was talking about is spontaneity. But the answer to your question comes from Nietzsche in the introduction to *Zarathustra*. It's curious to speak of Nietzsche in the same breath as Jesus because typically he's thought to be the anti-Christ; he even thought so himself a little bit. But these are two great teachers, and great teachers frequently say similar things in different languages.

Nietzsche says there are three stages to the spirit. The first is that of the camel. The camel gets down on his knees and says, "Put a load on me." This is the condition of youth and learning. When the camel is well loaded, he gets to his feet and runs out into the desert. This is the place where he's going to be alone to find himself and he's transformed into a lion. And the function and deed of the lion is to kill a dragon, and that dragon's name is "Thou shalt." On every scale of the dragon a law is written, some dating from 2000 B.C., others from yesterday's paper. When the camel is well loaded, the lion is potent and the dragon *is* killed. You see, there are two quite different things. One is submission, obedience, learning; the other is strong and assertive. And when the dragon is killed, the lion is transformed into a child.

In Nietzsche's words, "a wheel rolling out of its own center." That's what the child represents in this mystical language. The human being has recovered that spontaneity and innocence and thoughtlessness of rules which is so marvelous in childhood. The little one who comes up and says absolutely embarrassing things to the stranger who's visiting your house— that's the child; not the obedient child, but the innocent child who is spontaneous and has the courage to live its impulses.

How might we as individuals get in touch with the child that lives within us?

By killing the dragon, "Thou shalt."

By choosing not to live by other people's rules?

Right. Respecting them, but not living by them. Respecting them more or less in the way you respect the red and green lights on the highway. There are other rules which seem advisable—if, in your own intelligence, you see that such a rule represents human decency, for example. But a rule put on you as a rule—"Thou shalt not"—is another show. I think one can learn to take courage; it also involves taking responsibility for what you're doing—taking the rap, if you have made radical mistakes and hurt people. It can be done.

32 · REDEEMING THE INNER CHILD IN MARRIAGE AND IN THERAPY

· · · · · · ·

R O B E R T M. S T E I N

Robert M. Stein, M.D., a practicing Jungian analyst for thirty years, has written intelligently and persuasively on the subject of the inner child, always with honesty and compassion. His ideas about the inner child are original, grounded in a constructive and unsentimental approach to the real child.

Stein focuses on two forms of relationship, marriage and psychotherapy, because they represent two of the most viable—and threatened—vessels in our culture for what he calls "the cultivation of soul." He suggests that the neglected child within both partners dominates many marriage relationships, keeping husband and wife fixated in parent-child dynamics. The inner child suffering from wounding love relationships, according to Stein, is also what usually brings a person to seek psychotherapeutic help. We can look to marriage and therapy, therefore, to find and recover the inner child. This essay is both a challenging and provocative tool for redeeming the child.

Dr. Stein created this essay especially for this collection by updating the inner child material in his now-classic book, Incest and Human Love.

MARRIAGE AND THE NEGLECTED CHILD

Marriage is no marriage if it is not grounded in the essential maleness and femaleness of husband and wife. When the male/female polarity begins to deteriorate in marriage, this is a sure sign that the neglected child within both partners has assumed control. This condition is probably the source of many of the dissatisfactions in modern marriage. Pure maleness and pure femaleness are strongly attracted to each other. They are not enemies, not hostile opponents, as they seem to be in most marital relationships nowadays.

While the unformed maleness and femaleness of a child begins to emerge as soon as it is born—as soon as it is conceived, really—the child does not attain its own sexual identity until it becomes sexually conscious. And this cannot occur before its bodily centers of sexuality are fully awakened, not before its consciousness develops sufficiently to receive the dark mystery of sexual passion. In most cultures, the transition rites into manhood and womanhood center mainly around the mysteries of sexuality and sexual identity. Humanity has always found it necessary to help the child through this dangerous passage with the aid of complex rituals. Few of us today have successfully completed this psychological passage into manhood and womanhood; thus, the uninitiated and fearful child within us cries out continually for help and instruction. And this neglected child so dominates the marriage relationship that it quickly deteriorates into the asexual comfort and security of the archetypal parent-child relationship.

Not until the child has been initiated into the mysteries of manhood or womanhood will it be ready for marriage. Not until the child has become man or woman can it contain the mystery of its own dark sexual nature. Only then do husband and wife emerge into the full splendor and dignity of their own maleness and femaleness. Only then can they once again experience the powerful attraction of sexual polarity which the soul needs.

What is to be done for this neglected and dissatisfied child so that it may become truly man or woman? Obviously some initiation or healing rite is needed. Jungian analysis, I believe, can be such a rite. But it is a long, slow and still inadequate ritual. With or without analysis, the troubled child need not dominate if each partner at least attempts to assume responsibility for the care of his or her own inner child.

The demanding child is one who has encountered too much destructive resistance to its own development, who has been made to feel guilty and ashamed about the uniqueness of his own nature. The child inside the adult needs desperately to experience the full acceptance of its nature, and to be absolved from the crippling guilt which has arrested its development. Unfortunately, the demanding child usually evokes criticism and censure from others, especially when it speaks out of the body of an adult. What this child wants is to be allowed to live spontaneously and naturally. But when we ourselves are critical and rejecting of the child within us, how can we expect others to accept it? Besides, even when others have compassion for it, the Negative Parent archetype within our own psyches is even more rejecting than others; consequently the child's need for approval becomes insatiable and is never really gratified.

When the demanding child in us cries out to another person, it often provokes the other person to fall into the Negative Parent role. We then experience rejection and betrayal, and an even deeper sense of inadequacy and humiliation. When this happens in marriage, the flow of Eros is totally obstructed. Clearly, it is crucial to the re-awakening of the male-female connection to develop the capacity to contain the sufferings of the demanding child. We only prolong the process of its transformation each time we subject this child to further rejection and humiliation.

Containing the painful needs of the demanding child is difficult because they always seem so simple, so right and unpretentious to us: "Surely every human being has a right to a little love and understanding? Why should I suffer and contain a basic need which is so easy to fulfill? Now give me an important or meaningful cause and I'll show you what I can take! But why should I suffer just because you refuse to make a proper meal or keep the house properly? Why should I endure the pain I experience because of the way you sexually frustrate me? Why should I suffer because of your coldness and lack of understanding for my very simple, basic needs? A stranger would show more feeling for me than you do. I just won't tolerate it! You can talk all you like about meaningful suffering, shout it from the roof tops, but I know what I have a right to expect, and simple human kindness is not too much to demand. . . ."

So there you are. Do we have the right to deprive a baby of its milk? to deprive our loved ones of the milk of human kindness, of simple understanding? Well, an infant or child certainly has a right to expect certain basic needs to be fulfilled by its parents. A husband and wife, however, are not parents to each other; to expect more than honesty and openness kills the flow of love between them. And if the inner child still persists in demanding its rights from the other, the marriage will remain stuck in an archetypal Parent-Child pattern. There is no possibility for any vital male-female connection, then, and no real sex. So my answer to the man or woman who sees no reason to endure the "rightful" demands of his or her own neglected and frustrated child is this: There is no hope for any real change in your marriage, no hope for reconnecting to the great natural rhythms of your own being and of the cosmos, until this is fully realized and lived; your marriage can be only a sterile prison or a battlefield.

Now, the transformation of the demanding child cannot occur without a parallel internal change occurring in the Negative Parent archetype. As soon as one demands from another what one feels to be one's "right," the critical, rejecting Negative Parent is activated in the other person. I will take this one step further: The Negative Parent is also constellated within oneself as soon as we even *begin* to feel hurt or anger toward another for letting us down, for not giving us what we feel we have a "right" to expect.

Let me describe how I think the Negative Parent works internally. It enters as soon as the inner child begins to demand its rights, its simple needs for love, compassion and understanding. The Negative Parent makes us feel guilty about having such infantile and immature needs: "Are you not capable of standing on your own two feet? You are a worthless, dependent child—a nobody." So we are crushed by words such as these, and we make a determined effort to pull ourselves up by our own bootstraps. In the process, we reject the needs of our inner child. But the child is persistent and soon returns with its demands, even stronger than before. Now the battle is on in full fury and we are caught between these two opposing forces—the child of our own nature and the anti-life force of the Negative Parent. And we become devitalized, paralyzed by it all, not knowing which way to go. If we go with the Negative Parent, the life force within us falls into its iron grip and we feel imprisoned. But if we go with the demanding child in an attempt to get others to fulfill its needs, we only encounter the same Negative Parent reaction externally.

This dilemma can only be resolved once we gain the capacity to contain the struggle. This makes it possible for the internal Negative Parent to be ultimately transformed into a Positive Parent who supports and nourishes the child. Then this inner child begins to receive the compassion it needs, and we can discover the best possible means of fulfilling its neglected instinctual needs.

PSYCHOTHERAPY AND THE NEGLECTED CHILD

People seek psychotherapeutic help largely because of the pain, despair, rage and unfulfilled needs of the neglected inner child. A repetition of the patterns we have just described as occurring in marriage soon become manifest in the therapeutic relationship. Working through these deep wounds of childhood as they are activated in the so-called transference to the therapist can be enormously healing. The term transference describes the phenomenon in which an individual transfers (projects) a repressed experience from the past onto the therapist: i.e., the patient may experience the therapist as an unloving, critical, judgmental parental authority.

In childhood, all the psychic functions which eventually make a child human are first experienced as belonging to others. As long as vital portions of one's totality are not sufficiently internalized, one lives in a continual state of psychic dependency. Initiation into adulthood is primarily a process in which the archetypal projections carried by parental figures are gradually withdrawn and internalized. In our culture there has been a serious breakdown in this essential humanizing process. The phenomenon of one person becoming the carrier of an unconscious or neglected archetypal factor for another always occurs when one is powerfully drawn, by attraction or repulsion, to another person.

Archetypal projection does not necessarily diminish as one comes closer to inner balance. It is probably an essential factor in any dynamically creative relationship, turning negative and obstructive only when the archetypal constellation becomes frozen. Psychic internalization is never final, but a continual, individualized path which contains the key to the mystery of our psychological development. The parental fixations so characteristic of our culture are largely responsible for our arrested capacities to internalize. As a consequence we tend to become fixed, stuck in archetypal boxes in our most important relationships. Arrested internalization also prevents us from living our own "child"—that is, we lose our capacity for imaginal freedom. Only as we free ourselves of the parental fixations can we be the child and find our emotional imagination, since imagination is essential for psychological self-realization.

A disturbed relationship to the imaginal world may manifest itself not only as a failure or cramp of the imagination, but also as a lack of differentiation between the inner imaginal realm and the outer concrete world. Probably both the failure of the imagination and its undifferentiatedness belong together. For example, the apparently wild, uninhibited fantasy life that occurs in many psychotic states is quite frequently a defense against painful or unacceptable emotions and fantasies. Delusional fantasies in psychosis are often a consequence of severe repression that cramps the imagination. On the other hand, an individual whose imagination seems sparse and obstructed often fears opening himself to his inner images because he has no clear distinction between the inner imaginal realm of thought and feeling and the outer realm of expression and action.

Creative psychological development, individuation, is dependent on spiritual freedom. When we say, for example, a man has a free spirit, do we mean that he freely or necessarily transgresses the imposed manners, mores and taboos of his culture? I think not. But it does mean the freedom to do anything or go any place he desires in the imaginal realm. He is a man who has clearly distinguished the sacral, timeless world from the secular, historical world. He knows he can move with unashamed dignity among the gods and demons of the imaginal world without fear of transgressing the taboos which belong to the mundane world. Such freedom cannot occur with a primitive form of consciousness in which inner and outer reality are governed by the same laws and values. In this sense, our Judeo-Christian tradition is primitive in that our thoughts and desires are subject to the same dogma, the same regulation, as our deeds. Spiritual freedom requires a break with biblical tradition and the development of a new form of consciousness—a consciousness which promotes the cultivation of imaginal freedom.

In psychotherapy both therapist and patient are immediately thrown into the archetypal roles of Doctor-Patient, Teacher-Pupil or Parent-Child as soon as they begin working together. This is the usual initial transference constellation, but it is mutual rather than a one-sided phenomenon: the therapist projects the helpless or needy Child archetype onto the patient, at the same time the patient transfers the strong, helping Father or Mother archetype onto him/her. As long as this continues, both parties are primarily playing out roles for each other and the relationship is essentially impersonal.

Let us consider some of the ways in which transference can be used therapeutically: 1) as an instrument for increasing awareness and differentiation; 2) as a possibility for experiencing certain critical archetypal constellations with the analyst; 3) as a means of moving out of an archetypal fixation into a more individualized human relationship. This last, above all, is enormously healing. After a number of such healing experiences, the capacity to internalize begins to become a viable and reliable function, and the individual grows much less fearful of exposing his soul to others.

From these formulations we see that the right understanding of the transference helps provide an authentic healing experience. If the transference is unconscious or misused, the best that can be hoped for is an increase in ego-consciousness and, at its worst, an increase in the mind/body split and greater distrust for open human relationships. It also becomes apparent that the important questions concerning the resolution of the transference need to be reconsidered. Since it is part of the human condition to fall continually into archetypal constellations, the idea that the transference is resolved only when all the archetypal projections are withdrawn and internalized is a false and impossible objective. I would propose a more plausible objective for transference resolution: the development of the capacity to internalize, as evidenced by the individual's ability to recognize and eventually move out of any archetypal constellations.

So long as the analytical situation continues, it will not be possible to move permanently out of the archtypal situation which forces the analyst into the role of the carrier of greater consciousness. Although this archetypal constellation may have been transcended, the very nature of the situation makes it inevitable that both parties fall back into it. The definite termination of the analytical relationship is essential if one is to get out of this archetypal box. But termination is difficult because it generally means a termination of a relationship which may have become important as a thing in itself aside from its therapeutic or spiritual goals. The possibility of a vessel for a continued relationship must be there, or the relationship will become stuck in an archetypal situation where the analyst carries greater consciousness, whether or not the analysis continues or breaks off. Freud's student seminars and Jung's psychology club, which their analysands could join, were perhaps attempts to meet this need for some form in which the connection could be continued. This structure has in recent years moved toward a therapeutic group experience. One objection to these forms is that the analyst still ends up in the archetypal role of the carrier of consciousness, and there is no possibility for the analyst and analysand to realize the individualized dimension of the relationship, its value, meaning and place in the larger pattern of their lives.

Why is such a realization essential for the analytical process and the resolution of the transference? Is it not enough for the patient to have developed the capacity to internalize? Yes, that would be enough, but still the *possibility* of experiencing a more personal relationship is essential for both analyst and analysand, or the internalizing function becomes hollow and meaningless. If internalization is experienced as an end to a deeply meaningful human connection, who wants it? When a child or adolescent becomes stuck in a parental fixation, it is not necessarily because he is unable to get out of it, but as often as not he fears if he gets out of the archetypal role he will be cut off from the warm and positive human qualities so important to the soul. If analysis repeats this wounding parent-child archetypal experience, the patient ends up with the same sense of disillusionment and betrayal as does the child.

THE POSITIVE TRANSFERENCE

A sense of the inner child suffering from wounding love relationships is usually what brings a person into analysis. As a result of those childhood wounds to the soul, the eros function is generally undeveloped or damaged. This makes it extremely difficult, if not impossible, for one to experience an intimate and creatively evolving human connection. In this sense the wounded child also represents that aspect of the soul which needs and demands union with another. The analyst's compassion and desire to help this child constellates the fundamental human need for union, and the desire for union between analyst and analysand is set in motion. But the eros development of the child alone is not sufficient to enable it to enter into union. The child is primarily dependent on the other's love. Therefore the analyst's eros connection with the wounded child, and his desire to help it, initiates the positive transference.

Nevertheless, the patient is not a child. Unless he has been too severely damaged, the patient is generally capable of experiencing adult passion and desire for union. Although the wounded child is usually responsible for evoking the analyst's love, the consequent flow of love involves the totality of both analyst and analysand. Eros circulates not only around the inner child, but also between the two people involved with its care. Thus while the transference is of the nature of the parent-child relationship, it also includes the ingredients of an adult love and friendship. However, there is no possibility for fulfilling the soul's desire for union until the child is transformed and healed. Its neglected and abused nature must be attended to before it becomes capable of loving another.

This contamination of the instinctual needs of the sick, neglected child and the soul's need to love another is a primary source of the difficulties arising in the analytical relationship. That the child experiences the analyst as father, mother, healing God, etc., does not take away from the fact that the flow of love has been set in motion. It is vital for both analyst and analysand to maintain the eros connection, and whenever it is obstructed or cut off (most frequently because of the demands of the child) it is the child in need of healing who suffers most. But the soul in each of the participants also suffers because of its desire for union.

The mutual need of analyst and analysand for soul-connection is behind the entangling archetypal projections released in the transference. All attempts to further the psychological development of the patient, all attempts to understand and eliminate the obstructive resistances and other manifestations of the negative transference, are only partially due to the therapeutic concern and desire of the analyst. The deepest need of the soul in any human relationship is never therapeutic; it is the desire to unite with the other. Thus, the analyst's desire to heal is never pure. Even when the analyst attempts to assume an objective scientific stance, even though he attempts to focus on the wound or psychopathology, the flow of eros is set in motion and this activates his or her need for the human connection.

The capacity of both analyst and analysand to sustain the eros connection to the wounded child is largely dependent on the flow between them. A differentiation between the love for each other and for the child is artificial to some extent, but it is a necessary one to make. The parallel might be seen in the relationship of a husband and wife, when both are concerned with promoting the child's health and development. The love between parent and child, however, is largely one-sided, because the child's eros is undeveloped and largely bound to its basic instinctual needs. A mutual desire and capacity for communion is needed or the equality of a creative relationship is not possible. Psychologically, we know that when the parents suffer from a lack of connection to each other, the child becomes burdened with the parents' unfulfilled need for communion.

When the need for union between analyst and analysand is given less value than the therapeutic need of the relationship, this need for union will function autonomously and unconsciously just as it does in the typical negative parent-child relationship. Instead of the neglected child being healed in analysis, its wound will be further deepened. Moreover, by calling the need for union "transference" and attempting to interpret it away, therapy becomes the destructive reverse of itself. Both the child and the soul's individuation are damaged.

THE NEGATIVE TRANSFERENCE

The emotional frustration and disillusionment which the child experienced in relationship to the parent is reconstellated in the negative transference. This aspect of the analytical relationship must be resolved satisfactorily; if it isn't, the internal union between the masculine and feminine opposites does not occur. This experience is an essential step in the process of re-establishing a connection with one's soul.

The demands of the wounded child are largely responsible for the soul-splitting fixation which occurs in the negative transference. But, as we have seen, the child is wounded primarily because vital parts of its soul were not internalized and continued to be carried by parental figures. The patient initially experiences this lost part of himself as belonging to the analyst. Much of his frustration and anger comes from his inability to unite with this image which the analyst has incarnated. Since no such union is possible, acceptance of this reality is the only healing solution to the negative transference. The patient's need for union with his own soul is behind this idealized image. This phenomenon needs further elaboration.

The negative parental experience occurs when the child must carry vital aspects of a parent's soul, generally the consequence of lack of soul-connection between husband and wife. The typical incestuous triangle results and the child is robbed of the possibility of experiencing his totality in relationship to either parent. Instead of experiencing the basic attraction and harmony between the masculine and feminine opposites, the child experiences these archetypes—yang and yin, sun and moon, heaven and earth, and spirit and flesh—as hostile opponents. This above all seems responsible for the mind/body split which afflicts individuals today. The desperate need to heal this split, to become whole, is at the core of the negative transference. Whether it is the mother or father archetype or the hero-savior-lover archetype that constellates in the transference, still it is the need for the unification of the archetypal King and Queen, the *hierosgamos*, which is behind transference. Not until harmony is restored to the *internal* masculine/feminine opposites can a soul-connection be maintained. Analytical transference is resolved once there is a full acceptance on the part of both analyst and analysand that the fulfillment of this archtypal need in their relationship is neither possible nor desirable.

The nature of this mutually frustrating aspect of the analytical relationship needs to be understood and accepted before termination. If this does not occur, both parties end the analysis with the delusion that all is right and good between them. Such a delusion tends to perpetuate the internal split within the patient because he has not really been confronted with the impossibility of the archetypal situation. Since the soul's frustration in the negative transference is identical to the child's incestuous entanglement with the negative parent, this wounding experience of childhood is only repeated if analysis ends with the false premise that analyst and analysand are pleased by their connection with each other. Of course, it is also wounding when the patient terminates analysis with anger and disillusionment. There must be a mutual understanding and respect for the frustrating archetypal situation which analysis constellates. This recognition of the essentially *impersonal* nature of the obstructions that are interfering with soul-connection humanizes, and it is then possible to terminate with dignity, mutual respect and positive personal feelings, free of soul-splitting delusion. The idea that the negative transference can be changed within the analytical situation is dangerous and misleading. It tends to prolong greatly the analytical relationship. And the enormous value of terminating analysis with the negative transference still intact and out in the open is completely lost. To recapitulate: The full mutual acceptance of the negative transference promotes the internal reconciliation of the masculine and feminine opposites. This internalization of the archetypes of union (the incest archetype) is the key to soul-connection and individuation.

There is still another dimension to the transference dilemma. Especially in Jungian analysis, the analytical experience is often equivalent to being initiated into a spiritual order or mystery cult. The profound changes that occur constellate kinship libido, which then understandably tends to move toward other initiates. If one has experienced an authentic rebirth, one is ready to enter into a new life where kinship of spirit becomes a stronger bond than kinship of blood. It has been my experience that unless spiritual kinship develops between analyst and analysand, the process is too limited. This kinship connection is a bond which does not break with the termination of analysis. It can be destroyed, however, if the negative transference is not accepted, or consequently, if there is a denial of the validity of the analytical experience. The lack of firmly rooted kinship connections is perhaps more responsible for our sense of isolation and alienation today than any other single factor. Frequent renewal through kinship connections is basic nourishment for our spiritual and physical well-being.

TRANSFERENCE AND INNER WHOLENESS

Moving into the final stage of analysis would seem to necessitate the full and mutual recognition of the special unworldly nature of the analytical vessel and relationship. Both analyst and patient must be able to recognize their need, if it exists, to continue the relatively unobstructed relationship they have with each other and the impossibility of doing so. The conscious sacrifice they must make is similar to that which both a parent and child must make when the child is ready to leave the containment of the parental fold and enter the world. In a positive parent-child relationship, of which there are few nowadays, the child has no assurance that it will ever feel as closely connected to another as he or she has been to his parent. Yet the child must go and the parent must encourage her/him to leave. Of course, the situation is not identical in analysis; but it is a bitter pill to swallow when one realizes it is going to be extremely difficult to find or create a comparable vessel in everyday life which cultivates soul-connection and soul-transformation. If the patient is unable to fully accept and appreciate this reality, if he feels betrayed and disillusioned by it, the wound to his/her soul will remain unhealed. And if the analyst has a similar difficulty, he will experience a sense of failure and ultimate disillusionment with analysis.

The importance of viable creative vessels for the promotion of soul connection cannot be overemphasized. These vessels are the basic social forms and structures of society. They influence and determine the life patterns and life-style of a culture. There is a great need nowadays for new forms in marriage, friendship and community which will promote the development of eros and feelings of kinship connection. But it will probably be a long, long time before there will be any real creative change in the basic structural units of our society. What are we to do, in the meantime, about the great disparity between the reality of living in a sick and fragmented world and our vision of a better way of life? What is the patient who has completed analysis to do after he has re-connected with his soul's creative vision, after he has experienced the concrete reality of an open and *sustained* connection to another?

The exchange of soul-substance which occurs when two souls meet and touch is essential for the life and health of the body and spirit. Inner wholeness soon becomes cold, rigid and life-killing if the soul is not continually re-humanized and re-newed through the human connection. Still, it is just because soul-connections are so rare and difficult to have in our culture that the internal healing of the mind/body split and internal wholeness is so essential. This is another paradox which we cannot avoid.

The need to keep one's soul carefully hidden and protected disappears when one is no longer dependent on the connection to another for completion. There is no longer the fear of experiencing and expressing one's feelings, one's reactions to another, simply because the integrity and wholeness of one's being are not dependent on a particular relationship. This increases the possibility of having close human connections, and it decreases the demands and expectations which we are all prone to make upon those we care for. In addition, the revealed soul generally evokes the emotion of love, especially when it demands nothing from the other. Thus, inner wholeness opens the door to many more possibilities for soul-connection, in spite of the lack of eros promoting vessels in our culture.

But there is still another difficulty which continually threatens to undermine the connection to the inner child and wholeness: the vision of a new and better world. Regardless of the innumerable forms this vision may take, it has its origins in the Archetype of Union, expressed in such images as the Sacred Marriage of the Royal Couple (the *hierosgamos*), the Quaternity, the Mandala. A connection to this archetype, and the belief that it will eventually be fulfilled, gives direction, meaning and balance to life.

Realization and fulfillment can occur on many levels: internally, as inner harmony and union; externally, as union and openness with another, the community, the world, the cosmos. The images of an ideal world through which the archetype expresses itself have certain common characteristics: namely, a world in which peace, harmony and love are the rule; a kinship community in which each person moves with proud and quiet dignity, protected from invasion by alien forces; a community ruled by the Eros principle, where the aggressive instincts and the power principle are working creatively for truth, beauty and aesthetic values. These elements are the common ground upon which all celestial visions of Paradise, of a New Jerusalem, are based. *Analysis must be able to restore the individual's faith in these visions as a psychic reality, as the imaginal ground essential to the development of the inner child and the soul*, or it will fail in its promise to guide the individual along the path of self-realization and wholeness.

. . . .

INNER CHILD/ OUTER CHILD: THE FUTURE OF PARENTING

INTRODUCTION

. . . .

The way I treat my inner child is the way
I am going to treat my outer child.

—ROBERT M. STEIN

The feeling of being valuable—"I am a
valuable person"—is essential to mental
health and is a cornerstone of self-discipline.
It is a direct product of parental love. Such
a conviction must be gained in childhood;
it is extremely difficult to acquire it during
adulthood.

—M. SCOTT PECK

Childhood is not only important because
it is the starting point for possible crip-
plings of instinct, but also because this is
the time when, terrifying or encouraging,
those far-seeing dreams and images come
from the soul of the child, which prepare
his whole destiny.

—C. G. JUNG

As I suggested at the beginning of this book, the child-rearing task is under
siege now as never before. To know, value, and embody the inner child is
not, as some would have it, a further episode of self-involvement for the
me-generation. Awareness of the inner child must be seen in context as an
evolutionary process of transmitting the enlightened laws of individuality
to our children and their children. The signs in our culture and the stresses
on our children indicate that such explicit measures have become facts of
our destiny, the initiatory requirements for children born of an age of
millennial transition.

The child within the parent and the inner life of our actual children
intersect in the need for spiritual values that nurture wonder and the capacity
to experience the mysteries of life. As Robert M. Stein suggested in the

preceding essay, the inner child requires a vision of a new and better world. We need contact with the archetype of wholeness, and with the belief that it will eventually be fulfilled, in order for life to have direction, meaning, and balance.

The parents who have realized their own neglected child within also have drawn forward the inner resources of empathy and compassion to enhance the quality of their relations with their children. Such parents have fulfilled the old rabbinical dictum, "Don't limit children to your own learning, for they were born in another time." The child beneficiaries of such parents will be equipped to meet the difficult challenges of their time, knowing their own true worth and possessing an uninhibited capacity for renewal.

This section focuses on the benefits of inner-child awareness for improved parenting. All of the contributors are therapists or analysts, looking at the nature of the parental task with the inner child in mind.

The child's connection to the imaginal world is James Hillman's concern in his essay, "A Note on Story." Exposure to oral story enhances the ability to see and value the inner life. "It is good for the soul," says the author.

Bruno Bettelheim also is concerned with story and imagination, but from a different perspective. In "storying" their children, he suggests parents have the opportunity to recall important memories from their own childhoods, to realize their inner child while simultaneously stimulating the inner life of their children.

In his short tribute essay to Sigmund Freud, Erik H. Erikson acknowledges the debt we own to the founder of psychoanalysis for enlightened child attitudes. Freud gave us permission to become conscious of our childhood pasts and exhorted us to apply these insights to better parenting.

Theodore Reik speaks, like a kind and wise uncle, of the reality of the inner child who lives on in each of us, forever playful, forever young.

The final selection of this book is from Samuel O. Osherson, who reminds us of the wounded parent within the adult and of the necessity to bring to a close the unfinished business between the internalized parent and the inner child, so that the adult personality can honor both.

33 · A NOTE ON
STORY

· · · · · · ·

JAMES HILLMAN

This is a short and fascinating look at the enriching effects of "story-awareness" on the inner life of children. "The first task," as archetypal psychologist James Hillman sees it, "is restorying the adult—the teacher and the parent and the grandparent— in order to restore the imagination to a primary place in consciousness in each of us, regardless of age." Hillman's thoughts are always a cut above most psychologizing. Here, he is reaching toward a poetic basis to reality, a life grounded in symbolic reality. He exhorts us to give the child's imagination the early nurturance it deserves in order to sustain a long and healthy inner life.

This chapter is from the author's collection of essays entitled Loose Ends. *It was originally published in* Children's Literature: The Great Excluded, *vol. III.*

From my perspective as a depth psychologist, I see that those who have a connection with story are in better shape and have a better prognosis than those to whom story must be introduced. This is a large statement and I would like to take it apart in several ways. But I do not want to diminish its apodictic claim: to have "story-awareness" is *per se* psychologically therapeutic. It is good for soul.

To have had stories of any sort in childhood—and here I mean oral stories, those told or read (for reading has an oral aspect even if one reads to oneself) rather than watching them on a screen—puts a person into a basic recognition of and familiarity with the legitimate reality of story *per se*. It is something given with life, with speech and communication, and not something later that comes with learning and literature. Coming early with life it is already a perspective on life. One integrates life as a story because one has stories in the back of the mind (unconscious) as containers for organizing events into meaningful experiences. The stories are means of finding oneself in events that might not otherwise make psychological sense at all. (Economic, scientific, and historical explanations are sorts of "stories" that often fail to give the soul the kind of imaginative meaning it seeks for understanding its psychological life.)

Having had story built in with childhood, a person is usually in a better relationship with the pathologized material of obscene, grotesque, or cruel images which appear spontaneously in dream and fantasy. Those who hold to the rationalist and associationist theory of mind, who put reason against and superior to imagination, argue that if we did not introduce such grim tales in early impressionable years, we would have less pathology and more rationality in later years. My practice shows me rather that the more attuned and experienced is the imaginative side of personality, the less threatening the irrational, the less necessity for repression, and therefore the less actual pathology acted out in literal, daily events. In other words, through story the symbolic quality of pathological images and themes finds a place, so that these images and themes are less likely to be viewed naturalistically, with clinical literalism, as signs of sickness. These images find legitimate places in story. They *belong* to myths, legends, and fairy tales where, just as in dreams, all sorts of peculiar figures and twisted behaviors appear. After all, "The Greatest Story Ever Told," as some are fond of calling Easter, is replete with gruesome imagery in great pathologized detail.

Story-awareness provides a better way than clinical-awareness for coming to terms with one's own case history. Case history, too, is a fictional form written up by thousands of hands in thousands of clinics and consulting rooms, stored away in archives and rarely published. This fictional form called "case history" follows the genre of social realism; it believes in facts and events, and takes with excessive literalism all the tales it tells. In deep analysis, the analyst and the patient together rewrite the case history into a new story, creating the "fiction" in the collaborative work of the analysis. Some of the healing that goes on, maybe even the essence of it, is this collaborative fiction, this putting all the chaotic and traumatic events of a life into a new story. Jung said that patients need "healing fictions," but we have trouble coming to this perspective unless there is already a predilection for story-awareness.

Jungian therapy, at least as I practice it, brings about an awareness that fantasy is a creative activity which is continually telling a person into now this story, now that one. When we examine these fantasies we discover that they reflect the great impersonal themes of mankind as represented in tragedy, epic, folk tale, legend, and myth. Fantasy in our view is an attempt of the psyche itself to remythologize consciousness; we try to further this activity by encouraging familiarity with myth and folk tale. Soulmaking goes hand in hand with deliteralizing consciousness and restoring its connection to mythic and metaphorical thought patterns. Rather than interpret the stories into concepts and rational explanations, we prefer to see conceptual explanations as secondary elaborations upon basic stories which are containers and givers of vitality. As Owen Barfield and Norman Brown have written: "Literalism is the enemy." I would add: "Literalism is sickness." Whenever we are caught in a literal view, a literal belief, a literal statement, we have lost the imaginative metaphorical perspective to ourselves and our world. Story is prophylactic in that it presents itself always as "once upon a time," as an "as if," "make-believe" reality. It is the only mode of accounting or telling that does not posit itself as real, true, factual, revealed, i.e., literal.

This brings us to the question of content. Which stories need to be told? Here I am orthodox, holding for the old, the traditional, the ones of our own culture: Greek, Roman, Celtic, and Nordic myths; the Bible; legends and folk tales. And these with the least modern marketing (updating, cleaning up, editing, etc.), i.e., with the least interference by contemporary rationalism which is subject to the very narrowing of consciousness which the stories themselves would expand. Even if we be not Celtic or Nordic or Greek in ancestry, these collections are the fundamentals of our Western culture, and they work in our psyches whether we like it or not. We may consider them distorted in their pro-Aryan or pro-male or pro-warrior slant, but unless we understand that these tales depict the basic motifs of the Western psyche, we remain unaware of the basic motives in our psychological dynamics. Our ego psychology still resounds with the motif and motivation of the hero, just as much of the psychology of what we call "the feminine" today reflects the patterns of the goddesses and nymphs in Greek myth. These thematic tales channel fantasy. Platonists long ago and Jung more recently pointed out the therapeutic value of the great myths for bringing order to the chaotic, fragmented aspect of fantasy. The main body of biblical and classical tales directs fantasy into organized, deeply life-giving psychological patterns; these stories present the archetypal modes of experiencing.

I think children need less convincing of the importance of story than do adults. To be adult has come to mean to be adulterated with rationalist explanations, and to shun such childishness as we find in fairy stories. I have tried to show in my work how adult and child have come to be set against each other: childhood tends to mean wonder, imagination, creative spontaneity, while adulthood, the loss of these perspectives.[1] So the first task as I see it, is restorying the adult—the teacher and the parent and the grandparent—in order to restore the imagination to a primary place in consciousness in each of us, regardless of age.

I have come at this from a psychological viewpoint, partly because I wish to remove story from its too close association with both education and literature—something taught and studied. My interest in story is as something lived in and lived through, a way in which the soul finds itself in life.

34 · EXPLORING CHILDHOOD AS AN ADULT

· · · · · · ·

BRUNO BETTELHEIM

Bruno Bettelheim, an eminent child psychologist, encourages parents to go beyond empathy with their offspring and reexplore "the steps we made in becoming ourselves." Here is sage advice on how to achieve greater closeness with children by recapturing one's own child of experience. This article is from his most recent book on child-rearing, A Good Enough Parent.

> We shall not cease from exploration
> And the end of all our exploring
> Will be to arrive where we started
> And know the place for the first time.
>
> —T. S. ELIOT

Among the most valuable but least appreciated experiences parenthood can provide are the opportunities it offers for exploring, reliving, and resolving one's own childhood problems in the context of one's relationship to one's child. As T. S. Eliot reminds us, only by exploring and reexploring the steps we made in becoming ourselves can we truly *know* what our childhood experiences were and what they have signified in our lives. If we achieve this knowledge, the impact of these events on our personality will be altered. Our attitude toward our experience will change, as well as our attitude toward parallel experiences with our children. Our growth in self-knowledge must inevitably result in a better comprehension of our children, even more so when the new insights are in consequence of experiences involving these children.

Unfortunately, nearly all of our primary experiences are lost to conscious memory, because they happened too early to leave more than the vaguest traces in our minds. We cannot reexperience them, but we can at least explore imaginatively some of their aspects as we observe how our infant responds to his inner processes, to us, and to his world.

For example, if we realize that the infant's waking world consists of only two opposite experiences—happiness and physical well-being, and unhappiness and pain—this can help us also understand the origin and ambivalent nature of all strong emotions. Since it is normally the parents who change the negative state of the infant's existence, such as hunger pains or the discomfort of soiled diapers, into one of satisfaction by feeding or by changing him, he experiences his parents as all-powerful and the source of all happiness and unhappiness; also as all-giving and all-frustrating. Thus ambivalence is built into our unconscious, particularly in regard to our parents. Later on they and their surrogates, our foremost educators, continue to dispense both pleasure and pain, by praising us, for example, or by criticizing and frustrating us. In this way the original ambivalent feelings, so deeply rooted in our unconsciousness, continue to be fed by the innumerable experiences of daily life.

Understanding this infantile origin of ambivalence, particularly in regard to our parents, can help us comprehend our children better when we are confronted with expressions of ambivalence about us. The more we can accept their ambivalent feelings in relation to us, the greater chance they will have, as they grow up, to neutralize and control these ambivalences—and the less they will need to blow hot one moment and cold the next. By accepting that the negative aspects of this ambivalence must occasionally be ventilated, we reduce the need for our children to repress them; and the less they are repressed, the more accessible they are to rational scrutiny and modification.

As children, we too were torn by our ambivalent emotions. But when we acted out their negative aspects, our parents' disapproval was usually so strong that we were forced to repress these feelings, which thus retained their full force in our unconsciousness. When we are confronted as parents with similar feelings in our children, the experience tends to reactivate some of this repressed material. We can accept that our children will have much less control than we do, as long as their behavior does not awaken in us feelings we wish to keep repressed; but when our own repressions become remobilized, then we can no longer deal realistically with the negativism of our children.

That we repress the negative aspects of our feelings about our parents is understandable; after all, we need them and don't want to offend or alienate them by openly displaying our hostility. It is harder to comprehend why we also repress our identification with what to us as children seem negative aspects of our parents. Most of us are quite aware that we have made our own many of the things we like about our parents, but we're *not* aware that we have also identified with and internalized the negative aspects of their attitude toward us. Of this we become cognizant—usually to our great surprise—when we hear ourselves scold our children in exactly the same tone, even with the very same words, that our parents used with us. And this although we had objected to their doing so and have thought that we would never behave to our children in such a manner.

On the other hand, when we speak lovingly to our children, we are not at all compelled to use the same terms our parents employed. In our positive expressions and behavior we are quite our own persons and speak very much with our own voice. The reason for this is once again because there was no cause to repress our positive identification with our parents, it did not become encapsulated in the unconscious but remained accessible to modification as we ourselves developed. The negative identification, in contrast, was repressed and thus remained unchanged.

Very often the relations of the child to the parent of the same sex are more beset by ambivalence than are those to the parent of the other sex. The reason for this is that in relating to the child of our own sex we tend to reexperience some of the more difficult aspects of our own relation to our same-sex parent. Thus it is more likely that a mother will catch herself talking like her own mother when she criticizes her daughter, while a father will find himself repeating in his negative interactions with his son those that took place in his childhood between him and his father.

This is just one example of our tendency to project our own unresolved conflicts onto our children. If we take advantage of the opportunity such situations offer to examine what causes us to behave this way, we may be able at last to solve childhood conflicts we have not resolved before. Such openness to one's feelings will also facilitate our understanding that it is exactly our tremendous importance to our children, and their love for us, that spawns their occasional hostility. It will be clear that when hostility breaks out into the open, what we are being confronted with is but the obverse of their great affection for us. This realization will alter our attitude from annoyance or worse to one of understanding acceptance of the underlying emotional forces, although we still may have to inhibit our child's aggressive behavior. It may even make us recognize that in restraining him, we are reproducing our parents' conduct in parallel situations. Recalling how unfair we thought our parents were will keep us from overreacting to our child's behavior. With such deliberations, things ought to fall into their rightful place, and what now annoys us about our child will not be fed and aggravated by its connection with all the hostile feelings we have repressed into our unconscious. Most of all, as we realize that despite all the aggressive tendencies we had as children, we did grow up to be nonviolent, law-abiding adults, we will be less likely to bear down too hard on our child's aggressive behavior out of anxiety that it will become unmanageable once he is grown up.

The repression of the negative side of a child's ambivalent feelings about his parents, if done too severely, can have the consequence of interfering with the expression of the positive feelings, which are but the other side of this ambivalence. I have known many children who were able to form loving attachments to their parents only after they no longer felt the compulsion to repress all their negative feelings about them.

Of course, if we are able to recognize, through introspection, that our feelings toward our children are not entirely free of ambivalence, we no longer need to repress whatever negative feelings may well up in us from time to time. The pretense that our child, because of his immaturity and lack of control, is occasionally having negative feelings about us but that we are entirely free of such feelings about him can cause serious problems in the relations.

UNDERSTANDING NIGHTMARES

What has been said about the origins of our ambivalent feelings about our parents holds true, *mutatis mutandis*, for the entire period of childhood. Our earliest experiences, and those of our child, are mostly unconscious and thus not available in direct form to our memory, but later stages of his development replicate some of our experiences that were not necessarily unconscious or repressed by us, or if so, not so deeply. These memories can be recalled more readily, although this may still require considerable effort.

Few of us can remember in any detail the nightmares from which we suffered, as all children do; even those who can recall to some extent the contents of their nightmares and how upsetting they were have little notion what caused them, beyond the obvious fact that the young child feels help-lessly anxious about many things which are incomprehensible to him. Not many people realize that a major source of the nightmares of young children is their developing superegos, which try to punish them for their "unac-ceptable," if not "sinful," tendencies. Among others, these may be sexual urges, or the wish to rebel against authority or to get rid of a parent or sibling. As forerunner, an early stage of a more fully integrated conscience, the nightmare plays an important role in the personality development of all of us; it had this role in our development as it now has in that of our child.

Realizing this will help us to treat our child's nightmares with greater care and the respect which a developing conscience deserves. The more we understand about our own nightmares (of which we are not entirely free even in adult life), the better equipped we will be to help our children with theirs. The fact that we have forgotten so much about them suggests that we repressed the childish desires and fears which found expression in those haunting dreams. Underlying such alienation from our childhood experi-ences is the wish not to know what they were all about, maybe even some dim recognition that the terror we then felt has left in us some residues from which we have failed to free ourselves entirely. Witness the unrealistic anxiety many people still suffer, for example, when confronted with harm-less animals, such as garden snakes. Their fear is often rooted in forgotten childhood nightmares in which snakes threatened to devour them.

Thus we can use our children's nightmares as an opportunity to explore and reexplore—as T. S. Eliot suggested—what may have been behind our own, and whatever remnants of them we may still carry with us. Then we shall indeed, for the first time, truly know our nightmares and their meaning in our lives. To the degree we achieve this it will be a boon to us and to our children, since we shall then be able, by understanding ourselves, to help them with their nightmares with a personal sympathy for both the immediate suffering and the significance of such experiences in the formation of their personality, a depth of empathy which otherwise might never be available to either of us.

Unlike our nightmares, which we only vaguely recollect, our anxieties about entering school have stayed with many of us; in fact, some people spend a lifetime demonstrating, to themselves much more than to others, that their childish fears of academic and social failure were unrealistic. Because these worries are usually part of our conscious memoires, although often in fragmentary form, we have considerable compassion for our child's anxieties about his first entry into school. Unfortunately, some parents run out of compassion when an older child develops a school phobia for parallel reasons. This is when an understanding based on one's own experiences would be particularly helpful.

These situations stand for many others which may occur in our interactions with our children; efforts to understand the role played by parallel events in our own development always bring about beneficial changes as they provide new clarity about ourselves. We gain a deeper understanding of what certain experiences have meant in our lives and in our relation to our parents, as well as how these experiences now shape our attitude toward what our child experiences and expresses around some similar occurrence. Such understanding permits us to empathize with whatever moves our child, and this nearly always gives our relation greater depth and meaning, making it a more enjoyable experience for both of us. Thus around some common experience, we not only influence our children's attitudes, but we also change our own, because of a better understanding of what similar events meant to us as children.

Children are very sensitive to their parents' reasons for doing something with or for them. Do parents think they *ought* to do this, or do they really enjoy it? Is Mother reading a story because she wants to quiet me down? Or is it because she thinks it's her duty? Perhaps she thinks I'll enjoy this particular story, or being read to by her, or both? Obviously it is a more rewarding experience for a child if he can sense his mother's desire to give him pleasure.

The child's experience when being read to is radically different from that of the parent, although they engage together in a single activity. However, when parents respond to the story themselves, the two can really share the experience. Perhaps the parent will be moved by the story to recall important memories from his own childhood. I have been told that people who read my book on fairy tales, *The Uses of Enchantment*, suddenly understood why a particular story had been especially significant to them in their childhood. Then it had captivated them in some way, had aroused anxiety or pleasure, or both; but only now did they see why this had been so, with what personal experiences or problems the tale had been connected, so that it became uniquely meaningful to them.

As children these people had wanted a parent to read the story over and over again because, unbeknownst to them at the time but understood now, they had subconsciously hoped that it would convey an important message to the reader. For one it was *The Swiss Family Robinson*; by spinning fantasies about this story, she had found solace from her unhappy family situation. The same book was also very meaningful to another young girl who suffered from the repeated and prolonged absences of her parents, during which she was left in the care of relatives who physically took good care of her but whom she hated, mostly because they took her parents' place. Only as an adult did she realize that she had pestered her parents and relatives to read *The Swiss Family Robinson* aloud to her because she hoped they would get the message that children need to have their parents present. Subconsciously she had hoped that from the story they would understand how much she wanted her parents to either stop traveling or take her with them.

As soon as this woman realized that a child's desire to hear a certain story again and again may derive from his hope that his parent will get the message he thinks the story conveys, reading stories to her own child became a much more rewarding experience for her. Moreover, she began to pay quite different attention to the stories her child requested, for she remembered with particular poignancy how severely disappointed she had been that neither her parents nor her relatives had gotten the message she had tried to send through *The Swiss Family Robinson*.

Reading stories to her son now took on new levels of meaning for her. Before, she had read to him because she remembered how important this activity had been to her, and she wanted to give him this pleasure. Now it occurred to her that by asking for a particular tale, her son might be trying to give something to her—namely, a message about some matter that was of great importance to him. She enjoyed this demonstration of this confidence in her, his desire to tell her—in whatever roundabout form—something of personal significance.

Her experience of the importance *The Swiss Family Robinson* had once had for her gave this mother a new perspective on her own childhood. What she had previously recalled and viewed only as an escape into wish-fulfilling fantasies she now recognized as an intelligent, goal-directed action with a specific purpose: to secure relief from a distressing situation, the long and frequent absence of her parents. Before, she had remembered herself as having been unable to improve the conditions that oppressed her, but now she saw that she had actually done her best to persuade her family to change their ways. Thereafter, when she read stories to her son, she always remembered that this was the experience through which she had gained a more positive image of herself as a child, and with it of herself as a person.

What is said here in respect to story-reading holds true, with the appropriate variations, for many other aspects of child-rearing. Comprehending one's childhood experiences as an adult can provide new and important insights. When this happens, both parent and child have a significant experience through what they are doing together; although they are on different levels, the differences are of less importance than the fact that each is beholden to the other for having gained new insights, and for having provided the setting for such growth. The element of equality in such a shared experience is especially important to the child, because each participant becomes provider and beneficiary at the same time.

Many childhood experiences have become, of necessity, deeply buried in the unconscious during the process of developing one's adult personality. This separation or distancing from one's childhood is no longer needed when the adult personality is fully and securely formed, but by then, the distancing has for most people become a part of that very personality. Separation from one's childhood is temporarily necessary, but if it is permanently maintained it deprives us of inner experiences which, when restored to us, can keep us young in spirit and also permit greater closeness to our children.

35 · THE HISTORICAL RELEVANCE OF HUMAN CHILDHOOD

· · · · · · ·

ERIK H. ERIKSON

In keeping with the theme of improved parenting, Freudian psychoanalyst Erik H. Erikson gives us the context from which psychological restoration of the child has arisen, namely the work of Sigmund Freud. A man of indomitable intellect and courage, Freud actually resurrected childhood from its submerged status. "He invented," says Erikson, "a specific method for the detection of that which universally spoils the genius of the child in every human being."

This chapter pays tribute to the pioneering contribution Freud made, to his perception of the creative potentials in the child, both inner and outer. An excerpt from the author's collection of essays Insight and Responsibility, *it is a portion of a talk he delivered on May 6, 1956, at the University of Frankfurt, in celebration of the 100th birthday of Freud.*

> The real value of psychoanalysis is to improve parenting.
>
> —SIGMUND FREUD

That shift in self-awareness [that Freud's discoveries brought about] cannot remain confined to professional partnerships such as the observer's with the observed, or the doctor's with his patient. It implies a fundamentally new *ethical orientation of adult man's relationship to childhood*: to his own childhood, now behind and within him; to his own child before him; and to every man's children around him.

The fields dealing with man's historical dimension are far apart in their appraisal of childhood. Academic minds, whose long-range perspectives can ignore the everyday urgencies of the curative and educative arts, blithely go on writing whole world histories without a trace of women and children, whole anthropological accounts without any reference to the varying styles of childhood. As they record what causal chain can be discerned in political and economic realities, they seem to shrug off as historical accidents due to "human nature" such fears and rages in leaders and masses as are clearly the residue of childish emotions. True, scholars may have been justly repelled by the first enthusiastic intrusion of doctors of the mind into their ancient disciplines. But their refusal to consider the *historical relevance of human childhood* can be due only to that deeper and more universal emotional aversion and repression which Freud himself foresaw. On the other hand, it must be admitted that in clinical literature (and in literature turned altogether clinical) aversion has given place to a faddish preoccupation with the more sordid aspects of childhood as though they were the final determinants of human destiny.

Neither of these trends can hinder the emergence of a new truth, namely, that the collective life of mankind, in all its historical lawfulness, is fed by the energies and images of successive generations; and that each generation brings to human fate an inescapable conflict between its ethical and rational aims and its infantile fixations. This conflict helps drive man toward the astonishing things he does—and it can be his undoing. It is a condition of man's humanity—and the prime cause of his bottomless inhumanity. For whenever and wherever man abandons his ethical position, he does so only at the cost of massive regressions endangering the very safeguards of his nature.

Freud revealed this regressive trend by dissecting its pathological manifestations in individuals. But he also pointed to what is so largely and so regularly lost in the ambivalent gains of civilization: he spoke of "the child's radiant intelligence"—the naive zest, the natural courage, the unconditional faith of childhood, which become submerged by excessive ambitions, by fearful teaching and by limited and limiting information.

Now and again, we are moved to say that a genius preserved in himself the clear eye of the child. But do we not all too easily justify man's mass regressions by pointing to the occasional appearance of leaders of genius? Yet, we know (and are morbidly eager to know) how tortured a genius is driven to destroy with one hand as he created with the other.

In Freud, a genius turned a new instrument of observation back on his childhood, back on all childhood. He invented a specific method for the detection of that which universally spoils the genius of the child in every human being. In teaching us to recognize the daimonic evil in children, he urged us not to smother the creatively good. Since then, the nature of growth has been studied by ingenious observers all over the world: never before has mankind known more about its own past—phylogenetic and ontogeny. Thus, we may see Freud as a pioneer in a self-healing, balancing trend in human awareness. For now that technical invention readies itself to conquer the moon, generations to come may well be in need of being more enlightened in their drivenness, and more conscious of the laws of individuality; they may well need to appreciate and to preserve more genuine childlikeness in order to avoid utter cosmic childishness.

36 · OUT OF THE
MOUTHS OF
BABES

· · · · · · ·

THEODORE REIK

This anecdotal piece is a folksy acknowledgment of the inner child by a consum-
mate psychoanalyst, one of Freud's most brilliant disciples. Theodore Reik says that
the psychoanalyst must search for the child in the man, in himself, and in others.
"It would be a serious mistake on the part of the analyst," he says, "to under-
estimate the power of the ideas and ideals of the child who continues his existence
in the adult." Any parent or potential parent can enjoy the wisdom of this kind
man's words. This essay is a chapter from Listening with the Third Ear, *the*
author's fascinating account of the inner experience of a psychoanalyst, first published
in 1948.

Not everything the analyst labors to uncover is repressed material. The
area of the unconscious reaches far beyond the sphere attributed to it by
many psychoanalytic lecturers. It includes material which is displaced, distorted and disavowed. There are further events and emotions that were
never conscious because they happened when the person was too young to
grasp their meaning. They belong to the prehistoric period of the individual
personality.

We grown-ups are so far removed from the peculiar ways and forms
of our childhood that they have become strange to us. Everybody has
experiences of this sort. Our parents or old friends of the family have told
us that as a small boy we said or did this or that odd thing. In most cases
we do not remember the statement or action. And even when we do, we
can no longer discover why we acted or spoke like that. We cannot doubt
the truth of the story but we do not recognize ourselves in the picture it
shows to us. We have to admit that we were this little boy or that little
girl, but we cannot acknowledge any psychological identity with our past
self. It has vanished like the snows of yesteryear.

Memories of this order come up many times in psychoanalysis. They
are conscious in that their content can be ascertained, but their meaning has
been lost. This meaning was not repressed. It grew strange because a man

cannot recover the thought-processes peculiar to childhood. Loss of an old way of feeling or thinking can be observed already in children themselves. A little girl of eight cannot believe that, once when she was three, she had wanted to catch a snail and had been worried that the snail would run away. If, after some years, children cannot recognize themselves, how can we expect men and women to accept their psychological identity with an infant? The activities, joys, and griefs, the little games children sometimes remember represent their true selves, but the self from the past seems foreign. They are astonished at themselves and cannot imagine what made them so odd or say such funny things. The psychoanalyst frequently has a difficult time with memories of this kind, since no conscious effort on his part, either, can help him regain infantile ways of looking at the world. He would have to study children for a long time and with particular psychological skill in order to understand what his patients tell him about some episodes of their childhood days. Not longing for paradise lost, but his wish for psychological comprehension reminds him of the song by Brahms that goes: "Oh, if I but knew the way back, the dear way back to childhood days. . . ."

Sometimes we realize how remote we are from the child's way of feeling and thinking when we hear the funny things children say. I do not mean the "bright sayings," but remarks and comments that we call naive, which make us laugh because we are so charmed. I heard that a little girl on the beach complained about her playmate: "Mother, Bobby should not take so much water out of the sea. The sea will become quite empty." The other day I saw a cartoon showing a painter seated before his canvas in a field. He is immersed in his work and pays no attention to the little farm girl who is an attentive observer. The child interrupts the silence suddenly: "I have had the measles. . . ." The two instances, that of the little girl who is worried lest her playmate exhaust the sea, and that of the other child who wants to appear important and opens a conversation with the interesting news that she once had the measles, represent a whole group of sayings that show how differently the world reflects itself in little heads.

Sometimes, in the middle of psychoanalysis, memories occur that puzzle us because we cannot immediately understand what they mean, nor what they meant to the child who twenty or thirty years later is now a patient in our consultation room. Sometimes it is easy enough to grasp their meaning; we have no difficulty in putting ourselves in the emotional world of the child because we find ourselves echoes of the same feeling when we dig down deep enough in our own memories. I believe everybody will hear an echo when I tell what a patient remembered from her childhood.

When she was a very little girl she sneaked from her bedroom into the dining room in the dark because she wanted to know how the furniture, the table, the chairs, and the lamps behaved when they were alone, without people around. She was convinced that the room and the furniture would behave differently when they thought they were not being observed. Children's animistic conceptions of the world are further illustrated by another patient who remembered that he once asked his older brother whether the telegraphic poles speak with the lampposts. We understand immediately that the hum of the wires suggested the question.

Every psychoanalyst has met difficulties dealing with the childhood memories of patients who do not themselves understand the meaning of their recollections. A woman remembers, for example, that as a little girl she once began to cry when her father led her into the elevator of a hotel in which the family, interrupting a journey, was to spend the night. Her recollection tells her that the elevator was more spacious than any she has seen since and that there were plush benches along three sides. She is also sure that this was the first time she had ever been in an elevator. She clearly remembers that she was desperate when she entered it and that her father tried in vain to console her and stop her tears. Although the recollection recurred several times during her analysis, we could not figure out why she had behaved so strangely at that moment. She denied being scared when the elevator began to move because she was already sobbing before that happened. We—the patient and I—were both puzzled until all at once it occurred to her that she must have thought that the spacious elevator was a room, and that she, on this, her first visit to a hotel, would have to sleep in this room with her father. She had thought of the upholstered benches as couches. The memory was, of course, significant for the analytic understanding of the patient's relationship with her father.

In other cases the special meaning of a child's behavior or talk is not so easily grasped. There are times when no learning, no expenditure of conscious intellectual energy, and no hard thinking can penetrate to these lost ways of a child's emotional processes. There is no other path to this hidden area but unconscious identification with the patient as a child.

A man remembered that as a boy he once behaved very strangely on a bus with his mother. A woman who had stepped down from the bus while it was in motion, fell to the pavement without being seriously hurt. The little boy had protested desperately that he had not pushed the woman down. Actually he had been standing at some distance from her so that it would have been impossible for him to attempt anything of the sort. There was no doubt that his memory of the incident was correct. The analytic interpretation of this childhood memory started from the assumption that in some way his emotions must have been appropriate. We learned later that at this time he felt very hostile and aggressive toward his mother, who stood beside him in the bus. In a serious marital conflict between his parents, he had sided with his father. It seemed likely that his hostility against his mother had led to aggressive wishes, which reappeared when the accident on the bus occurred. His feelings toward his mother were displaced upon a stranger. The woman who was hurt was unconsciously thought of as a mother-substitute. When she was hurt he must have felt guilty, as if he were really responsible because he had entertained evil wishes against his mother. It was as if his wishes had become reality in the accident to the other woman. There are many instances that show grown-up people behaving similarly when a crime they wished for is actually committed by others.

I am choosing a relatively simple instance from my psychoanalytic practice in order to demonstrate that only a return to the thought-world of the child can solve the puzzle of a memory that has become unintelligible to the person himself.

A British patient remembered that as a small boy he had said something to his sister (two years older than he) that does not make sense to him now. He recalled the situation precisely. They stood at the window of their country house and it was early evening. They looked at the cows coming home along the village street. The little boy turned to his sister and asked her, "Can you imagine Uncle Harry being a cow?" Well, that sounds silly enough, and the patient was inclined to dismiss the remembered sentence as one of the funny thoughts children frequently have. He remembered that his sister had roared with laughter and quoted his saying teasingly to him later on.

I tried to convince him that the sentence must have made sense then. His associations seemed to lead him far away, to later memories of Uncle Harry and Aunt Mabel, his wife, to other relatives, and to the contrast between life in the country and in London. The only fact that seemed to be worthy of consideration in these associations was that shortly afterward Aunt Mabel had a baby. I guessed that something in the child's remark alluded to this event, perhaps to the pregnancy, which the little boy had noticed. But I still could not figure out what the sentence, "Can you imagine Uncle Harry being a cow?" meant. Nothing indicated that the boy had suspicions about Uncle Harry's lack of masculinity. On the contrary, this particular uncle came to be known as quite a philanderer. We did not arrive at a satisfactory solution of the puzzling memory that day. There was only the vague idea that the sentence might have something to do with Aunt Mabel's pregnancy.

The recognition of its meaning occurred to me much later, when the patient, on another occasion and in another context, mentioned that cows sometimes behave strangely in the spring. They jump at each other's backs as if imitating the bull. Everything suddenly became clear. The children, the boy and his sister, must have spoken before about what the grown-ups do in sexual intercourse and compared it with the playful sexual behavior of the cows. The question, "Can you imagine Uncle Harry being a cow?" had thus the meaning, "Can you imagine Uncle Harry behaving like a cow jumping at another cow's back?" It therefore meant: "Can you imagine Uncle Harry in sexual intercourse?" The children might at this time have noticed Aunt Mabel's pregnancy and their thoughts turned to the sexual experiences of their relatives. The boy's question is of a sexual nature. It makes sense now after we have translated it from the child's language into expressions now familiar to us. The laughter of his sister, we understand now, was not only determined by the way the question was put. The girl laughed as an adult would at a sexual allusion that is comical.

It turned out that this interpretation of an unintelligible childhood memory became crucial in the analysis of this patient. He had denied that he had any knowledge of sexual processes before a certain age. No longer understood by the adult, here was perfect proof that he knew what the sexual secret was before that age. His parents postponed sexual information; they seemed to wait with it indefinitely, "until the cows came home." But the children knew the secret long before, and the return of the cows only gave them an opportunity to review what they had learned. Often enough just such uncomprehended childhood memories, when psychoanalytically interpreted, give important clues to the life history and the character-formation of our patients.

The child is the father of the man. In reality, there are three persons in the consultation room of the psychoanalyst: the analyst, the patient as he is now, and the child who continues his existence within the patient. We recognized how old childhood convictions live subterraneously side by side with the opinions and views of the adult. Old values consciously discarded long ago operate in the dark and influence the lives of our patients. It would be a serious mistake on the part of the analyst to underestimate the power of the ideas and ideals of the child who continues his existence in the adult. They rise sometimes quite suddenly from their submergence into the bright daylight of conscious living. An adults feels suddenly afraid of the dark and imagines that a picture has come alive. He has revived the animistic belief of childhood days, when every inanimate object had a life and soul of its own. To our astonishment we often realize that childhood beliefs remain intact in us, are not dead and buried, only submerged.

It would be erroneous to neglect this phenomenon. The psychoanalyst must search for the child in the man, in himself, and in others. He will not understand the depth of the emotions if he is not aware of these vestiges of childhood in maturity. Those childhood ideas need not be childish because they are childlike. Some of them are built around a nucleus of early-understood truths and reveal an astonishingly clear vision of the social environment within the narrow circle that makes up the child's world.

About a hundred years ago there lived in Vienna a brilliant satirist and actor, John N. Nestroy, whose witty plays the Viennese loved. In one of them a figure speaks about cobblers' apprentices, who were known as very clever and impudent youngsters, prematurely wise, like the urchins of New York's lower East Side. "I would like to know," says this figure, "what becomes of all those clever, witty cobblers' boys?" Freud, who frequently quoted this line, replied, "They became stupid shoemakers." Freud said that at a certain point in childhood sexual repression begins to operate and puts an end to the natural and brilliant intelligence of the child. I think this answer is one-sided. The child learns also to accept authority and to suppress its natural aggressions, rebelliousness, and independence of thinking. Nevertheless, it is true that frequently very bright children suddenly show at a certain age a kind of weakening of their natural powers of observation and judgement, as if the adjustment to society forces them to sacrifice these early personal qualities.

These ideas of children, we said, often contain a grain of truth presented in a childlike manner that sometimes appears funny. A patient was enlightened about the sexual processes by his parents at an early age. Nevertheless, the boy puzzled about the sexuality of men because he tried to imagine it in terms of the animals and the flowers about which his parents had spoken. He imagined that a husband knocks at the bedroom door of his wife on certain evenings and says, "Mary, the seed is here." There is no blinking the fact that there is a certain biological truth in the boy's conception. When you remove the trimmings and arrive at the core, you will realize that as little Johnny sees the world, so it is.

We are often reminded in our analytic work that the child lives on in the man and the woman. Life itself bears witness to such survival. When my daughter Miriam was a little girl and we took her to the dentist for the second time, she crawled under a desk and no amount of persuasion could overcome her anxiety. Her mother appealed to her in vain, "Do you think that a lady would crawl on all fours under a desk in a dentist's office?" My little girl answered, "They would like to, but they are too big."

37 · THE WOUNDED
FATHER WITHIN

· · · · · · ·

SAMUEL OSHERSON

This touching piece comes from psychotherapist Samuel Osherson's very readable book about unfinished business between men and their fathers, Finding Our Fathers. *Although it focuses specifically on a man's inner conflicts, the feeling tones transcend gender: feelings of abandonment, longing, and neediness that both men and women have trouble accepting in themselves. "Because we have not been more able to nurture the needy, vulnerable parts of ourselves," Osherson says, "we carry around within an angry, sad, childlike residue, which often shapes our adult relationships."*

Yet this essay is specific to men and to male vulnerability: "My work with men convinces me that there is a male vulnerability in relationships that can be traced back to our early childhood experiences of separation and loss." Men have a task, suggests Osherson, one that no doubt parallels women's task, to let go of "distorted and painful misidentifications" with their parents. The clear message is that we must heal the wounded parent within in order to become more nurturing parents to our inner and our outer children. Osherson suggests that this is not only possible, but necessary in order to feel empowered in our lives. This is a liberating note on which to end this book, for both men and women.

Current family situations are rekindling issues of separation and loss that men have not had a chance to work out in growing up. The issues center on our own vulnerability and dependency as men; uncertainties about our identities and about what it means to be a man; and the needs for support and reassurance many of our own fathers masked beneath the surface of traditional family arrangements and passed along—unmet—to their sons. The normal demands of family life today are powerfully shaped by men's early experiences with father and mother, and by the lessons learned from those experiences about what it means to be male.

Often men's reactions to their wives' involvement with work or with their children reflect childlike feelings of abandonment and the hunger for parental attention and nurturance. When a wife goes off to work, we may feel without realizing it some of the vulnerability and anger we experienced as a child wanting to hold on to Mother and trying to let go of her. The fact that many of our fathers went off to work every day, leaving us alone with our mothers, increased their importance to us and weakened our fathers' roles as the transitional figures necessary to complete the normal process of separation-individuation from mother. And, too, having rarely observed his father taking a secondary place to his mother, a man may not know how confidently to support a wife who works.

One day a successful thirty-eight-year-old lawyer in a luxurious Manhattan office was telling me about his marriage. That confident, engaging man's tone suddenly became plaintive: "Without wanting to sound patronizing, I always assumed any wife of mine would have a career of her own. I just never anticipated it would be like *this*." The *this* referred to the mix of loss, feelings of abandonment, and unmet dependency needs he felt on evenings and weekends when his wife devoted her time and energy to her career rather than to him.

The plaintive lawyer was not alone in his feelings of abandonment. A successful university professor also talked about the darker side of a dual-career marriage. Thoughtful and gentle, he was clearly proud of his wife's achievements in becoming established in a counseling center now that the children were older. Yet he stopped at one point in our talk and reflected that "confidence is an illusion, you know, and I need my wife to bolster my belief that I *can* be successful, get the writing done I need every week, publish those articles in the tenure race. Since my wife's been working she has much less time to pay attention to me, and I know maintaining confidence in myself is a continuing struggle for me."

Similarly the arrival of children may rekindle some of our wishes to be taken care of in that blissful way, as well as our desperate desire to prove that we have given up such wishes and are independent. Becoming a father may also spark an identity struggle for the man who, lacking role models in his past, is not at all sure how to be a father who *is* present for his children.

A business executive told me with pride how involved he had been in the birth of his daughter. Yet he spoke sheepishly about how betrayed he felt by his wife's continuing commitment to her demanding career as a lawyer now that their first child was born. For ten years they had shared most of their spare time. Now with his wife juggling her law practice and the care of a one-year-old, it seemed to this man as if "she has time for everything but me." Spreading his hands in front of him in a shy gesture of embarrassed neediness, he exclaimed, "The new baby is doing fine, but how about the old baby? Me!"

There are numerous circumstances in adult life that leave us feeling childlike—needy, helpless, powerless to change things. In growing up men have great difficulty coming to terms with dependency and vulnerability, often because our fathers showed us that such feelings were unacceptable, that to be successful men, to win our fathers' approval, achievement was what counted. Our vulnerability and dependency became papered over by an instrumental, competent pose as adults or by focusing on what we do well: our ability to achieve in the work world.

Yet, despite our self-assurance about work, uncertainties abound there as well. Much of the uncertainty concerns how much of a commitment to make to career success; there is discomfort with the sense of self that the competitive workplace fosters. One puzzled Washington official, the associate director of a powerful government agency, said to me in dismay, after an interview filled with heroic stories of success: "One major concern does bother me . . . I feel more and more like a well-honed tool for my boss." Then the clue: "He's like a father to me." Many men today wonder, how much like my boss or my mentor do I have to live my life?

Clearly the capacity for autonomy, independence, and a separate identity is essential for healthy adult life. But our emphasis on those qualities in boys obscures the struggle they experience in separating from mother and father. Because we have not been more able to nurture the needy, vulnerable parts of ourselves, we carry them around within an angry, sad, childlike residue, which often shapes our adult relationships with wife, children, boss, and our own parents.

Men used to be protected from their unfinished business with mothers and fathers by the traditional division of labor. But those of us who have grown up during the decades in which the women's movement became a powerful force are experiencing social changes of epic proportions: the clear and direct movement of women into positions of greater power and equality in the workplace, and the movement of men into family life. Regardless of whether men truly are taking greater part in family life (and the evidence suggests there is indeed some small movement in that direction), men are not being sheltered from parts of life they had to repress or devalue in order to grow up.[1] Today, when a wife goes to work, when a baby arrives, or when the family reorganizes upon the departure of children to college, the man is less able to turn to traditional sex roles and expectations. He is often put back in touch with feelings of helplessness and powerlessness that he did not entirely master as a child and is caught by surprise, often feeling a pain he can't really understand.

The volatile nature of this situation is exacerbated by the mutual distrust between the sexes. In this time of changing sex roles men and women often look at each other with suspicion. Many women feel impatient with men's resistance to change, feeling that men are just trying to hold onto their power in relationships or are hopelessly deficient in their capacity for intimacy. Men in turn often become defensive around women, feeling accused and criticized by the women's movement. Some men then try to hide the powerlessness or incompetence they feel behind an emotionally armored posture. In many marriages today neither spouse has much sympathy or patience for the husband's childlike fears and anxieties as both try to develop new work-family arrangements in their life together.

Both sexes today seem to share a stereotype: that men are distant and unconnected, while relationships are the female specialty. Many people believe that women care more than men about love. Yet the division of the sexes into men as rational and women as feelers is simply untrue, a harmful and dangerous myth. For all that feminism has contributed to our culture, it has also brought with it a subtle idealization of women and a less subtle denigration or misunderstanding of men. My work with men convinces me that there is a male vulnerability in relationships that can be traced back to our early childhood experiences of separation and loss. The key to the unfinished business of manhood is unraveling and letting go of our distorted and painful misidentifications with our fathers.

In order to understand men's adult conflicts with work and intimacy in today's world we have to understand the ways the boy comes to experience himself, women, and men, as well as his ongoing relationships as a grown man with the mother and father of his childhood.

It is possible to heal the wounded father within. Men are not passive victims; much of our wish to be more involved with our children or to become mentors at work, much of the hunger for intimacy that many men reveal, is actually an attempt to heal the wound within ourselves, so that we can become more confident and nurturing as men. As we learn more about the adult life cycle, we are discovering that people reexperience issues of separation and individuation from parents throughout adulthood. Dr. George Vaillant, the director of the Grant Study, a longitudinal study of Harvard men, concludes: "Over and over throughout the study, the lesson was repeated: childhood does not end at 21. Even these men, selected in college for psychological health, continued for the next two decades to wean themselves from their parents.[2]

I have talked to enough men to know that both work and family can be a healing experience for men; particularly in our experiences as nurturing husbands and fathers, we can heal our relationship with our own fathers and mothers, letting go of oppressive fantasies about what happened to us growing up male. Yet too there are many men who continue to act out with bosses and wives unfinished business with their fathers and mothers.

Healing the wounded father within is a psychological and social process that unfolds over time and involves exploring one's own history, testing out and exploring a new sense of self, and understanding the complex crosscurrents within our families which affected us as we grew up. Certainly it means tolerating the angry and needy feelings that our work and family life provoke today, and not trying to discard too quickly those uncomfortable, childlike feelings of powerlessness beneath the pose of male competence and identity.

THE WOUNDED FATHER WITHIN

I saw this little boy within myself one summer day at our cabin in New Hampshire several years ago. It happened during a period when I felt stuck and frustrated in my work. Despite the sunshine outside, I was hard at work inside on a book whose point had completely escaped me. A sinking feeling came over me. I was walking through snowdrifts of words, knee-high, bored by what I was saying, angry and frustrated underneath.

My wife was watching my daily melodrama of frustration. One morning, to cheer me up, she suggested we take a hike on one of our favorite trails.

"No, I can't. I want to finish this chapter, Julie. I can't take time off," I replied through gritted teeth.

"Well, how's it going?"

"Terrible. I hate this writing. Why am I doing this? Does it have to be so hard?"

I saw an expression of sorrow, irritation, and boredom cross Julie's face, the sort of look people get when they see those they love hurting themselves again. And in the same way. For the nth time. This time she unloaded:

"You've said this a million times, Sam. When are you going to listen to yourself? Why don't you take time off and think things through? You're not sure what you want to say in that book, or even if you're going about it in the right way.

"You're like a kid walking down the street pulling this red wagon full of rocks behind you, crying and asking for help." As boys look to mother so too men look to their wives to provide us comfort and nurture without our having to take our pain seriously. As a little boy I would go to my mother with my pain (feeling embarrassed and inappropriate), but I never was able satisfactorily to go to my father with it.

I appreciated Julie's concern and ultimately did take her advice to put the book aside. Yet in identifying my expectations and the game I was playing, she was also calling off the game. I felt shamed and angry. An angry inner voice shouted back:

"You owe me!"

Here was the traditional bargain men make with women: I work hard and suffer, and she will be sympathetic and comforting and reassuring. Often men's inability to let go of mother seems like a consolation prize for the absence of a reassuring sense of father.

There I was in this beautiful New Hampshire countryside, suffering —and she was supposed to comfort me, not challenge me to grow up! She wasn't living up to her part in my passion play.

If my anger then had more voice, I might have said, "You're a woman, you wouldn't understand—you can't possibly know what it feels like to be a man."

An image of my father watching TV sullenly after a hard day's work comes to mind. My mother seemingly more cheerful, energetic, my father looking beaten down in a way that couldn't really be talked about. He was, after all, a big success at work, but the sense of entrapment he felt was not an appropriate topic for family talk, or so it seemed to me at the time.

To my shock, sitting in that summer cabin several years ago, I saw that as angry as I was at my father's sad, powerless face in our house, that part of him was in me as well. And my wife had pointed to an angry, trapped part of myself that I was afraid to confront.

In some remote recess where we see ourselves clearly, I bumped into a frightening truth: I felt powerless to take control of my life. I was making Julie into my mother while I'd become my father in this passion play, or at least my image of my father. John Updike's lesson came to mind, explored in Rabbi Angstrom's journey through adulthood: The fate of American men is to remain little boys, never gaining their freedom from mother or father.

For men to feel empowered, to come to terms with our identities and deal honestly with our wives, our children, and the demands of careers, means healing the wounded father within, an angry-sad version of ourselves that feels unloved and unlovable. That means coming to terms with that distorted person we never knew well enough: father.

EPILOGUE: "MAY YOU STAY FOREVER YOUNG"

· · · · · · ·

The child [within] is therefore . . . both
beginning and end, an initial and a terminal creature. The initial creature existed before man was, and the terminal
creature will be when man is not. Psychologically speaking, this means that the
"child" symbolizes the pre-conscious and
the post-conscious essence of man. His
pre-conscious essence is the unconscious
state of earliest childhood; his post-conscious essence is an anticipation by analogy of life after death. In this idea the
all-embracing nature of psychic wholeness is expressed.

—C. G. JUNG

The child survives within us, joined to us for life: perennially the child,
fully alive, an inner possibility awaiting our full and conscious acknowledgment. However, to fixate on the inner child or overidentify with the
archetype is inappropriate, psychologically debilitating, just as any unconscious identification with an idea is dangerous.

But to embrace the child, embody it consciously as a healthy expression
of our psychic wholeness, is to receive the inner child's gift.

The process begins somewhere, probably in the obvious and the
commonplace. A simple recognition, a playful gleam or a grin, and there
you go!

At heart, we are all simply children. "We are but older children, dear,"
said Lewis Carroll in *Through the Looking Glass*, "Who fret to find our
bedtime near."

Alice Miller, in *Pictures of Childhood*, confessed her moment of choice
in this way:

301

Probably I, too, would have remained trapped by this compulsion to protect the parents . . . had I not come into contact with the Child Within Me, who appeared late in my life, wanting to tell me her secret . . . now I was standing at an open door . . . filled with an adult's fear of the darkness . . . But I could not close the door and leave the child alone until my death. . . . I made a decision that was to change my life profoundly . . . to put my trust in this nearly autistic being who had survived the isolation of decades.

I learned the lesson of embracing the child within at a time when I was most vulnerable. It was the sudden death of my father; I was twenty-one. I came by the experience through the words of two loving friends who sent me a telegram. It was an instantaneous recognition, as soon as I read the words:

> Life is a child's spirit within you which does not answer to the question why, but she is a loving being and you must embrace her no matter how she misbehaves. She is joyful and sorrowful, beautiful and enriching. Yet remember she is always for you (never against).

• • • • • •

When you experience the child within, it brings you into the world. We are all here to live out the child's destiny.

"The great ship," said Whitman, "the ship of the World. Mariners, Mariners, gather your skills."

NOTES

· · · · · · ·

ABBREVIATIONS USED IN NOTES

CW *Collected Works* of C. G. Jung (Bollingen Series XX), translated by R. F. C. Hull and edited by H. Read, M. Fordham, G. Adler, and William McGuire (Princeton, N.J.: Princeton University Press; and London: Routledge and Kegan Paul, 1953–) cited below by volume number and paragraph or page.

MDR C. G. Jung, *Memories, Dreams, and Reflections* (New York: Random House, 1961).

PC "The Psychology of the Child Archetype," in *CW*, vol. 9, part 1, *The Archetypes and the Collective Unconscious*.

Introduction/Abrams

All contributors' quotes are from the sources of their respective essays, except where otherwise noted. The subheadings are quoted as follows: "Where is the life we have lost in living?"—T. S. Eliot; "It takes a long time to become young."—Picasso; "Sing, Muse, the Child!"—Homer.

Chapter opening quote: C. G. Jung, *CW*, vol. 17, p. 286.

1. C. G. Jung, *CW*, vol. 16, *The Practice of Psychotherapy* (Princeton, N.J.: Bollingen, 1954), p. 32.

2. Culver Barker, "Healing the Child Within," in *The Wake of Jung* (London: Coventure, 1983), p. 48–49.

3. Ronald W. Clark, *Einstein: The Life and Times* (New York: Abrams, 1984), p. 13.

4. Paul A. Schlipp, ed., *Albert Einstein: Philosopher-Scientist* (New York: Tudor, 1951), p. 17 (as quoted in the Goertzels' *Cradles of Eminence*; see bibliography).

5. As quoted in Marshall McLuhan and Quentin Fiore, *The Medium Is the Massage* (New York: Bantam Books, 1967), p. 93.

6. Johann Wolfgang von Goethe, "The Holy Longing," 1814, trans. Robert Bly, as printed in *News of the Universe* (San Francisco: Sierra Club Books, 1980), p. 70.

7. C. G. Jung, 1932, from the Introduction to M. Esther Harding's *The Way of All Women* (New York: C. G. Jung Foundation, 1970), p. xvii.

8. William Butler Yeats, "The Second Coming," *Selected Poems and Two Plays of William Butler Yeats*, ed. M. L. Rosenthal (New York: Collier, 1962), p. 91.

9. "To Find Our Life," after Ramon Medina Silva, as published in *Technicians of the Sacred*, ed. Jerome Rothenberg (Berkeley: University of California Press, 1968, 1985), p. 232.

Chapter 1/Sullwold

1. George Bernard Shaw, "Essay on Parents and Children," in *Prefaces* (London: Constable & Co., 1934), p. 47.

2. William Wordsworth, "Ode: Intimations of Immortality . . ." in Laurel Poetry Series (New York: Dell, 1968), p. 115.

3. *PC*, p. 170.

Chapter 2/Jung

1. It may not be superfluous to point out that lay prejudice is always inclined to identify the child motif with the concrete experience "child," as though the real child were the cause and precondition of the existence of the child motif. In psychological reality, however, the empirical idea "child" is simply the means (and not the only one) by which to express a psychic fact that cannot be formulated more exactly. Hence by the same token the mythological idea of the child is emphatically not a copy of the empirical child but a *symbol* clearly recognizable as such: it is a wonder-child, a divine child, begotten, born, and brought up in quite extraordinary circumstances, and not—this is the point—a human child. Its deeds are as miraculous or monstrous as its nature and physical constitution. Only on account of these highly unempirical properties is it necessary to speak of a "child motif" at all. Moreover, the mythological "child" has various forms: now a god, giant, Tom Thumb, animal, etc., and this points to a causality that is anything but rational or concretely human. The same is true of the "father" and "mother" archetypes which, mythologically speaking, are equally irrational symbols.

2. C. G. Jung, *Psychological Types*, in *CW*, vol. 6 (alternative source: trans. by H. G. Baynes [London and New York: 1923]) Def. 48; and *Two Essays on Analytical Psychology*, in *CW*, vol. 7, 2d ed. (New York and London: 1966), Index, s.v. "persona."

3. ——— *Psychological Types*, in *CW*, vol. 6, ch. V, 3: "The Significance of the Uniting Symbol."

4. ——— *Psychology and Alchemy*, in *CW*, vol. 12, 2d ed. (New York and London: 1968).

5. ——— *Two Essays on Analytical Psychology*, in *CW*, vol. 7, pars. 399ff.

6. ——— *Psychology and Alchemy*, in *CW*, vol. 12, pars. 328ff.

Chapter 3/Young

1. C. G. Jung, "The Psychology of the Child Archetype," in *Psyche and Symbol*, ed. Violet S. de Laszlo (Garden City, N.Y.: Doubleday & Co., 1958), p. 124n.

2. This tale appears in Heinrich Zimmer, *Myths and Symbols in Indian Art and Civilization*, ed. Joseph Campbell (New York: Harper and Row, 1962), pp. 4–10.

3. Heinrich Zimmer, *The King and the Corpse: Tales of the Soul's Conquest of Evil*, ed. Joseph Campbell, Princeton/Bollingen (Princeton, N.J.: Princeton University Press, 1971), p. 134n.

4. Zimmer, *The King and the Corpse*, p. 192.

5. My discussion of Jung's ideas regarding the child archetype is based on C. G. Jung, "The Psychology of the Child Archetype" and "The Special Phenomenology of the Child Archetype," in *Psyche and Symbol*, ed. Violet S. de Laszlo.

6. Quotations of Wordsworth's poetry are from *Wordsworth: Poetical Works*, ed. Thomas Hutchinson, revised by Ernest de Selincourt (London: Oxford University Press, 1969).

7. Erich Neumann, *The Origins and History of Consciousness*, trans. R. F. C. Hull (New York: Harper and Brothers, 1962), p. 23.

8. Jung, "Psychology of the Child Archetype," p. 131.

9. Jung, "Special Phenomenology of the Child Archetype," p. 135.

10. My summary is based on Jung, "Psychology of the Child Archetype," p. 125ff.

11. *Ibid.*, p. 135.

12. *Ibid.*, p. 130.

13. Richard J. Onorato, *The Character of the Poet: Wordsworth in the Prelude* (Princeton, N.J.: Princeton University Press, 1971), p. 203.

14. A. Charles Babenroth, *English Childhood: Wordsworth's Treatment of Children in the Light of English Poetry* (New York: Columbia University Press, 1922), p. 314.

15. Zimmer, *The King and the Corpse*, p. 131.

Chapter 4/Bachelard

1. Alain Bosquet, *Premier testament* (Paris: Gallimard), p. 17.

2. Charles Plisnier, *Sacre*, XXI.

3. Paul Chaulot, *Jours de beton*, ed. Amis de Rochefort, p. 98.

4. Count of Villiers de L'Isle-Adam, *Isis* (Brussels and Paris: Librairie Internationale, 1862), p. 85.

5. Vincent Huidobro, *Altaible*, trans. Vincent Verhesen, p. 56.

6. Gerhard de Nerval writes: "The memories of childhood come back to life when one reaches the halfway point in life" (*Les filles du feu, Angelique*, 6th letter, ed. du Divan, p. 80). Our childhood waits a long time before being reintegrated into our life. This reintegration is doubtless possible only in the last half of life when one goes back down the hill. Jung writes (*Die Psychology der Uebertragung*, p. 167): "The integration of the Self, taken in its profounder sense, is a matter for the second half of life." As long as one is in the bloom of life, it seems that the adolescence which survives within us puts up a barrier to the childhood which is waiting to be relived. This childhood is the reign of the self, of the *Selbst*, set forth by Jung. Psychoanalysis should be practiced by old men.

7. Jean Follain, *Exister*, p. 37.

8. Baudelaire, *Les paradis artificiels*, p. 329.

9. Pierre Emmanuel, *Tombeau d'Orphee*, p. 49.

10. Robert Ganzo, *L'oeuvre poetique*, Grasset, p. 46.

11. Alexandre Arnoux, *Petits poemes* (Paris: Seghers), p. 31.

12. Jean Rousselot, *Il n'y pas d'exil* (Paris: Seghers), p. 41.

13. Edmond Vandercammen, *Faucher plus pres du ciel*, p. 42.

14. Henry David Thoreau, *Walden*, p. 48.

15. Lamartine, *Les foyers du peuple*, 1st series, p. 172.

Chapter 5/Singer

1. William Blake, *A Song of Liberty*.

2. *PC*, in *CW* vol. 9, p. i.

3. Cf. also Bacchus, Dionysus.

4. Marie-Louise von Franz, *The Problem of the Puer Aeternus*.

5. Ibid.

6. A full discussion of this archetype and the preceding one appears in James Hillman's essay, "Senex and Puer: An Aspect of the Historical and Psychological Present," in *Eranos-Jahrbuch* XXXVI/1967 (Zurich: Rhein-Verlag, 1968).

Chapter 6/Metzner

1. Ramana Maharshi, *The Spiritual Teachings of Ramana Maharshi*, with foreword by C. G. Jung (Boulder, Colo.: Shambhala, 1972).

2. *PC*, p. 164. Jung continues: "In the psychology of the individual, the 'child' paves the way for a future change of personality. In the individuation process, it anticipates the figure that comes from the synthesis of conscious and unconscious elements in the personality. It is therefore a symbol which unites the opposites; a mediator, a bringer of healing, that is, one who makes whole."

3. Michael Harner, *The Way of the Shaman* (San Francisco: Harper and Row, 1980).

4. Meister Eckhart, *Meister Eckhart*, trans. Raymond B. Blakney (New York: Harper and Row, 1941).

5. Fritz Meier, "The Transformation of Man in Mystical Islam," in *Man and Transformation*, ed. Joseph Campbell; Eranos Yearbooks, vol. 5; Bollingen Series, no. 30 (Princeton, N.J.: Princeton University Press, 1964).

6. King James Version Bible: New Testament, John 3:3.

7. C. G. Jung, "Concerning Rebirth," in *The Archetypes and the Collective Unconscious*, p. 121. *CW*, vol. 9, part 1.

8. Evelyn Underhill, "Treatise of the Resurrection," in *Mysticism* (New York: New American Library, 1955).

9. *PC*, pp. 151–181.

10. Chuang Tsu, *Inner Chapters*, trans. Gia-Fu Feng and Jane English (New York: Random House, 1974).

Chapter 7/Frantz

1. *PC*, para. 287.

2. M. Woodman, "Psyche/Soma Awareness" (Paper presented at Conference of Jungian Analysts in New York, May 3–6, 1984).

3. N. Schwartz-Salant, *Narcissism and Character Transformation* (Toronto: Inner City Books, 1982).

4. *MDR*, p. 152.

5. *CW*, vol. 5, *Symbols of Transformation*, para. 165.

6. E. Tripp, *The Meridian Handbook of Classical Mythology* (New York and Scarborough, Ontario: New American Library, 1970).

7. *CW*, vol. 17, *The Development of Personality*, 1954, p. 173.

8. M-L. von Franz, *Creation Myths* (New York: Spring Publications, 1972).

9. *CW*, vol. 7, *Two Essays on Analytical Psychology*, 1966, para. 342.

10. J. Blofeld, *Bodhisattva of Compassion: The Mystical Tradition of Kuan Yin* (Boulder, Colo.: Shambhala, 1978).

11. Von Franz, *Creation Myths*, p. 237.

12. H. Kirsch, "Reveries on Jung," in *Professional Reports* from Annual Conference of the Society of Jungian Analysts of Northern and Southern California, privately printed by C. G. Jung Institute of San Francisco, 1975.

13. Von Franz, *Creation Myths*, p. 122.

14. *I Ching*, 1950, p. 81.

15. J. Blofeld, *Bodhisattva of Compassion*, 1978.

16. G. A. Foy, "On Feeling: The Feeling Function Revisited" (Paper presented at 13th Biennial Bruno Klopfer Workshop, Asilomar, Calif., 1983).

17. Dalai Lama, the XIVth, *The Opening of the Wisdom-Eye* (Wheaton, Ill.: The Theosophical Publishing House, 1966), p. 142.

18. *Ibid.*, pp. 142–143.

19. A. de Vries, *Dictionary of Symbols and Imagery* (Amsterdam and London: North-Holland Publishing Co., 1974).

20. J. Dallett, "Active Imagination in Practice," in *Jungian Analysis*, ed. M. Stein (La Salle, Ill.: Open Court, 1982), pp. 173–191.

21. J. Harrison, 1903, *Prolegomena to the Study of Greek Religion* (New York: Meridian Books, 1955), p. 574.

22. *Ibid.*, p. 575.

23. *CW*, vol. 5, *Symbols of Transformation*, 1956.

24. L. Taylor, *Mourning Dress: A Costume and Social History* (London: George Allen & Unwin, 1983), p. 48.

25. *Ibid.*, p. 49.

26. *Ibid.*, p. 51.

27. *Ibid.*, pp. 48–60.

28. *Ibid.*, p. 56.

29. H. Feifel, *The Meaning of Death*, rev. ed. (New York and London: McGraw Hill Book Co., 1965), p. 124.

30. G. Frantz, "On the Meaning of Loneliness," in *Chaos to Eros*, ed. R. Lockhart (Los Angeles: C. G. Jung Institute, 1976).

31. Harrison, *Prolegomena*.

32. G. Frantz, "Images and Imagination: Wounding and Healing" (Paper presented at the C. G. Jung Institute of San Francisco, 1980).

33. *MDR*, pp. 173–174.

Chapter 8/Hillman

1. P. Aries, *Centuries of Childhood* [trans. R. Baldrick from *L'Enfant et la vie familiale sous l'ancien regime*, Paris: Plon, 1960] (New York: Knopf and London: Cape, 1962), Part I.

2. M. Foucault, *Madness and Civilization* [trans. R. Howard from *Histoire de la Folie*, Paris: Plon, 1961] (New York: Pantheon, 1965).

3. S. Freud, *Collected Papers*, vol. II (London: Hogarth, 1924, 1925), p. 177.

4. S. Freud, *New Introductory Lectures on Psycho-Analysis*, trans. Sprott (London: Hogarth, 1933, 1957), p. 190.

5. Rousseau, *Emile*, II.

6. Freud, "From the history of an infantile neurosis (1918)," in *Collected Papers*, vol. III (London: Hogarth, 1924, 1925), pp. 577–578.

7. Cf. *Collected Papers*, vol. III., p. 470: the last paragraph of Freud's discussion of the Schreber case.

8. Freud, *New Introductory Lectures*, p. 190.

9. Freud, *Collected Papers*, vol. II, p. 188.

10. *CW*, vol. 9, 1, 2d ed. (London: Routledge, 1968), p. 161fn.

11. *CW*, vol. 9, 1 para. 300.

12. *CW*, vol. 5, passim.

13. *CW*, vol. 6, para. 422f, 442.

14. Freud, *Collected Papers*, vol. III, p. 562f.

15. *CW*, vol. 9,1, para. 276.

16. *CW*, vols. 14 and 16, passim.

17. *CW*, 331c and following.

18. St. Augustine, *Enar. in Ps.* XLIV, 1.

19. St. Augustine, *Confessions*, I, 7, 11.

20. Freud, *New Introductory Lectures*, p. 106.

Chapter 10/Woodman

1. *King James Version Bible*: Psalms 118:22.

2. C. G. Jung, "The Tavistock Lectures," in *CW*, vol. 18, *The Symbolic Life*, para. 389.

Chapter 13/Covitz

1. Maria Montessori, *The Child in the Family* (New York: Hearst Corporation, Aron Books, 1970), pp. 14–15.

2. Alice Miller, *Prisoners of Childhood* (retitled *Drama of the Gifted Child*) (New York: Basic Books, 1981), p. 69.

3. *CW*, vol. 17, *The Development of Personality*, pp. 40–41.

4. *Ibid.*, p. 44.

5. *Ibid.*

6. John Bowlby, *Child Care and the Growth of Love* (Middlesex, England: Penguin Books, Ltd., 1965), pp. 77–78.

7. C. G. Jung, "On Psychical Energy," in *CW*, vol. 8, p. 52.

Chapter 14/Miller

1. M. Mahler, *On Human Symbiosis and the Vicissitudes of Individuation* (New York: International Universities Press, 1968), p. 11.

2. Alice Miller, "Zur Behandlungstechnik bei Sogenannten Narzisstischen Neurosen," *Psyche* 25:641–668.

3. J. Habermas, "Der universalitatsanspruch der Hermeneutik," in *Kultur und Kritik* (Frankfurt: M. Suhrkamp, 1973).

4. D. W. Winnicott, "The use of an object," *International Journal of Psychoanalysis* 50:700, 716, 1969.

Chapter 15/von Franz

1. Ovid, *Metamorphoses*, vol. IV (London and Cambridge, Mass.: Loeb Classical Library, 1946), pp. 18–20.

2. C. G. Jung, *CW*, vol. 5, *Symbols of Transformation*.

3. J. G. Magee, Jr., "High Flight," in *The Family Album of Favorite Poems*, ed. P. E. Ernest (New York: Grosset & Dunlap, 1959).

4. Gerhard Adler and Aniela Jaffé, eds. *C. G. Jung: Letters*, 2 vols. (Princeton: Princeton University Press, 1973) vol. 1, p. 82, letter dated February 23, 1931.

Chapter 17/Luke

1. Antoine de Saint-Exupéry, *The Little Prince*, trans. Katherine Woods (New York: Harcourt, Brace and World, 1943).

2. C. G. Jung, and C. Kerenyi, *Essays on a Science of Mythology* (New York: Harper Torchbooks, 1963), p. 96.

Chapter 18/Whitfield

1. Anna Freud, *The Ego and the Mechanisms of Defense*, rev. ed. (New York: International Universities Press, 1986).

2. George Valliant, *The Natural History of Alcoholism* (Cambridge, Mass.: Harvard University Press, 1983).

3. H. L. Gravitz and J. D. Bowden, *Guide to Recovery: A Book for Adult Children of Alcoholics* (Holmes Beach, Fla.: Learning Publications, 1985).

4. M. Ferguson, *The Aquarian Conspiracy: Personal and Social Transformation in the 1980's* (*Los Angeles: Tarcher*, 1980).

5. J. Campbell, *The Hero with a Thousand Faces* (Princeton, N.J.: Princeton Press, 1949).

6. Ferguson, *Aquarian Conspiracy*; C. L. Whitfield, *Alcoholism, Other Drug Problems, and Other Attachments and Spirituality: Stress Management and Serenity During Recovery, A Transpersonal Approach* (Baltimore, Md.: The Resource Group, 1985).

7. Gravitz and Bowden, *Guide to Recovery*.

8. T. L. Cermak and S. Brown, "International group therapy with the adult children of alcoholics," *International Journal Group Psychotherapy* 32:375–389, 1982.

9. B. Fischer, *Workshop on Shame* (Baltimore, Md.: The Resource Group, 1985).

Chapter 19/Stone and Winkelman

1. Lucia Capacchione, *The Power of Your Other Hand* (Van Nuys, Calif.: Newcastle Co., Inc. 1988).

Chapter 22/Stein

1. C. Kerenyi and C. G. Jung, *Essays on a Science of Mythology* (New York: Pantheon Books Inc., 1949), p. 40.

2. Alice Miller, *Prisoners of Childhood* (New York: Basic Books, Inc., 1981).

3. Alice Miller, *Thou Shalt Not Be Aware* (New York: Farrar, Straus, Giroux, 1984).

4. Sigmund Freud, *Standard Edition*, vol. VII.

5. Robert M. Stein, *Incest and Human Love: The Betrayal of the Soul in Psychotherapy* (Dallas: Spring Publications, Inc., 1984).

6. Harold Searles, "Oedipal Love in the Countertransference" (1959), in *Collected Papers on Schizophrenia and Related Subjects* (New York: International University Press, 1965), p. 284.

7. *Ibid.*

8. *Ibid.*, p. 295.

9. *Ibid.*, p. 296.

Chapter 23/Short

1. *CW*, vol. 17, *The Development of Personality*, para. 153.

2. D. H. Lawrence, *The Complete Short Stories* (Penguin Books, 1983), pp. 790–791.

3. T. S. Eliot, *The Complete Poems and Plays* (New York: Harcourt, Brace & Co., 1952), p. 260.

4. *CW*, vol. 17, para. 217a.

5. *Ibid.*, para. 154.

6. *Ibid.*, para. 84.

7. *Ibid.*

8. *Ibid.*

9. G. K. Chesterton, *Orthodoxy* (New York, Vintage Books, 1959), p. 80.

10. *Ibid.*, para. 286.

11. *Ibid.*

Chapter 25/Mills and Crowley

1. V. Axline, *Play Therapy* (New York: Ballantine, 1969 (originally published in 1947). See also, A. Freud, *The Psychoanalytic Treatment of Children* (London: Imago, 1946); R. Gardner, *Therapeutic Communication with Children: The Mutual Story-telling Technique* (New York: Science House, 1971); G. Gardner and K. Olness, *Hypnosis and Hypnotherapy with Children* (New York: Grune & Stratton, 1981); V. Oaklander, *Windows to Our Children* (Moab, Utah: Real People Press, 1978); and S. Russo, "Adaptations in behavioral therapy with children," *Behavior Research & Therapy* 2:43–47.

2. *MDR*, pp. 173–174.

3. *Ibid.*, pp. 174–175.

4. *PC*

5. C. G. Jung, *Psyche and Symbol* (New York: Doubleday, 1958), pp. 125–128.

6. *Ibid.*, pp. 135–136.

7. E. Rossi and M. Ryan, eds., *Life Reframing in Hypnosis. II. The Seminars, Workshops, and Lectures of Milton H. Erikson* (New York: Irvington, 1985), p. 51.

8. *Ibid.*, p. 65.

Part 6: Introduction

Chapter opening quote: "On Psychic Energy." C. G. Jung, *CW*, vol. 8, p. 52.

Chapter 33/Hillman

1. James Hillman, "Abandoning the Child," in *Loose Ends: Primary Papers in Archetypal Psychology* (Dallas: Spring Publications and the University of Dallas, 1975).

Chapter 37/Osherson

1. J. M. Ross, "In Search of Fathering: A Review," in *Father and Child*, ed. Cath, Gurwitz, and Ross.

2. D. Hall, "My Son, My Executioner," in *The Alligator Bride* (New York: Harper & Row, 1969).

Epilogue/Abrams

"May You Stay Forever Young": Bob Dylan, "Forever Young," 1973, Ram's Horn Music.

Chapter opening quote: C. G. Jung, "The Psychology of the Child Archetype," *CW*, vol. 9, i, para. 299.

NOTES ON CONTRIBUTORS

· · · · · · ·

GASTON BACHELARD was one of the most significant thinkers of modern France. A philosopher and psychology writer, Bachelard was said to have been a truly free mind who recognized imagination as the fundamental substance of the world. He held the chair of history and philosophy of science at the Sorbonne from 1940 until his death in 1962.

BRUNO BETTELHEIM is Distinguished Professor of Education Emeritus and Professor Emeritus of both psychology and psychiatry at the University of Chicago. His books include *A Good Enough Parent*, *Love Is Not Enough*, *Children of the Dream*, *Freud and Man's Soul*, and *The Uses of Enchantment*. The last won both the National Book Award and the National Book Critics Circle Award in 1977.

JOHN BRADSHAW has worked for the past twenty years as a counselor, theologian, management consultant, and public speaker. He is host of the nationally televised PBS series *Bradshaw On: The Family* and author of a book by the same title. *Healing the Shame That Binds You* is his most recent work.

NATHANIEL BRANDEN is a practicing psychologist at the Biocentric Institute in Los Angeles. He has written extensively on psychology, including the books *The Psychology of Romantic Love*, *The Psychology of Self-Esteem*, and *How to Raise Your Self-Esteem*.

ADELAIDE BRY has written books on a number of psychological themes, including *The TA Primer*, *Inside Psychotherapy*, *How to Get Angry Without Feeling Guilty*, *est: 60 Hours That Transform Your Life*, and *Visualization: Directing the Movies of Your Mind*.

JOSEPH CAMPBELL, the great bard and scholar of mythology who died in October 1987, is best known for his work in comparative world mythology. He taught at Sarah Lawrence College in New York City for almost forty years, where the Joseph Campbell Chair in Comparative Mythology was established in his honor. His written works include *The Mythic Image*, *The Masks of God* (4 volumes), *The Hero with a Thousand Faces*, *Myths to Live By*, *The Atlas of World Mythology*, and the posthumous interview transcripts *The Power of Myth* and *An Open Life*.

LUCIA CAPACCHIONE is a registered art therapist, consultant, and workshop leader. Her books include *The Creative Journal*, *The WellBeing Journal*, and

The Power of Your Other Hand. Her methods are currently being used with AIDS and cancer patients and in 12-step recovery programs.

JOEL COVITZ is a clinical psychologist and Jungian analyst in Brookline, Massachusetts, where he lives with his wife and two children. He is the author of *Emotional Child Abuse* and the forthcoming *Visions of the Night: A Study of Jewish Dream Interpretation.*

ERIK H. ERIKSON is one of the leading figures in the field of psychoanalysis and human development. Winner of both the Pulitzer Prize and the National Book Award, he is the author of *Gandhi's Truth, Young Man Luther, Identity: Youth and Crisis, Childhood and Society,* and *Insight and Responsibility.*

GILDA FRANTZ is a Jungian analyst in private practice in Santa Monica, California, and a founding editor of the journal *Psychological Perspectives,* published by the C. G. Jung Institute of Los Angeles.

MARIE-LOUISE VON FRANZ, a Swiss psychoanalyst, is probably Carl Jung's most important living disciple, having worked directly with him for 31 years. Her work fully embodies the essence of his teachings, although she is in her own right an original and provocative thinker. Many of her lectures have been published and are available in English. Her books include *Number and Time, The Grail Legend* (with Emma Jung), *Puer Aeternus, Projection and Re-Collection in Jungian Psychology, The Feminine in Fairy Tales,* and *On Dreams and Death.*

JAMES HILLMAN, representing the third generation in Jungian thought, is rapidly coming to be seen as one of the most original psychological thinkers in America today. Trained as a Jungian analyst, he calls himself an imaginal or archetypal psychologist, and his writings have captured the imaginations of novelists, poets, feminists, cultural historians, as well as his fellow analysts. He lectures widely and is the editor of the journal *Spring.* His books include *Suicide and the Soul, The Myth of Analysis, Re-Visioning Psychology, Anima,* and *Loose Ends.*

JEAN HOUSTON is director of the Foundation for Mind Research in New York. She conducts innovative seminars and works in human development in over thirty-five countries, and has authored more than ten books, including *The Search for the Beloved, The Possible Human, Life Force, and Mind Games.*

C. G. JUNG, who died in 1961, one of the great personalities of our time, is probably best known as one of the founders of psychoanalysis. His reflections covered the full range of human problems and concerns of the modern soul. His overriding interest was the mystery of consciousness and personality, and their relationship with the great unconscious. His books include *Collected Works* (20 volumes), *Man In Search of a Soul,* and his popular autobiography, *Memories, Dreams, and Reflections.*

URSULA K. LEGUIN is a well-known and beloved novelist and short story writer. Among her books are *Planet of Exile, The Left Hand of Darkness, The Dispossessed,* and the collection *The Wind's Twelve Quarters.* She lives with her family in Portland, Oregon.

JOHN LOUDON was the original editor of the journal *Parabola*. He has served as editor of the religious/general books division of Harper and Row in New York and San Francisco. He makes his home in Northern California.

ALEXANDER LOWEN, director of the Institute for Bioenergetic Analysis in New York, is the creator of bioenergetics, a practice that incorporates direct work on the body into psychoanalytic process. He is the author of numerous books, including *Love and Orgasm*; *Betrayal of the Body*; *Pleasure, Depression and the Body*; and *Bioenergetics*.

HELEN M. LUKE is a Jungian counselor and director of Apple Farm, a retreat center in Three Rivers, Michigan. She is the author of *The Way of Woman: Ancient and Modern*; *Woman: Earth and Spirit*; *White Rose*; and *The Inner Story*.

RALPH METZNER has been a researcher and teacher in the area of consciousness for over 25 years. He is a psychotherapist and professor of East-West psychology at the California Institute of Integral Studies in San Francisco. His books include *Maps of Consciousness* and *Opening to the Light*.

ALICE MILLER, who lives in Zurich, has devoted herself to writing since 1979, after having practiced and taught for over twenty years as a psychoanalyst. Her best-selling books, *Prisoners of Childhood* (retitled *The Drama of the Gifted Child*), *For Your Own Good*, and *Thou Shalt Not Be Aware*, have created ferment and spawned a movement of activists on behalf of children.

JOYCE C. MILLS and RICHARD J. CROWLEY are child therapists practicing in Southern California. Their collaboration has produced *Therapeutic Metaphors for Children and the Child Within*, and a therapeutic comic book for abused children, *Gardenstone: Fred Protects the Vegetables*.

SAMUEL OSHERSON is a research psychologist and practicing psychotherapist in Cambridge, Massachusetts. He is the author of *Holding On or Letting Go* and *Finding Our Fathers* and has written a monthly column for *Boston* magazine.

M. SCOTT PECK is a psychiatrist practicing in New Milford, Connecticut. He is the author of the enormously popular book *The Road Less Traveled*, its sequel *People of the Lie*, and *The Different Drum*.

THEODORE REIK, born in Vienna in 1888, was one of Freud's earliest pupils. He wrote the first doctoral dissertation on psychoanalysis at the University of Vienna. He came to the United States in 1938 and practiced psychoanalysis in New York for many years. His books include *Masochism in Modern Man*, *A Psychologist Looks at Love*, and *Listening with the Third Ear*.

ROSE-EMILY ROTHENBERG is a Jungian analyst in private practice in Los Angeles. She was the editor of *A Well of Living Waters*, a tribute to psychoanalyst and mentor Hilde Kirsch.

JEFFREY SATINOVER is a Fellow of the Child Study Center at the Yale University School of Medicine, a director of the Sterling Institute in Weston, Connecticut, and a Jungian analyst in private practice.

SUSANNE SHORT is a Jungian analyst in private practice in New York City.

JUNE SINGER is a Jungian analyst, author, and member of the faculty at the Institute of Transpersonal Psychology, Palo Alto, California. Her books include *Androgyny, Energies of Love, The Unholy Bible, Boundaries of the Soul,* and *Seeing Through the Visible World.*

ROBERT M. STEIN is a senior training analyst at the Jung Institute of Los Angeles and is in private practice in Beverly Hills. He is author of numerous articles and the book *Incest and Human Love: The Betrayal of the Soul in Psychotherapy.*

HAL STONE is a clinical psychologist and teacher and the director of the Academy of Delos in Northern California, where he and his wife, Sidra Winkelman, offer training groups in Voice Dialogue. He is author of *Embracing Heaven and Earth* and co-author of *Embracing Our Selves* and *Embracing Each Other.*

EDITH SULLWOLD founded the Hilde Kirsch Children's Center at the C. G. Jung Institute of Los Angeles. She was director of Turning Point, a professional group working with seriously ill children. She now teaches and supervises therapists in various parts of the world, most recently in Kenya.

CHARLES L. WHITFIELD is a psychotherapist and author of *Healing the Child Within* and the companion workbook, *A Gift to Myself.* He is on the faculty of Rutgers University Summer School of Alcohol Studies and the University of Maryland School of Medicine.

SIDRA WINKELMAN is a psychotherapist, mother, and co-creator of the Voice Dialogue process, which she and her husband, Hal Stone, teach in the United States and abroad. She is co-author of *Embracing Our Selves* and *Embracing Each Other.*

MARION WOODMAN is a Jungian analyst in private practice in Toronto. She travels and lectures widely. Her books include *The Owl Was a Baker's Daughter: Obesity, Anorexia Nervosa, and the Repressed Feminine; Addiction to Perfection: The Still Unravished Bride;* and *The Pregnant Virgin.*

JAMES H. YOUNG is a contributing writer for *Quadrant,* the journal of the C. G. Jung Foundation of New York.

BIBLIOGRAPHY

· · · · · · ·

The works cited below include the sources of the essays in this book, as well as other relevant and related materials on the themes of this collection. I recommend these to the reader, as well as the reference bibliographies in the source books themselves.

Armstrong, Thomas. *The Radiant Child*. Wheaton, Ill.: Quest, 1985.

Bachelard, Gaston. *The Poetics of Reverie*. Translated by Daniel Russell. Boston: Beacon Press, 1971.

————. *Water and Dreams*. Translated by Edith R. Farrell. Dallas: Pegasus Foundation, 1983.

Bettelheim, Bruno. *A Good Enough Parent*. New York: A. Knopf, 1987.

Bly, Robert, ed. *News of the Universe: Poems of Two-fold Consciousness*. San Francisco: Sierra Club, 1980.

Boer, Charles, trans. *The Homeric Hymns*. Dallas: Spring Publications, 1979.

Bradshaw, John. *Bradshaw On: The Family*. Deerfield Beach, Fla.: Health Communications, 1988.

————. *Healing the Shame That Binds You*. Deerfield Beach, Fla.: Health Communications, 1988.

Branden, Nathaniel. *How to Raise Your Self-Esteem*. New York: Bantam, 1987.

Bry, Adelaide, with Marjorie Bair. *Visualization: Directing the Movies of Your Mind*. New York: Barnes and Noble, 1979.

Campbell, Joseph. *The Hero with a Thousand Faces*. Princeton, N.J.: Princeton University Press, Bollingen Series XVII, 1949.

Campbell, Joseph, with Bill Moyers. *The Power of Myth*. New York: Doubleday, 1988.

Campbell, Joseph, with Michael Toms. *An Open Life: Joseph Campbell in Conversation with Michael Toms*. Edited by J. M. Maher and D. Briggs. Burdett, N.Y.: Larsen Publications, 1988.

Capacchione, Lucia. *The Power of Your Other Hand*. North Hollywood, Calif.: Newcastle Publishing, 1988.

Carroll, Lewis. *Through the Looking Glass*. New York: Random House, 1946.

Cott, Jonathan. *Pipers at the Gates of Dawn: The Wisdom of Children's Literature*. New York: Random House, 1981.

Covitz, Joel. *Emotional Child Abuse: The Family Curse*. Boston: Sigo Press, 1986.

Dieckmann, Hans. "The Favorite Fairy Tale from Childhood," in *The Analytic Process*. Edited by Joseph Wheelwright. New York: Putnam's, C. G. Jung Foundation, 1971: 77–84.

Elkind, David. *The Hurried Child*. Reading, Mass.: Addison-Wesley, 1981.

Erikson, Erik H. *Insight and Responsibility*. New York: W. W. Norton, 1964.

Fordham, Michael. "Religious Experience in Childhood," in *The Well-Tended Tree*. Edited by Hilde Kirsch. New York: Putnam's, C. G. Jung Foundation, 79–89, 1971.

Frantz, Gilda. "Birth's Cruel Secret/O I Am My Own Lost Mother/To My Own Sad Child." *Chiron, 1985*: 157–172.

Franz, Marie-Louis von. *C. G. Jung: His Myth in Our Time*. Translated by W. H. Kennedy. New York: Putnam's, C. G. Jung Foundation for Analytical Psychology, 1975.

———. *Individuation in Fairytales*. Dallas: Spring Publications, 1977.

———. *Puer Aeternus*. Boston: Sigo Press, 1981.

Ghiselin, Brewster, ed. *The Creative Process*. New York: New American Library, 1952.

Giannini, John. "The Dynamics of the Wounded Child." *Creation*, vol. 4, no. 6: 32–35.

Goertzel, Victor and Mildred G. *Cradles of Eminence*. Boston: Little Brown, 1962.

Harding, M. Esther. *The 'I' and the 'Not-I'*. Princeton, N.J.: Princeton University Press, Bollingen Series LXXIX, 1965.

Hillman, James. *Loose Ends*. Dallas: Spring Publications, 1975.

———. *Re-Visioning Psychology*. New York: Harper and Row, 1975.

Hillman, James, with Laura Pozzo. *Inter Views*. New York: Harper and Row, 1983.

Hillman, James, et al. *Puer Papers*. Dallas: Spring Publications, 1979.

Houston, Jean. *The Possible Human*. Los Angeles: Jeremy Tarcher, 1982.

Jaffe, Aniela, ed. *C. G. Jung: Word and Image*. Princeton, N.J.: Princeton University Press, Bollingen Series XCVII, 1979.

James, Muriel, and Dorothy Jongeward. *Born to Win: Transactional Analysis with Gestalt Experiments*. Reading, Mass.: Addison-Wesley, 1971.

Jung, Carl Gustav. *Collected Works*, vols. 1–20. Translated by R. F. C. Hull and edited by H. Read, M. Fordham, G. Adler, and William McGuire. (Especially vols. 9i, 16, 17). Princeton, N.J.: Princeton University Press, Bollingen Series XX, 1953–.

———. *Psyche and Symbol*. Edited by Violet de Laszlo. Garden City, N.Y.: Doubleday, 1958.

———. *Memories, Dreams, and Reflections*. Edited by Aniela Jaffe. New York: Random House, Pantheon Books, 1961.

———. *Psychological Reflections*. Edited by Jolanda Jacobi and R. F. C. Hull. Princeton, N.J.: Princeton University Press, Bollingen Series XXXI, 1970.

Jung, Carl Gustav, and Karl Kerenyi. *Essays on A Science of Mythology*. Princeton, N.J.: Princeton University Press, Bollingen Series XXII, 1969.

Keen, Sam. *Apology for Wonder*. New York: Harper and Row, Torchbooks, 1969.

Kehl, Richard. *Silver Departures*. La Jolla, Calif.: Green Tiger, 1983.

Kohut, Heinz. *The Restoration of the Self*. New York: International Universities, 1977.

Lawrence, D. H. *Fantasia of the Unconscious and Psychoanalysis and the Unconscious*. New York: Viking Penguin, 1960.

Liedloff, Jean. *The Continuum Concept*. Reading, Mass.: Addison-Wesley, 1977.

Loudon, John. "Becoming a Child." *Parabola*, vol. IV, no. 3 (August 1979): 35–41.

Lowen, Alexander. *Pleasure: A Creative Approach to Life*. New York: Coward, McCann, 1970.

———. *Bioenergetics*. New York: Coward, McCann, 1975.

———. *Narcissism: Denial of the True Self*. New York: Macmillan, Collier Books, 1983.

Luke, Helen. *The Inner Story: Myth and Symbol in the Bible and Literature*. New York: Crossroad, 1982.

———. *Woman: Earth and Spirit*, New York: Crossroad, 1984.

Mahdi, Louise, Steven Foster, and Meredith Little. *Betwixt and Between: Patterns of Masculine and Feminine Initiation*. LaSalle, Ill.: Open Court, 1987.

Metzner, Ralph. *Opening to the Light*. Los Angeles: Jeremy Tarcher, 1986.

Middelton-Moz, Jane, and Lorie Dwinell. *After the Tears: Reclaiming the Personal Losses of Childhood*. Deerfield Beach, Fla.: Health Communications, Inc., 1986.

Miller, Alice. *The Drama of the Gifted Child* (original title *Prisoners of Childhood*). New York: Basic Books, 1981.

———. *For Your Own Good: Hidden Cruelty in Child-Rearing and the Roots of Violence*. New York: Farrar, Straus, Giroux, 1983.

———. *Thou Shalt Not Be Aware: Society's Betrayal of the Child*. New York: Farrar, Straus, Giroux, 1984.

———. *Pictures of Childhood*. New York: Farrar, Straus, Giroux, 1986.

Mills, Joyce C., and Richard J. Crowley, with Margaret O. Ryan. *Therapeutic Metaphors for Children and the Child Within*. New York: Brunner/Mazel, 1986.

Missildine, W. Hugh. *Your Inner Child of the Past*. New York: Simon and Schuster, 1963.

Neary, John M. "The Dickens Child: From Infantilism to Wholeness," *Psychological Perspectives*, Fall, 1982: 138–155.

Neumann, Erich. *The Child*. New York: Putnam's, C. G. Jung Foundation, 1973.

Osherson, Samuel O. *Finding Our Fathers: The Unfinished Business of Manhood*. New York: Random House, Ballantine Books, 1986.

Pearce, Joseph C. *Magical Child: Rediscovering Nature's Plan for Our Children*. New York: Bantam, 1986.

Pearson, Carol. *The Hero Within*. San Francisco: Harper and Row, 1986.

Peck, M. Scott. *The Road Less Traveled*. New York: Simon and Schuster, Touchstone, 1978.

Reik, Theodore. *Listening with the Third Ear*. New York: Arena Books, 1972.

Richards, M. C. "Recovery of the Child in Manhood," in *Centering*. Middletown, Conn.: Wesleyan, 1962.

Rothenberg, Rose-Emily. "The Orphan Archetype." *Psychological Perspectives*, 1983: 181–194.

Rubin, Theodore. *Compassion and Self-Hate*. New York: Macmillan, Collier, 1975.

Samuels, Andrew. *Jung and the Post-Jungians*. New York: Routledge & Kegan Paul, 1985.

Samuels, Andrew, Bani Shorter, and Fred Plaut, eds. *A Critical Dictionary of Jungian Analysis*. London: Routledge & Kegan Paul, 1986.

Satinover, Jeffrey. "The Mirror of Doctor Faustus: The Decline of Art in the Pursuit of Eternal Adolescence." *Quadrant*, Spring, 1984: 23–38.

———. "*Puer Aeternus*: The Narcissistic Relation to the Self." *Quadrant*, Fall, 1980: 75–108.

Schwartz-Salant, Nathan. *Narcissim and Character Transformation*. Toronto: Inner City, 1982.

Short, Susanne. "Understanding Our Childhood: The Hidden Secret." *Psychological Perspectives*, Fall, 1989.

Singer, June K. *Boundaries of the Soul*. Garden City, N.Y.: Doubleday, 1972.

Stein, Robert M. *Incest and Human Love: The Betrayal of the Soul in Psychotherapy*. Dallas: Spring Publications, 1973.

———. "On Incest and Child Abuse." *Spring 1987*: 61–65.

Stevens, Anthony. *Archetypes: A Natural History of the Self*. New York: Quill, 1983.

Stone, Hal, and Sidra Winkelman. *Embracing Our Selves: The Voice Dialogue Manual*. San Rafael, Calif.: New World Library, 1989.

———. *Embracing Each Other: Relationship as Teacher, Healer, and Guide*. San Rafael, Calif.: New World Library, 1990.

Sullwold, Edith. "The Ritual-Maker Within at Adolescence," in *Betwixt and Between*. Edited by Louise Mahdi, Steven Foster, and Meredith Little. LaSalle, Ill.: Open Court, 1987, 111–131.

Tuby, Molly, ed. *In the Wake of Jung*. London: Coventure, 1983.

Viorst, Judith. *Necessary Losses*. New York: Ballantine, Fawcett, 1986.

Weinrib, Estelle L. *Images of the Self: The Sandplay Therapy Process*. Boston: Sigo Press, 1983.

Whitfield, Charles L. *Healing the Child Within*. Deerfield Beach, Fla.: Health Communications, 1987.

———. *A Gift to Myself: A Workbook and Guide to Healing My Child Within*. Deerfield Beach, Fla.: Health Communications, 1989.

Wickes, Frances G. *The Inner World of Choice*. New York: Harper and Row, 1963.

Woodman, Marion. *The Pregnant Virgin: A Process of Psychological Transformation*. Toronto: Inner City Books, 1985.

Young, James H. "The Child Archetype." *Quadrant*, Winter, 1977: 63–72.

PERMISSIONS AND COPYRIGHTS

. . . .

Chapter 1 is an original essay created especially for this collection by Edith Sullwold. Copyright © 1989 by Edith Sullwold. Used by permission of the author.

Chapter 2 is comprised of excerpts from the essay "The Psychology of the Child Archetype" by C. G. Jung, from *The Collected Works of C. G. Jung*, trans. R. F. C. Hull, Bollingen Series XX, vol. 9, no. i, *The Archetypes and the Collective Unconscious*. Copyright © 1959, 1969. Reprinted by permission of Princeton University Press.

Chapter 3 is an essay by James H. Young. Copyright © 1977 by *Quadrant*, Journal of Analytical Psychology, reprinted by permission of the C. G. Jung Foundation of New York.

Chapter 4 is comprised of excerpts from *The Poetics of Reverie* by Gaston Bachelard, translated from the French by Daniel Russell. Copyright 1960 by Presses Universitaires de France. English translation, copyright © 1969 by Grossman Publishers, Inc. Reprinted by permission of Viking Penguin, a division of Penguin Books USA Inc.

Chapter 5 is an excerpt from *Boundaries of the Soul* by June K. Singer. Copyright © 1972 by June Singer. Reprinted by permission of Doubleday, a division of Bantam, Doubleday, Dell Publishing Group, Inc.

Chapter 6 is an excerpt from *Opening to the Light* by Ralph Metzner. Copyright © 1986 by Ralph Metzner. Reprinted by permission of Jeremy P. Tarcher, Inc., Los Angeles.

Part 2's Introduction contains the poem "I Live My Life," by Rainer Maria Rilke, translated by Robert Bly. It is reprinted from *News of the Universe*, copyright 1980, © Robert Bly, used by permission of Robert Bly.

Chapter 7 is an essay by Gilda Frantz. Copyright © 1985 by Gilda Frantz. Reprinted by permission of the author.

Chapter 8 is comprised of excerpts from *Loose Ends* by James Hillman. Copyright © 1975 by James Hillman. Reprinted by permission of the author and Spring Publications, Inc., Dallas.

Chapter 9 is an essay by Rose-Emily Rothenberg. Copyright © 1983 by Rose-Emily Rothenberg. Reprinted by permission of the author.

Chapter 10 is comprised of excerpts from *The Pregnant Virgin: A Process of Psychological Transformation* by Marion Woodman (Studies in Jungian Psychology by Jungian Analysts, no. 21). Copyright © 1985 by Marion Woodman. Reprinted by permission of Inner City Books, Toronto.

Chapter 11 is an excerpt from *The Road Less Traveled* by M. Scott Peck. Copyright

ABOUT THE EDITOR

JEREMIAH ABRAMS has worked for the past twenty years as a Jungian therapist, dream analyst, writer, counselor, and consultant. He is currently the director of the Mount Vision Institute, a Center for Individuation, in Sausalito, California. He lives with his wife and two children in Northern California.